4
T
H
-
Edition

CELEBRITY
DIRECTORY™

4 T H - Edition

CELEBRITY DIRECTORY™

 **Axiom Information Resources**

Library of Congress Catalog Card Number: 91-78325

ISBN 0-943213-06-1

Printed in the United States of America

SPECIAL SALES

The Celebrity Directory™ is available at special quantity discounts. For information, write:

Axiom Information Resources, P.O. Box 8015-T1, Ann Arbor, Michigan 48107 U.S.A.

Introduction

Welcome to the expanded fourth edition of the Celebrity Directory™. This new edition incorporates many changes suggested by our readers' enthusiastic response to previous editions. As always, our aim is to provide the reference librarian, speaking engagement coordinator, general researcher or fan with the easiest-to-use, most accurate and comprehensive collection of celebrity names and addresses available anywhere.

The editors have researched and arranged data on thousands of prominent persons engaged in all fields of human accomplishment throughout the world. If a person is famous and worth locating, it's almost certain that his or her name and address is listed in the convenient, alphabetically-arranged Celebrity Directory™.

Most of the celebrities listed in the directory welcome correspondence concerning their lives and work. Please remember when writing to a celebrity, as well as writing to Axiom Information Resources, it is always best to enclose a stamped, self-addressed envelope. Of course, the editorial staff and publisher cannot guarantee that listed celebrities will respond to correspondence.

We have made every effort to ensure that the information contained in the Celebrity Directory™ is up-to-date and accurate. We cannot accept responsibility for inaccuracies created by a celebrity's moving or changing his or her mail arrangements after the directory went to press.

We welcome any suggestions or inquiries concerning the Celebrity Directory™, and we sincerely hope this new edition will provide our readers with even more entertainment and information. All inquiries concerning this book should be sent to Axiom Information Resources, P.O. Box 8015-T1, Ann Arbor, Michigan 48107 U.S.A.

Willie Aames
901 Bringham Avenue
Los Angeles, CA 90049
"Actor, Dancer"

Tommy Aaron
P.O. Box 12458
Palm Beach Gardens, FL 33410
"Golfer"

Henry Aaron
1611 Adams Drive S.W.
Atlanta, GA 30311
"Baseball Player"

ABBA
Box 26072 S-100 41
Stockholm SWEDEN
"Rock & Roll Group"

Dihanne Abbott
12121 Wilshire Blvd. #1100
Los Angeles, CA 90025
"Actress"

George Abbott
1270 Sixth Avenue
New York, NY 10020
"Director, Writer, Producer"

Gregory Abbott
P.O. Box 68
Bergenfield, NJ 07621
"Singer"

John Abbott
6424 Ivarene Avenue
Los Angeles, CA 90068
"Actor"

Philip Abbott
5400 Shirley Avenue
Tarzana, CA 91356
"Actor, Director"

Paula Abdul
14046 Aubrey Road
Beverly Hills, CA 90210
"Singer"

Kareem Abdul-Jabbar
1170 Stone Canyon Road
Los Angeles, CA 90077
"Basketball Player"

Abdullah The Butcher
1000 South Industrial Blvd.
Dallas, TX 75207
"Wrestler"

F. Murray Abraham
888-7th Avenue #1800
New York, NY 10019
"Actor"

Ray Abruzzo
20334 Pacific Coast Hwy.
Malibu, CA 90265
"Actor"

Bella Abzug
2 Fifth Avenue
New York, NY 10011
"Politician"

AC/DC
11 Leominster Road
Morden Surrey
SM4 6HN ENGLAND
"Rock & Roll Group"

Sharon Acker
9744 Wilshire Blvd. #312
Beverly Hills, CA 90212
"Actress"

Bettye Ackerman
302 North Alpine Drive
Beverly Hills, CA 90210
"Actress"

Rep. Gary Ackerman (NY)
House Longworth Bidg. #1725
Washington, DC 20515
"Politician"

Forrest Ackerman
2495 Glendower
Los Angeles, CA 90027
"Author"

Leslie Ackerman
950-2nd Street #201
Santa Monica, CA 90403
"Actress"

Jay Acovone
151 South El Camino Drive
Beverly Hills, CA 90212
"Actor"

Roy Acuff
2804 Opryland Drive
Nashville, TN 37214
"Singer"

Deborah Adair
10100 Santa Monica Blvd. #700
Los Angeles, CA 90067
"Actress"

Red Adair
8705 Katy Freeway #302
Huston, TX 77024
"Fire Extinguishing Expert"

Brooke Adams
2451 Holly Drive
Los Angeles, CA 90068
"Actress"

Bryan Adams
406-68 Water Street
Vancouver BC 1A4 CANADA
"Singer"

Cindy Adams
1050 Fifth Avenue
New York, NY 10028
"Actress"

Don Adams
6310 San Vicente Blvd. #407
Los Angeles, CA 90048
"Actor, Writer, Director"

Edie Adams
8040 Okean Terrace
Los Angeles, CA 90046
"Singer"

Joey Adams
1050 Fifth Avenue
New York, NY 10028
"Actor, Writer, Director"

Julie Adams
5915 Corbin Avenue
Tarzana, CA 91356
"Actress"

Mason Adams
900 Fifth Avenue
New York, NY 10021
Actor"

Maud Adams
12700 Ventura Blvd. #350
Studio City, CA 91604
"Actress, Model"

Richard Adams
26 Church Street
Whitechurch, Hants. ENGLAND
"Author"

Tom Adams
29-31 Kings Road
London SW3 ENGLAND
"Actor"

ADC Band
17397 Santa Barbara
Detroit, MI 48221
"Rock & Roll Group"

Wesley Addy
88 Central Park West
New York, NY 10023
"Actor"

Merv Adelson
600 Sarbonne Road
Los Angeles, CA 90077
"TV Producer"

Isabelle Adjani
2 rue Gaston de St. Paul
75016 Paris, FRANCE
"Actress"

Lou Adler
3969 Villa Costera
Malibu, CA 90265
"Director, Producer"

Margot Adler
c/o National Public Radio
2025 "M" Street N.W.
Washington, DC 20036
"News Correspondent"

Stella Adler
1016 Fifth Avenue
New York, NY 10028
"Actor, Director"

Iris Adrian
3341 Floyd Terrace
Los Angeles, CA 90028
"Actress"

King Bhumibol Adulyadey
Villa Chiralada
Bangkok, THAILAND
"King Of Thailand"

John Agar
639 North Hollywood Way
Burbank, CA 91505
"Actor"

Andre Agassi
6739 Tara Avenue
Las Vegas, NV 89102
"Tennis Player"

Mehmet Ali Agca
Rebibbia Prison
Rome, ITALY
"Prisoner"

Spiro T. Agnew
78 Columbia Drive
Rancho Mirage, CA 92270
"Politician"

Art Agnos
42 Graystone Terrace
San Francisco, CA 94114
"Mayor of San Francisco"

Martin Agronsky
4001 Brandywine Street
Washington, DC 20016
"TV Producer"

Jenny Agutter
6882 Camrose Drive
Los Angeles, CA 90068
"Actress"

A-Ha
Box 203
Watford WD1 3YA ENGLAND
"Rock & Roll Group"

Charles Aidman
525 North Palm Drive
Beverly Hills, CA 90210
"Actor, Writer, Driector"

Danny Aiello
4 Thornhill Drive
Ramsey, NH 07446
"Actor"

Troy Aikman
1 Cowboys Parkway
Irving, TX 75063
"Football Player"

Anouk Aimee
4 rue de Ponthieu
F-75008 Paris, FRANCE
"Actress"

Air Supply
1990 Bundy Drive #590
Los Angeles, CA 90025
"Rock & Roll Group"

Franklin Ajaye
1312 South Orange Drive
Los Angeles, CA 90019
"Comedian, Actor"

Rep. Daniel Akaka (HI)
House Rayburn Bldg. #2301
Washington, DC 20515
"Politician"

Emperor Akihoto
The Imperial Palace
1-1 Chiyoda - Chiyoda-Ku
Tokyo, JAPAN
"Emperor of Japan"

Claude Akins
1927 Midlothian Drive
Altadena, CA 91001
"Actor"

Alabama
P.O. Box 529
Ft. Payne, AL 35967
"C&W Group"

Buddy Alan
1225 North Chester Avenue
Bakersfield, CA 93308
"Singer"

Alarm
47 Bernard Street
St. Albans, Herts ENGLAND
"Rock & Roll Group"

President Hafez Al-Assad
Presidential Office
Damascus, SYRIA
"President of Syria"

Capt. Lou Albano
P.O. Box 3859
Stamford, CT 06905
"Wrestler, Manager"

Edward Albee
14 Harrison Street
New York, NY 10013
"Writer, Producer"

Anna Marie Alberghetti
293 South Reeves Drive
Beverly Hills, CA 90212
"Actress, Singer"

Carl Albert
Rt. #2
McAlester, OK 74501
"Politician"

Eddie Albert
719 Amalfi Drive
Pacific Palisades, CA 90272
"Actor"

Edward Albert
10100 Santa Monica Blvd. #1600
Los Angeles, CA 90067
"Actor"

Prince Albert
Palais De Monaco
Boite Postal 158
98015 Monte Carlo Monaco
"Prince of Monaco"

Dolores Albin
13006 Woodbridge
Studio City, CA 91604
"Actress"

Lola Albright
P.O. Box 6067
Glendale, CA 91225
"Actress"

Dr. Tenley Albright
2 Commonwealth
Boston, MA 02117
"Skater"

Alan Alda
641 Lexington Avenue #1400
New York, NY 10022
"Actor"

Antony Alda
15 Seaview Drive North
Rolling Hills, CA 90274
"Actor"

Ginger Alden
4152 Royal Crest Place
Memphis, TN 38138
"Model"

Norman Alden
9300 Wilshire Blvd. #410
Beverly Hills, CA 90212
"Actor"

Dr. Ed "Buzz" Aldrin, Jr.
233 Emerald Bay
Laguna Beach, CA 92651
"Astronaut"

Frank Aletter
5430 Corbin Avenue
Tarzana, CA 91356
"Actor"

Rep. Bill Alexander (AR)
House Cannon Bldg. #233
Washington, DC 20515
"Politician"

Denise Alexander
345 North Maple Drive #183
Beverly Hills, CA 90210
"Actress"

Jane Alexander
Gordon Road, RFD #2
Carmel, NY 10512
"Actress"

Kim Alexis
3575 Cahuenga Blvd. West #217
Los Angeles, CA 90068
"Model"

ALF
8660 Hayden Place
Culver City, CA 90230
"Actor"

Kristian Alfonso
P.O. Box 93-1628
Los Angeles, CA 90093
"Actress"

Muhammad Ali
P.O. Box 187
Berrien Springs, MI 59103
"Former Boxing Champion"

Ana Alicia
9744 Wilshire Blvd. #308
Beverly Hills, CA 90212
"Actress"

Jed Allan
11759 Iowa Avenue
Los Angeles, CA 90025
"Actor"

Betty Allen
645 St. Nicholas Avenue
New York, NY 10030
"Mezzo-Soprano"

Byron Allen
1875 Century Park East #2200
Los Angeles, CA 90067
"Comedian"

Chad Allen
12049 Smokey Lane
Cerritos, CA 90701
"Actor"

Corey Allen
8642 Hollywood Blvd.
Los Angeles, CA 90046
Actor, Writer, Director"

Debbie Allen
607 Magueritta Avenue
Santa Monica, CA 90402
"Actress, Dancer, Singer"

J. Presson Allen
1500 Broadway
New York, NY 10036
"Filmwriter, Producer"

Karen Allen
122 East 10th Street
New York, NY 10013
"Actress"

Marcus Allen
11745 Montana Avenue
Los Angeles, CA 90049
"Football Player"

Marty Allen
5750 Wilshire Blvd. #580
Los Angeles, CA 90036
"Actor, Comedian"

Nancy Allen
409 North Camden Drive #105
Beverly Hills, CA 90210
"Actress"

Peter Allen
6 West 77th Street
New York, NY 10022
"Singer, Composer"

Rex Allen
P.O. Box 430
Sonoita, AZ 85637
"Singer"

Sean Barbara Allen
1622 Sierra Bonita Avenue
Los Angeles, CA 90046
"Actress, Writer"

Steve Allen
16185 Woodvale
Encino, CA 91316
"Actor, Writer, Comedian"

Woody Allen
930 Fifth Avenue
New York, NY 10018
"Actor, Director, Comedian"

Kirstie Alley
4875 Louis
Encino, CA 91316
"Actress"

Bobby Allison
140 Church Street
Hueytown, AL 35020
"Auto Racer"

Mose Allison
34 Dogwood Street
Smithtown, NY 11787
"Pianist, Composer"

Greg Allman
P.O. Box 4332
Marietta, GA 30061
"Singer, Musican"

Christopher Allport
121 North San Vicente Blvd.
Beverly Hills, CA 90211
"Actor"

Gloria Allred
6380 Wilshire Blvd. #1404
Los Angeles, CA 90048
"Lawyer, Feminist"

June Allyson
1651 Foothill Road
Ojai, CA 93020
"Actress"

Maria Conchita Alonso
P.O. Box 537
Beverly Hills, CA 90213
"Actress"

Felipe Alou
1501 West 16th Street
Indianapolis, IN 46202
"Baseball Player"

Herb Alpert
31930 Pacific Coast Hwy.
Malibu, CA 90265
"Musician"

Hollis Alpert
P.O. Box 142
Shelter Island, NY 11964
"Writer"

Carol Alt
163 John Street
Greenwich, CT 06831
"Model"

Jeff Altman
345 North Maple Drive #183
Beverly Hills, CA 90210
"Comedian, Actor"

Robert Altman
502 Park Avenue #15G
New York, NY 10022
"Writer, Producer, Director"

Robert Altman
5051 Klingle Street
Washington, DC 20016
"Financier"

Alvin & The Chipmunks
4400 Coldwater Canyon #300
Studio City, CA 91604
"Music Group"

Rodney Amateau
133 1/2 South Linden Drive
Beverly Hills, CA 90212
"Film Writer, Producer

Lou Ambers
4235 North 16th Avenue
Phoenix, AZ 85015
"Boxer"

Don Ameche
2121 Avenue of the Stars #950
Los Angeles, CA 90067
"Actor"

America
8730 Sunset Blvd. PH
Los Angeles, CA 90069
"Rock & Roll Group"

Ed Ames
1457 Claridge
Beverly Hills, CA 90210
"Singer"

Leon Ames
1015 Goldenrod Avenue
Corona Del Mar, CA 92625
"Actor"

Rachel Ames
12711 Hacienda Drive
Studio City, CA 91604
"Author"

Trey Ames
15760 Ventura Blvd. #1730
Encino, CA 91436
"Actor"

Idi Amin
Box 8948
Jidda 21492
SAUDI ARABIA
"Deposed Ruler"

Clevland Amory
200 West 57th Street
New York, NY 10019
"Writer"

Deborah Amos
c/o National Public Radio
2025 "M" Street N.W.
Washington, DC 20036
"News Correspondent"

Famous Amos (Wally)
215 Lanipo Drive
Kailua, HI 96734
"Cookie Entrepreneur"

John Amos
431 West 162nd Street
New York, NY 10032
"Actor"

Morey Amsterdam
1012 North Hillcrest Road
Beverly Hills, CA 90210
"Actor, Comedian"

Barbara Anderson
4345 Enoro Drive
Los Angeles, CA 90008
"Actress"

Bill Anderson
P.O. Box 888
Hermitage, TN 37076
"Singer"

Daryl Anderson
5923 Wilbur Avenue
Tarzana, CA 91356
"Actor"

Ernie Anderson
4075 Troost
Studio City, CA 91604
"Actor"

Harry Anderson
1420 N. W. Gilman Blvd. #2123
Issaguah, WA 98027
"Actor, Comedian"

Jack Anderson
1531 "P" Street N.W.
Washington, DC 20005
"News Correspondent"

John Anderson
Nova University
Center for Law
Ft. Lauderdale, FL 33314
"Politician"

Lindsay Anderson
9 Stirling Mansions
Canfield Gardens
London NW6 ENGLAND
"Filmwriter, Producer"

Loni Anderson
1001 Indiantown Road
Jupiter, FL 33458
"Actress"

Louie Anderson
8033 Sunset Blvd. #605
Los Angeles, CA 90046
"Comedian"

Lynn Anderson
4925 Tyne Valley Blvd.
Nashville, TN 37220
"Singer"

Marian Anderson
Marianna Farms
Joe's Hill Road
Danbury, CT 06811
"Singer"

Mary Anderson
1127 Norman Place
Los Angeles, CA 90049
"Actress"

Melissa Sue Anderson
20722 Pacific Coast Hwy
Malibu, CA 90265
"Actress"

Melody Anderson
10433 Wilshire Blvd. #1203
Los Angeles, CA 90024
"Actress"

Michael Anderson, Jr.
132-B South Lasky Drive
Beverly Hills, CA 90212
"Actor"

Paul Anderson
1603 McIntosh Street
Vidalia, GA 30474
"Weightlifter"

Richard Anderson
10120 Cielo Drive
Beverly Hills, CA 90210
"Actor"

Richard Dean Anderson
16030 Ventura Blvd. #380
Encino, CA 91436
"Actor"

Sparky Anderson
c/o Tiger Stadium
Detroit, MI 48216
"Baseball Manager"

Andre The Giant
P.O. Box 3859
Stamford, CT 06905
"Wrestler"

Ursula Andress
Danikhofenweg 95
Ostermundingen, SWITZERLAND
"Actress"

Mario Andretti
53 Victory Lane
Nazareth, PA 18064
"Auto Racer"

Andy Andrews
1514 Shamrock Drive
Helena, AL 35080
"Comedian"

Anthony Andrews
13 Manor Place
Oxford, Oxon, ENGLAND
"Actor"

Prince Andrew
Sunninghill Park
Windsor, ENGLAND
"England Royalty"

Dana Andrews
1021 North Crescent Heights Blvd.
3rd Floor
Los Angeles, CA 90046
"Actor"

Julie Andrews
P.O. Box 666
Beverly Hills, CA 90213
"Singer"

Maxene Andrews
14200 Carriage Oak Lane
Auburn, CA 95603
"Singer"

Rep. Michael Andrews (TX)
House Cannon Bldg. #322
Washington, DC 20515
"Politician"

Patti Andrews
9823 Aldea Avenue
Northridge, CA 91354
"Singer"

Tige Andrews
4914 Encino Terrace
Encino, CA 91316
"Actor, Writer"

Vanessa Angel
853-7th Avenue #9-A
New York, NY 10019
"Actress"

Maya Angelo
51 Church Street
Boston, MA 02116
"Writer, Poet"

The Angels
P.O. Box 262
Carteret, NJ 07008
"Vocal Group"

Kenneth Anger
6028 Barton Avenue
Los Angeles, CA 90038
"Film Director"

Jim Angle
c/o National Public Radio
2025 "M" Street N.W.
Washington, DC 20036
"News Correspondent"

Philip Anglim
2404 Grand Canal
Venice, CA 90291
"Actor"

Edward Anhalt
500 Amalfi Drive
Pacific Palisades, CA 90272
"Writer, Producer"

John Aniston
3307 Bonnie Hill Drive
Los Angeles, CA 90068
"Actor"

Paul Anka
721 Fifth Avenue
New York, NY 10022
"Singer"

Annabella
1 rue Pierret
92200 Neuilly, FRANCE
"Actress"

Princess Anne
Gatombe Park
Glouchestershire, ENGLAND
"England Royalty"

Wallis Annenberg
1026 Ridgedale Drive
Beverly Hills, CA 90210
"Magazine Executive"

Walter Annenberg
P.O. Box 98
Rancho Mirage, CA 92270
"Philanthropist"

Francesca Annis
2 Vicarage Court
London W8 ENGLAND
"Actress"

Rep. Frank Annunzio
House Rayburn Bldg. #2303
Washington, DC 20515
"Politician"

Michael Ansara
4624 Park Mirasol
Calabasas, CA 91302
"Actor"

Susan Anspach
473-16th Street
Santa Monica, CA 90402
"Actress"

Adam Ant
P.O. Box 866
London SE1 3AP ENGLAND
"Singer"

Rep. Beryl Anthony (AR)
House Longworth Bldg. #1117
Washington, DC 20515
"Politician"

Ray Anthony
9288 Kinglet Drive
Los Angeles, CA 90069
"Orchestra Leader"

Susan Anton
1853 Noel Place
Beverly Hills, CA 90210
"Actress"

Laura Antonelli
Lungotevere Michelangelo 9
1-00192 Rome, ITALY
"Actress"

Lou Antonio
534 Gaylord Drive
Burbank, CA 91505
"Actor, Writer, Director"

Michelangelo Antonioni
Via Vincenzo Tiberio 18
Rome, ITALY
"Film Director"

Rocky Aoki
8685 N.W. 53rd Terrace
Miami, FL 33155
"Food Entrepreneur"

Luis Aparicio
Calle 73 #14-53
Maraciabo, VENEZUELA
"Baseball Player"

Apollonia (Kotero)
8200 Wilshire Blvd. #218
Beverly Hills, CA 90212
"Actress"

Christina Applegate
4527 Park Allegra
Calabasas, CA 91302
"Actress"

Rep. Douglas Applegate (OH)
House Rayburn Bldg. #2183
Washington, DC 20515
"Politician"

John Aprea
1930 Century Park West #303
Los Angeles, CA 90067
"Actor"

Michael Apted
1051 Villa View Drive
Pacific Palisades, CA 90272
"Film Director"

Corazon Aquino
Malacanang Palace
Manila, PHILIPPINES
"Politician"

Yassir Arafat
Arnestconseil 17 Belvedere
1002 Tunis, TUNISIA
"Politician"

Alan Arbus
2208 North. Beverly Glen
Los Angeles, CA 90077
"Actor"

Loreen Arbus
8841 Appian Way
Los Angeles, CA 90046
"Writer"

Eddie Arcaro
11111 Biscayne Blvd.
Miami, FL 33161
"Tennis Player"

Anne Archer
13201 Old Oak Lane
Los Angeles, CA 90049
"Writer"

Rep. Bill Archer (TX)
House Longworth Bldg. #1135
Washington, DC 20515
"Politician"

Jeffrey Archer
93 Albert Embankment
London SE1 ENGLAND
"Author"

Army Archerd
442 Hilgard Avenue
Los Angeles, CA 90024
"Columnist"

Dotti Archibald
10372 Tennessee Avenue
Los Angeles, CA 90064
"Comedienne"

Toni Arden
34-34 75th Street
Jackson Heights, NY 11372
"Singer"

Moshe Arens
49 Hagderat
Savyon, ISRAEL
"Politician"

Adam Arkin
50 Ridge Drive
Chappauqua, NY 10514
"Actor, Director"

Alan Arkin
31 Bank Street
New York, NY 10014
"Actor"

Oscar Arias
Casa Presidencia
San Jose, COSTA RICA
"Politician"

Samuel Z. Arkoff
3205 Oakdell Lane
Studio City, CA 91604
"Film Producer"

Roone Arledge
535 Park Avenue #13A
New York, NY 10021
"TV Producer"

Arletty
14 rue De Rimusat
75016 Paris, FRANCE
"Actress"

Giorgio Armani
650 Fifth Avenue
New York, NY 10019
"Fashion Designer"

Joan Armatrading
27 Queensdale Place
London W11 ENGLAND
"Singer, Guitarist"

Rep. Dick Armey (TX)
House Cannon Bldg. #514
Washington, DC 20515
"Politician"

Anne Armstrong
Armstrong Ranch
Armstrong, TX 78338
"Politician"

Bess Armstrong
1518 North Doheny Drive
Los Angeles, CA 90069
"Actress"

Curtis Armstrong
6306 Ivarene
Los Angeles, CA 90068
"Actor"

Garner Ted Armstrong
P.O. Box 2525
Tyler, TX 75710
"Evangelist, Author"

Neil Armstrong
1739 North State, Rt. 123
Lebanon, OH 45036
"Astronaut"

Desi Arnaz, Jr.
P.O. Box 2000
Ojai, CA 93023
"Actor"

Lucie Arnaz
470 Main Street #K
Ridgefield, CT 06877
"Actress"

James Arness
P.O. Box 49003
Los Angeles, CA 90049
"Actor"

Jeanetta Arnette
840 North Huntley Drive #3
Los Angeles, CA 90069
"Actress"

Peter Arnett
111 Massachusetts N.W.
Washington, DC 20001
"News Correspondent"

Alison Arngrim
1340 North Poinsettia #422
Los Angeles, CA 90046
"Actress"

Danny Arnold
1293 Sunset Plaza Drive
Los Angeles, CA 90069
"Writer, Producer"

Eddy Arnold
P.O. Box 97
Brentwood, TN 37027
"Singer"

Stefan Arnsten
1017 Laurel Way
Beverly Hills, CA 90210
"Actor"

David Arquette
616 North Gower Street
Los Angeles, CA 90004
"Actor"

Rosanna Arquette
1201 Alta Loma Road
Los Angeles, CA 90069
"Actress"

Rod Arrants
9113 Sunset Blvd.
Los Angeles, CA 90069
"Actor"

Beatrice Arthur
2000 Old Ranch Road
Los Angeles, CA 90049
"Actress"

Maureen Arthur
9200 Sunset Blvd. #909
Los Angeles, CA 90069
"Actress"

Mary Kay Ash
8787 North Stemmons Freeway
Dallas, TX 75247
"Cosmetic Executive"

Dana Ashbrook
2634 North Beachwood Drive
Los Angeles, CA 90069
"Actress"

Daphne Ashbrook
335 North Maple Drive #250
Beverly Hills, CA 90210
"Actress"

Arthur Ashe
370 East 76th Street #A-1402
New York, NY 10021
"Tennis Player"

Jane Asher
644 North Doheny Drive
Los Angeles, CA 90069
"Actress"

Peter Asher
644 North Doheny Drive
Los Angeles, CA 90069
"Record Producer"

William Asher
2341 Canyon Back Road
Los Angeles, CA 90049
"Writer, Producer"

Ashford & Simpson
254 West 72nd Street #1-A
New York, NY 10023
"Vocal Duo"

Vladimir Ashkenazy
Sonnehof 4
6004 Lucerne, SWITZERLAND
"Pianist"

Edward Ashley
1879 Benecia Avenue
Los Angeles, CA 90025
"Actor"

Elizabeth Ashley
9010 Dorrington Avenue
Los Angeles, CA 90048
"Actress"

Jennifer Ashley
200 North Robertson Blvd. #219
Beverly Hills, CA 90211
"Actress"

John Ashley
18067 Lake Encino Drive
Encino, CA 91316
"Actor, Producer"

John Ashton
P.O. Box 49698
Los Angeles, CA 90049
"Actor"

Isaac Asimov
10 West 66th Sreet #33A
New York, NY 10023
"Author"

Leon Askin
625 North Rexford Drive
Beverly Hills, CA 90210
"Actor, Director"

Asleep At The Wheel
6060 N. Central Expressway #428
Dallas, TX 75205
"Rock & Roll Group"

Edward Asner
P.O. Box 7407
Studio City, CA 91604
"Actor"

Rep. Les Aspin (WI)
House Rayburn Bldg. #2336
Washington, DC 20515
"Politician"

Armand Assante
RD #1, Box 561
Campbell Hall, NY 10916
"Actor"

Pat Ast
205 South Beverly Drive #210
Beverly Hills, CA 90212
"Actress"

Robyn Astaire
1155 San Ysidro Drive
Beverly Hills, CA 90210
"Widower of Fred Astaire"

John Astin
P.O. Box 49698
Los Angeles, CA 90049
"Actor, Director, Writer"

Mackenzie Astin
P.O. Box 385
Beverly Hills, CA 90213
"Actor"

Sean Astin
5824 Norwich Avenue
Van Nuys, CA 91411
"Actor"

Rick Astley
4-7 The Vineyard Sancyuary
London SE1 1QL ENGLAND
"Singer"

William Atherton
1527 Veteran Avenue #4
Los Angeles, CA 90024
"Actor"

Rep. Chester Atkins (MA)
House Cannon Bldg. #504
Washington, DC 20515
"Politician"

Chet Atkins
33 Music Square West #106-B
Nashville, TN 37203
"Guitarist"

Christopher Atkins
3751 Sunswept Drive
Studio City, CA 91604
"Actor"

Tom Atkins
9301 Wilshire Blvd. #312
Beverly Hills, CA 90210
"Actor"

Atlantic Rhythm Section
3927 Northcrest Road #203
Doraville, GA 30340
"Music Group"

Sir Richard Attenborough
Old Friars
Richard Green, Surrey
ENGLAND
"Writer, Producer"

Malcolm Atterbury
605 North Camden Drive
Beverly Hills, CA 90210
"Actor, Director, Writer"

Rene Auberjonois
448 South Arden Blvd.
Los Angeles, CA 90020
"Actress"

Lenore Aubert
505 East 79th Street
New York, NY 10021
"Actress"

James Aubrey
67 Duriston Road
London, A58 RP, ENGLAND
"Actor"

Jacques Aubuchon
20978 Rios Street
Woodland Hills, CA 91364
"Actor"

Louis Auchincloss
1111 Park Avenue
New York, NY 10028
"Author, Critic"

Rep. Les Aucoin (OR)
House Rayburn Bldg. #2159
Washington, DC 20515
"Politician"

Stephanie Audran
95 Bis rue de Chezy
92200 Neuilly-sur-seine, FRANCE
"Actor"

Red Auerbach
4200 Massachusetts Avenue N.W.
Washington, DC 20016
"Basketball Executive"

Ira Augustain
3900 Ramboz Drive
Los Angeles, CA 90063
"Actor"

Jean Pierre Aumont
27 Rue de Richelieu
75001 Paris, FRANCE
"Author"

Jean Aurel
40 rue Lauriston
75116 Paris, FRANCE
"Writer"

Karen Austin
141 El Camino Drive #205
Beverly Hills, CA 90212
"Actress"

Teri Austin
4245 Laurel Grove
Studio City, CA 91604
"Actress"

Tracy Austin
1025 Thomas Jefferson Street
Suite #450-E
Washington, DC 20007
"Tennis Player"

Alan Autry
200 Bay Street #901
Ottawa, Ont. K1R 7W8 CANADA
"Actor"

Gene Autry
5858 Sunset Blvd.
P.O. Box 710
Los Angeles, CA 90028
"Actor, Singer, Executive"

Frankie Avalon
6311 DeSoto Street #1
Woodland Hills, CA 91367
"Singer"

Michael Angelo Avaloone
80 Hilltop Blvd.
East Brunswick, NJ 08816
"Author"

Richard Avedon
407 East 75th Street
New York, NY 10021
"Photographer"

Average White Band
273-287 Regent Street
London, ENGLAND
"Rock & Roll Group"

Margaret Avery
P.O. Box 3494
Hollywood, CA 90078
"Actress"

Hoyt Axton
3135 Cedarwood, Box 614
Tahoe City, CA 95730
"Singer, Songwriter"

Dan Aykroyd
3960 Laurel Canyon Blvd.
Studio City, CA 91604
"Actor"

Leah Ayres
16 Fleet Street #8
Marina del Rey, CA 90292
"Actress"

Lew Ayres
675 Walther Way
Los Angeles, CA 90049
"Actor"

Charles Aznavour
rue de Ponthieu
F-75008 Paris, FRANCE
"Singer"

Candy Azzara
1155 North La Cienega Blvd. #307
Los Angeles, CA 90069
"Actress"

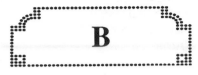

B-52
P.O. Box 506
Canal Street Station
New York, NY 10013
"Rock & Roll Group"

Shirley Babashoff
17254 Santa Clara Street
Santa Ana, CA 92708
"Swimmer"

Bruce Babbitt
1700 West Washington Street
Phoenix, AZ 85007
"Ex-Governor"

Harry Babbitt
7 Rue St. Cloud
Newport Beach, CA 91660
"Conductor"

Tai Babilonia
933-21st Street #6
Santa Monica, CA 90402
"Ice Skater"

Baby's
1545 Archer Road
Bronx, NY 10462
"Music Group"

Babyface
P.O. Box 921729
Atlanta, GA 30092
"R&B Group"

Lauren Bacall
1 West 72nd Street #43
New York, NY 10023
"Actress"

Barbara Bach
24 Avenue Princess Grace
Monte Carlo, MONACO
"Actress"

Cathrine Bach
14000 Davana Terrace
Sherman Oaks, CA 91403
"Actress"

Burt Bacharach
658 Nimes Road
Los Angeles, CA 90077
"Composer, Pianist"

Don Bachardy
145 Adelaide Drive
Santa Monica, CA 90402
"Writer"

Wally Backman
160 S.E. 39th Street
Hillsboro, OR 97123
"Baseball Player"

Henny Backus
10914 Bellagio Road
Los Angeles, CA 90077
"Actress"

Francis Bacon
6 Albermarle Street
London W1X 3HF ENGLAND
"Statesman, Essayist"

James Bacon
10982 Topeka Drive
Northridge, CA 91324
"Actor"

Kevin Bacon
800 West End Avenue #7-A
New York, NY 10025
"Actor"

John Badham
100 Universal City Plaza
Bldg. #507, 3E
Universal City, CA 91608
"Film Director"

Jane Badler
8383 Wilshire Blvd. #840
Beverly Hills, CA 90211
"Actress"

Max Baer, Jr.
10433 Wilshire Blvd. #103
Los Angeles, CA 90024
"Film Director"

Parley Baer
4967 Bilmoor Avenue
Tarzana, CA 91356
"Actor"

Joan Baez
P.O. Box 1026
Menlo Park, CA 94025
"Singer"

Vince Bagetta
3928 Madelia Avenue
Sherman Oak, CA 91403
"Actor"

F. Lee Bailey
66 Long Wharf
Boston, MA 02109
"Lawyer"

G.W. Bailey
4972 Calvin
Tarzana, CA 91356
"Actor"

Joel Bailey
6550 Murietta Road
Van Nuys, CA 91401
"Actor"

Razzy Bailey
417 Saundrers Ferry
Hendersonville, TN 37075
"Singer"

Baillie & The Boys
1103-16th Avenue South
Nashville, TN 37212
"C&W Group"

Barbara Bain
23717 Long Valley Road
Calabasas, CA 91302
"Actress"

Conrad Bain
1230 Chickory Lane
Los Angeles, CA 90049
"Actress"

Beryl Bainbridge
42 Albert Street
London NW1 7NU ENGLAND
"Author"

Jimmy Baio
9229 Sunset Blvd. #607
Los Angeles, CA 90069
"Actor"

Scott Baio
11662 Duque Drive
Studio City, CA 91604
"Actor"

Richard Bakalyan
1070 South Bedford Street
Los Angeles, CA 90035
"Actor, Writer"

Anita Baker
804 North Crescent Drive
Beverly Hills, CA 90210
"Singer"

Benny Baker
5004 Canoga Avenue
Woodland Hills, CA 91364
"Actor"

Blanche Baker
70 Flower Avenue
Hastings-on-Hudson, NY 10706
"Actress"

Carroll Baker
70 Flower Avenue
Hastings-on-Hudson, NY 10706
"Actress"

Diane Baker
2585 La Paloma Court
Thousand Oaks, CA 91360
"Actress, Director"

Howard Baker
Box 8
Huntsville, TN 37756
"Former Senator"

James Baker III
2201 "C" Street N.W.
Washington, DC 20001
"Secretary of State"

Janet Abbott Baker
450 Edgeware Road
London W2 ENGLAND
"Mezzo-Soprano"

Joe Don Baker
23339 Hatteras
Woodland Hills, CA 91364
"Actor"

Raymond Baker
10100 Santa Monica Blvd. #1600
Los Angeles, CA 90067
"Actor"

Rep. Richard Baker (LA)
House Cannon Bldg. #506
Washington, DC 20515
"Politician"

William Bakewell
1745 Selby Avenue #16
Los Angeles, CA 90024
"Actor"

James (Jim) Bakker
Federal Medical Center
2110 Center Street East
Rochester, MN 55901
"TV Evangelist, Prisoner"

Tammy Faye Bakker
P.O. Box 690788
Orlando, FL 32869
"TV Evangelist"

Adam Baldwin
8882 Lookout Mountain Rd.
Los Angeles, CA 90046
"Actor"

Alec Baldwin
300 Central Park West
New York, NY 10024
"Actor"

Stephen Baldwin
10100 Santa Monica Blvd. #1600
Los Angeles, CA 90067
"Actor"

Carla Balenda
15848 Woodvale
Encino, CA 91316
"Actress"

Christine Ballard
11501 Chandler Blvd.
North Hollywood, CA 91601
"TV Writer, Director"

Kaye Ballard
1204-3rd Avenue #152
New York, NY 10121
"Actress, Singer"

Lucinda Ballard
180 East End Avenue
New York, NY 10028
"Costume Designer"

Rep. Cass Ballenger (NC)
House Cannon Bldg. #116
Washington, DC 20515
"Politician"

Mark Ballou
9169 Sunset Blvd.
Los Angeles, CA 90069
"Actor"

Martin Balsam
Hotel Olcott
27 West 72nd Street
New York, NY 10011
"Actor"

Talia Balsam
1331 North Hayworth Avenue
Los Angeles, CA 90036
"Actress"

Anne Bancroft
2301 La Mesa Drive
Santa Monica, CA 90405
"Actress, Writer, Director"

Prince Bandar al-Saud
601 New Hampshire Avenue N.W.
Washington, DC 20037
"Politician"

Sal Bando
104 West Juniper Lane
Mequon, WI 52092
"Baseball Player"

Moe Bandy
P.O. Box 40661
Nashville, TN 37204
"Singer"

Victor Banerjee
10 East Harrington
Calcutta 700071 INDIA
"Actor"

Abolhassan Bani Sadr
Auvers-Sur-Oise
FRANCE
"Politician"

Ernie Banks
P.O. Box 24302
Los Angeles, CA 90024
"Baseball Player"

Jonathan Banks
909 Euclid Street #8
Santa Monica, CA 90403
"Actor"

Ian Bannen
1999 Avenue of the Stars #2850
Los Angeles, CA 90067
"Actor"

Bob Banner
2409 Briarcrest Drive
Beverly Hills, CA 90210
"Director, Producer"

Sir Roger Bannister
16 Edward Square
London W8 ENGLAND
"Actor"

Jack Bannon
5832 Nagle Avenue
Van Nuys, CA 91401
"Actor"

Adrienne Barbeau
P.O. Box 1334
North Hollywood, CA 91604
"Actress"

Glynis Barber
113 Wardour Street
London W1V 3TD ENGLAND
"Actress"

Red Barber
3013 Brookmont Drive
Tallahassee, FL 32312
"Sportcaster"

Joseph Barbera
3617 Alomar Drive
Sherman Oaks, CA 91403
"Film Producer"

John Barbour
4254 Forman Avenue
Toluca Lake, CA 91602
"Writer, Comedian"

Pete Barbutti
3000 Ocean Park Blvd. #2006
Santa Monica, CA 90405
"Comedian"

Brigitte Bardot
La Madrigue 83990
St. Tropez Var, FRANCE
"Actress"

Bobby Bare
1210 West Main Street
Hendersonville, TN 37075
"Singer, Songwriter"

Bob Barker
1851 Outpost Drive
Los Angeles, CA 90068
"TV Show Host"

Ellen Barkin
3007 Lake Glen
Beverly Hills, CA 90210
"Actress"

Randy Barlow
5514 Kelly Road
Brentwood, TN 37027
"Singer"

Dr. Christian Barnard
The Moorings
Flamingo Crescent
Capetown, SOUTH AFRICA
"Medical Doctor"

Rep. Doug Barnard, Jr. (GA)
House Rayburn Bldg. #2227
Washington, DC 20515
"Politician"

Binnie Barnes Frankovich
838 North Doheny Drive #B
Los Angeles, CA 90069
"Actress"

Joanna Barnes
2160 Century Park East #2101-N
Los Angeles, CA 90067
"TV Writer"

Priscilla Barnes
3500 West Olive Avenue #1400
Burbank, CA 91505
"Actress"

Doug Barr
515 South Irving Blvd.
Los Angeles, CA 90020
"Actor"

Roseanne Barr-Arnold
12916 Evanston
Los Angeles, CA 90049
"Actress"

Jean Louis Barrault
18 Ave. du President Wilson
Paris 8e FRANCE
"Actor"

Marie-Christine Barrault
De Lisbonne 19
75008 Paris, FRANCE
"Actress"

Premier Raymond Barre
4-6 Ave. Emile-Acollas
F-75007 Paris, FRANCE
"Government Official"

Rona Barrett
P.O. Box 1410
Beverly Hills, CA 90213
"TV Personality"

Barbara Barrie
465 West End Avenue
New York, NY 10024
"Actress"

Maurice Barrier
18 rue de Gravelle
F-75012 Paris, FRANCE
"Actor"

Chuck Barris
17 East 76th Street
New York, NY 10021
"TV Host, Producer"

Blue Barron
P.O. Box 18049
Cleveland, OH 44118
"Band Leader"

Sydney Biddle Barrows
210 West 70th Street
New York, NY 10023
"Alleged Madam, Socialite"

Dave Barry
614 North Palm Drive
Beverly Hills, CA 90210
"Comedian"

Gene Barry
622 North Maple Drive
Beverly Hills, CA 90210
"Actor"

John Barry
540 Centre Island Road
Oyster Bay, NY 11771
"Composer"

Patricia Barry
12742 Highwood Street
Los Angeles, CA 90049
"Actress"

Philip Barry, Jr.
12742 Highwood Street
Los Angeles, CA 90049
"Writer, Producer"

Sy Barry
34 Saratoga Drive
Jericho, NY 11753
"Cartoonist"

Drew Barrymore
3960 Laurel Canyon Blvd. #159
Studio City, CA 91604
"Actress"

John Blyth Barrymore
144 South Peck Drive
Beverly Hills, CA 90212
"Actor"

Lionel Bart
200 Fulham Road
London SW10 9PN ENGLAND
"Lyricist, Composer"

Peter Bart
2270 Betty Lane
Beverly Hills, CA 90210
"Film Producer"

Jean Bartel
229 Bronwood Avenue
Los Angeles, CA 90049
"Actress"

Paul Bartel
7860 Fareholm Drive
Los Angeles, CA 90046
"Actor, Director"

Bonnie Bartlett
12802 Hortense Street
Studio City, CA 91604
"Actress"

Hall Bartlett
861 Stone Canyon Road
Los Angeles, CA 90077
"Writer, Producer"

Martine Bartlett
1233 North Harper #9
Los Angeles, CA 90046
"Actress"

Rep. Steve Barlett
House Longworth Bldg. 1709
Washington, DC 20515
"Politician"

Rep. Joe L. Barton (TX)
House Longworth Bldg. 1225
Washington, DC 20515
"Politician"

Peter Barton
2265 Westwood Blvd. #2619
Los Angeles, 90064
"Actor"

Billy Barty
4502 Framdale Avenue
North Hollywood, CA 91602
"Actor"

Andre Baruch
9955 Durant Drive
Beverly Hills, CA 90212
"Radio Personality"

Mikhail Baryshnikov
35 East 12th Street #5-D
New York, NY 10018
"Ballet Dancer"

Basia
40/42 Newman Street
London W1P 3PA ENGLAND
"Rock & Roll Group"

Carmen Basillo
67 Boxwood Drive
Rochester, NY 14617
"Boxer"

Kim Basinger
3960 Laurel Canyon Blvd. #414
Studio City, CA 91604
"Actress"

Lina Basquette
Shawod Hill Road #1
Wheeling, W.VA 26003
"Actress"

Dick Bass
506 Montana
Santa Monica, CA 90403
"Director, Producer"

Saul Bass
337 South Las Palmas Avenue
Los Angeles, CA 90020
"Director, Producer"

Jennifer Bassey
Chelsea Hotel
222 West 23rd Street
New York, NY 10019
"Actress"

Shirley Bassey
c/o Sergio Novak
villa Capricorn
55 Via Campione
6816 Bissone SWITERLAND
"Singer"

William Bast
6691 Whitley Terrace
Los Angeles, CA 90068
"Screenwriter"

Amelia Batchelor
14811 Mulholland Drive
Beverly Hills, CA 90210
"Model"

Rep. Herbert H. Bateman (VA)
House Longworth Bldg. #1527
Washington, DC 20515
"Politician"

Jason Bateman
2628-2nd Street
Santa Monica, CA 90405
"Actor"

Justine Bateman
3960 Laurel Canyon Blvd. #193
Studio City, CA 91604
"Actress"

Alan Bates
122 Hamilton Terrace
London NW8 ENGLAND
"Actor"

Rep. Jim Bates (CA)
House Longworth Bldg. #1404
Washington, DC 20515
"Politician"

Kathy Bates
121 North San Vicente Blvd.
Beverly Hills, CA 90211
"Actress"

Randall Batinkoff
P.O. Box 555
Ferndale, NY 12734
"Actor"

Belinda Bauder
15301 Ventura Blvd. #345
Sherman Oaks, CA 91403
"Actress"

Bruce Bauer
12456 Ventura Blvd. #1
Studio City, CA 91604
"Actor"

Hank Bauer
12705 West 108th Street
Overland Park, KS 66210
"Baseball Player"

Jamie Lyn Bauer
3500 West Olive Avenue #1400
Burbank, CA 91505
"Actress"

Sammy Baugh
c/o General Delivery
Rotan, Texas 79546
"Football Player"

Steven Bauer
5233 Strohm Avenue
North Hollywood, CA 91601
"Actor"

Jon "Bowzer" Bauman
3168 Oakshire Drive
Los Angeles, CA 90068
"Actor, Singer"

Meredith Baxter
10100 Santa Monica Blvd. #700
Los Angeles, CA 90067
"Actress"

Bay City Rollers
27 Preston Grange Road
Lothian, SCOTLAND
"Rock & Roll Group"

Birch Bayh
1 Indiana Square #240
Indianapolis, IN 46204
"Politician"

Don Baylor
5 Fieldstone Lane
South Natick, MA 01760
"Baseball Player"

Elgin Baylor
3939 South Figueroa Street
Los Angeles, CA 90037
"Basketball Player"

Beach Boys
101 Mesa Lane
Santa Barbara, CA 93109
"Rock & Roll Group"

Stephanie Beacham
31538 Broad Beach Road
Malibu, CA 90264
"Actress"

John Beal
205 West 54th Street
New York, NY 10019
"Actor"

Jennifer Beals
8899 Beverly Blvd.
Los Angeles, CA 90048
"Actress"

Abe Beame
1111-20 Street N.W.
Washington, DC 20575
"Politician"

Alan Bean
26 Sugarberry Circle
Houston, TX 77024
"Astronaut, Painter"

Orsen Bean
9255 Sunset Blvd. #515
Los Angeles, CA 90069
"Actor, Comedian"

Amanda Bearse
1907 Lucille Avenue
Los Angeles, CA 90039
"Actress"

Allyce Beasley
2415 Castilian
Los Angeles, CA 90068
"Actress"

Beastie Boys
298 Elizabeth Street
New York, NY 10012
"Rap Group"

Beatlemania
8665 Wilshire Blvd. #208
Beverly Hills, CA 90211
"Music Group"

Queen Beatrix
Kasteel Drakesteijn
Lage Vuursche 3744 BA
HOLLAND
"Royalty"

Ned Beatty
2706 North Beachwood Drive
Los Angeles, CA 90027
"Actor"

Warren Beatty
13671 Mulholland Drive
Beverly Hills, CA 90210
"Actor, Director, Writer"

Gilbert Becaud
24 rue de Longchamp
Paris 16e FRANCE
"Singer, Songwriter"

Jeff Beck
11 Old South Lincolns Inn
London WC2 ENGLAND
"Singer, Guitarist"

John Beck
822 South Robertson Blvd. #200
Los Angeles, CA 90035
"Actor"

Marilyn Beck
2132 El Roble Lane #655
Beverly Hills, CA 90210
"Columnist, Critic"

Michael Beck
1999 Avenue of the Stars
Suite #2850
Los Angeles, CA 90067
"Actor"

Boris Becker
Nusslocher Str. 51
6906 Leiman, GERMANY
"Tennis Player"

Don Beddor
26801 Via Grande
Mission Viejo, CA 92675
"Actor"

Bonnie Bedelia
1021 Georgina Avenue
Santa Monica, CA 90407
"Actress"

Brian Bedford
9301 Wilshire Blvd. #312
Beverly Hills, CA 90210
"Actor"

The Bee Gee
1735-149th Street N.E.
Miami Beach, FL 33181
"Rock & Roll Group"

Geoffrey Beene
550-7th Avenue
New York, NY 10018
"Fashion Designer"

Noah Beery, Jr.
P.O. Box 108
Keene, CA 93531
"Actor"

Leslie Bega
6451 Deep Dell Place
Los Angeles, CA 90048
"Actress"

David Begelman
705 North Linden Drive
Beverly Hills, CA 90210
"Film Executive"

Memachem Begin
1 Rosenbaum Street
Tel Aviv, ISRAEL
"Politician"

Ed Begley, Jr.
3850 Moundview Avenue
Studio City, CA 91604
"Actor"

Sam Behrens
10000 Santa Monica Blvd. #305
Los Angeles, CA 90049
"Actor"

Rep. Anthony C. Beilenson (CA)
House Longworth Bldg. #1025
Washington, DC 20515
"Politician"

Nina Beilina
400 West 43rd Street #7D
New York, NY 10036
"Violinist"

Harry Belafonte
300 West End Avenue
New York, NY 10023
"Singer, Actor"

Shari Belafonte-Harper
3546 Longridge Avenue
Sherman Oaks, CA 91423
"Actress, Model"

Christine Belford
201-A North Robertson Blvd.
Beverly Hills, CA 90211
"Actress"

Barbara Bel Geddes
15 Mill Street
Putnam Valley, NY 10579
"Actress"

Belita
Rose Cottage
44 Crabtress Lane
London SW6 6LW ENGLAND
"Actress, Belleria"

Greg Bell
110-12th Street
Logansport, IN 46947
"Track Athlete"

Tom Bell
108 Torriano Avenue
London NW5 ENGLAND
"Actor"

Bellamy Brothers
Rt. 2, Box 294
Dade City, FL 33525
"Vocal Duo"

Harry Bellaver
116 Summit Avenue
Tappan, NY 10983
"Actor"

Kathleen Beller
2018 North Whitley
Los Angeles, CA 90068
"Actress"

Melvin Belli
574 Pacific Avenue
San Francisco, CA 94133
"Lawyer"

Marco Bellocchio
Viale Mazzini 117
00195 Rome, ITALY
"Film Director"

Louie Bellson
P.O. Box 2608
Lake Havasu City, AZ 86405
"Drummer"

Pamela Bellwood
7444 Woodrow Wilson Drive
Los Angeles, CA 90046
"Actress, Photographer"

Jean-Paul Belmondo
77 Avenue Donfert Rochereaux
Paris 16e FRANCE
"Actor"

James Belushi
9830 Wilshire Blvd.
Beverly Hills, CA 90212
"Actor"

Pat Benatar
3575 Cahuenga Blvd. West
Suite #470
Los Angeles, CA 90068
"Singer"

Johnny Bench
661 Reisling Knoll
Cincinnati, OH 45226
"Baseball Player"

Peter Benchley
35 Boudinot Street
Princeton, NJ 08540
"Author"

Billy Benedict
1347 North Orange Grove Avenue
Los Angeles, CA 90046
"Actor"

Dirk Benedict
1637 Wellesley Drive
Santa Monica, CA 90406
"Actor"

Paul Benedict
P.O. Box 451
Chilmark, MA 02535
"Actor"

Tex Beneke
2275 Faust Avenue
Long Beach, CA 90815
"Orchestra Leader"

Annette Bening
5646 Tuxedo Tarrace
Los Angeles, CA 90068
"Actress"

Richard Benjamin
719 North Foothill Road
Beverly Hills, CA 90210
"Actor, Director"

Bruce Bennett
2702 Forester Road
Los Angeles, CA 90064
"Actor"

Rep. Charles E. Bennett (FL)
House Rayburn Bldg. #2107
Washington, DC 20515
"Politician"

Hywell Bennett
15 Golden Square #300
London W1R 3AG ENGLAND
"Actor"

Tony Bennett
101 West 55th Street #9A
New York, NY 10019
"Singer"

William Bennet
1150-17th Street N.W.
Washington, DC 20036
"Fomer Drug Czar"

Joan Benoit
R.R. #1 - Box 145AA
Freeport, ME 04302
"Track Athlete"

George Benson
19 Holomakani Place
La Haina, HI 96761
"Singer, Guitarist"

Robby Benson
15760 Ventura Blvd. #1730
Encino, CA 91436
"Actor, Writer"

Rep. Helen D. Bentley (MD)
House Longworth Bldg. #1610
Washington, DC 20515
"Politician"

Barbi Benton
P.O. Box 549
Carbondale, CO 81623
"Actress, Model"

Lloyd Bentsen (TX)
703 Senate Hart Bldg.
Washington, DC 20510
"Politician"

John Beradino
1719 Ambassador Drive
Beverly Hills, CA 90210
"Actor"

Tom Berenger
P.O. Box 1842
Beaufort, SC 29901
"Actor"

Berry Berenson
2840 Seattle Drive
Los Angeles, CA 90046
"Mrs. Anthony Perkins"

Marisa Berenson
80 Avenue Charles de Gaulle
F92200 Neuilly, FRANCE
"Actress"

Rep. Doug Bereuter (NE)
House Rayburn Bldg. #2446
Washington, DC 20515
"Politician"

Patty Berg
P.O. Box 9227
Ft. Meyers, FL 33902
"Golfer"

Candice Bergen
955 South Carrillo Drive #200
Los Angeles, CA 90048
"Actress"

Mrs. Edgar Bergen
1485 Carla Ridge
Beverly Hills, CA 90210
"Actress"

Polly Bergen
1400 Devlin Drive
Los Angeles, CA 90069
"Actress"

Helmut Berger
Pertallstrasse 6
8000 Munchen 80 GERMANY
"Actor"

Senta Berger
Robert-Koch-Stasse 10
022 Grunwald, GERMANY
"Actress"

Lee Bergere
2385 Century Hill
Los Angeles, CA 90067
"Actor"

Herbert Berghof
11310 Shoshone Avenue
Granada Hills, CA 91344
"Actor"

Alan Bergman
714 North Maple Drive
Beverly Hills, CA 90210
"Lyricist"

Ingmar Bergman
Titurelstrasse 2 D-8000
Munich 81 Germany
"Film Director"

Marilyn Bergman
714 North Maple Drive
Beverly Hills, CA 90210
"Lyricist"

Sandahl Bergman
9903 Santa Monica Blvd. #274
Beverly Hills, CA 90212
"Actress, Model"

Luciano Berio
II Colombaig Radiocobdoli
53100 Siena, ITALY
"Composer, Conductor"

Howard Berkes
c/o National Public Radio
2025 "M" Street N.W.
Washington, DC 20036
"New Correspondent

Milton Berle
10750 Wilshire Blvd. #1003
Los Angeles, CA 90024
"Actor, Comedian"

Berlin
10642 Arnel Place
Chatsworth, CA 91311
"Rock & Roll Group"

Warren Berlinger
10642 Arnel Place
Chatsworth, CA 91311
"Actor"

Alan Berlow
c/o National Public Radio
2025 "M" Street N.W.
Washington, DC 20036
"News Correspondent"

Rep. Howard L. Berman (CA)
House Cannon Bldg. #137
Washington, DC 20515
"Politician"

Pandro S. Berman
914 North Roxbury Drive
Beverly Hills, CA 90210
"Film Producer"

Shelley Berman
268 Bell Canyon Road
Bell Canyon, CA 91307
"Comedian"

Lazar Bermann
155 West 68th Street
New York, NY 10023
"Pianist"

Crystal Bernard
10100 Santa Monica Blvd. #1600
Los Angeles, CA 90067
"Actress"

Ed Bernard
18851 Braemore Road
Northridge, CA 91326
"Actor"

Sandra Bernhard
11233 Blix Street
North Hollywood, CA 91602
"Comedianne"

Kevin Bernhardt
9300 Wilshire Blvd. #410
Beverly Hills, CA 90212
"Actor"

Collin Bernsen
401 North Poinsettia Place
Los Angeles, CA 90036
"Actor"

Corbin Bernsen
3500 West Olive #920
Burbank, CA 91505
"Actor"

Carl Bernstein
242 East 62nd Street
New York, NY 10021
"Writer"

Elmer Bernstein
859 Pichaco Lane
Montecito, CA 93103
"Composer, Conductor"

Jay Bernstein
9360 Beverly Crest Drive
Beverly Hills, CA 90210
"Talent Agent"

Kenny Bernstein
1105 Seminole
Richardson, TX 75080
"Auto Racer"

Yogi Berra
19 Highland Avenue
Montclair, NJ 07042
"Baseball Player & Manager"

Chuck Berry
Buckner Road
Wentzville, MO 63386
"Singer, Songwriter"

Ken Berry
1900 Outpost Drive
Los Angeles, CA 90068
"Actor, Dancer"

HRH Prince Bertil
Hertigens av Halland
Hungl Slottet
11130 Stockholm, SWEDEN
"Royalty"

Valerie Bertinelli
15760 Ventura Blvd. #700
Encino, CA 91436
"Actress"

Bibi Besch
3500 West Olive Avenue #1400
Burbank, CA 91505
"Actress"

Ted Bessel
1415 Stone Canyon Road
Los Angeles, CA 90077
"Actor, Dancer"

Martine Bestwicke
131 South Sycamore Avenue
Los Angeles, CA 90036
"Actress"

Ivy Bethune
3096 Lake Hollywood Drive
Los Angeles, CA 90068
"Actress"

Zina Bethune
3096 Lake Hollywood Drive
Los Angeles, CA 90028
"Actress"

Gary Bettenhausen
2550 Tree Farm Road
Martinsville, IN 46151
"Auto Racer"

Tony Bettenhausen
5234 Wilton Wood Court
Indianapolis, IN 46254
"Auto Racer"

Lyle Bettger
7060 Hollywood Blvd. #610
Los Angeles, CA 90028
"Actor"

Rep. Tom Bevill (AL)
House Rayburn Bldg. #2302
Washington, DC 20515
"Politician"

Turhan Bey
Paradisgasse Ave. 47
1190 XIX Vienna, AUSTRIA
"Actor"

Troy Beyer
3800 Barham Blvd
Los Angeles, CA 90068
"Actress"

Richard Beymer
9744 Wilshire Blvd. #308
Beverly Hills, CA 90212
"Actor"

Benazir Bhutto
70 Clifton Road
Karachi, PAKISTAN
"Politician"

Mayim Bialik
11350 Ventura Blvd. #206
Studio City, CA 91603
"Actress"

Sen. Joseph Biden, Jr. (DE)
6 Montchan Drive
Wilmington, DE 19807
"Politician"

Michael Biehn
3737 Deervale Drive
Sherman Oaks, CA 91403
"Actor"

Thom Bierdz
1435 North Stanley
Los Angeles, CA 90046
"Actor"

Ronald Biggs
201 rua Monte Alegre
Santa Teresa
Rio de Janiero, BRAZIL
"Train Robber"

Theodore Bikel
1131 Alta Loma Road #523
Los Angeles, CA 90069
"Actor, Singer"

Rep. James Bilbray (NV)
House Longworth Bldg. #1431
Washington, DC 20515
"Politician"

Rep. Michael Bilirakis (FL)
House Longworth Bldg. #1530
Washington, DC 20515
"Politician"

Tony Bill
73 Market Street
Venice, CA 90291
"Actor, Director"

Barbara Billingsley
800 San Lorenzo Street
Santa Monica, CA 90402
"Actress"

Peter Billingsley
11350 Ventura Blvd. #206
Studio City, CA 91604
"Child Actor"

Sir Rudolph Bing
160 Central Park South
New York, NY 10019
"Opera Executive"

Matt Biondi
1404 Rimer Drive
Morage, CA 94556
"Swimmer"

Billie Bird
9229 Sunset Blvd. #515
Los Angeles, CA 90069
"Actress"

Larry Bird
151 Merrimac Street
Boston, MA 02114
"Basketball Player"

Rose Elizabeth Brid
350 McAllister Street
San Francisco, CA 94102
"Former Judge"

Jane Birkin
28 rue de la Tour
F-75016 Paris, FRANCE
"Actress"

David Birney
20 Ocean Park Blvd. #11
Sanata Monica, CA 90405
"Actor"

Joey Bishop
1221 West Coast Highway
Newport Beach, CA 92663
"Actor, Comedian"

Stephen Bishop
2310 Apollo Drive
Los Angeles, CA 90047
"Singer Composer"

Whit Bissell
23388 Mulholland Hwy.
Calabasas, CA 91364
"Actor"

Jacqueline Bisset
1815 Benedict Canyon Drive
Beverly Hills, CA 90210
"Actress"

Bill Bixby
200 North Robertson Blvd. #223
Beverly Hills, CA 90211
"Actor, Director"

Cilla Black
Tilenouse Lane
Denholm, Buckinghamshire
ENGLAND
"Singer, Actress"

Clint Black
P.O. Box 19647
Houston, TX 77024
"Singer"

Karen Black
280 South Beverly Drive #400
Beverly Hills, CA 90212
"Actress"

Blackfoot
17650 West 12 Mile Road
Southfield, MI 48076
"Rock & Roll Group"

Blackjack
35 Brentwood
Farmingville, NY 11738
"Rock & Roll Group"

Black Oak Arkansas
1487 Red Fox Run
Lilburn, GA 30247
"C&W Group"

Honor Blackman
8 Harley Street
London W1N 2AB ENGLAND
"Actress"

Stephanie Blackmore
205 South Beverly Drive #210
Beverly Hills, CA 90212
"Actress"

Harry Blackstone, Jr.
P.O. Box 15428
San Diego, CA 92115
"Magician"

Mr. Earl Blackwell
171 West 57th Street
New York, NY 10019
"Publisher, Designer"

Nina Blackwood
8145 Mulholland Drive
Los Angeles, CA 90046
"Music Correspondent"

Taurean Blacque
4207 Don Ortega Place
Los Angeles, CA 90008
"Actor"

Ruben Blades
1234 1/2 North Crescent Hgts.
Los Angeles, CA 90046
"Singer, Actor, Songwriter"

Nell Walden Blaine
3 Ledge Road
Gloucester, MA 01930
"Painter"

Vivian Blaine
20 East 35th Street
New York, NY 10016
"Actress"

Betsy Blair
11 Chalcot Gardens
England's Lane
London NW3 ENGLAND
"Actress"

Janet Blair
21535 Irwin Street #126
Woodland Hills, CA 91367
"Actress"

Linda Blair
8033 Sunset Blvd. #204
Los Angeles, CA 90046
"Actress"

Robert Blake
11604 Dilling Street
North Hollywood, CA 91608
"Actor"

Whitney Blake
P.O. Box 6088
Malibu, CA 90265
"Actress"

Ronee Blakley
8033 Sunset Blvd. #693
Los Angeles, CA 90046
"Singer, Actress"

Susan Blakely
1829 Franklin Canyon
Beverly Hills, CA 90210
"Actress"

Noel Blanc
702 North Rodeo Drive
Beverly Hills, CA 90210
"Writer"

Nina Blanchard
957 North Cole Avenue
Los Angeles, CA 90028
"Talent Agent"

Bobby "Blue" Bland
108 North Auburndale #1010
Memphis, TN 38104
"Singer"

George Blanda
P.O. Box 1153
La Quinta, CA 92253
"Football Player"

Sally Blane
1114 South Roxbury Drive
Los Angeles, CA 90035
"Actress"

Fanny Blankers-Koen
"Nachtegaal"
Strat #67
Utrecht, HOLLAND
"Track Athlete"

Mark Blankfield
141 South El Camino Drive #205
Beverly Hills, CA 90212
"Actor"

Bill Blass
444 East 57th Street
New York, NY 10021
"Fashion Designer"

Freddie Blassie
P.O. Box 3859
Stamford, CT 06905
"Wrestler, Manager"

The Blasters
2667 North Beverly Glen
Los Angeles, CA 90077
"Rock & Roll Group"

Richard Blasucci
353 1/2 North Gardner
Los Angeles, CA 90036
"Actor, Writer"

Jeff Blatnick
848 Whitney Drive
Schenectady, NY 12309
"Wrestler"

Rep. Ben Blaz (GU)
House Longworth Bldg. #1130
Washington, DC 20515
"Politician"

Tempest Bledsoe
8230 Beverly Blvd. #23
Los Angeles, CA 90048
"Actress"

Rocky Bleier
580 Squal Run Road East
Pittsburgh, PA 15238
"Football Player"

Brian Blessed
St. James's Street
22 Groom Place
London SW1 ENGLAND
"Actor"

Rep. Thomas J. Bliley, Jr. (VA)
House Rayburn Bldg. #2241
Washington, DC 20515
"Politician"

Hunt Block
8370 Wilshire Blvd. #310
Beverly Hills, CA 90211
"Cartoonist"

Dirk Blocker
11726 San Vicente Blvd. #300
Los Angeles, CA 90049
"Actor"

Michael Blodgett
10485 National Blvd. #22
Los Angeles, CA 90034
"Actor"

Anne Bloom
656 West Knoll Drive #303
Los Angeles, CA 90069
"Actress, Comedienne"

Brian Bloom
11 Croydon Court
Dix Hills, NY 11746
"Actor"

Claire Bloom
109 Jermyn Street
London W1 ENGLAND
"Actress"

Lindsay Bloom
3751 Reklaw
Studio City, CA 91604
"Actress"

Verna Bloom
327 East 82nd Street
New York, NY 10028
"Actress"

Betsy Bloomingdale
131 Delfern Drive
Los Angeles, CA 90024
"Business Executive"

Lisa Blount
3957 Albright Avenue
Los Angeles, CA 90066
"Actress"

Mel Blount
R.D. 1, Box 91
Claysville, PA 15323
"Football Player"

Judy Blume
54 Riverside Drive
New York, NY 10023
"Writer"

Ann Blyth
P.O. Box 9754
Rancho Santa Fe, CA 92067
"Actress"

Eleanor Boardman
240 Santa Rosa Lane
Montecito, CA 93108
"Actress"

True Boardman
2951 Paisano Road
Pebble Beach, CA 93593
"Actor"

Steven Bochco
694 Amalfi Drive
Pacific Palisades, CA 90272
"Writer, Producer"

Hart Bochner
42 Haldeman Road
Santa Monica, CA 90402
"Actor"

Lloyd Bochner
42 Haldeman Road
Santa Monica, CA 90402
"Actor"

Rep. Sherwood Boehlert (NY)
House Longworth Bldg. #1127
Washington, DC 20515
"Politician"

Ivan Boesky
650-5th Avenue
New York, NY 10019
"Criminal, Financier"

Dirk Bogarde
235 Regent Street
London W1 ENGLAND
"Actor"

Peter Bogdanovich
212 Copa de Oro Road
Los Angeles, CA 90024
"Film Writer, Director"

Wade Boggs
14615 Village Glenn Circle
Tampa, FL 33624
"Baseball Player"

Eric Bogosian
151 El Camino Drive
Beverly Hills, CA 90212
"Performance Artist"

Heidi Bohay
4304 Farmdale Avenue
Studio City, CA 91604
"Actress"

Corinne Bohrer
8075 West 3rd Street
Los Angeles, CA 90048
"Actress"

Brian Boitano
1384 Francisco
San Francisco, CA 94123
"Ice Skater"

Tiffany Bolling
12483 Braddock Drive
Los Angeles, CA 90066
"Actress"

Joseph Bologna
613 North Arden Drive
Beverly Hills, CA 90210
"Actor, Writer, Director"

Michael Bolton
201 West 85th Street #15A
New York, NY 10024
"Singer"

Erma Bombeck
1703 Kaiser Avenue
Irvine, CA 92714
"Writer, TV Personality"

Julian Bond
361 West View Drive
Atlanta, GA 30310
"Politician"

Steve Bond
10201 West Pico Blvd. #54-6
Los Angeles, CA 90035
"Actor"

Tommy "Butch" Bond
14704 Road 36
Madera, CA 93638
"Actor"

Sergei Bondarchuk
Gorky Street 9-75
Moscow 8 RUSSIA
"Film Director"

Gary U.S. Bonds
141 Dunbar Avenue
Fords, NJ 08863
"Singer"

Peter Bonerz
3637 Lowry Road
Los Angeles, CA 90027
"Actor, Director"

Lisa Bonet
6435 Balcom
Reseda, CA 91335
"Actress"

Bon Jovi
240 Central Park South
New York, NY 10019
"Rock & Roll Group"

Rep. David E. Bonior (MI)
House Rayburn Bldg. #2242
Washington, DC 20515
"Politician"

Elayna Bonner
Uliza Tschakalowa 48
Moscow, RUSSIA
"Politician"

Frank Bonner
10100 Santa Monica Blvd. #700
Los Angeles, CA 90067
"Actor, Director"

Chastity Bono
9200 Sunset Blvd. #1001
Los Angeles, CA 90069
"Cher's Daughter"

Sonny Bono
1700 North Indian Avenue
Palm Springs, CA 92262
"Singer, Actor, Politician"

Brian Bonsall
11712 Moorpark Street #204
Studio City, CA 91604
"Actor"

Sorrell Booke
P.O. Box 1105
Studio City, CA 91604
"Actor, Director, Writer"

The Boomtown Rats
44 Seymour
London W1 ENGLAND
"Rock & Roll Group"

Debby Boone
4334 Kester Avenue
Sherman Oaks, CA 91403
"Singer"

Larry Boone
P.O. Box 23795
Nashville, TN 37212
"Singer"

Pat Boone
904 North Beverly Drive
Beverly Hills, CA 90210
"Actor, Singer"

Randy Boone
7060 Hollywood Blvd. #504
Los Angeles, CA 90028
"Actor"

Charley Boorman
"The Glebe"
Annanoe County Wicklow
IRELAND
"Film Director"

Elayne Boosler
11061 Wrightwood Lane
North Hollywood, CA 91604
"Comedienne"

Adrian Booth
3922 Glenridge Drive
Sherman Oaks, CA 91423
"Actor"

Connie Booth
Chatto & Linnit
Shaftsbury
London W1 ENGLAND
"Actress"

Shirley Booth
P.O. Box 103
Chatham, MA 02633
"Actress"

Powers Boothe
4319 Manson Avenue
Woodland Hills, CA 91364
"Actor"

Carla Borelli
2836 North Beachwood Drive
Los Angeles, CA 90068
"Actress"

Bjorn Borg
Via Aristo 10
Milan, ITALY
"Tennis Player"

Victor Borge
Fieldpoint Park
Greenwich, CT 06830
"Pianist, Comedian"

Jorge Luis Borges
Maipu 994
Buenos Aires, ARGENTINA
"Author, Poet"

Ernest Borgnine
3055 Lake Glen Drive
Beverly Hills, CA 90210
"Actor"

Tova Borgnine
3055 Lake Glen Drive
Beverly Hills, CA 90210
"Actress"

Robert Bork
1150-17th Street N.W.
Washington, DC 20036
"Judge"

Carroll Borland
275 Los Ranchitos Road #142
San Rafael, CA 94903
"Actress"

Major Frank Borman
6628 Vista Hermosa
Las Cruces, NM 88005
"Astronaut"

Roscoe Born
8444 Wilshire Blvd. #800
Beverly Hills, CA 90211
"Actor"

Julius Boros
2900 N.E. 40th Street
Ft. Lauderdale, FL 33308
"Golfer"

Rep. Robert A. Borski (PA)
House Cannon Bldg. #407
Washington, DC 20515
"Politician"

Tom Bosley
2822 Royston Place
Beverly Hills, CA 90210
"Actor"

Barbara Bosson
694 Amalfi Drive
Pacific Palisades, CA 90272
"Actress"

Ralph Boston
3301 Woodbine Avenue
Knoxville, TN 37914
"Track Athlete"

Barry Bostwick
2770 Hutton Drive
Beverly Hills, CA 90210
"Actor"

Brian Bosworth
230 Park Avenue #527
New York, NY 10169
"Actor, Football Player"

Pres. Pieter W. Botha
Union Building
Pretoria 0001
REPUBLIC OF SOUTH AFRICA
"Politician"

Joe Bottoms
1015 Gayley Avenue #300
Los Angeles, CA 90024
"Actor"

Sam Bottoms
4719 Willowcrest Avenue
Toluca Lake, CA 91602
"Actor"

Timothy Bottoms
532 Hot Springs Road
Santa Barbara, CA 93108
"Actor"

Rep. Rick Boucher (VA)
House Cannon Bldg. #405
Washington, DC 20515
"Politician"

Lou Boudreau
15600 Ellis Avenue
Dolton, IL 60419
"Baseball Player"

Pierre Boulez
Postgach 22
Baden-Baden
GERMANY
"Composer, Conductor"

Jim Bouton
6 Myron Court
Teaneck, NJ 07666
"Baseball Player"

Julie Bovasso
251 West 19th Street #6A
New York, NY 10011
"Dramatist"

Antoinette Bower
1354 Los Robles Drive
Palm Springs, CA 92262
"Actress"

David Bowie
641-5th Avenue #22-Q
New York, NY 10022
"Singer, Actor"

Judi Bowker
31 Soho Square
London W1V 5DG ENGLAND
"Actress"

Peter Bowles
125 Gloucester Road
London SW7 ENGLAND
"Actor"

Christopher Bowman
5653 Kester
Van Nuys, CA 91405
"Skater"

John Box
41 Meredyth Road
Barnes
London SW13 ENGLAND
"Motion Picture Producer"

Boxcar Willie
1300 Division Street #103
Nashville, TN 37203
"Singer"

Rep. Barbara Boxer (CA)
House Cannon Bldg. #307
Washington, DC 20515
"Politician"

Bruce Boxleitner
24500 Jonh Colter Road
Hidden Hills, CA 91302
"Actor"

Jimmy Boyd
901 Bringham
Los Angeles, CA 90049
"Actor, Singer"

Lara Flynn Boyle
828 Venezia
Venice, CA 90291
"Actress"

Peter Boyle
12065 Laurel Lane
Studio City, CA 91604
"Actor"

The Boys
6255 Sunset Blvd. #1700
Los Angeles, CA 90068
"Rock & Roll Group"

Boys Don't Cry
3 Wansdown Place
Fulham, Broadway
London SW6 1DN ENGLAND
"Rock & Roll Group"

Boys II Men
6255 Sunset Blvd. #1700
Los Angeles, CA 90028
"R&B Group"

Lorraine Bracco
P.O. Box 49
Palisades, NY 10964
"Actress"

Eddie Bracken
69 Douglas Road
Glen Ridge, NJ 07028
"Actor"

Barbara Taylor Bradford
425 East 58 Street
New York, NY 10022
"Writer"

Greg Bradford
3752 Redwood Avenue
Los Angeles, CA 90066
"Actor"

Richard Bradford
6605 Hollywood Blvd. #220
Los Angeles, CA 90028
"Actor"

Benjamin Bradlee
1150-15th Street N.W.
Washington, DC 20071
"Journalist"

Sen. Bill Bradley (NJ)
731 Hart Office Building
Washington DC 20510
"Politician"

Ed Bradley
285 Central Park West
New York, NY 10024
"Newcaster"

Owen Bradley
P.O. Box 120838
Nashville, TN 37212
"Pianist"

Tom Bradley
605 South Irving Blvd.
Los Angeles, CA 90005
"Mayor of Los Angeles"

Terry Bradshaw
Rt. 1, Box 227
Gordonville, TX 76254
"Football Player"

Eric Braeden
13723 Romany Drive
Pacific Palisades, CA 90272
"Actor"

Sonia Braga
210 East 58th Street
New York, NY 10022
"Actress"

Don Bragg
P.O. Box 171
New Gretna, NJ 08224
"Track Athlete"

Kenneth Branagh
56 Kings Road
Kingston-upon- Thames
KT2 5HF ENGLAND
"Actor, Director"

Klaus Maria Brandauer
Fischernforf 76
8992 Alta-Ausse, AUSTRIA
"Actress"

Christian Brando
P.O. Box 809
Beverly Hills, CA 90213
"Son of Marlon Brando"

Marlon Brando
P.O. Box 809
Beverly Hills, CA 90213
"Actor"

Clark Brandon
9000 Sunset Blvd. #1200
Los Angeles, CA 90069
"Actor"

Michael Brandon
9320 Wilshire Blvd. #300
Beverly Hills, CA 90212
"Actor"

Brand X
17171 Roscoe Blvd. #104
Northridge, CA 91325
"Actor"

Willy Brandt
Erich-Ollenhauser-Str.1
5300 Bonn 1 GERMANY
"Politician"

Claude Brasseur
1 rue Seguier
75006 Paris, FRANCE
"Actor"

Asher Brauner
190 North Canon Drive #201
Beverly Hills, CA 90210
"Actor"

Bart Braverman
524 North Laurel Avenue
Los Angeles, CA 90048
"Actor"

Rosanno Brazzi
Giovanni Batista Martini 13
Rome, ITALY
"Actor"

Julian Bream
122 Wigmore Street
London W1 ENGLAND
"Guitarist"

Peter Breck
238 East 1st Street
Vancouver, B.C. V7L 1B3
CANADA
"Actor"

Buddy Bregman
11288 Ventura Blvd. #700
Studio City, CA 91604
"Director, Producer"

Tracey Bremer-Recht
10351 Santa Monica Blvd. #211
Los Angeles, CA 90025
"Actress"

Arthur Bremer
Maryland Correctional Institute
Hagerstown, MD 21740
"Assasin"

Melissa Bremnan
23643 Califa Street
Woodland Hills, CA 91367
"Actress"

Eileen Brennan
P.O. Box 1777
Ojai, CA 93023
"Actress"

David Brenner
229 East 62nd Street
New York, NY 10021
"Comedian"

Dori Brenner
2106 Canyon Drive
Los Angeles, CA 90068
"Actress"

Jimmy Breslin
220 East 42nd Street
New York, NY 10017
"Author, Columnist"

Martin Brest
831 Paseo Miramar
Pacific Palisades, CA 90272
"Film Writer, Director"

George Brett
P.O. Box 1969
Kansas City, MO 64141
"Baseball Player"

Jeremy Brett
151 South El Camino Drive
Beverly Hills, CA 90212
"Actor"

Teresa Brewer
384 Pinebrook Blvd.
New Rochelle, NY 10803
"Singer"

Carol Brewster
8721 Sunset Blvd. #203
Los Angeles, CA 90069
"Actress"

David Brian
3922 Glenridge
Sherman Oaks, CA 91403
"Actor"

Mary Brian
4107 Troost Avenue
North Hollywood, CA 90212
"Actress"

Beth Brickell
9933 Robbins Drive #2
Beverly Hills, CA 90212
"Writer, Director"

Beau Bridges
5525 North Jed Smith Road
Hidden Hills, CA 91302
"Actor, Director"

James Bridges
449 Skyeway Road
Los Angeles, CA 90049
"Film Writer, Director"

Jeff Bridges
1223 Wilshire Blvd. #593
Santa Monica, CA 90403
"Actor"

Lloyd Bridges
225 Lorina Avenue
Los Angeles, CA 90024
"Actor"

Todd Bridges
7550 Zombar Avenue #1
Van Nuys, CA 91406
"Actor"

Charlie Brill
3635 Wrightwood Drive
Studio City, CA 91604
"Actor"

Bernie Brillstein
9200 Sunset Blvd. #428
Los Angeles, CA 90069
"Talent Agent"

Wilfred Brimley
9830 Wilshire Blvd.
Beverly Hills, CA 90212
"Actor"

Christie Brinkley
344 East 59th Street
New York, NY 10022
"Model"

David Brinkley
4001 Nebraska Avenue
Washington DC 20016
"TV Show Host"

Valerie Brisco-Hooks
P.O. Box 21053
Long Beach, CA 90801
"Runner"

Danielle Brisebois
8075 West 3rd Street #303
Los Angeles, CA 90048
"Actress"

May Britt
P.O. Box 525
Zephyr Cove, NV 89448
"Actress"

Morgan Brittany
3434 Cornell Road
Agoura Hills, CA 91301
"Actress, Model"

Albert "Cubby" Broccoli
809 North Hillcrest Road
Beverly Hills, CA 90210
"Motion Picture Producer"

Lou Brock
12595 Durbin Drive
St. Louis, MO 63141
"Baseball Player"

Matthew Broderick
9830 Wilshire Blvd.
Beverly Hills, CA 90212
"Actor"

Kevin Brodie
4424 Moorpark Way
North Hollywood, CA 91602
"Actor"

Steve Brodie
6742 Sunny Brae Avenue
Canoga Park, CA 91306
"Actor"

Lane Brody
P.O. Box 24775
Nashville, TN 37202
"Singer"

Norman Brokaw
530 Vick Place
Beverly Hills, CA 90210
"Talent Agent"

Tom Brokaw
941 Park Avenue #14C
New York, NY 10025
"Newscaster"

James Brolin
2401 Colorado Avenue #160
Santa Monica, CA 90404
"Actor"

Josh Brolin
2401 Colorado Avenue #160
Santa Monica, CA 90404
"Actor"

John Bromfield
1750 Whittier Avenue
Costa Mesa, CA 92627
"Actor"

Edgar M. Bronfman
375 Park Avenue
New York, NY 10022
"Distillery Executive"

Charles Bronson
P.O. Box 2644
Malibu, CA 90265
"Actor"

Lillian Bronson
32591 Seven Seas Drive
Laguna Niguel, CA 92677
"Actress"

Hilary Brooke Klune
40 Via Casitas
Bonsall, CA 92003
"Actress"

Gary Brooker
5 Cranley Gardens
London SW7 ENGLAND
"Singer, Composer"

Brooklyn Bridge
P.O. Box 262
Carteret, NJ 07008
"Rock & Roll Group"

Brooklyn Dreams
1224 North Vine Street
Los Angeles, CA 90038
"Vocal Group"

Albert Brooks
3600 Longridge Avenue
Sherman Oaks, CA 91403
"Actor, Writer, Director"

Avery Brooks
20 Layne Road
Summerset, NJ 08873
"Actor"

Foster Brooks
315 South Beverly Drive #216
Beverly Hills, CA 90212
"Comedian"

Garth Brooks
1109-17th Avenue South
Nashville, TN 37212
"Singer"

Rep. Jack Brooks (TX)
House Rayburn Bldg. #2449
Washington, DC 20515
"Politician"

Mel Brooks
2301 La Mesa Drive
Santa Monica, CA 90405
"Actor, Writer, Director"

Phyllis Brooks
P.O. Box 14
Cape Neddick, ME 03902
"Actress"

Rand Brooks
1701 Capistrano Circle
Glendale, CA 91207
"Actress"

Randi Brooks
1459 Irving Avenue
Glendale, CA 91201
"Actress"

Richard Brooks
2900 Deep Canyon Drive
Beverly Hills, CA 90210
"Author, Director"

Rep. William S. Broomfield (MI)
House Rayburn Bldg. #2306
Washington, DC 20515
"Politician"

Kevin Brophy
15010 Hamlin Street
Van Nuys, CA 91411
"Actor"

Pierce Brosnan
28011 North Parquet Place
Malibu, CA 90265
"Actor, Model"

The Brothers Four
P.O. Box 135
Vashon, WA 98070
"Vocal Duo"

Dr. Joyce Brothers
1530 Palisades Avenue
Fort Lee, NJ 07024
"Psychologist"

Louise Brough
1808 Voluntary Road
Vista, CA 92083
"Tennis Player"

Haywood Hale Brown
312 Plochman
Woodstock, NY 12498
"Sportswriter, Sportscaster"

Blair Brown
8899 Beverly Blvd.
Los Angeles, CA 90048
"Actress"

Bobby Brown
3350 Peachtree Road N.E.
Atlanta, GA 30326
"Singer"

Bryan Brown
9830 Wilshire Blvd.
Beverly Hills, CA 90212
"Actor"

Edmund G. "Pat" Brown
9918 Kip Drive
Beverly Hills, CA 90210
"Ex-Governor"

Georg Stanford Brown
4049-C Radford Avenue
Studio City, CA 91604
"Actor, Director"

Rep. George E. Brown, Jr. (CA)
House Rayburn Bldg. 2300
Washington, DC 20515
"Politician"

Helen Brown
1811 Whiley Avenue #200
Los Angeles, CA 90028
"Actress"

Helen Gurley Brown
1 West 81st Street #22D
New York, NY 10024
"Author, Editor"

Hubie Brown
6 Cobblewood Road
Livingston, NJ 07039
"Basketball Coach"

Georgia Brown
1902 Coldwarter Canyon
Beverly Hills, CA 90210
"Actress"

James Brown
810-7th Avenue
New York, NY 10019
"Singer

James L. Brown
3800 Barham Blvd. #303
Los Angeles, CA 90068
"Actor"

Edmund "Jerry" Brown, Jr.
646 North Beachwood Drive
Los Angeles, CA 900404
"Ex-Governor"

Jim Brown
1851 Sunset Plaza Drive
Los Angeles, CA 90069
"Football Player, Actor"

Jim Ed Brown
P.O. Box 121089
Nashville, TN 37212
"Singer"

Johnny Brown
9229 Sunset Blvd. #306
Los Angeles, CA 90069
"Performer"

Julie Brown
P.O. Box 12186
San Diego, CA 92112
"Actress"

Les Brown
603 Ocean Avenue #5-S
Santa Monica, CA 90402
"Orchestra Leader"

Peter Brown
854 Cypress Avenue
Herman Beach, CA 90254
"Actor"

Reb Brown
5454 Las Virgines Road
Calabasas, CA 91302
"Actor"

Ron Brown
430 South Capitol Street S.E.
Washington, DC 20002
"Democrat Party Chairman"

Ruth Brown
600 West 165th Street #4-H
New York, NY 10032
"Singer"

T. Graham Brown
1516-16 Avenue South
Nashville, TN 37212
"Singer"

Thomas Wilson Brown
5918 Van Nuys Blvd.
Van Nuys, CA 91401
"Actor"

Vanessa Brown
14340 Milholland Drive
Los Angeles, CA 90024
"Actress"

Willie L. Brown, Jr.
1200 Gough Street #10-A
San Francisco, CA 94109
"Politician"

Woody Brown
6548 Colbath Avenue
Van Nuys, CA 91604
"Actor"

Jackson Browne
3208 Cahuenga Blvd. West
Suite #108
Los Angeles, CA 90068
"Singer, Composer"

Kathy Browne
8643 Holly Plaza
Los Angeles, CA 90069
"Actress"

Roscoe Lee Browne
3531 Wonderview Drive
Los Angeles, CA 90068
"Actor, Writer, Director

Herbert Brownell
25 Broadway
New York, NY 10004
"Government Official"

Frank Browning
c/o National Public Radio
2025 "M" Street N.W.
Washington, DC 20036
"News Correspondent"

Dave Brubeck
221 Millstone Road
Wilton, CT 06897
"Pianist"

Carol Bruce
1361 North Laurel #9
Los Angeles, CA 90046
"Actress"

Ed Bruce
1022-16th Avenue South
Nashville, TN 37203
"Singer"

Kitty Bruce
31 Harrison Street
New York, NY 10019
"Singer"

Rep. Terry L. Bruce (IL)
House Cannon Bldg. #419
Washington, DC 20515
"Politician"

Ellen Bry
2800 Neilson Way #1113
Santa Monica, CA 90405
"Actress"

Dora Bryan
11 Marine Parade
Brighton Sussex ENGLAND
"Actress"

Jane Bryan
P.O. Box 1033
Pebble Beach, CA 93953
"Actress"

Rep. John Bryant (TX)
House Cannon Bldg. #208
Washington, DC 20515
"Politician"

Zbigniew Brzezinski
c/o School of Government
Columbia University
New York, NY 10027
"Politician"

Patrick J. Buchanan
1017 Savile Lane North
McLean, VA 22101
"Politician, Columnist"

Horst Buchholz
7078 Lenzer Heibe
SWITZERLAND
"Actor"

Art Buchwald
1750 Pennsylvania Avenue NW
Suite #1331
Washington DC 20006
"Columnist"

Bill Bucker
3 McDonald Circle
Andover, MA 01810
"Baseball Player"

Lindsay Buckingham
900 Airole Way
Los Angleles, CA 90077
"Singer, Songwriter"

The Buckinghams
P.O. Box 82
Great Neck, NY 11021
"Rock & Roll Group"

Betty Buckley
530 West End Avenue
New York, NY 10024
"Actress"

William F. Buckley, Jr.
150 East 35th Street
New York, NY 10016
"Author, Editor"

Julie Budd
4433 Bergamo Drive
Encino, CA 91436
"Actress"

Terence Budd
29 Rylette Road
London W12 ENGLANG
"Actor"

Zola Budd
1 Church Row
Wandsworth Plain
London SW18 ENGLAND
"Runner"

Don Budge
P.O. Box 789
Dingman's Ferry, PA 18328
"Tennis Player"

Maria Bueno
Rua Consolagao 3414 #10
1001 Edificio Augustus
Sao Paulo, BRAZIL
"Tennis Player"

Buffalo Springfield
1616 Butler Avenue
Los Angeles, CA 90025
"Rock & Roll Group"

Jimmy Buffet
500 Duval Street #B
Key West, FL 33040
"Singer, Songwriter"

Zev Bufman
1466 Broadway
New York, NY 10036
"Theater Producer"

The Buggles
22 St. Peters Square
London W69 NW ENGLAND
"Rock & Roll Group"

Vincent T. Bugliosi
9300 Wilshire Blvd. #470
Beverly Hills, CA 90210
"Lawyer, Author"

Genevieve Bujold
27258 Pacific Coast Hwy.
Malibu, CA 90265
"Actress"

Ray Buktenica
15301 Ventura Blvd. #345
Sherman Oaks, CA 91403
"Actor"

Richard Bull
651 North Wilcox Avenue #3-G
Los Angeles, CA 90036
"Actor"

Jim J. Bullock
6210 Temple Hill Drive
Los Angeles, CA 90069
"Actor"

Grace Bumbry
165 West 57th Street
New York, NY 10019
"Opera Singer"

Brooke Bundy
833 North Martel Avenue
Los Angeles, CA 90046
"Actress"

Rep. Jim Bunning (KY)
116 Cannon House Building
Washington DC 20515
"Politician, Baseball Player"

Lou Burdette
2019 Beveva Road
Sarasota, FL 34232
"Baseball Player"

Warren E. Burger
3111 North Rochester Street
Arlington, VA 22213
"Supreme Court Justice"

Anthony Burgess
44 rue Grimaldi
Monte Carlo, MONACO
"Actor"

Gary Burghoff
P.O. Box 33018, #315
St. Petersburg, FL 33733
"Actor"

Delta Burke
1290 Inverness
Pasadena, CA 91011
"Actress"

Paul Burke
2217 Avenida Caballeros
Palm Springs, CA 92262
"Actor"

Dennis Burkley
5145 Costello Avenue
Sherman Oaks, CA 91423
"Actor"

Carol Burnett
P.O. Box 1298
Pasadena, CA 91031
"Actress, Comedienne"

John Burnett
c/o National Public Radio
2025 "M" Street N.W.
Washington, DC 20036
"Newscaster"

T-Bone Burnett
c/o Nancy Clarke
211-20th Street
Santa Monica, CA 90402
"Singer"

Rocky Burnette
c/o Jim Seiter
21009 Valerio
Canoga Park, CA 91303
"Singer"

George Burns
720 North Maple Drive
Beverly Hills, CA 90210
"Actor, Comedian"

James MacGregor Burns
Bee Hill Road
Williamstown, MA 01267
"Political Scientist, Historian"

Jere Burns
5513 Oaken Court
Agoura Hills, CA 91301
"Actor"

Ken Burns
Maple Grove Road
Walpole, NH 03608
"Documentary Producer"

Raymond Burr
P.O. Box 678
Geyserville, CA 95441
"Actor, Director"

James Burrows
5555 Melrose Avenue #D-208
Los Angeles, CA 90038
"Writer, Producer"

Ellen Burstyn
Ferry House, Box 217
Washington Spring Road
Snedens Landing
Palisades, NY 10964
"Actress"

Rep. Dan Burton (IN)
House Cannon Bldg. #120
Washington, DC 20515
"Politician"

Kate Burton
121 North San Vincente Blvd.
Beverly Hills, CA 90211
"Actress"

Levar Burton
13417 Inwood
Sherman Oaks, CA 91423
"Actor"

Mrs. Sally Burton
Pays de Galles
Coligny, SWITZERLAND
"Widower of Richard Burton"

Tim Burton
1605 Marmont
Los Angeles, CA 90069
"Actor"

Wendell Burton
6526 Costello Drive
Van Nuys, CA 91401
"Actor"

Gary Busey
2914 Searidge Street
Malibu, CA 90265
"Actor"

Timothy Busfield
2416 "G" Street #D
Sacramento, CA 95816
"Actor"

Barbara Bush
The White House
1600 Pennsylvania Avenue
Washington, DC 20500
"First Lady"

George Bush
The White House
1600 Pennsylvania Avenue
Washington, DC 20500
"President of United States"

Kate Bush
20 Manchester Square
London W1 ENGLAND
"Singer, Songwriter"

Joe Bushkin
435 East 52nd Street
New York, NY 10022
"Pianist, Composer"

Dr. Jerry Buss
P.O. Box 10
Inglewood, CA 90306
"Basketball Team Owner"

Albert G. Bustamante (TX)
House Longworth Bldg. #1116
Washington, DC 20515
"Politician"

Dick Butkus
3500 West Olive #1400
Burbank, CA 91505
"Football Player"

Dean Butler
6220 Rogerton Drive
Los Angeles, CA 90068
"Actor"

Dick Button
250 West 57th Street #1818
New York, NY 10107
"TV Producer"

Red Buttons
778 Tortuoso Way
Los Angeles, CA 90024
"Actor"

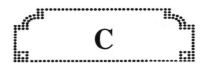

Pat Buttram
13906 Ventura Blvd. #302
Sherman Oaks, CA 91423
"Actor"

Bill Buzenberg
c/o National Public Radio
2025 "M" Street N.W.
Washington, DC 20036
"Newscaster"

Ruth Buzzi
2309 Malaga Road
Los Angeles, CA 90068
"Actress"

John Byner
475 South Bedford Drive
Beverly Hills, CA 90212
"Comedian, Writer"

Charlie Byrd Trio
P.O. Box 1515
New York, NY 10023
"Jazz Trio"

Tom Byrd
121 North San Vincente Blvd.
Beverly Hills, CA 90211
"Actor"

Rep. Beverly Byron (MD)
House Rayburn Bldg. #2430
Washington, DC 20515
"Politician"

David Byrne
7964 Willow Glen Road
Los Angeles, CA 90046
"Singer, Songwriter"

Edd Byrnes
1201 1/2 Cabrillo
Venice, CA 90292
"Actor"

Kathleen Byron
6 Kassala Road
London SW11 ENGLAND
"Actress"

James Caan
1435 Stone Canyon Road
Los Angeles, CA 90024
"Actor"

Frank Cady
110 East 9th Street #1005
Los Angeles, CA 90079
"Actor"

Herb Caen
901 Mission Street
San Francisco, CA 94119
"Columnist"

Irving Caesar
Hotel Park Sheraton
870 - 7th Avenue
New York, NY 10019
"Lyricist, Composer"

Shirley Caesar
10100 Santa Monica Blvd.#1600
Los Angeles, CA 90067
"Singer"

Sid Caesar
1910 Loma Vista
Beverly Hills, CA 90210
"Actor, Comedian"

John Cage
101 West 18th Street
New York, NY 10011
"Composer"

Nicholas Cage
5647 Tryon
Los Angeles, CA 90068
"Actor"

Mrs. James Cagney
P.O. Box 281, Verney Farm
Stanfordville, NY 12581
"Widower of James Cagney"

Sammy Cahn
704 North Canon Drive
Beverly Hills, CA 90210
"Actor"

Michael Caine
315 Trousdale Place
Beverly Hills, CA 90210
"Actor"

Sarah Caldwell
539 Washington Street
Boston, MA 02111
"Author"

J.J. Cale
P.O. Box 210103
Nashville, TN 37202
"Singer, Guitarist"

Rory Calhoun
10637 Burbank Blvd.
North Hollywood, CA 91601
"Actor"

Joseph Cali
5033 Campo Road
Woodland Hills, CA 91304
"Actor"

Joseph Califano
1775 Pennsylvania Avenue NW
Washington, DC 20006
"Politician"

Anthony Call
305 Madison Avenue #4419
New York, NY 10165
"Actor"

Brandon Call
5918 Van Nuys Blvd.
Van Nuys, CA 91401
"Actor"

John Callahan
342 North Alfred Street
Los Angeles, CA 90048
"Actor"

Rep. Sonny Callahan (AL)
House Longworth Bldg. #1330
Washington, DC 20515
"Politician"

K. Callan
4957 Matilija Ave.
Sherman Oaks, CA 91423
"Actress"

Michael (Mickey) Callan
8711 Burton Way #406
Los Angeles, CA 90048
"Actor"

Charlie Callas
P.O. Box 67869
Los Angeles, CA 90067
"Comedian, Actor"

Thomas Callaway
10000 Santa Monica Blvd. #305
Los Angeles, CA 90067
"Actor"

Lt. William Calley
V.V. Vicks Jewelry
Cross Country Plaza
Columbus, GA 31906
"Ex-Military"

Simon Callow
60 Finborough Road
London SW5 ENGLAND
"Actor"

Cab Calloway
1040 Knollwood Road
White Plains, NY 10603
"Singer, Composer"

Corinne Calvet
1431 Ocean Avenue #109
Santa Monica, CA 90401
"Actress"

John Calvin
1794 Washington Way
Venice, CA 90292
"Actor"

Hector Camacho
Star Rt., Box 113
Clewiston, FL 33440
"Boxer"

Candace Cameron
P.O. Box 80515
Conyers, GA 30208
"Actress"

Kirk Cameron
9560 Wilshire Blvd #500
Beverly Hills, CA 90212
"Actor"

Colleen Camp
2050 Fairburn Avenue
Los Angeles, CA 90025
"Actress"

Joseph Campanella
4647 Arcola Avenue
North Hollywood, CA 91602
"Actor"

Roy Campanella
6213 Capistrano
Woodland Hills, CA 91367
"Baseball Player"

Bert Campaneria
P.O. Box 8232
Scottsdale, AZ 85232
"Baseball Player"

Alan Campbell
2254-15th Street
Santa Monica, CA 90405
"Actor"

Archie Campbell
P.O. Box 189
Brentwood, TN 37027
"Comedian, Actor"

Ben Nighthouse Campbell (CO)
House Longworth Bldg. #1530
Washington, DC 20515
"Politician"

Cheryl Campbell
5 Milner Place
London N1 ENGLAND
"Actress"

Earl Campbell
University of Texas Football
P.O. Box 7399
Austin, TX 78713
"Football Player"

Glen Campbell
5290 Exeter Blvd
Phoenix, AZ 85018
"Singer, Actor, Composer"

Julia Campbell
570 North Rossmore Avenue
Los Angeles, CA 90004
"Actress"

Luther Campbell
8400 N.E. 2nd Avenue
Miami, FL 33138
"Rap Singer"

Nicholas Campbell
11342 Dona Lisa Drive
Studio City, CA 91604
"Actor"

Rep. Tom Campbell (CA)
House Cannon Bldg. #313
Washington, DC 20515
"Politician"

William Campbell
21502 Velicata Street
Woodland Hills, CA 91364
"Actor"

David Canary
903 South Mansfield Avenue
Los Angeles, CA 90036
"Actor"

Pete Candoli
12451 Mulholland Drive
Beverly HIlls, CA 90210
"Actor, Trumpeter"

John Candy
11454 San Vicente Blvd.
Los Angeles, CA 90049
"Actor, Comedian"

Elias Canetti
Klosbachstrasse 88
Zurich, SWITZERLAND
"Writer"

Stephen Cannell
7083 Hollywood Blvd.
Los Angeles, CA 90028
"TV Writer, Producer"

Billy Cannon
1640 Sherwood Forest Blvd.
Baton Rouge, LA 70815
"Football Player"

Dyan Cannon
8033 Sunset Blvd. #254
Los Angeles, CA 90046
"Actress, Writer"

Freddie Cannon
18641 Cassandra Street
Tarzana, CA 91356
"Singer, Songwriter"

J. D. Cannon
9255 Sunset Blvd. #515
Los Angeles, CA 90069
"Actor"

Katherine Cannon
10100 Santa Monica Blvd. #700
Los Angeles, CA 90067
"Actress"

The Cannons
1522 Demonbreun Street
Nashville, TN 37203
"C&W Group"

Diana Canova
8370 Wilshire Blvd. #310
Beverly Hills, CA 90211
"Actress"

Jose Canseco
4525 Sheridan Avenue
Miami Beach, FL 33140
"Baseball Player"

Cantinflas
Ave. Insurgentes Sur 377
Mexico D.F. MEXICO
"Comedian, Actor"

Lana Cantrell
300 East 71st Street
New York, NY 10021
"Singer, Actress"

Canyon
65 Music Square West
Nashville, TN 37203
"C&W Group"

Virginia Capers
390 South Hauser Blvd.
Los Angeles, CA 90036
"Actress"

Anna Capri
8227 Fountain Avenue
Los Angeles, CA 90046
"Actress"

Jennifer Capriatti
100 Saddle Brook Way
Wesley Chapel, FL 33543
"Tennis Player"

Kate Capshaw
P.O. Box 6190
Malibu, CA 90265
"Actress"

Captain & Tennille
(Toni & Daryl Dragon)
P.O. Box 262
Glenbrook, NV 89413
"Music Duo"

Irene Cara
8033 Sunset Blvd. #735
Los Angeles, CA 90046
"Actress, Singer"

Roger Caras
22108 Slab Bridge Road
Freeland, MD 21053
"News Correspondent"

Rep. Ben Cardin (MD)
House Cannon Bldg. #117
Washington, DC 20515
"Politician"

Pierre Cardin
59 rue du Faubourg
St-Honore 8e Paris, FRANCE
"Fashion Designer"

Claudia Cardinale
Salita di Castel Giubeleo
1-00100 Rome, ITALY
"Actress"

Rod Carew
5144 East Crescent Drive
Anaheim, CA 92807
"Baseball Player"

Harry Carey, Jr.
14159 Dickens #303
Sherman Oaks, CA 91423
"Baseball Executive"

Hugh Carey
9 Prospect Place
Brooklyn, NY 11215
"Ex-Governor"

MacDonald Carey
1543 Benedict Canyon Drive
Beverly Hills, CA 90210
"Actor"

Mariah Carey
9830 Wilshire Blvd.
Beverly Hills, CA 90212
"Singer"

Rick Carey
119 Rockland Avenue
Larchmont, NY 10538
"Swimmer"

Ron Carey
151 El Camino Drive
Beverly Hills, CA 90212
"Actor"

Timothy Carey
P.O. Box 1254
Temple City, CA 91780
"Actor"

Len Cariou
888-7th Avenue #201
New York, NY 10019
"Actor"

Frankie Carle
P.O. Box 7415
Mesa, AZ 85216
"Band Leader"

George Carlin
901 Bringham Avenue
Los Angeles, CA 90049
"Comedian"

Lynn Carlin
15301 Ventura Blvd. #345
Sherman Oaks, CA 91403
"Actress"

Belinda Carlisle
3907 West Alameda Avenue #200
Burbank, CA 91505
"Singer, Songwriter"

Kitty Carlisle-Hart
32 East 64th Street
New York, NY 10021
"Actress"

Mary Carlisle
517 North Rodeo Drive
Beverly Hills, CA 90210
"Actress"

King Juan Carlos
Palacio de La Carcuela
Madrid, SPAIN
"Royalty"

Gail Rae Carlson
11818 Riverside Drive #125
North Hollywood, CA 91607
"Actress"

Karen Carlson
3700 Ventura Canyon Avenue
Sherman Oaks, CA 91423
"Actress"

Larry Carlton
27815 Lorjen
Canyon Country, CA 91351
"Guitarist"

Ian Carmichael
The Priory, Grosmont
Whitby, Yorks. YO22 SQT
ENGLAND
"Actor, Producer"

Jean Carne
1 Bedford Avenue
London WC1B 3DT
ENGLAND
"Singer"

Judy Carne
300 West 12th Street
New York, NY 10014
"Actress"

Kim Carnes
737 Latimer Road
Santa Monica, CA 90402
"Singer, Songwriter"

Art Carney
RR 20, Box 911
Westbrook, CT 06498
"Actor"

Princess Caroline
La Maisonde la Source
St. Remy Prov. FRANCE
"Royalty"

Leslie Caron
9169 Sunset Blvd.
Los Angeles, CA 90069
"Actress"

Morris Carnovsky
422 Rock House Road
Easton, CT 06612
"Actor"

A.J. Carothers
217 South Burlingame Avenue
Los Angeles, CA 90049
"Screenwriter"

Carleton Carpenter
R.D. #2 Chardavoyne Road
Warwick, NY 10990
"Actor"

John Carpenter
8532 Hollywood Blvd.
Los Angeles, CA 90046
"Actor"

Richard Capenter
8341 Lubec Avenue
Downey, CA 90240
"Pianist, Composer"

Scott Carpenter
1183 Stradella Road
Los Angeles, CA 90007
"Astronaut"

Rep. Thomas Carper (DE)
House Cannon Bldg. #131
Washington, DC 20515
"Politician"

Allan Carr
P.O. Box 691670
Los Angeles, CA 90069
"Film Writer, Producer"

Rep. Bob Carr (MI)
House Rayburn Bldg. #2439
Washington, DC 20515
"Politician"

Darlene Carr
1930 Century Park West #403
Los Angeles, CA 90067
"Actress"

Jane Carr
121 North San Vicente Blvd.
Beverly Hills, CA 90212
"Actress"

Vikki Carr
2289 Betty Lane
Beverly Hills, CA 90210
"Singer, Songwriter"

David Carradine
9753 La Tuna Canyon Road
Sun Valley, CA 91352
"Actor"

Keith Carradine
20800 Hillside Drive
Topanga Canyon, CA 90290
"Actor, Singer"

Robert Carradine
1999 Avenue of the Stars #2850
Los Angeles, CA 90067
"Actor"

Barbara Carrera
15430 Milldale Drive
Los Angeles, CA 90077
"Actress, Model"

Jose Carreras
via Augusta 59
E-08006 Barcelona
SPAIN
"Tenor"

Tia Carrere
201-A North Roberson Blvd.
Beverly Hills, CA 90211
"Actress"

Lord Carrington
Manor House
Bledlow, Aylesbury
Buckinghamshire HP17 9PE
ENGLAND
"Politician"

Diahann Carroll
P.O. Box 2999
Beverly Hills, CA 90213
"Actress, Singer"

Pat Carroll
6523 West Olympic Blvd.
Los Angeles, CA 90048
"Actress"

Vinette Carroll
227 West 17th Street
New York, NY 10011
"Actor, Writer, Director"

Kitty Carruthers
22 East 71st Street
New York, NY 10021
"Ice Skater"

Peter Carruthers
22 East 71st Street
New York, NY 10021
"Ice Skater"

Marcey Carsey
4024 Redford Avenue #3
Studio City, CA 91604
"TV Producer"

Joanna Carson
400 St. Cloud Road
Los Angeles, CA 90024
"Ex-Wife of Johnny Carson"

Johnny Carson
6962 Wildlife
Malibu, CA 90265
"TV Host, Comedian"

Amy Carter
1 Woodland Drive
Plains, GA 31780
"Ex-President's Daughter"

Benny Carter
8321 Skyline Drive
Los Angeles, CA 90046
"Saxophonist"

Dixie Carter
618 South Lucerne Blvd.
Los Angeles, CA 90005
"Actress"

Carter Family
P.O. Box 508
Hendersonville, TN 37075
"Music Group"

Helena Carter
1655 Gilcrest
Beverly Hills, CA 90210
"Actress"

Helena Bonham Carter
109 Jermyn Street
London W1 ENGLAND
"Actress"

Hodding Carter III
211 South St. Asaph
Alexandria, VA 22314
"News Correspondent"

Jack Carter
1023 Chevy Chase Drive
Beverly Hills, CA 90210
"Comedian, Actor"

Jimmy Carter
1 Woodland Drive
Plains, GA 31780
"Former President of USA"

Lynda Carter
9200 Harrington Drive
Potomac, MD 20854
"Actress, Singer"

Nell Carter
133-60 Java Drive
Beverly Hills, CA 90210
"Actress, Singer"

Ralph Carter
104-60 Queens Blvd. #1D
Forest Hills, NY 11375
"Actor"

Rosalyn Carter
1 Woodland Drive
Plains, GA 31780
"Former First Lady"

Rubin "Hurricane" Carter
1313 Brookedge Drive
Hamlin, NY 14464
"Boxer, Ex-Convict"

Terry Carter
447-9th Street
Santa Monica, CA 90402
"Actor"

Thomas Carter
10958 Strathmore Drive
Los Angeles, CA 90024
"Actor, Director"

Barbara Cartland
Camfield Place, Hatfield
Hertfordshire ENGLAND
"Novelist"

Angela Cartwright
10112 Riverside Drive
Toluca Lake, CA 91602
"Actress"

Veronica Cartwright
161 West 15th Street #2-H
New York, NY 10011
"Actress"

Anthony Caruso
721 East Grinnell Drive
Burbank, CA 91501
"Actor"

Dana Carvey
17333 Rancho
Encino, CA 91316
"Comedienne"

Rosie Casals
1505 Bridgeway #208
Sausalito, CA 94965
"Tennis Player"

Harold Case
34 Cunningham Park
Harrow, Middlesex
HA1 4AL ENGLAND
"Cinematographer"

Adriana Caselotti
201 North Larchmont Blvd.
Los Angeles, CA 90004
"Entertainer"

Bernie Casey
6145 Flight Avenue
Los Angeles, CA 90056
"Actor, Football Player"

Lawrence Casey
4139 Vanetta Place
North Hollywood, CA 91604
"Actor"

Johnny Cash
711 Summerfield Drive
Hendersonville, TN 37075
"Singer"

June Carter Cash
711 Summerfield Drive
Hendersonville, TN 37075
"Singer"

Kellye Cash
1935 Sunset Drive #98
Escondido, CA 92025
Former Miss America"

Pat Cash
281 Clarence Street
Sydney NSW 2000 AUSTRALIA
"Tennis Player"

Rosalind Cash
118 Park Place #D
Venice, CA 90291
"Actress"

Rosanne Cash
1775 Broadway #700
New York, NY 10019
"Singer, Songwriter"

Philip Casnoff
201 West 85th Street #16-C
New York, NY 10024
"Actor"

Billy Casper
14 Quiet Meadow Lane
Mapleton, UT 84663
"Golfer"

Peggy Cass
200 East 62nd Street
New York, NY 10021
"Actress"

Seymour Cassell
P.O. Box 5617
Beverly Hills, CA 90210
"Actor"

David Cassidy
701 North Oakhurst Drive
Beverly Hills, CA 90210
"Actor, Singer"

Joanna Cassidy
463 Mesa Road
Santa Monica, CA 90402
"Actress"

Patrick Cassidy
10433 Wilshire Blvd. #605
Los Angeles, CA 90024
"Actor"

Ryan Cassidy
701 North Oakhurst Drive
Beverly Hills, CA 90210
"Actor"

Shaun Cassidy
8899 Beverly Blvd.
Los Angeles, CA 90077
"Actor, Singer"

Oleg Cassini
135 East 19th Street
New York, NY 10003
"Fashion Designer"

Tricia Cast
221 North Dianthus
Manhattan Beach, CA 90266
"Actress"

John Castle
126 Kennington Park Road
London W1 ENGLAND
"Mezzo-Soprano"

Roy Castle
235 Regent Street
London W1A ENGLAND
"Actor"

Fidel Castro
Palacio del Gobierno
Havana, CUBA
"Politician"

Phoebe Cates
136 East 57th Street #1001
New York, NY 10022
"Actress"

Dick Cathcart
6414 Lubao Avenue
Woodland Hills, CA 91364
"Composer"

Mary Jo Catlett
4375 Farmdale
Studio City, CA 91604
"Actress"

Kim Cattrell
760 North La Cienega Blvd.
Los Angeles, CA 90069
"Actress"

Maxwell Caufield
4036 Foothill Road
Carpinteria, CA 93013
"Actor"

Tracy Caulkins
213 Ocella
Nashville, TN 37209
"Swimmer"

Steve Cauthen
Barry Hills
Lambourne, ENGLAND
"Horse Racer"

Dick Cavett
2200 Fletcher Avenue
Ft. Lee, NJ 07024
"TV Host, Comedian"

Evonne Goolagong Cawley
80 Duntroon Avenue
Roseville NSW AUSTRALIA
"Tennis Player"

Christopher Cazenove
9169 Sunset Blvd.
Los Angeles, CA 90069
"Actor"

Eugene Cernan
900 Town & Country Lane #210
Houston, TX 77024
"Astronaut"

Rick Cerrone
63 Eisenhower
Cresskill, NJ 07626
"Baseball Player"

Peter Cetera
1880 Century Park East #900
Los Angeles, CA 90067
"Singer, Musician"

Ron Cey
22714 Creole Road
Woodland HIlls, CA 91364
"Baseball Player"

Alex Chadwick
c/o National Public Radio
2025 "M" Street N.W.
Washington, DC 20036
"News Correspondent"

Florence Chadwick
814 Armada Terrace
San Diego, CA 92106
"Swimmer"

Suzie Chaffee
140 Hollister Avenue
Santa Monica, CA 90405
"TV Personality, Skier"

Mme. Chaing Kai-Shek
Locust Valley
Lattingtown, NY 11560
"Politician"

Chairman of the Board
2300 East Independence Blvd.
Charlotte, NC 28205
"Music Group"

George Chakiris
7266 Clinton Street
Los Angeles, CA 90036
"Actor"

Richard Chamberlain
87/829 Farrington Highway
Waianac, HI 96792
"Actor, Producer"

Wilt Chamberlain
15216 Antelo Place
Los Angeles, CA 90024
"Basketball Player"

The Chambers Brothers
5218 Almont Street
Los Angeles, CA 90032
"R&B Group"

Marilyn Chambers
4528 West Charleston Blvd.
Las Vegas, NV 89102
"Actress"

Chris Chambliss
140 Prospect Street #11-N
Hackensack, NJ 07601
"Baseball Player"

Violetta Chamorro
Presidential Palace
Managua, NICARAGUA
"Politician"

Marge Champion
484 West 43rd Street
New York, NY 10036
"Actress, Dancer"

Charles Champlin
2169 Linda Flora Drive
Los Angeles, CA 90024
"Film Critic"

John Chancellor
30 Rockefeller Plaza
New York, NY 10112
"Newscaster"

Otis Chandler
1421 Emerson
Oxnard, CA 93033
"Publisher"

Rep. Rod Chandler (WA)
House Cannon Bldg. #223
Washington, DC 20515
"Politician"

Micheal Chang
1025 North Holt Drive
Placentia, CA 92670
"Tennis Player"

Carol Channing
9301 Flicker Way
Los Angeles, CA 90069
"Actress"

Stockard Channing
10390 Santa Monica Blvd. #300
Los Angeles, CA 90025
"Actress"

The Chantels
5218 Almont Street
Los Angeles, CA 90069
"Vocal Group"

Rosalind Chao
11726 San Vicente Blvd. #300
Los Angeles, CA 90049
"Actress"

Lauren Chapin
P.O. Box 922
Killeen, TX 76541
"Actress"

Tom Chapin
57 Piermont Place
Piermont, NY 10968
"Singer"

Geraldine Chaplin
6 rue Asseline
75015 Paris, FRANCE
"Actress"

Lita Grey Chaplin
8440 Fountain Ave. #302
Los Angeles, CA 90069
"Actress"

Sydney Chaplin
69950 Frank Sinatra Drive
Rancho Mirage, CA 92270
"Son of Charlie Chaplin"

Rep. Jim Chapman (TX)
House Cannon Bldg. #429
Washington, DC 20515
"Politician"

Judith Chapman
11670 Sunset Blvd. #312
Los Angeles, CA 90049
"Actress"

Lonny Chapman
3973 Goodland Avenue
Studio City, CA 91604
"Actor"

Marguerite Chapman
11558 Riverside Drive #304
Hollywood, CA 91602
"Actress"

Mark David Chapman
Attica State Prison
Attica, NY 14011
"John Lennon's Killer"

Mark Lindsay Chapman
6565 Sunset Blvd. #300
Los Angeles, CA 90028
"Actor"

Tracy Chapman
506 Santa Monica Blvd. #400
Santa Monica, CA 90401
"Actress"

Patricia Charbonneau
8899 Beverly Blvd.
Los Angeles, CA 90069
"Actress"

Cyd Charisse
10390 Wilshire Blvd. #1507
Los Angeles, CA 90024
"Actress, Dancer"

HRH Prince Charles
Kensington Pa,lace
London W8 ENGLAND
"Royalty"

Ray Charles
4863 Southridge Avenue
Los Angeles, CA 90008
"Singer, Pianist"

Suzette Charles
1930 Century Park West #403
Los Angeles, CA 90067
"Former Miss America"

Leslie Charleson
2314 Live Oak Drive East
Los Angeles, CA 90068
"Actress"

Tony Charmoli
1271 Sunset Plaza Drive
Los Angeles, CA 90069
"Director, Choreography"

Charo
P.O. Box 1007
Hanalei, HI 96714
"Singer"

Melanie Chartoff
444-A South Roxbury Drive
Beverly Hills, CA 90212
"Actress"

Barry Chase
3750 Beverly Ridge Drive
Sherman Oaks, CA 91423
"Actress, Dancer"

Chevy Chase
17492 Camino de Yatasto
Pacific Palisades, CA 90272
"Actor, Writer"

Lorraine Chase
68 Old Brompton Road
London SW7 ENGLAND
"Actress"

Cesar Chavez
P.O. Box 62
La Paz
Keene, CA 93531
"Union Leader, Activist"

Cheap Trick
315 West Gorham Street
Madison, WI 53703
"Rock & Roll Group"

Maree Cheatham
3377 Canton Lane
Studio City, CA 91604
"Actress"

Chubby Checker
1650 Broadway #1011
New York, NY 10019
"Singer, Songwriter"

Tommy Chong
(Cheech & Chong)
11661 San Vicente #1010
Los Angeles, CA 90049
"Comedian, Actor"

Molly Cheek
13038 Landale
Studio City, CA 91604
"Actress"

Joan Chen
148 South Occidental Blvd. #204
Los Angeles, CA 90057
"Actress"

Mrs. Anna Chenault
2510 Virgina Avenue NW #1404
Washington, DC 20005
"Author, Journalist"

Dick Cheney
Department of Defense
The Pentagon
Washington, DC 20301
"Secretary of Defense"

Cher
9200 Sunset #1001
Los Angeles, CA 90069
"Actress, Singer"

Neneh Cherry
8800 Sunset Blvd. #401
Los Angeles, CA 90069
"Singer"

Colby Chester
1245 North Orchard Drive
Burbank, CA 91506
"Actor"

Sam Chew, Jr.
8075 West 3rd Street #303
Los Angeles, CA 90048
"Actor"

Chicago
345 North Maple Drive #235
Beverly Hills, CA 90210
"Rock & Roll Group"

The Chiffons
185 Clinton Avenue
Staten Island, NY 10301
"Vocal Group"

Julia Child
103 Irving Street
Cambridge, MA 02138
"TV Personality"

Toni Childs
888-7th Avenue #1602
New York, NY 10019
"Singer, Songwriter"

Linden Chiles
2521 Topanga Skyline
Topanga, CA 90290
"Actor"

Lois Chiles
644 San Lorenzo
Santa Monica, CA 90402
"Actress"

Tiffany Chin
2331 Century Hill
Los Angeles, CA 90057
"Skater"

Shirley Chisholm
48 Crestwood Lane
Williamsville, NY 14221
"Politician"

Chocolate Milk
P.O. Box 82
Great Neck, NY 11021
"R&B Group"

Rae Dawn Chong
P.O. Box 181
Bearville, NY 12409
"Actress"

Thomas Chong
1625 Casale Road
Pacific Palisades, CA 90272
"Actor, Writer, Director"

Raymond Chow
23 Barker Road
Craigside Mansion #5B
HONG KONG (BCC)
"Film Director"

Todd Christensen
991 Sunburst Lane
Alpine, UT 84004
"Football Player"

Claudia Christian
9200 Sunset Blvd. #625
Los Angeles, CA 90069
"Actress"

Marc Christian
1801 Century Park East
Suite 1900
Los Angeles, CA 90067
"Musician"

Julie Christie
23 Linden Gardens
London W2 ENGLAND
"Actress"

Virginia Christine
12348 Rochedale Lane
Los Angeles, CA 90049
"Actress"

Dennis Christopher
175 Fifth Avenue #2413
New York, NY 10010
"Actor"

Warren Christopher
400 South Hope Street
Los Angeles, CA 90071
"Lawyer"

William Christopher
P.O. Box 50698
Pasadena, CA 91105
"Actor"

"Cicciolina"
Via Europa 300
Rome, ITALY
"Actress"

Connie Chung
c/o CBS News
524 West 57th Street
New York, NY 10019
"Newscaster"

Michael Cimino
9015 Alta Cedro
Beverly Hills, CA 90210
"Writer Producer"

Charles Cioffi
Glover Avenue
Norwalk, CT 06850
"Actor"

Liz Claiborne
1441 Broadway
New York, NY 10018
"Fashion Designer"

Eric Clapton
67 Brook Street
London W1 ENGLAND
"Singer, Guitarist"

Candy Clark
P.O. Box 632
Oldwick, NJ 08853
"Actress"

Christie Clark
3800 Barham Blvd. #303
Los Angeles, CA 90068
"Actress"

Dane Clark
1680 Old Oak Road
Los Angeles, CA 90049
"Actor, Director"

Dick Clark
3003 West Olive Avenue
Burbank, CA 91505
"TV Host, Producer"

Doran Clark
9301 Wilshire Blvd. #312
Beverly Hills, CA 90210
"Actress"

Joe Clark
366 South Ridgewood Road
South Orange, NJ 07079
"High School Principal"

Petula Clark
410 Park Avenue, 10th Floor
New York, NY 10022
"Singer, Actress"

Ramsey Clark
36 East 12th Street
New York, NY 10003
"Politician"

Roy Clark
1800 Forrest Blvd.
Tulsa, OK 74114
"Singer, Guitarist"

Susan Clark
7943 Woodrow Wilson Drive
Los Angeles, CA 90046
"Actress"

Ted Clark
c/o National Public Radio
2025 "M" Street N.W.
Washington, DC 20036
"News Correspondent"

Angela Clarke
7557 Mulholland Drive
Los Angeles, CA 90046
"Actress"

Brian Patrick Clarke
333-D Kenwood
Burbank, CA 91505
"Actor"

Mae Clarke
Motion Picture Country Home
23450 Calabasas Road
Woodland Hills, CA 91364
"Actress"

Stanley Clarke
1807 Benedict Canyon
Beverly Hills, CA 90210
"Guitarist, Composer"

Robert Clary
10001 Sun Dial Lane
Beverly Hills, CA 90210
"Actor"

The Clash
268 Camden Road
London NW1 ENGLAND
"Rock & Roll Group"

James Clavell
2006 Thayer Avenue
Los Angeles, CA 90025
"Writer, Producer"

Andrew Dice Clay
48 East 50th Street #400
New York, NY 10022
"Comedian, Actor"

Nicholas Clay
31 Kings Road
London SW3 ENGLAND
"Actor"

Rep. William L. Clay (MO)
House Rayburn Bldg. #2470
Washington, DC 20515
"Politician"

Jill Clayburgh
225 McLain Street
Mt. Kisco, NY 10549
"Actress"

Jack Clayton
Herons Flight
Marlow, Buckinghamshire
ENGLAND
"Film Director"

John Cleese
82 Ladbroke Road
London W11 3NU ENGLAND
"Actor, Writer"

Roger Clemens
10131 Beekman Place
Houston, TX 77043
"Baseball Player"

Van Cliburn
455 Wilder Place
Shreveport, LA 71104
"Pianist"

Clark Clifford
9421 Rockville Pike
Bethesda, MD 20814
"Lawyer"

Eleanor Clift
1750 Pennsylvania Avenue N.W.
Washington, DC 20001
"News Correspondent"

Debra Clinger
4415 Auckland Avenue
North Hollywood, CA 91602
"Actress"

Rep. William F. Clinger (PA)
House Rayburn Bldg. #2160
Washington, DC 20515
"Politician"

Bill Clinton
1800 Center Street
Little Rock, AR 72206
"Governor"

George Clooney
11655 Laurelcrest Drive
Studio City, CA 91604
"Actor"

Rosemary Clooney
1019 North Roxbury Drive
Beverly Hills, CA 90210
"Singer"

Glenn Close
9830 Wilshire Blvd
Beverly Hills, CA 90212
"Actress"

Jerry Clower
P.O. Box 121089
Nashville, TN 37212
"Comedian"

The Coasters
4484 Pennwood #233
Las Vegas, NV 89102
"Vocal Group"

Phyllis Coates
P.O. Box S-3024
Carmel, CA 93921
"Actress"

Sen. Dan Coats (IN)
Senate Russell Bldg. #407
Washington, DC 20510
"Politician"

Joe Cobb
3746 1/2 Clarington
Culver City, CA 90230
"Actor"

Rep. Howard Coble (NC)
House Cannon Bldg. #430
Washington, DC 20515
"Politician"

James Coburn
3930 Holly Line
Sherman Oaks, CA 91403
"Actor, Director"

Imogene Coca
200 East 66th Street #1803D
New York, NY 10021
"Actress"

Bruce Cockburn
151 John Street #301
Toronto, Ontario M5V 2T2
CANADA
"Singer, Songwriter"

Joe Cocker
48 East 50th Street
New York, NY 10022
"Singer"

Iron Eyes Cody
2017 Griffith Park Blvd.
Los Angeles, CA 90039
"Actor"

David Allan Coe
P.O. Box 152
Elden, MO 65026
"Singer, Songwriter"

Peter Coe
518 Pier Avenue #9
Santa Monica, CA 90405
"Film Director"

Sebastian Coe
37 Marlborough Road
Sheffield, South Yorkshire
ENGLAND
"Runner"

Susie Coelho
2814 Hutton
Beverly Hills, CA 90210
"Actress, Model"

Tony Coelho
787-7th Avenue
New York, NY 10036
"Ex-Congressman"

Tris Coffin
5601 Warwick Place
Chevy Chase, MD 20015
"Actor"

Alexander Cohen
25 West 54th Street #5-F
New York, NY 10019
"TV/Theater Producer"

Mindy Cohn
9606 Yoakum Avenue
Beverly Hills, CA 90210
"Actress"

Claudette Colbert
Bellerive St. Peter
Barbados, WEST INDIES
"Actress"

Robert Colbert
151 Ocean Park
Santa Monica, CA 90405
"Actor"

Anita Colby
Flagler River Club
447 East 52nd Street
New York, NY 10022
"Actress, Model, Editor"

Dennis Cole
2160 Century Park East
Los Angeles, CA 90067
"Actor"

Gary Cole
1122 South Robertson Blvd.
Los Angeles, CA 90035
"Actor"

George Cole
Donnelly, Newham Hill
Bottom Nettleford
Oxon, ENGLAND
"Actor"

Michael Cole
6332 Costello Avenue
Van Nuys, CA 91401
"Actor"

Natalie Cole
4201 3/4 Cahuenga Blvd.
North Hollywood, CA 91602
"Singer"

Mrs. Nat King Cole-Devore
South House
Tyringham, MA 01264
"Widower of Nat Cole"

Olivia Cole
9744 Wilshire Blvd. #308
Beverly Hills, CA 90212
"Actress"

Tina Cole
2126 Cahuenga Blvd.
Los Angeles, CA 90068
"Actress"

Dabney Coleman
360 North Kenter
Los Angeles, CA 90049
"Actor"

Rep. E. Thomas Coleman (MO)
House Rayburn Bldg. #2468
Washington, DC 20515
"Politician"

Gary Coleman
900 Sunset Blvd. #1200
Los Angeles, CA 90069
"Actor"

Jack Coleman
7358 Woodrow Wilson Drive
Los Angeles, CA 90046
"Actor"

Nancy Coleman
Manhattan Plaza
484 West 43rd Street
New York, NY 10036
"Actress"

Rep. Ronald Coleman (TX)
House Cannon Bldg. #440
Washington, DC 20515
"Politician"

Charles "Honi" Coles
19 West 44th Street #1500
New York, NY 10036
"Actor"

Margaret Colin
10 East 44th Street
New York, NY 10017
"Actress"

Rep. Cardiss Collins (IL)
House Rayburn Bldg. #2264
Washington, DC 20515
"Politician"

Cora Sue Collins
116 West Granada
Phoenix, AZ 85003
"Actress"

Gary Collins
2751 Hutton Drive
Beverly Hills, CA 90210
"Actor, TV Host"

Jackie Collins
710 North Foohill Road
Beverly Hills, CA 90210
"TV-Host, Author"

Joan Collins
19 Eaton Place #2
London SW1 ENGLAND
"Actress, Producer"

Judy Collins
845 West End Avenue
New York, NY 10024
"Singer, Songwriter"

Kate Collins
1410 York Avenue #4-D
New York, NY 10021
"Actress"

Marva Collins
4146 West Chicago Avenue
Chicago, IL 60651
"Educator"

Michael Collins
4206-48th Place N.W.
Washington, DC 200016
"Actor"

Phil Collins
Lockswood
Sussex, ENGLAND
"Singer, Drummer"

Stephen Collins
7920 Sunset Blvd. #350
Los Angeles, CA 90046
"Actor"

Scott Colomby
8730 Sunset Blvd. #408
Los Angeles, CA 90069
"Actor"

Color Me Badd
345 North Maple Drive #205
Beverly Hills, CA 90210
"Music Group"

Charles Colson
P.O. Box 40562
Washington, DC 20016
"Author"

Marshall Colt
151 South El Camino Drive
Beverly Hills, CA 90212
"Actor"

Jessie Colter
1117-17th Avenue South
Nashville, TN 37212
"Singer"

Chi Coltrane
5955 Tuxedo Terrace
Los Angeles, CA 90068
"Singer"

Franco Columbu
2947 South Sepulveda Blvd.
Los Angeles, CA 90064
"Actor, Bodybuilder"

Chris Columbus
290 West End Avenue
New York, NY 10023
"Screenwriter"

Rep. Larry Combest (TX)
House Longworth Bldg. #1527
Washington, DC 20515
"Politician"

Anjanette Comer
2357 Kimridge Drive
Beverly Hills, CA 90210
"Actress"

Paul Comi
1665 Oak Knoll Avenue
San Marino, CA 91108
"Actor"

Commodores
3151 Cahuenga Blvd. West
Suite #235
Los Angeles, CA 90068
"R&B Group"

Perry Como
305 Northern Blvd. #3-A
Great Neck, NY 11021
"Singer"

Joyce Compton
23388 Mulholland Drive
Woodland Hills, CA 91364
"Actress"

Jeff Conaway
10351 Santa Monica Blvd. #211
Los Angeles, CA 90025
"Actor"

Richard T. Condon
3436 Ashbury
Dallas, TX 75205
"Author"

Gino Conforti
132-B South Lasky Drive
Beverly Hills, CA 90212
"Actor"

Ray Coniff
2154 Hercules Drive
Los Angeles, CA 90046
"Composer"

Tony Conigliaro
339 Nahant Road
Nahant, MA 01808
"Baseball Player"

John Conlee
38 Music Square East #117
Nashville, TN 37203
"Singer, Songwriter"

Darlene Conley
4647 Willis Street #212
Sherman Oaks, CA 91403
"Actress"

Earl Thomas Conley
1222-16 Avenue South
Nashville, TN 37212
"Singer, Songwriter"

Billy Conn
544 Gettysburg Street
Pittsburgh, PA 15206
"Boxer"

Didi Conn
14820 Valley Vista Blvd.
Sherman Oaks, CA 91403
"Actress"

Jennifer Connelly
8899 Beverly Blvd.
Los Angeles, CA 90048
"Actress"

Bart Conner
2325 Westwood Drive
Norman, OK 73069
"Athlete"

Dennis Conner
2225 Hancock Street #B
San Diego, CA 92110
"Yachtsman"

Jason Connery
22 Bishops Road
London SW6 7AB ENGLAND
"Actor"

Sean Connery
2220 Avenue of the Stars
Suite #2305
Los Angeles, CA 90067
"Actor"

Harry Connick, Jr.
298 Mulberry Street
New York, NY 10012
"Pianist, Singer"

Billy Connolly
151 South El Camino Drive
Beverly Hills, CA 90212
"Comedian"

Carol Connors
1709 Ferrari Drive
Beverly Hills, CA 90210
"Songwriter"

Chuck Connors
P.O. Box 4440-73
Tehachapi, CA 93561
"Actor, Baseball Player"

Jimmy Connors
200 South Refugio Road
Santa Ynez, CA 93460
"Tennis Player"

Mike Connors
4810 Louise Avenue
Encino, CA 91316
"Actor"

Barnaby Conrad
3530 Pine Valley Drive
Sarasota, FL 34239
"Author, Painter"

Charles Conrad, Jr.
5301 Bolsa Avenue
Huntington Beach, CA 92647
"Astronaut"

Christian Conrad
15301 Ventura Blvd. #345
Sherman Oaks, CA 91403
"Actor"

Kimberly Conrad
10236 Charing Cross Road
Los Angeles, CA 90024
"Mrs. Hugh Hefner"

Paul Conrad
28649 Crestridge Road
Palos Verdes, CA 90274
"Cartoonist"

Robert Conrad
21355 Pacific Coast Hwy.
Malibu, CA 90265
"Actor, Writer"

Shane Conrad
21355 Pacific Coast Hwy.
Suite #200
Malibu, CA 90265
"Actor"

William Conrad
4031 Longridge
Sherman Oaks, CA 91403
"Actor, Radio Personality"

John Considine
16 1/2 Red Coat
Greenwich, CT 06830
"Actor, Writer"

Tim Considine
10328 Viretta Lane
Los Angeles, CA 90024
"Actor, Writer, Director"

Michel Constantin
17 Blvd. Bartole Beauvallon
8321 Sainte Maxime, FRANCE
"Actor"

Eddie Constantine
Bodenstedt 3
6200 Wiesbaden, GERMANY
"Actor"

Ex-King Constantine
4 Linnell Drive
Hampstead Way
London NW11 ENGLAND
"Royalty"

John Conte
75600 Beryl Drive
Indian Wells, CA 92260
"Actor"

Bill Conti
117 Fremont Place
Los Angeles, CA 90005
"Composer, Arranger"

Tom Conti
9000 Sunset Blvd #1200
Los Angeles, CA 90069
"Actor"

Frank Converse
19 West Street #1500
New York, NY 10017
"Actor"

Peggy Converse
2525 Briarcrest Drive
Beverly Hills, CA 90210
"Actress"

Gary Conway
2035 Mandeville Canyon
Los Angeles, CA 90049
"Actor"

Kevin Conway
9301 Wilshire Blvd. #312
Beverly Hills, CA 90210
"Actor"

Tim Conway
P.O. Box 17047
Encino, CA 91416
"Actor, Director"

Rep. John Conyers (MI)
House Rayburn Bldg. #2426
Washington, DC 20515
"Politician"

Ry Cooder
321 Fulham Road
London SW10 9QL ENGLAND
"Guitarist, Songwriter"

Keith Coogan
3500 West Olive Avenue #1400
Burbank, CA 91505
"Actor"

Barbara Cook
c/o Kravet
205 Lexington Avenue #100
New York, NY 10016
"News Correspondent"

Carole Cook
8829 Ashcroft
Los Angeles, CA 90048
"Actress"

Elisha Cook, Jr.
429 Mandich Lane,
P.O. Box 335
Bishop, CA 93514
"Actor"

Peter Cook
24 Perrins Walk
London NW3 ENGLAND
"Actor, Comedian"

Robin Cook
22 Prince Albert Road
London NW1 7ST ENGLAND
"Screenwriter"

Alistair Cook
Nassau Point
Cutchogue, NY 11935
"Journalist, TV Announcer"

Jack Kent Cooke
Kent Farms
Middleburg, VA 22117
"Laywer, Football Team Owner"

Danny Cooksey
11350 Ventura Blvd. #206
Studio City, CA 91604
"Singer"

Peter Cookson
30 Norfolk Road
Southfield, MA 01259
"Actor"

Dr. Denton Cooley
3014 Del Monte Drive
Houston, TX 77019
"Heart Surgeon"

Rita Coolidge
1330 North Wetherly Drive
Los Angeles, CA 90069
"Singer, Actress"

Alice Cooper
4135 East Keim Drive
Paradise Valley, AZ 85253
"Singer, Songwriter"

Ann Cooper
c/o National Public Radio
2025 "M" Street N.W.
Washington, DC 20036
"News Correspondent"

Ben Cooper
20838 Exhibit Court
Woodland Hills, CA 91367
"Actor"

Henry Cooper
36 Brampton Grove
London NW4 ENGLAND
"TV Personality"

Jackie Cooper
9621 Royalton
Beverly Hills, CA 90210
"Actor, Director"

Jeanne Cooper
2472 Coldwater Canyon
Beverly Hills, CA 90210
"Actress"

Rep. Jim Cooper (TN)
House Cannon Bldg. #125
Washington, DC 25105
"Politician"

L. Gordon Cooper
5011 Woodley Avenue
Encino, CA 91436
"Astronaut"

Mark Copage
P.O. Box 461677
Los Angeles, CA 90046
"Actor"

Joan Copeland
88 Central Park West
New York, NY 10023
"Actress"

Stewart Copeland
9313 Doheny Road
Beverly Hills, CA 90210
"Drummer, Songwriter"

Teri Copley
4535 Coldwater #103
North Hollywood, CA 91604
"Actress"

David Copperfield
2181 Broadview Terrace
Los Angeles, CA 90068
"Magician"

Francis Coppola
916 Kearny Street
San Francisco, CA 94133
"Writer, Producer"

Sofia Coppola
781-5th Avenue
New York, NY 10022
"Actress"

Gretchen Corbett
2600 Rinconia Drive
Los Angeles, CA 90068
"Actress"

Ronnie Corbett
57 Gt. Cumberland Place
London W1H 7LJ ENGLAND
"Comedian"

Barry Corbin
11726 San Vincente Blvd #300
Los Angeles, CA 90049
"Actor"

Ellen Corby
9026 Harratt
Los Angeles, CA 90069
"Actress"

Kevin Corcoran
8617 Balcom
Northridge, CA 91325
"Actor"

Alex Cord
10100 Santa Monica Blvd. #700
Los Angeles, CA 90067
"Actor"

Barbara Corday
532 North Cherokee
Los Angeles, CA 90004
"TV Writer, Producer"

Mara Corday
25932 Mendoza Drive
Valencia, CA 91355
"Actress"

Paula Corday
14101 Greenleaf Street
Van Nuys, CA 91403
"Actress"

Angel Cordero
P.O. Box 90
Jamaica, NY 11411
"Horse Jockey"

Chick Corea
2635 Griffith Park Blvd.
Los Angeles, CA 90039
"Musician"

Prof. Irwin Corey
58 Nassau Drive
Great Neck, NY 11022
"Comedian"

Jeff Corey
29445 Bluewater Road
Malibu, CA 90265
"Actor, Director"

Ann Corio
721 East Grinnell Drive
Burbank, CA 91501
"Burlesque"

Al Corley
3330 Purdue Avenue
Los Angeles, CA 90066
"Singer"

Roger Corman
11611 San Vicente Blvd.
Los Angeles, CA 90049
"Writer, Producer"

**Cornelius Bros. &
Sister Sledge**
203 Culver
Charleston, SC 29407
"Vocal Group"

Don Cornelius
P.O. Box C
River Edge, NJ 07661
"TV Producer"

Helen Cornelius
724 State Street
Hannibal, MO 63401
"Singer"

Lydia Cornell
142 South Bedford Drive
Beverly Hills, CA 90212
"Actress, Model"

Bernie Cornfield
1100 Carolyn Way
Beverly Hills, CA 90210
"Investment Manager"

Adrienne Corri
26 Springfield Road
London SW3 ENGLAND
"Actress"

Douglas Corrigan
2828 North Flower
Santa Ana, CA 92706
"Actor"

Aneta Corsaut
4313 Agnes Avenue
Studio City, CA 91604
"Actress"

Bud Cort
606 North Larchmont Blvd. #309
Los Angeles, CA 90004
"Actor"

Valentina Cortese
Pretta S. Erasmo 6
Milan, ITALY
"Actress"

Norman Corwin
1840 Fairburn Avenue #302
Los Angeles, CA 90025
"Writer, Producer"

Bill Cosby
P.O. Box 88
Greenfield, MA 01301
"Actor, Comedian"

Howard Cosell
150 East 69th Street
New York, NY 10021
"Sportscaster"

Pierre Cossette
8899 Beverly Blvd. #100
Los Angeles, CA 90048
"Film Producer"

Mary Costa
321 Barton Avenue
Palm Beach, FL 33480
"Soprano"

Constantin Costa-Gavras
244 rue Saint-Jacques
75005 Paris, FRANCE
"Filmwriter, Director"

Midge Costanza
11811 West Olympic Blvd.
Los Angeles, CA 90210
"Ex-President Aide"

Bob Costas
c/o NBC Sports
30 Rockefeller Plaza
New York, NY 10112
"Sportscaster"

Elvis Costello.
9028 Great West Road
Middlesex TW8 9EW ENGLAND
"Singer"

Rep. Jerry F. Costello (IL)
House Cannon Bldg. #119
Washington, DC 20515
"Politician"

Mariclare Costello
8271 Melrose Avenue #110
Los Angeles, CA 90046
"Actress"

Nicholas Coster
9301 Wilshire Blvd. #312
Beverly Hills, CA 90210
"Actor"

Kevin Costner
P.O. Box 275
Torrance, CA 91021
"Actor"

Joseph Cotten
White Gables
1993 Mesa Drive
Palm Springs, CA 92264
"Actor"

David Coulier
5016 Bellaire Avenue
North Hollywood, CA 91606
"Actor"

Katherine Couric
30 Rockefeller Plaza
New York, NY 10020
"TV Host"

Jim Courier
1 Eriview Plaza #1300
Cleveland, OH 44114
"Tennis Player"

Hazel Court Taylor
1111 San Vicent Blvd
Santa Monica, CA 90402
"Actress"

Tom Courtenay
30 Charlywood Road
London SW15 ENGLAND
"Actor"

Jerome Courtland
P.O. Box 802650
Santa Clarita, CA 91380
"Film Director"

Robin Cousins
2887 Hollyridge Drive
Los Angeles, CA 90068
"Ice Skater"

Jacques Cousteau
425 East 52nd Street
New York, NY 10022
"Oceanographer"

Bob Cousy
459 Salisbury Street
Worchester, MA 01609
"Basketball Player"

Franklin Cover
1422 North Sweetzer #402
Los Angeles, CA 90069
"Actor"

Archibald Cox
Glesen Lane
Wayland, MA 01778
"Politician"

Rep. C. Christopher Cox (CA)
House Cannon Bldg. #412
Washington, DC 20515
Politician"

Courteney Cox
8816 Appian Way
Los Angeles, CA 90046
"Actress"

Ronny Cox
13948 Magnolia Blvd.
Sherman Oaks, CA 91423
"Actor, Film Producer"

Rep. William J. Coyne (PA)
House Rayburn Bldg. #2455
Washington, DC 20515
"Politician"

Peter Coyote
121 North Vicente Blvd.
Beverly Hills, CA 90211
"Actor"

Cuffy Crabbe
11216 North 74th Street
Scottsdale, AZ 85260
"Actor"

Billy "Crash" Craddock
1020 East Wendover Avenue #202
Greensboro, NC 27405
"Singer, Songwriter"

Christine Craft
500 Media Place
Sacramento, CA 95815
"TV Personality"

Jimmy Craig
445 Marine View Drive #300
Del Mar, CA 92014
"Physical Director"

Jim Craig
36 North Main Street
North Easton, MA 02156
"Hockey Player"

Roger Craig
2453 Canora Avenue
Alpine, CA 92331
"Football Player"

Yvonne Craig
1221 Ocean Avenue #202
Santa Monica, CA 90401
"Actress"

Jeanne Crain
354 Hilgard Avenue
Los Angeles, CA 90024
"Actress"

Douglass Cramer
738 Sarbonne Road
Los Angeles, CA 90077
"TV Writer, Producer"

Floyd Cramer
5109 Oak Haven Lane
Tampa, FL 33617
"Pianist"

Grant Cramer
291 South La Cienega Blvd. #307
Beverly Hills, CA 90211
"Actor"

Barbara Crampton
10000 Santa Monica Blvd. #305
Los Angeles, CA 90067
"Actress"

Bruce Crampton
7107 Spanky Ranch Drive
Dallas, TX 75248
"Golfer"

Cheryl Crane
9055 Sunset Blvd.
Los Angeles, CA 90069
"Lana Turner's Daughter"

Les Crane
424 South Rexford Drive
Beverly Hills, CA 90212
"TV-Radio Host"

Rep. Philip Crane (IL)
House Longworth Bldg. #1035
Washington, DC 20515
"Politician"

Sen. Alan Cranston (CA)
2024 Camden Avenue
Los Angeles, CA 90025
"Politician"

Gemma Craven
41 Hazelburg Road
London SW6 ENGLAND
"Actress"

Wes Craven
2015 Navy Street
Santa Monica, CA 90405
"Writer, Producer"

Christina Crawford
3530 Pine Valley Drive
Sarasota, FL 34239
"Author"

Cindy Crawford
9115 Cordell Drive
Los Angeles, CA 90069
"Model"

Johnny Crawford
8721 Sunset Blvd. #101
Los Angeles, CA 90069
"Actor"

Michael Crawford
162 Wardour Street
London W1 ENGLAND
"Actor"

Randy Crawford
911 Park Street S.W.
Grand Rapids, MI 49504
"Singer"

Bettino Craxi
Palazzo Chigi
Piazza Colonna
I-00100 Rome, ITALY
"Prime Minister"

Poppa John Creach
1122 South La Jolla Avenue
Los Angeles, CA 90035
"Singer, Guitarist"

Richard Crenna
3951 Valley Meadow Road
Encino, CA 91316
"Actor, Director"

Ben Crenshaw
1811 West 35th Street
Austin, TX 78703
"Golfer"

The Crew-Cuts
29 Cedar Street
Creskill, NJ 07626
"Vocal Group"

Michael Crichton
2210 Wilshire Blvd. #433
Santa Monica, CA 90403
"Filmwriter, Director"

The Crickets
Route 1, Box 222
Lyles, TN 37098
"Rock & Roll Group"

Quentin Crisp
46 East 3rd Street
New York, NY 10003
"Actor"

Peter Criss
645 Madison Avenue
New York, NY 10022
"Drummer, Singer"

Judith Crist
180 Riverside Drive
New York, NY 10024
"Film Critic"

Linda Cristal
9129 Hazen Drive
Beverly Hills, CA 90210
"Actress"

Phyllis Crockett
c/o National Public Radio
2025 "M" Street N.W.
Washington, DC 20036
"News Correspondent"

James Cromwell
4433 Bergamo Drive
Encino, CA 91436
"Actor"

David Cronenberg
184 Cottingham Street
Toronto, Ontario, CANADA
"Film Writer, Directorr"

Walter Cronkite
519 East 84th Street
New York, NY 10028
"Broadcast Journalist"

Hume Cronyn
63-23 Carlton Street
Rego Park, NY 11374
"Actor"

Bob Crosby
939 Coast Blvd.
La Jolla, CA 92037
"Musician"

Cathy Lee Crosby
1223 Wilshire Blvd. #404
Santa Monica, CA 90403
"Actress"

David Crosby
584 North Lachmont Blvd.
Hollywood, CA 90004
"Singer, Songwriter"

Denise Crosby
43 Navy Street #B
Venice, CA 90291
"Actor"

Mrs. Kathryn Crosby
P.O. Box 85
Genda, NV 89411
"Widower of Bing Crosby"

Mary Crosby
2875 Barrymore
Malibu, CA 90265
"Actress"

Norm Crosby
1400 Londonderry Place
Los Angeles, CA 90069
"Comedian, Actor"

Philip Crosby
21801 Providencia
Woodland Hills, CA 91364
"Actor"

Ben Cross
8 Harley Street
London W1 2AB ENGLAND
"Actor"

Christopher Cross
P.O. Box 23021
Santa Barbara, CA 93103
"Singer, Songwriter"

Andrae Crouch
1821 Wilshire Blvd. #200
Santa Monica, CA 90403
"Singer, Songwriter"

Lindsay Crouse
8428 Melrose Place #C
Los Angeles, CA 90069
"Actress"

J. D. Crowe
P.O. Box 1210
Hamilton, OH 45012
"Bluegrass"

Tanya Crowe
13030 Mindanao Way #4
Marina del Rey, CA 90291
"Actress"

Rodney Crowell
1114-17th Avenue South #101
Nashville, TN 37212
"Singer, Songwriter"

Patricia Crowley
150 West 56th Street #4603
New York, NY 10019
"Actress"

Tom Cruise
14 East 4th Street
New York, NY 10012
"Actor"

Denny Crumm
23015 Third Street
Louisville, KY 40292
"College Basketball Coach"

Jon Cryer
10000 West Washington #3018
Culver City, CA 90232
"Actor"

Billy Crystal
850 Chautauqua Blvd.
Pacific Palisades, CA 90272
"Actor, Comedian"

The Crystals
5218 Almont Street
Los Angeles, CA 90032
"Vocal Group"

Melinda Culea
5504 Calhoun Avenue
Van Nuys, CA 91401
"Actress"

Macaulay Culkin
40 West 57th Street
New York, NY 10019
"Actor"

Brett Cullen
P.O. Box 5617
Beverly Hills, CA 90210
"Actor"

William Kirby Cullen
9021 Melrose Avenue #308
Los Angeles, CA 90069
"Actor"

Robert Culp
357 Crown Drive
Los Angeles, CA 90049
"Actor, Writer, Director"

Culture Club
34A Green Lane
Northwood, Middlesex
ENGLAND
"Rock & Roll Group"

Constance Cummings
66 Old Church Street
London SW3 ENGLAND
"Actress"

e.e. Cummings
4 Patchin Place
New York, NY 10011
"Author, Painter"

Quinn Cummings
121 North San Vicente Blvd.
Beverly Hills, CA 90211
"Actress"

Randall Cunningham
c/o Veterans Stadium
Philadelphia, PA 19148
"Football Player"

Mario Cuomo (NY)
Governor, State Capitol
Albany, NY 12224
"Governor"

Mike Curb
1820 Carla Ridge Drive
Beverly Hills, CA 90210
"Record Producer"

Tim Curry
2401 Wild Oak Drive
Los Angeles, CA 90068
"Actor"

Jane Curtin
35 West 11th Street
New York, NY 10011
"Actress"

Valerie Curtin
15622 Meadowgate Road
Encino, CA 91316
"Actress, Writer"

Dan Curtis
9911 West Pico Blvd. #306
Los Angeles, CA 90035
"Director, Producer"

Jamie Lee Curtis
1242 South Camden Drive
Los Angeles, CA 90035
"Actress"

Keene Curtis
6363 Ivarene Avenue
Los Angeles, CA 90068
"Actor"

Tony Curtis
11831 Folkstone Lane
Los Angeles, CA 90077
"Actor, Director"

Cyril Cusack
30 Lower Hatch Street
Dublin 2 IRELAND
"Actor"

Peter Cushing
Seasalter
Whitstable, Kent
ENGLAND
"Actor"

Jon Cypher
4053 San Rafael Avenue
Los Angeles, CA 90065
"Actor"

Larry Czonka
37256 Hunter Camp Road
Lisbon, OH 44128
"Football Player"

Maryan d'Abo
9301 Wilshire Blvd. #312
Beverly Hills, CA 90210
"Actress"

Olivia d'Abo
7495 Mulholland Drive
Los Angeles, CA 90046
"Actress"

Willem Dafoe
33 Wooster Street #200
New York, NY 10013
"Actor"

Tim Daggett
53 Harmon Street
Long Beach, NY 11561
"Gymnast"

Arlene Dahl
P.O. Box 116
Sparkill, NY 10976
"Actress"

Bill Dailey
5245 East Coldwater Canyon
Van Nuys, CA 91401
"Actor"

Janet Dailey
Star Rt. 4, Box 2197
Branson, MO 65616
"Author"

Dick Dale
909 Parkview Avenue
Lodi, CA 95240
"Singer, Guitarist"

Jim Dale
26 Pembridge Villas
London W11 ENGLAND
"Actor"

The Dalai Lama
Thekchen Choling
McLeod Gunji, Hangra Dist.
Himachal Pradesh, INDIA
"Religious Leader"

Richard M. Daley
121 North Main Street
Chicago, IL 60602
"Mayor of Chicago"

Joe Dallesandro
711 North Formosa Avenue
Los Angeles, CA 90046
"Actress"

Abby Dalton
10000 Santa Monica Blvd. #305
Los Angeles, CA 90067
"Actress"

Audrey Dalton
15227 Del Gado Drive
Sherman Oaks, CA 91403
"Actress"

Lacy J. Dalton
1010-16th Avenue South
Nashville, TN 37212
"Singer"

Timothy Dalton
15 Golden Square #315
London W1 ENGLAND
"Actor"

Roger Daltry
48 Harley House
Marylebone Road
London NW1 5HL ENGLAND
"Singer, Actor"

Rad Daly
2901 West Alameda
Burbank, CA 91505
"Actor"

Timothy Daly
401 East 88th Street #11-G
New York, NY 10128
"Actor"

Tyne Daly
2934 1/2 Beverly Glen Circle #404
Los Angeles, CA 90077
"Actress"

Jacques D'Amboise
244 West 71st Street
New York, NY 10023
"Choreographer"

Leo Damian
303 South Crescent Heights
Los Angeles, CA 90048
"Conductor"

Michael Damian
24337 Mulholland Hwy.
Calabasas, CA 91302
"Actor"

Mark Damon
2781 Benedict Canyon
Beverly Hills, CA 90210
"Actor"

Stuart Damon
367 North Van Ness Avenue
Los Angeles, CA 90004
"Actor"

Vic Damone
P.O. Box 2999
Beverly Hills, CA 90213
"Singer"

Bill Dana
5965 Peacock Ridge Road #563
Rancho Palos Verdes, CA 90274
"Actor, Comedian"

Justin Dana
16130 Ventura Blvd. #300
Encino, CA 91436
"Actor"

Charles Dance
31 Kings Road
London SW3 4RP
ENGLAND
"Actor"

Sen. John Danforth (MO)
249 Senate Russell Bldg.
Washington, DC 20510
"Politician"

Beverly D'Angelo
2168 Outpost Drive
Los Angeles, CA 90068
"Actress"

Rodney Dangerfield
530 East 76th Street
New York, NY 10021
"Comedian, Actor"

Clifton Daniel
830 Park Avenue
New York, NY 10028
"Journalist"

Margaret Truman Daniel
830 Park Avenue
New York, NY 10028
"Author"

Charlie Daniels Band
Route 6, Box 156-A
Lebanon, TN 37087
"C&W Group"

David Mason Daniels
427 North Camden Drive #205
Beverly Hills, CA 90210
"Actor"

William Daniels
12805 Hortense Street
Studio City, CA 91604
"Actor"

Nicholas Daniloff
2400 "N" Street NW
Washington, D C 20037
"News Correspondent"

Alexandra Danilov
100 West 57th Street
New York, NY 10019
"Ballerina"

Rep. William Dannemeyer (CA)
House Rayburn Bldg. #2351
Washington, DC 20515
"Politician"

Blythe Danner
304-21st Street
Santa Monica, CA 90402
"Actress"

Sybil Danning
3575 Cahuenga Blvd. West #200
Los Angeles, CA 90068
"Actress"

Danny & The Juniors
168 Orchid Drive
Pearl River, NY 10965
"Vocal Group"

Royal Dano
517-20th Street
Santa Monica, CA 90402
"Actor"

Cesare Danova
4910 Libbit Avenue
Encino, CA 91316
"Actor"

Ted Danson
31504 Victoria Pointe Road
Malibu, CA 90265
"Actor"

Michael Dante
9827 Burgen Avenue
Los Angeles, CA 90034
"Actor"

Nikki Dantine
9744 Wilshire Blvd. #308
"Actress"

Ray Danton
1850 Holmby Avenue
Los Angeles, CA 90025
"Actor, Director"

Tony Danza
19722 Trull Brook Drive
Tarzana, CA 91356
"Actor"

Patti D'Arbanville
432-15th Street
Santa Monica, CA 90403
"Actress"

Kim Darby
4255 Laurel Grove
Studio City, CA 91604
"Actress"

Terence Trent D'Arby
Churchworks No. Villas
London NW1 9AY ENGLAND
"Singer"

Alex D'Arcy
930 North Spalding Avenue #2
Los Angeles, CA 90046
"Actor"

Severn Darden
3220 Laurel Canyon Blvd
Studio City, CA 91604
"Actor"

Mireille Darc
78 Blvd. Malesherbes
75008 Paris, FRANCE
"Actress"

Rep. George Darden (GA)
House Cannon Bldg. #228
Washington, DC 20515
"Politician"

Alvin Dark
103 Cranberry Way
Easley, SC 29640
"Baseball Player"

Johnny Dark
1100 North Alta Loma #707
Los Angeles, CA 90069
"Comedian"

Joan Darling
P.O. Box 6700
Tesuque, NM 87574
"Writer, Director"

Ron Darling
19 Woodland Street
Millbury, MA 01527
"Baseball Player"

James Darren
P.O. Box 1088
Beverly Hills, CA 90213
"Actor, Singer"

Danielle Darrieux
3, Quai Malaquais
75006 Paris, FRANCE
"Actress"

Henry Darrow
9169 Sunset Blvd
Los Angeles, CA 90069
"Actor"

Sam Dash
110 Newlands
Chevy Chase, MD 20015
"Watergate Participate"

Jules Dassin
Anagnostopoulon 25
Ahtens, GREECE
"Actor, Director"

Roberto d'Aubuisson
Presidential Palacio
San Salvador, EL SALVADOR
"Politician"

Elyssa Davalos
8271 Melrose Avenue #110
Los Angeles, CA 90046
"Actress"

Richard Davalos
1958 Vestal Avenue
Los Angeles, CA 90026
"Actor, Director"

Nigel Davenport
5 Ann's Close
Kinnerton Street
London SW1 ENGLAND
"Actor"

Willie Davenport
4876 Campbell Drive
Baton Rouge, LA 70807
"Track Athlete"

Marty Davich
530 South Greenwood Lane
Pasadena, CA 91107
"Actor"

Hal David
5253 Lankershim Blvd
North Hollywood, CA 91601
"Lyricist"

Lolita Davidovich
151 El Camino Drive
Beverly Hills, CA 90212
"Actress"

Doug Davidson
3641 East Chevy Chase Drive
Glendale, CA 91206
"Actor"

Eileen Davidson
620 Vollambrosa
Pasadena, CA 91107
"Actress"

Gordon Davidson
165 Mabery Road
Santa Monica, CA 90406
"Director"

John Davidson
6051 Spring Valley Road
Hidden Hills, CA 91302
"Singer, Actor"

John Rhys Davies
4 Court Lodge
48 Sloane Square
London SW1 ENGLAND
"Actor"

Lane Davies
9200 Sunset Blvd. #625
Los Angeles, CA 90069
"Actor"

Altovise Davis
279 South Beverly Drive #1006
Beverly Hills, CA 90212
"Mrs. Sammy Davis, Jr."

Angela Davis
San Francisco State University
Ehtnic Studies Dept.
1600 Holloway
San Francisco, CA 94132
"Author, Politician"

Ann B. Davis
1427 Beaver Road
Ambridge, PA 15003
"Actress"

Benjamin Davis
1001 Wilson Blvd. #906
Arlington, VA 22209
"Black Military General"

Clifton Davis
500 North Rossmore Avenue #502
Los Angeles, CA 90004
"Actor, Clergyman"

Eric Davis
6606 Denver Avenue #1
Los Angeles, CA 90044
"Actor"

Geena Davis
6201 Sunset Blvd. #7
Los Angeles, CA 90028
"Actress"

Glenn Davis
47-650 Eisenhower Drive
La Quinta, CA 92253
"Actor"

Jim Davis
200 Park Avenue
New York, NY 10166
"Cartoonist"

Jimme Davis
P.O. Box 15826
Baton Rouge, LA 70895
"Ex-Govenor"

Mac Davis
759 Nimes Road
Los Angeles, CA 90024
"Singer, Actor"

Martha Davis
10513 Cushdon Avenue
Los Angeles, CA 90064
"Singer"

Marvin Davis
1120 Schuyler Road
Beverly Hills, CA 90210
"Film Executive"

Ossie Davis
44 Cortland Avenue
New Rochelle, NY 10801
"Actor, Writer, Director"

Patti Davis
959-22nd Street
Santa Monica, CA 90403
"Author"

Rep. Robert W. Davis (MI)
House Rayburn Bldg. #2417
Washington, DC 20515
"Politician"

Skeeter Davis
508 Seward Road
Brentwood, TN 37027
"Singer"

Todd Davis
245 South Keystone Street
Burbank, CA 91506
"Actor"

Willie Davis
4419 Buena Vista #203
Dallas, TX 75202
"Baseball Player"

Bruce Davison
P.O. Box 57593
Sherman Oaks, CA 91403
"Musician"

Pam Dawber
2236-A Encinitas Blvd
Encinitas, CA 92024
"Actress"

Andre Dawson
10301 S.W. 144th Street
Miami, FL 33176
"Baseball Player"

Richard Dawson
1117 Angelo Drive
Beverly Hills, CA 90210
"Actor"

Doris Day
P.O. Box 223163
Carmel, CA 93922
"Actress"

Laraine Day
10313 Lauriston Avenue
Los Angeles, CA 90025
"Actress"

Linda Day
3335 Coy Drive
Sherman Oaks, CA 91423
"Actress"

Morris Day
3580 Wilshire Blvd. #184
Los Angeles, CA 90010
"Singer"

Taylor Day
2288 Jerusalem Avenue
North Bellmore, NY 11710
"Singer"

Jimmy Dean
28035 Dorothy Drive #210-A
Agoura, CA 91301
"Singer"

John Dean
9496 Rembert Lane
Beverly Hills, CA 90210
"Author"

Blossom Dearie
P.O. Box 21
East Durham, NY 12423
"Singer"

Dr. Michael De Bakey
Baylor College fo Medicine
1200 Moursund Avenue
Houston, TX 77030
"Heart Surgeon"

Debarge
205 Hill Street
Santa Monica, CA 90405
"Musician"

Burr De Benning
4235 Kingfisher Road
Calabasas, CA 91302
"Actor"

Dorothy DeBorba
1810 Montecito Avenue
Livermore, CA 94550
"Actress"

Chris De Burge
Bargy Castle, Tonhaggard
Wesxord, IRELAND
"Singer, Guitarist"

Rosemary De Camp
317 Camino de Las Colinas
Redondo Beach, CA 90277
"Actress"

Yvonne De Carlo
4 Martine Avenue #501
White Plains, NY 10606
"Actress"

Doug De Cinces
9411 Hazel Circle
Villa Park, CA 92667
"Baseball Player"

Mary Decker Slaney
2923 Flintlock Street
Eugene, OR 97401
"Track Athlete"

Fred de Cordova
1875 Carla Ridge Drive
Beverly Hills, CA 90210
"Film-TV Director"

Javier Perez de Cuellar
3 Sutton Place
New York, NY 10022
"United Nation Executive"

Frances Dee
Route 1
Camarillo, CA 93010
"Actress"

Joey Dee
141 Dunbar Avenue
Fords, NJ 08863
"Singer"

Ruby Dee
44 Cortland Avenue
New Rochelle, NY 10801
"Actress"

Sandra Dee
10351 Santa Monica Blvd #211
Los Angeles, CA 90025
"Actress"

Frances Dee McCrea
Route 3, Box 575
Camarillo, CA 93010
"Actress"

Mickey Deems
13114 Weddington Street
Van Nuys, CA 90401
"Actor, Director"

Deep Pruple
P.O. Box 254
Sheffield S6 1DF ENGLAND
"Rock & Roll Group"

Morris Dees
Rolling Hills Ranch
Route #1
Mathews, AL 36052
"Lawyer"

Rick Dees
8 Toluca Estates Drive
Toluca Lake, CA 91602
"Radio-TV Personality"

Rep. Peter A. DeFazio (OR)
House Longworth Bldg. #1233
Washington, DC 20515
"Politician"

Eddie Deezen
1570 North Edgemont #602
Los Angeles, CA 90027
"Actor"

Def Leppard
80 Warwick Gardens
London W14 8PR ENGLAND
"Rock & Roll Group"

Don Defore
2496 Mandeville Lane
Los Angeles, CA 90049
"Actor"

Buddy DeFranco
660 Madison Avenue
New York, NY 10021
"Jazz Musician"

Hubert De Givenchy
3 Avenue George V
75008 Paris, FRANCE
"Fashion Designer"

Gloria DeHaven
73 Devonshire Road
Cedar Grove, NJ 07009
"Actress"

Penny DeHaven
P.O. Box 83
Brentwood, TN 37027
"Singer"

Olivia DeHavilland
Boite Postal 156-16
Paris Cedex 75764 FRANCE
"Actress"

John Dehner
P.O. Box 5196
Bear Valley, CA 95223
"Actor"

Deja Vu
1 Touchstone Lane
Chard, Somerset TA20 IRF
ENGLAND
"Rock & Roll Group"

Frederick deKlerk
Union Building
Pretoria 0001
Republic of South Africa
"Politician"

Rep. E. "Kika" de la Garza (TX)
House Longworth Bldg. #1401
Washington, DC 20515
"Politician"

Kim Delaney
4724 Poe Avenue
Woodland Hills, CA 91364
"Actress"

Dana Delany
2521-6th Street
Santa Monica, CA 90405
"Actress"

Oscar de la Renta
Brook Hill Farm
Skiff Mountain Road
Kent, CT 06757
"Fashion Designer"

Dino De Laurentis
Via Poutina Ku 23270
Rome, ITALY
"Producer"

Rep. Thomas D. Delay (TX)
House Cannon Bldg. #308
Washington, DC 20515
"Politician"

Myrna Dell
21958 Valley Heart Drive
Studio City, CA 91604
"Actress"

Rep. Ronald V. Dellums (CA)
House Rayburn Bldg. #2136
Washington, DC 20515
"Politician"

Alain Delon
4 Chambiges, Trois Etage
75008 Paris, FRANCE
"Actor"

Nathalie Delon
3 Qual Malaquais
75006 Paris, ENGLAND
"Actor"

John Z. DeLorean
834 Fifth Avenue
New York, NY 10028
"Car Builder"

Daniele Delorme
16 rue de Marignan
75008 Paris, FRANCE
"Actor"

George Deloy
11460 Amanda Drive
Studio City, CA 91604
"Actor"

Milton De Lugg
2740 Claray Drive
Los Angeles, CA 90024
"Composer, Conductor"

Rep. Ron de Lugo (VI)
House Rayburn Bldg. #2238
Washington, DC 20515
"Politician"

Dom Deluise
1186 Corsica Drive
Pacific Palisades, CA 90272
"Actor, Director"

Peter Deluise
5643 Burnett
Van Nuys, CA 91411
"Actor"

The Del Vikings
P.O. Box 70218
Ft. Lauderdale, FL 33307
"Music Group"

Agnes De Mille
25 West 9th Street
New York, NY 10003
"Choreographer"

Rebecca De Mornay
760 North La Cienega Blvd.
Los Angeles, CA 90069
"Actress"

Patrick Dempsey
431 Lincoln Blvd.
Santa Monica, CA 90402
"Actor"

Nigel Dempster
10 Buckingham Street
London WC2 ENGLAND
"Writer"

Catherine Deneuve
76 rue Bonaparte
Paris 6 FRANCE
"Actress"

Maurice Denham
44 Brunswick Gardens #2
London W8 ENGLAND
"Actor"

Robert DeNiro
375 Greenwich Street
New York, NY 10013
"Actor"

Brian Dennehy
121 North San Vincente Blvd.
Beverly Hills, CA 90211
"Actor"

Sandy Dennis
93 North Sylvan Road
Westport, CT 06880
"Actress"

John Densmore
927 Berkeley Street
Santa Monica, CA 90403
"Musician"

Bucky Dent
5540 East Coach House Circle
Boca Raton, FL 33432
"Baseball Player"

Bob Denver
P.O. Box 196
Bearsville, NY 12409
"Actor"

John Denver
P.O. Box 1587
Aspen, CO 81612
"Singer, Songwriter"

James DePaiva
880 Greenleaf Canyon
Topanga, CA 90290
"Actor"

Brian De Palma
270 North Canyon Drive #1195
Beverly Hills, CA 90210
"Writer, Producer"

Gerard Depardieu
4 Place de la Chapelle
Bougival, FRANCE
"Actor"

Suzanne De Passe
1100 North Altal Loma #805
Los Angeles, CA 90069
"TV Writer"

Depeche Mode
429 Harrow Road
London W10 4RE ENGLAND
"Rock & Roll Group"

Johnny Depp
9229 Sunset Blvd. #414
Los Angeles, CA 90069
"Actor"

Bo Derek
3625 Roblar
Santa Ynez, CA 93460
"Actress, Model"

John Derek
3625 Roblar
Santa Ynez, CA 93460
"Actor, Writer, Director"

Bruce Dern
23430 Malibu Colony
Malibu, CA 90265
"Actor"

Laura Dern
760 North La Cienega Blvd.
Los Angeles, CA 90069
"Actress"

Richard Derr
8965 Cynthia Street
Los Angeles, CA 90069
"Actor"

Rep. Butler Derrick (SC)
House Cannon Bldg. #201
Washington, DC 20515
"Politician"

Cleavant Derricks
533 West End Avenue #3-A
Los Angeles, CA 90024
"Actor"

Alan Dershowitz
2 Tudor City Place
New York, NY 10017
"Lawyer"

Jean Desailly
53 quai des Gr. Augustina
75006 Paris, FRANCE
"Actor"

Jackie DeShannon
7526 Sunnywood Lane
Los Angeles, CA 90069
"Singer"

William Devane
11567 Acama Street
Studio City, CA 91604
"Actor"

Donna Devarona
30 Lincoln Place
New York, NY 10023
"Swimmer, Sportscaster"

Danny Devito
31020 Broad Beach Road
Malibu, CA 90265
"Actor"

William DeVrees
Human Heart Institute
One Audubon Plaza Drive
Louisville, KY 40202
"Medical Doctor"

Peter DeVries
170 Cross Highway
Westport, CT 06880
"Author, Editor"

Joyce De Witt
101 Ocean Avenue #1-4
Santa Monica, CA 90402
"Actress"

Susan Dey
10390 Santa Monica Blvd. #300
Los Angeles, CA 90025
"Actress"

Cliff DeYoung
766 Kingman Avenue
Santa Monica, CA 90402
"Actor"

Bobby Diamond
633 Calle Arroyo
Thousand Oaks, CA 91360
"Actor"

Neil Diamond
161 South Mapleton Drive
Los Angeles, CA 90024
"Singer, Songwriter"

Don Diamont
15045 Sherview Place
Sherman Oaks, CA 91403
"Actor"

HRH Princess Diana
Kensington Palace
London W8 ENGLAND
"Royalty"

George Di Cenzo
RD 1, Box 728
Stone Hollow Farm
Pipersville, CA 18947
"Actor"

Misha Dichter
40 West 47th Street
New York, NY 10019
"Pianist"

Douglas Dick
604 Gretna Green Way
Los Angeles, CA 90049
"Actor"

Jimmy Dickens
510 West Concord
Brentwood, TN 37027
"Singer"

Eric Dickerson
P.O. Box 535000
Indianapolis, IN 46253
"Football Player"

Nancy Dickerson
1811 Karlorama Square N.W.
Washington, DC 20008
"News Correspondent"

Bill Dickey
5817 South Country Club Blvd.
Little Rock, AR 72207
"Baseball Player"

James Dickey
4620 Lelias Court
Lake Katherine
Columbia, SC 29206
"Poet, Novelist"

Angie Dickinson
9580 Lime Orchard Road
Beverly Hills, CA 90210
"Actress"

Rep. William Dickinson (AL)
House Rayburn Bldg. #2406
Washington, DC 20515
"Politician"

Rep. Norman D. Dicks (WA)
House Rayburn Bldg. #2429
Washington, DC 20515
"Politician"

Brenda Dickson
10366 Wilshire Blvd. #5
Los Angeles, CA 90024
"Actress"

Bo Diddley
200 West 57th Street #907
New York, NY 10019
"Singer, Guitarist"

Charles Dierkop
10637 Burbank Blvd.
North Hollywood, CA 91601
"Actor"

Dena Dietrich
122 North La Cienega Blvd. #303
Los Angeles, CA 90069
"Actress"

Marlene Dietrich
12 Avenue Montaigne
75008 (8 EME) Paris, FRANCE
"Actress"

Barry Diller
1940 Coldwater Canyon
Beverly Hills, CA 90210
"Film Executive"

Phyllis Diller
163 South Rockingham Avenue
Los Angeles, CA 90049
"Actress, Comedienne"

Bradford Dillman
770 Hot Springs Road
Santa Barbara, CA 93103
"Actor"

C. Douglas Dillon
1270 Ave. of the Americas #2300
New York, NY 10020
"Banker, Diplomat"

Kevin Dillon
49 West 9th Street
New York, NY 10010
"Actor"

Matt Dillon
P.O. Box 800
Old Chelsea Station
New York, NY 10010
"Actor"

Melinda Dillon
3949 Rambla Orienta
Malibu, CA 90265
"Actress"

Dom DiMaggio
162 Point Road
Marion, MA 02738
"Baseball Player"

Joe DiMaggio
2150 Beach Street
San Francisco, CA 94123
"Baseball Player"

Dion Di Mucci
2639 N.W. 42nd Street
Boca Raton, FL 33434
"Singer"

Rep. John D. Dingell (MI)
House Rayburn Bldg. #2328
Washington, DC 20515
"Politician"

David N. Dinkins
Gracie Mansion
888-9th Avenue
New York, NY 10010
"Mayor of New York"

Colleen Dion
10637 Burbank Blvd.
North Hollywood, CA 91601
"Actress"

The Dirt Band
P.O. Box 1915
Aspen, CO 81611
"Music Group"

Dire Straits
#10 Southwick Mews
London W2 ENGLAND
"Rock & Roll Group"

Bob Dishy
20 East 9th Street
New York, NY 10003
"Actor, Writer"

Roy Disney
500 South Buena Vista Street
Burbank, CA 91521
"Writer, Producer"

Mrs. Lillian Disney
1333 Flower Street
Glendale, CA 91201
"Mrs. Walt Disney"

Mike Ditka
233 West Ontario
Chicago, IL 60616
"Football Coach"

Donna Dixon
8955 Norma Place
Los Angeles, CA 90069
"Actress"

Ivan Dixon
3432 North Marengo
Altadena, CA 91101
"Actor, Director"

Jeanne Dixon
1225 Connecticut Avenue NW
Suite #411
Washington, DC 20036
"Astrologer"

Rep. Julian C. Dixon (CA)
House Rayburn Bldg. #2400
Washington, DC 20515
"Politician"

Lawrence Dobkin
1788 Old Ranch Road
Los Angeles, CA 90049
"Actor, Writer, Director"

Kevin Dobson
11930 Iredell Street
Studio City, CA 91604
"Actor"

Larry Doby
Nishuana Road #45
Montclair, NJ 07042
"Baseball Manager"

Shannon Doherty
6525 Sunset Blvd. #600
Los Angeles, CA 90028
"Actress"

Don Dolan
14228 Emelita Street
Van Nuys, CA 91401
"Actor"

Thomas Dolby
20 Manchester Square
London W1 ENGLAND
"Singer, Songwriter"

Elizabeth Dole
2510 Virgina Avenue N.W. #112
Washington, DC 20037
"President of Red Cross"

Sen. Robert J. Dole (KS)
141 Hart Office Bldg.
Washington, DC 20510
"Politician"

Ami Dolenz
6058 St. Clair Avenue
North Hollywood, CA 91607
"Actress"

Mickey Dolenz
2921 West Alameda Avenue
Burbank, CA 91505
"Musician, Actor"

Placido Domingo
10601 Wilshire Blvd. #1502
Los Angeles, CA 90024
"Tenor"

Fats Domino
5515 Marais Street
New Orleans, LA 70117
"Singer, Pianist"

Elinor Donahue
4525 Lemp Avenue
North Hollywood, CA 91602
"Actress"

Phil Donahue
420 East 54th St. #22-F
New York, NY 10022
"TV Host"

Troy Donahue
1022 Euclid Avenue #1
Santa Monica, CA 90403
"Actor"

Elyse Donaldson
5330 Lankershim Blvd. #210
North Hollywood, CA 91610
"Actress"

Sam Donaldson
1717 DeSales N.W.
Washington, DC 20007
"Broadcast Journalist"

Peter Donat
1030 Broderick Street
San Francisco, CA 94115
"Actor"

Stanley Donen
300 Stone Canyon Road
Los Angeles, CA 90024
"Film Director"

Donfeld
2900 Hutton Drive
Beverly Hills, CA 90210
"Costume Designer"

Rep. Brian J. Donnelly (MA)
House Rayburn Bldg. #2229
Washington, DC 20515
"Politician"

Clive Donner
1466 North Kings Road
Los Angeles, CA 90069
"Film Director"

Jorn Donner
Pohjoisranta 12
00170 Helsinki 17
FINLAND
"Film Director"

Richard Donner
4000 Warner Blvd., Bldg. #102
Burbank, CA 91522
"Film Director"

Amanda Donohue
8899 Beverly Blvd.
Los Angeles, CA 90048
"Actress"

Terry Donohue
11918 Laurelwood
Studio City, CA 91604
"Football Coach"

Donovan
P.O. Box 472
London SW1 2QB ENGLAND
"Singer, Songwriter"

Art Donovan
1512 Jeffers Road
Baltimore, MD 21204
"Football Player"

Doobie Brother
15140 Sonoma Highway
Glen Ellen, CA 95442
"Rock & Roll Group"

James Doohan
5533 Matilija Avenue
Van Nuys, CA 91401
"Actor"

James H. Doolittle
8545 Carmel Valley Road #28-A
Carmel, CA 93923
"Military Leader"

The Doors
2548 Hutton Drive
Beverly Hills, CA 90210
"Rock & Roll Group"

Karin Dor
Tsintauerstrasse 80
D-8000 Munich 82
GERMANY
"Actress"

Ann Doran
1610 North Orange Grove Avenue
Los Angeles, CA 90046
"Actress"

Rep. Byron L. Dorgan (ND)
House Cannon Bldg #203
Washington, DC 20515
"Politician"

Dolores Dorn
7461 Beverly Blvd. #400
Los Angeles, CA 90036
"Actress"

Michael Dorn
3751 Multiview Drive
Los Angeles, CA 90068
"Actor"

Rep. Robert Dornan (CA)
12387 Lewis Street #301
Garden Grove, CA 92640
"Politician"

Tony Dorsett
1 Cowboy Parkway
Irving, TX 75063
"Football Player"

David Dortort
133 Udine Way
Los Angeles, CA 90024
"Writer, Producer"

Roy Dotrice
Talbot House
St. Martin's Lane
London WC2 ENGLAND
"Actor"

John Doucette
P.O. Box 252
Cabazon, CA 92230
"Actor"

Donna Douglas
P.O. Box 49455
Los Angeles, CA 90049
"Actress, Singer"

Eric Douglas
9000 Sunset Blvd. #405
Los Angeles, CA 90069
"Actor"

James "Buster" Douglas
2525 Oakstone Drive #C
Columbus, OH 43231
"Boxer"

Jerry Douglas
8600 Hillside Avenue
Los Angeles, CA 90069
"Actor"

Kirk Douglas
805 North Rexford Drive
Beverly Hills, CA 90210
"Actor, Director"

Michael Douglas
P.O. Box 49054
Los Angeles, CA 90049
"Actor, Producer"

Mike Douglas
602 North Arden Drive
Beverly Hills, CA 90210
"TV Host, Singer"

Robert Doulas
1810 Parliament Road
Leucadia, CA 92024
"Actor, Director"

Brad Dourif
213 1/2 South Arnaz Drive
Beverly Hills, CA 90211
"Actress"

Billie Dove
70612 Highway 111
P.O. Box 5005
Rancho Mirage, CA 92270
"Actress"

Peggy Dow
3003 South Rockford Road
Tulsa, OK 74114
"Actress"

Tony Dow
1731 Gunnison Trail
Topanga, CA 90290
"Actor"

Doris Dowling
9026 Elevado Avenue
Los Angeles, CA 90069
"Actress"

Lesley-Anne Down
6509 Wandermere Road
Malibu, CA 90265
"Actress"

Morton Downey, Jr.
10351 Santa Monica Blvd. #211
Los Angeles, CA 90025
"TV Host"

Robert Downey, Jr.
1494 North King Road
Los Angeles, CA 90069
"Actor"

Rep. Thomas J. Downey (NY)
House Rayburn Bldg. #2232
Washington, DC 20515
"Politician"

Hugh Downs
P.O. Box 1132
Carefree, AZ 85331
"TV-Journalist"

David Doyle
4731 Noeline Avenue
Encino, CA 91316
"Actor, Director"

Stan Dragoti
755 Stradella Road
Los Angeles, CA 90024
"Writer, Producer"

Victor Drai
1201 Des Resto Drive
Beverly Hills, CA 90210
Film Producer"

Alfred Drake
50 East 89th Street #26-A
New York, NY 10128
"Singer, Actor, Director"

Frances Drake
1511 Summit Ridge Drive
Beverly Hills, CA 90210
"Actress"

Larry Drake
2294 Bronson Hills Drive
Los Angeles, CA 90069
"Actor"

Pete Drake
809-18th Avenue South
Nashville, TN 37203
"Dobroist"

Polly Draper
11487 Laurelcrest Drive
Studio City, CA 91604
"Actress"

Dave Dravecky
P.O. Box 3505
Boardman, OH 44513
"Baseball Player"

Tom Dreesen
14570 Benefit Street #201
Sherman Oaks, CA 91403
"Comedian"

Rep. David Dreier (CA)
House Cannon Bldg. #411
Washington, DC 20515
"Politician"

Ellen Drew
P.O. Box 343
Palm Desert, CA 92260
"Actress"

Richard Dreyfuss
2809 Nichols Canyon
Los Angeles, CA 90046
"Actor"

Moosie Drier
8485-E Melrose Place
Los Angeles, CA 90069
"Actor"

The Drifter
10 Chelsea Court
Neptune, NJ 07753
"Vocal Group"

Joanne Dru
1459 Carla Ridge Road
Beverly Hills, CA 90210
"Actress"

Allen Drury
P.O. Box 674
Tiburon, CA 94920
"Author"

James Drury
12755 Mill Ridge #622
Cyprus, TX 77429
"Actor"

Roy Drusky
131 Trivett Drive
Portland, TN 37148
"Singer, Songwriter"

Fred Dryer
11911 Mayfield
Los Angeles, CA 90049
"Actor, Football Player"

Don Drysdale
1488 Rutherford Drive
Pasadena, CA 91103
"Baseball Player"

Alexander Dubcek
ulize Vinohradska 1
CS-110 00 Prague 1
CZECHOSLAVAKIA
"Politician"

Al Dubin
1000 North Orange Drive
Los Angeles, CA 90038
"Lyricist"

Ja'Net DuBois
405 West Ivy Street #204
Glendale, CA 91204
"Actress"

Peter Duchin
305 Madison Avenue #956
New York, NY 10165
"Pianist"

Rick Ducommun
7967 Woodrow Wilson Drive
Los Angeles, CA 90046
"Comedian"

Michael Dudikoff
8485 Melrose Place
Los Angeles, CA 90069
"Actor"

Julia Duffy
10100 Santa Monica Blvd. #700
Los Angeles, CA 90067
"Actress, Director"

Patrick Duffy
P.O. Box "D"
Tarzana, CA 91356
"Actor, Director"

Dennis Dugan
1755 Old Ranch Road
Los Angeles, CA 90049
"Actor"

Kitty Dukakis
85 Perry Street
Brookline, MA 02146
"Author, Wife of Michael"

Michael Dukakis
85 Perry Street
Brookline, MA 02146
"Ex-Govornor"

Olympia Dukakis
222 Upper Mountain Road
Montclair, NJ 07043
"Actress"

Angier Biddle Duke
435 East 52nd Street
New York, NY 10022
"Diplomat, Businessman"

David Duke
500 North Arnoult
Metairie, LA 70001
"White Supremacist, Politician"

Doris Duke
1 East 78th Street
New York, NY 10021
"Heiress, Philathropist"

Patty Duke
17815 Valley Vista Blvd.
Encino, CA 91316
"Actress"

David Dukes
255 South Lorraine Blvd.
Los Angeles, CA 90004
"Actor"

The Dukes
11 Chartfield Square
London SW15 ENGLAND
"Rock & Roll Group"

Keir Dullea
6 Dogwood Lane
Westport, CT 06880
"Actor"

Jane Dulo
904 Hilldale Avenue #2
Los Angeles, CA 90069
"Actress"

Melvin Dummar
Dummar's Restaurant
Gabbs, NV 89409
"Alleged in Howard Hughes' Will"

Steffi Duna
1448 North Beverly Drive
Beverly Hills, CA 90210
"Dancer, Actress"

Faye Dunaway
1435 Linda Crest Drive
Beverly Hills, CA 90210
"Actress"

Rep. John Duncan, Jr. (TN)
House Rayburn Bldg. #115
Washington, DC 20515
"Politician"

Sandy Duncan
10390 Santa Monica Blvd. #300
Los Angeles, CA 90025
"Actress"

Angelo Dundee
1700 Washington Avenue
Miami Beach, FL 33142
"Boxing Trainer"

Holly Dunn
P.O. Box 128037
Nashville, TN 37212
"C&W Singer"

Dominick Dunne
155 East 49th Street
New York, NY 10017
"Author, Producer"

Griffin Dunne
40 West 12th Street
New York, NY 10011
"Actor, Producer"

Pierre duPont
Patterns
Rockland, DE 19732
"Ex-Govenor"

Duran Duran
P.O. Box 600
London NW18 1EN ENGLAND
"Rock & Roll Group"

Roberto Duran
P.O. Box 157 Arena Colon
Panama City, PANAMA
"Boxer"

Margie Durante
511 North Beverly Drive
Beverly Hills, CA 90210
"Mrs. Jimmy Durante"

Deanna Durbin
B.P. 7677
75123 Paris Cedex 03
FRANCE
"Actress"

Rep. Richard Durbin (IL)
House Cannon Bldg. #129
Washington, DC 20515
"Politician"

Sen. David Durenberger (VA)
Senate Russell Bldg. #154
Washington, DC 20510
"Politician"

Charles Durning
10590 Wilshire Blvd. #506
Los Angeles, CA 90024
"Actor"

Melvin Durslag
523 Dalehurst Avenue
Los Angeles, CA 90024
"Columnist"

Marj Dusay
1930 Century Park West #303
Los Angeles, CA 90067
"Actress"

Ann Dusenberry
9000 Sunset Blvd. #1200
Los Angeles, CA 90069
"Actress"

Nancy Dussault
12211 Fredell Street
Studio City, CA 91604
"Actress"

John Duttine
Pebro House
13 St. Martins Road
London SW9 ENGLAND
"Actor"

Jean-Claude Duvalier
Hotel de l'Abbaye
Talloires, FRANCE
"Politician"

Robert Duvall
257 West 86th Street
New York, NY 10024
"Actor"

Shelley Duvall
12725 Ventura Blvd.
Studio City, CA 91604
"Actress"

Rep. Bernard J. Dwyer (NJ)
House Rayburn Bldg. #2428
Washington, DC 20515
"Politician"

Len Dykstra
908 Rashford Drive
Placentia, CA 92670
"Baseball Player"

Bob Dylan
P.O. Box 264
Cooper Station
New York, NY 10003
"Singer, Songwriter"

Rep. Mervyn Dymally (CA)
House Longworth Bldg. #1717
Washington, DC 20515
"Politician"

Richard Dysart
654 Copeland Court
Santa Monica, CA 90405
"Actor"

George Dzundza
151 South El Camino Drive
Beverly Hills, CA 90212
"Actor"

Thomas F. Eagleton
1 Mercantile Center
St. Louis, MO 63101
"Former Senator"

Dale Earnhardt
Rt. 8, Box 463
Moresville, NC 28115
"Auto Racer"

Rep. Joseph D. Early (MA)
House Rayburn Bldg. #2349
Washington, DC 20510
"Politician"

Earth, Wind & Fire
4323 West Verdugo Avenue
Burbank, CA 91505
"R&B Group"

Tony Eason
1000 Fulton Road
Hempstead, NY 11550
"Football Player"

Jeff East
5521 Rainbow Crest Drive
Agoura, CA 91301
"Actor"

Leslie Easterbrook
17352 Sunset Blvd. #401-D
Pacific Palisades, CA 90272
"Actress"

Richard Eastham
1529 Oriole Lane
Los Angeles, CA 90069
"Actor"

Robert Easton
9169 Sunset Blvd.
Los Angeles, CA 90069
"Actor"

Sheena Easton
3575 Cahuenga Blvd. West #470
Los Angeles, CA 90068
"Singer, Songwriter"

Clint Eastwood
P.O. Box 4366
Carmel, CA 93921
"Actor"

Shirley Eaton
8 Harley Street
London W1N 2AB ENGLAND
"Actress"

Fred Ebb
146 Central Park West #14D
New York, NY 10020
"Lyricist"

Jose Eber
1277 St. Ives Place
Los Angeles, CA 90069
"Hair Stylist"

Christine Ebersole
4323 Ben Avenue
Studio City, CA 91604
"Actress"

Roger Ebert
2114 North Cleveland
Chicago, IL 60614
"Film Critic"

Bonnie Ebsen
P.O. Box 356
Agoura, CA 91301
"Actress"

Buddy Ebsen
605 Via Horquilla
Polos Verdes Estates, CA 90274
"Actor"

Rep. Dennis Eckart (OH)
House Longworth Bldg. #1111
Washington, DC 20515
"Politician"

Dennis Eckersley
263 Morse Road
Sudbury, MA 01776
"Baseball Player"

Billy Eckstine
1118-15th Street #4
Santa Monica, CA 90403
"Singer"

Stefan Edberg
Spinnaregaten 6
S-59300 Vastervik SWEDEN
"Tennis Player"

Helen Jerome Eddy
1428 South Marengo Avenue
Alhambra, CA 91803
"Actress"

Herbert Edelman
15301 Ventura Blvd. #345
Sherman Oaks, CA 91403
"Actor"

Barbara Eden
9816 Denbigh
Beverly Hills, CA 90210
"Actress"

Gertrude Ederle
4465 S.W. 37th Avenue
Ft. Lauderdale, FL 33312
"Swimmer"

Lee Edler
1725 "K" Street NW #1201
Washington, DC 20006
"Golfer"

Donna Edmonson
10236 Charing Cross Road
Los Angeles, CA 900024
"Model, Actress"

HRH The Prince Edward
Buckingham Palace
London SW1 ENGLAND
"Royalty"

Anthony Edwards
8820 Lookout Mountain
Los Angeles, CA 90046
"Actor"

Blake Edwards
P.O. Box 666
Beverly Hills, CA 90213
"Writer, Producer, Director"

Rep Don Edwards (CA)
House Rayburn Blgd. #2307
Washington, DC 20515
"Politician"

Edwin Edwards
P.O. Box 94004
Baton Rouge, LA 70804
"Governor"

Gail Edwards
P.O. Box 5617
Beverly Hills, CA 90213
"Actress"

Jennifer Edwards
6805 Dume Drive
Malibu, CA 90265
"Actress"

Rep. Mickey Edwards (OK)
House Rayburn Bldg. #2330
Washington, DC 20515
"Politician"

Ralph Edwards
1717 North Highland Avenue
10th Floor
Los Angeles, CA 90028
"TV Host, Producer"

Stephanie Edwards
533-18th Street
Santa Monica, CA 90402
"Actress"

Steve Edwards
3980 Royal Oaks Place
Encino, CA 91436
"TV Host"

Vincent Edwards
P.O. Box 642
Malibu, CA 90265
"Actor, Writer, Director"

Samantha Eggar
15430 Mulholland Drive
Los Angeles, CA 90024
"Actress"

Marta Eggerth Kiepura
Park Drive North
Rye, NY 10508
"Actress, Singer"

Nicole Eggert
20591 Queens Park
Huntington Beach, CA 92646
"Actress"

Beth Ehlers
233 East 88th Street
New York, NY 10028
"Actress"

John Ehrlichman
P.O. Box 5559
Santa Fe, NM 87502
"Author"

Lisa Eichorn
19 West 44th Street #1100
New York, NY 10036
"Actress"

Jill Eikenberry
2183 Mandeville Canyon
Los Angeles, CA 90049
"Actress"

Lisa Eilbacher
10100 Santa Monica Blvd. #1600
Los Angeles, CA 90067
"Actress"

Bob Einstein
2949 Deep Canyon Drive
Beverly Hills, CA 90210
"Actor, Writer"

John Eisenhower
12333 Wooded Way
Westchester, PA 19380
"Ike's Son"

Michael Eisner
500 South Buena Vista
Burbank, CA 91521
"Disney Executive"

Stuart Eizenstat
1110 Vermont Avenue NW #1050
Washington, DC 20005
"Lawyer, Government Official"

Anita Ekberg
00045 Genzano di Roma
Italy
"Actress"

Britt Ekland
1744 North Doheny Drive
Los Angeles, CA 90069
"Actress"

Jack Elam
P.O. Box 5718
Santa Barbara, CA 93108
"Actor"

Taina Elg
114 East 28th Street
New York, NY 10016
"Actress"

Larry Elgart
55 East 74th Street
New York, NY 10021
"Orchestra Leader"

HRH Elizabeth II
Buckingham Palace
London SW1 ENGLAND
"Royalty

HM Queen Elizabeth
Clarence House
London SW1 ENGLAND
"The Queen's Mother"

Hector Elizando
5040 Nobel Avenue
Sherman Oaks, CA 91403
"Actor"

Robert Ellenstein
5215 Sepulveda Blvd. #23-F
Culver City, CA 90230
"Actor, Director"

Linda Ellerbee
17 St. Lukes Place
New York, NY 10014
"Journalist"

Denholm Elliott
235-241 Regent Street
London W1A 2JT ENGLAND
"Actor"

Ross Elliott
5702 Graves Avenue
Encino, CA 91316
"Actor"

Sam Elliott
33050 Pacific Coast Hwy.
Malibu, CA 90265
"Actor"

Stephen Elliott
3948 Woodfield Drive
Sherman Oaks, CA 91403
"Actor"

Daniel Ellsberg
90 Norwood Avenue
Kensington, CA 94707
"Author"

Michael Elphick
37 Dennington Park Road
London SW6 ENGLAND
"Actor"

Elvira (Cassandra Peterson)
P.O. Box 38246
Los Angeles, CA 90038
"Actress"

John Elway
5700 Logan Street
Denver, CO 80216
"Football Player"

Cary Elwes
131 North Rodeo Drive #300
Beverly Hills, CA 90212
"Actor"

Ron Ely
4161 Mariposa Drive
Santa Barbara, CA 93110
"Actor"

Kelly Emberg
1608 North Poinsettia
Manhattan Beach, CA 90266
"Model"

Rep. Bill Emerson (MO)
House Longworth Bldg. #1213
Washington, DC 20515
"Politician"

Robert Emhardt
P.O. Box 303
Ojai, CA 93023
"Actor"

Emir of Kuwait
Bayan Palace
Kuwait City Kuwait
"Royalty"

Emmanuel
1406 Georgette Street
Santurce PUERTO RICO 00910
"Fashion Designer"

Guildermo Endara
Presidential Palace
Panama City, PANAMA
"President of Panama""

Michael Ende
via Montegiove 13
00045 Ganzano di Roma
ITALY
"Author"

Rep. Eliot Engel (NY)
House Longworth Bldg. #1213
Washington, DC 20515
"Politician"

Georgia Engel
350 West 57th Street #10E
New York, NY 10019
"Actress"

England Dan
P.O. Box 82
Great Neck, NY 11021
"Singer, Songwriter"

Rep. Glenn English (OK)
House Rayburn Bldg. #2206
Washington, DC 20515
"Politician"

Robert Englund
2451 Horseshoe Canyon
Los Angeles, CA 90046
"Actor"

Philippe Entremont
Schwarzenbergplatz 10/7
A-1040 Vienna, AUSTRIA
"Pianist"

John Entwhistle
1705 Queen Court
Los Angeles, CA 90069
"Musician, Singer"

Henry Ephron
176 East 71st Street
New York, NY 10021
"Screenwriter"

Nora Ephron
2211 Broadway
New York, NY 10024
"Screenwriter"

Richard Erdman
12256 Dehouge Street
North Hollywood, CA 91605
"Actor, Director"

Rep. Ben Erdreich (AL)
House Cannon Bldg. #439
Washington, DC 20515
"Politician"

John Ericson
12659 Moorpark #12
Studio City, CA 91604
"Actor"

Carl Erskine
6214 South Madison Avenue
Anderson, IN 46013
"Baseball Player"

Julius Erving
Upper Brookville
Long Island, NY 11545
"Basketball Player"

Bill Erwin
12325 Moorpark Street
Studio City, CA 91604
"Actor"

Christoph Eschenbach
2 Avenue d'Alena
75016 Paris, FRANCE
"Pianist"

"Boomer" Esiason
14 Pete Rose Pier
Covington, KY 41011
"Football Player"

Carl Esmond
576 Tigertail Road
Los Angeles, CA 90049
"Actor"

Rep. Mike Espy (MS)
House Cannon Bldg. #216
Washington, DC 20515
"Politician"

William Grey Espy
205 West 54th Street #3D
New York, NY 10019
"Actor"

Gary Essert
3612 Woodhill Canyon Road
North Hollywood, CA 91604
"Actor"

David Essex
109 Eastbourne Mews
London W2 ENGLAND
"Singer, Actor"

Gloria Estefan
8390 S.W. 4th Street
Miami, FL 33125
"Singer"

Billie Sol Estes
c/o General Delivery
Brady, TX 76825
"Financier, Ex-Convict"

Emilio Estevez
31709 Sea Level Drive
Malibu, CA 90265
"Actor, Writer"

Erik Estrada
3768 Eureka Drive
Studio City, CA 91604
"Actor"

Susan Estrich
124 South Las Palmas
Los Angeles, CA 90004
"Actress"

Melissa Etheridge
3800 Barham Blvd. #309
Los Angeles, CA 90068
"Singer"

Bob Eubanks
23801 Calabasas Road #2050
Calabasas, CA 91302
"TV Host"

Europe
Box 22036, S-104 22
Stockholm, SWEDEN
"Rock & Roll Group"

Eurythmics
P.O. Box 245
London N8 Q0G ENGLAND
"Rock & Roll Group"

Linda Evangelista
121 rue Legendre
F-75017 Paris, FRANCE
"Model"

Andrea Evans
310 West 72nd Street #7G
New York, NY 10023
"Actress"

Dale Evans Rogers
P.O. Box 1223
Apple Valley, CA 92307
"Actress"

Evans Evans
3114 Abington Drive
Beverly Hills, CA 90210
"Actress"

Gene Evans
P.O. Box 93
Medon, TN 38356
"Actor"

Sir Geraint Evans
17 Highcliffe
32 Albermarle Street
Beckenham, Kent, ENGLAND
"Opera Singer"

Janet Evans
424 Brower
Placentia, CA 92670
"Swimmer"

Rep. Lane Evans (IL)
House Longworth Bldg. #1121
Washington, DC 20515
"Politician"

Linda Evans
6015 West 6th Street
Los Angeles, CA 90077
"Actress"

Mary Beth Evans
106 North Grand
Pasadena, CA 91103
"Actress"

Mike Evans
12530 Collins Street
North Hollywood, CA 91605
"Actor"

Robert Evans
10033 Woodlawn Drive
Beverly Hills, CA 90210
"Producer, Actor"

Roland Evans
1750 Pennsylvania Avenue NW
Suite #1312
Washington, DC 20006
"Columnist"

Trevor Eve
60 St. James's Street
London W1 ENGLAND
"Actor"

Chad Everett
19901 Northridge Road
Chatsworth, CA 91311
"Actor"

Leon Everette
P.O. Box "D"
Johnston, SC 29832
"Singer, Guitarist

Don Everly
10100 Santa Monica Blvd. #1600
Los Angeles, CA 90067
"Singer"

Phil Everly
10414 Camarillo Street
North Hollywood, CA 91602
"Singer"

Don Everly
10100 Santa Monica Blvd. #1600
Los Angeles, CA 90067
"Singer"

Charles Evers
1072 Lynch Street
Jackson, MS 39203
"Civil Rights Worker"

Jason Evers
232 North Crescent Drive #101
Beverly Hills, CA 90210
"Actor"

Cory Everson
7324 Reseda Blvd. #208
Reseda, CA 91335
"Bodybuilder"

Chris Evert
7100 West Camino Real #203
Boca Raton, FL 33433
"Tennis Player"

Greg Evigan
5070 Arundel Drive
Woodland Hills, CA 91364
"Actor, Singer"

Weeb Ewbank
7 Patrick Drive
Oxford, OH 45056
"Football Coach"

Tom Ewell
53 Aspen Way
Rolling Hills, CA 90274
"Actor"

Patrick Ewing
4 Pennsylvania Plaza
New York, NY 10001
"Basketball Player"

Sen. J. James Exon (NE)
Senate Hart Bldg. #528
Washington, DC 20510
"Politician"

Shelley Fabaras
P.O. Box 6010 #85
Sherman Oaks, CA 91413
"Actress"

Nanette Fabray
14360 Sunset Blvd.
Pacific Palisades, CA 90272
"Actress"

Max Factor III
9777 Wilshire Blvd. #1015
Beverly Hills, CA 90212
"Lawyer, Finance"

Clifton Fadiman
3222 Campanil Drive
Santa Barbara, CA 93109
"TV Personality"

HM King Fahd
Royal Palace
Riyadh, SAUDI ARABIA
"Royalty"

Bruce Fairbairn
9744 Wilshire Blvd. #308
Beverly Hills, CA 90212
"Actor"

Douglas Fairbanks, Jr.
575 Park Avenue
New York, NY 10021
"Actor"

Morgan Fairchild
3321 Dixie Canyon Lane
Beverly Hills, CA 90210
"Actress"

Ron Fairley
23140 Park Sorrento
Calabasas, CA 90302
"Sportscaster"

Princess Faisa
10747 Wilshire Blvd. #1504
Los Angeles, CA 90024
"Royalty"

Adam Faith
Crockham Hill
Edenbridge Kent, ENGLAND
"Singer, Actor"

Marianne Faithfull
Yew Tree Cottage
Aldworth, Berks. ENGLAND
"Singer, Songwriter"

Lola Falana
P.O. Box 50369
Henderson, NV 89016
"Singer, Actress"

Falco
Mohlstrasse 16
D-8000 Munich 80
GERMANY
"Singer, Actress"

Peter Falk
1004 North Roxbury Drive
Beverly Hills, CA 90210
"Actor, Director"

Jinx Falkenburg
10 Shelter Rock Road
Manhasset, NY 11030
"Actress, Model"

Rev. Jerry Falwell
P.O. Box 1111
Lynchburg, VA 24505
"Evangelist"

Hampton Fancher III
262 Old Topanga Canyon
Topanga, CA 90290
"Screenwriter"

Stephanie Faracy
8765 Lookout Mountain Road
Los Angeles, CA 90046
"Actress"

James Farentino
1340 Londonderry Place
Los Angeles, CA 90069
"Actor"

Antonio Fargas
1930 Century Park West #403
Los Angeles, CA 90067
"Actor"

Donna Fargo
PO. Box 15743
Nashville, TN 37215
"Singer"

Dennis Farina
8457 Melrose Place #200
Los Angeles, CA 90069
"Actor"

Lillian Farley
84 Kenneth Avenue
Huntington, NY 11743
"Model"

Shannon Farnon
12743 Milbank Street
Studio City, CA 91604
"Actress"

Richard Farnsworth
3800 Barham Blvd. #303
Los Angeles, CA 90068
"Actor"

Felica Farr
141 South El Camino Drive #201
Beverly Hills, CA 90212
"Actress"

Jamie Farr
53 Ranchero
Bell Canyon, CA 91307
"Actor, Director"

Louis Farrakhan
813 East Broadway
Phoenix, AZ 85001
"Religious Leader"

Eileen Farrell
72 Louis Street
Staten Island, NY 10304
"Opera Singer"

Mike Farrell
P.O. Box 5961-306
Sherman Oaks, CA 91413
"Actor, Writer, Director"

Sharon Farrell
10637 Burbank Blvd
North Hollywood, CA 91601
"Actress"

Shea Farrell
125 South Green Way
Los Angeles, CA 90049
"Actor"

Mia Farrow
135 Central Park West
New York, NY 10018
"Actress"

Rep. Dante B. Fascell (FL)
House Rayburn Bldg. #2354
Washington, DC 20515
"Politician"

Howard Fast
c/o Howard
2 Park Street
Boston, MA 02107
"Writer"

Fat Boys
250 West 57th Street #1723
New York, NY 10107
"Rap Group"

David Faustino
1320 North Maple Street
Burbank, CA 91505
"Actor"

Dan Fauts
9449 Friars Road
San Diego, CA 92120
"Football Player"

Allen Fawcett
9113 Sunset Blvd.
Los Angeles, CA 90069
"Actor, TV Host"

Farrah Fawcett
3130 Antelo Road
Los Angeles, CA 90024
"Actress, Model"

Rep. Harris W. Fawell (IL)
House Cannon Bldg. #435
Washington, DC 20515
"Politician"

Alice Faye
49400 JFK Trail
Palm Desert, CA 92260
"Actress, Singer"

Rep. Vic Fazio (CA)
House Rayburn Bldg. #2113
Washington, DC 20515
"Politician"

Tom Fears
41470 Woodhaven Drive West
Palm Desert,CA 92260
"Football Player"

Leonard Feather
13833 Riverside Drive
Sherman Oaks, CA 91423
"Music Critic"

Jules Feiffner
325 West End Avenue
New York, NY 10023
"Writer"

Rep. Edward Feighan (OH)
House Longworth Bldg. #1124
Washington, DC 20515
"Politician"

Alan Feinstein
432 South Ogeden Drive
Los Angeles, CA 90036
"Actor"

Dianne Feinstein
30 Presidio Terrace
San Francisco, CA 94118
"Ex-Mayor"

Michael Feinstein
2233 Cheremoya Avenue
Los Angeles, CA 90068
"Actor"

Fritz Feld
12348 Rochedale Lane
Los Angeles, CA 90049
"Actor"

Corey Feldman
454 North Oakhurst Drive
Beverly Hills, CA 90210
"Actor"

Barbara Feldon
14 East 74th Street
New York, NY 10021
"Actress, Model"

Tovah Feldshuh
110 Riverside Drive #16
New York, NY 10024
"Actress"

Martin Feldstein
147 Clifton Street
Belmont, MA 02178
"Economist"

Jose Feliciano
266 Lyons Plain Road
Weston, CT 06883
"Singer, Guitarist"

Maria Felix
Melchor Ocampo 309-403
Mexico D.F. MEXICO
"Actress"

Norman Fell
113 North San Vicente Blvd. #202
Beverly Hills, CA 90211
"Actor"

Bob Feller
P.O. Box 157
Gates Mills, OH 44040
"Baseball Player"

Federico Fellini
141a Via Margutta 110
Rome, ITALY
"Writer, Producer"

Edith Fellows
2016 1/2 North Vista Del Mar
Los Angeles, CA 90068
"Actress"

John Femia
1650 Boradway #714
New York, NY 10019
"Singer"

Freddy Fender
5626 Brock Street
Houston, TX 77023
"Singer, Songwriter"

Sherilyn Fenn
7266 Franklin Avenue #310
Los Angeles, CA 90046
"Actress"

George Fenneman
13214 Moorpark #206
Sherman Oaks, CA 91423
"TV Host"

Maynard Ferguson
P.O. Box 716
Ojai, CA 93023
"Trumpeter"

Ferrante & Teicher
P.O. Box 12403, NS Station
Atlanta, GA 30355
"Piano Duo"

Cristina Ferrare
1280 Stone Canyon
Los Angeles, CA 90077
"Actress, Model"

Geraldine Ferraro
22 Deepdene Road
Forest Hills, NY 11375
"Ex-Congresswoman"

Tina Ferrari
3901 South Las Vegas Blvd.
Las Vegas, NV 89109
"Wrestler"

Conchata Ferrell
3147 North Seward Street
Los Angeles, CA 90028
"Actress"

Lupita Ferrer
861 Stone Canyon Road
Los Angeles, CA 90024
"Actress"

Mel Ferrer
6590 Camino Carreta
Carpenteria, CA 93013
"Actor"

Miguel Ferrer
4334 Kester Avenue
Sherman Oaks, CA 91403
"Actor"

Lou Ferrrigno
621-17th Street
Santa Monica, CA 90402
"Actor, Bodybuilder"

Brian Ferry
321 Fulham Road
London SW10 9QL ENGLAND
"Singer, Songwriter"

Mark Fidrych
259 Crawford
Northborough, MA 01532
"Baseball Player"

John Fiedler
225 Adams Street #10B
Brooklyn, NY 11201
"Actor"

Chelsea Field
10390 Santa Monica Blvd. #300
Los Angeles, CA 90025
"Actress"

Sally Field
825 South Barrington #204
Los Angeles, CA 90049
"Actress"

Shirley Anne Field
4206 Arcola Avenue
Toluca Lake, CA 91602
"Actress"

Sylvia Field
3263 Via Alta Mira
Fallbrook, CA 92028
"Actress"

Freddie Fields
1005 Benedict Canyon Drive
Beverly Hills, CA 90210
"Motion Picture Producer"

Rep. Jack Fields (TX)
House Cannon Bldg. #108
Washington, DC 20515
"Politician"

Kim Fields
23460 Hatteras Street
Woodland Hills, CA 91367
"Actress"

Harvey Fierstein
1479 Carla Ridge Drive
Beverly Hills, CA 90210
"Dramatist, Actor"

Jon Finch
135 New Kings Road
London SW6 ENGLAND
"Actor"

Sylvia Fine Kaye
1103 San Ysidro Drive
Beverly Hills, CA 90210
"Mrs. Danny Kaye"

Travis Fine
200 North Robertson Blvd. #219
Beverly Hills, CA 90211
"Actor"

Fine Young Young Cannibals
1680 North Vine Street #1101
Los Angeles, CA 90028
"Rock & Roll Group"

Rollie Fingers
11582 Avenida Sirvita
San Diego, CA 92128
"Baseball Player"

Albert Finney
39 Seymour Walk
London W1 ENGLAND
"Actor"

Linda Fiorentino
c/o ICM
388 Oxford Street
Los Angeles, CA 90069
"Actress"

Eddie Firestone
303 South Crescent Heights
Los Angeles, CA 90048
"Actor"

The Firm
57A Great Titchfield Street
London W1P 7FL ENGLAND
"Rock & Roll Group"

Peter Firth
4 Windmill Street
London W1 England
"Actor"

Bobby Fischer
186 Route 9-W
New Windsor, NY 12550
"Chess Player"

Dietrich Fischer-Diskau
Lindenalle 22
1000 Berlin 19 GERMANY
"Baritone"

Rep. Hamilton Fish, Jr. (NY)
House Rayburn Bldg. #2269
Washington, DC 20515
"Politician"

Carrie Fisher
9555 Oak Pass Road
Beverly Hills, CA 90210
"Actress"

Eddie Fisher
1000 North Point Street #1802
San Francisco, CA 94109
"Actor, Singer"

Gail Fisher
1150 South Hayworth
Los Angeles, CA 90035
"Actress"

Todd Fisher
9555 Oak Pass Road
Beverly Hills, CA 90210
"Evangelist, TV Performer"

Carlton Fisk
16612 Catawba Road
Lockport, IL 60441
"Baseball Player"

Ella Fitzgerald
908 North Whittier Drive
Beverly Hills, CA 90210
"Singer"

Tom Fitzsimmons
247 South Beverly Drive #102
Beverly Hills, CA 90212
"Actor"

Marlin Fitzwater
2001 Swan Terrace
Alexandria, VA 22307
"Politician"

Roberta Flack
1 West 72nd Street
New York, NY 10023
"Singer, Songwriter"

Fanny Flagg
1520 Willina Lane
Montecito, CA 93108
"Actress"

Rep. Floyd Flake (NY)
House Longworth Bldg. #1031
Washington, DC 20515
"Politician"

The Flamingos
25 High Street
Southboro, MA 01772
"Vocal Group"

Fionnula Flanagan
13438 Java Drive
Beverly Hills, CA 90210
"Actress"

Ed Flanders
P.O. Box 210
Willowcreek, CA 95573
"Actor"

Susan Flannery
480 Pimiento Lane
Santa Monica, CA 93108
"Actress"

Flash Cadillac
P.O. Box 6588
San Antonio, TX 78209
"Rock & Roll Group"

Fleetwood Mac
29169 Heathercliff #574
Malibu, CA 90265
"Rock & Roll Group"

Mick Fleetwood
129169 Heathercliff #574
Malibu, CA 90265
"Drummer, Songwriter"

Charles Fleischer
749 North Crescent Heights Blvd.
Los Angeles, CA 90038
"Actor"

Richard Fleischer
169 South Rockingham Avenue
Los Angeles, CA 90049
"Film Director"

Peggy Fleming
16387 Aztec Ridge
Los Gatos, CA 95030
"Ice Skater"

Rhonda Fleming-Mann
2129 Century Woods Way
Los Angeles, CA 90067
"Actress"

Louise Fletcher
1520 Camden Avenue #105
Los Angeles, CA 90025
"Actress"

Flock of Seagulls
526 Nicollett Mall
Minneapolis, MN 55402
"Rock & Roll Group"

Curt Flood
4139 Cloverdale Avenue
Los Angeles, CA 90008
"Baseball Player"

Myron Floran
26 Georgeff Road
Rolling Hills, CA 90274
"Composer"

Doug Flutie
21 Spring Valley Road
Natick, MA 01760
"Football Player"

Larry Flynt
9211 Robin Drive
Los Angeles, CA 90069
"Publisher"

Nina Foch
P.O. Box 1884
Beverly Hills, CA 90213
"Actress"

Dan Fogelberg
Mountain Bird Ranch
P.O. Box 824
Pagosa Springs, CO 81147
"Singer, Songwriter"

John Fogerty
2830 Royston Place
Beverly Hills, CA 90210
"Singer, Songwriter"

Rep. Thomas Foglietta (PA)
House Cannon Bldg. #231
Washington, DC 20515
"Politician"

Rep. Thomas Foley (WA)
House Longworth Bldg. #1201
Washington, DC 20515
"Politician, House Speaker"

Ken Follett
P.O. Box 708
London SW10 0DH ENGLAND
"Author"

Bridget Fonda
9560 Wilshire Blvd. #500
Beverly Hills, CA 90212
"Actress"

Jane Fonda
914 Montana Avenue #200
Santa Monica, CA 90402
"Actress, Writer"

Peter Fonda
RR#38
Livingston, MT 59047
"Actor, Writer, Director"

Shirlee Fonda
110 East 57th Street
New York, NY 10022
"Mrs. Henry Fonda"

Kam Fong
9430 Washington Blvd. #5
Culver City, CA 90230
"Actress"

Joan Fontaine
P.O. Box 222600
Carmel, CA 93922
"Actress"

Wayne Fontana
P.O. Box 262
Carteret, NJ 07108
"Rock & Roll"

Horton Foote
95 Horatio Street #332
New York, NY 10014
"Screenwriter"

June Foray
22745 Erwin Street
Woodland Hills, CA 91367
"Actress"

Brenda Forbes
430 East 57th Street
New York, NY 10022
"Actress"

Brian Forbes
Seven Pines
Wentworth, Surrey, ENGLAND
"Writer, Director"

Bette Ford
1999 Avenue of the Stars
Suite #2850
Los Angeles, CA 90067
"Actress"

Mrs. Betty Ford
2100 Century Park West
Los Angeles, CA 90067
"Ex-First Lady, Author"

Charlotte Ford
25 Sutton Place
New York, NY 10023
"Daughter of Henry Ford II"

Doug Ford
4701 Oak Terrace
Lake Worth, FL 33463
"Golfer"

Faith Ford
9229 Sunset Blvd. #306
Los Angeles, CA 90069
"Actress, Model"

Gerald R. Ford
40365 San Dune Road
Rancho Mirage, CA 92270
"Former President"

Glenn Ford
911 Oxford Way
Beverly Hills, CA 90210
"Actor"

Harrison Ford
P.O. Box 49344
Los Angeles, CA 90049
"Actor"

Rep. Harold E. Ford (TN)
House Rayburn Bldg. #2305
Washington, DC 20515
"Politician"

Mick Ford
47 Glengarry Road
Dulwich
London SE22 ENGLAND
"Actor"

Stephen Ford
Rt. 1, Box 90
San Luis Obispo, CA 93401
"Actor"

"Tennessee "Ernie" Ford
255 Mathache Drive
Portola Valley, CA 94025
"Singer"

Sen. Wendell Ford (KY)
Senate Russell Bldg. #173A
Washington, DC 20510
"Politician"

Whitey Ford
38 Schoolhouse Lane
Lake Success, NY 11020
"Baseball Player"

Rep. William Ford (MI)
House Rayburn Bldg. #2371
Washington, DC 20515
"Politician"

Foreigner
1790 Broadway, PH
New York, NY 10019
"Rock & Roll Group"

Deborah Foreman
1341 Ocean Avenue #213
Santa Monica, CA 90401
"Actress"

George Foreman
7639 Pin Oak Drive
Humble, TX 77397
"Boxer"

Forester Sisters
128 Volunteer Drive
Hendersonville, TN 37075
"C&W Group"

Milos Forman
Hampshire House
150 Central Park South
New York, NY 10019
"Film Director"

Frederick Forrest
111 Hortense Street
North Hollywood, CA 91602
"Actor"

Helen Forrest
1870 Caminito del Cielo
Glendale, CA 91208
"Singer"

Sally Forrest
1125 Angelo Drive
Beverly Hills, CA 90210
"Actress"

Steve Forrest
1605 Michael Lane
Pacific Palisades, CA 90272
"Actor"

Constance Forslund
853-7th Avenue #9-A
New York, NY 10019
"Actress"

Robert Forster
8550 Hollywood Drive #402
Los Angeles, CA 90069
"Actor"

Bruce Forsyth
Kent House
Upper Ground
London SE1 ENGLAND
"TV Personality"

Rosemary Forsyth
1591 Benedict Canyon
Beverly Hills, CA 90210
"Actress"

Bill Forsythe
20 Winton Drive
Glasgow G12 SCOTLAND
"Guitarist"

Frederick Forsythe
17-21 Conway Street
London W1P 6JD ENGLAND
"Writer"

John Forsythe
9229 Sunset Blvd. 813
Los Angeles, CA 90069
"Actor"

Fabian Forte
6671 Sunset Blvd. #1502
Los Angeles, CA 90028
"Actor, Singer"

Dick Fosbury
c/o General Delivery
Ketchum, ID 83440
"Track Athlete"

Gen. Joe Foss
P.O. Box 566
Scottsdale, AZ 85252
"Firearms Assoc. Executive"

Brigitte Fossey
18 rue Troyon
75017 Paris, FRANCE
"Actress"

David Foster
6173 Bonsall Drive
Malibu, CA 90265
"Musician, Songwriter"

Jodie Foster
10960 Wilshire Blvd. #1428
Los Angeles, CA 90024
"Actress"

Kimberly Foster
957 North Cole Avenue
Los Angeles, CA 90038
"Actress"

Meg Foster
9301 Wilshire Blvd. #312
Beverly Hills, CA 90210
"Actress"

Susanna Foster
11255 West Morrison Street
North Hollywood, CA 91601
"Actress"

Pete Fountain
2 Poldras Street
New Orleans, LA 70140
"Clarienetist"

Four Aces
12 Marshall Street #8Q
Irvington, NJ 07111
"Vocal Group"

Four Freshmen
P.O. Box 60404
Las Vegas, NV 89160
"Vocal Group"

Four Guys
P.O. Box 2138
Nashville, TN 37214
"Vocal Group"

Four Lads
32500 Concord Drive #221
Madison Heights, MI 49071
"Vocal Group"

The Four Seasons
P.O. Box 262
Carteret, NJ 07008
"Rock & Roll Group"

Gene Fowler, Jr.
7261 Outpost
Los Angeles, CA 90068
"Film Director"

Sen. Wyche Fowler (GA)
Senate Russell Bldg. #204
Washington, DC 20510
"Politician"

John Fowles
52 Floral Street
London WC2 ENGLAND
"Author"

Douglas V. Fowley
38510 Glen Abbey Lane
Murietta, CA 92362
"Actor"

Fox Brothers
Rt. 6, Bending Chestnut
Franklin, TN 37064
"Gospel Group"

Edward Fox
25 Maida Avenue
London W2 ENGLAND
"Actor"

Michael J. Fox
3960 Laurel Canyon #281
Studio City, CA 91604
"Actor, Director"

Samantha Fox
11 Mt. Pleasant Villas
London 4HH ENGLAND
"Singer, Model"

Robert Foxworth
1230 Benedict Canyon Drive
Beverly Hills, CA 90210
"Actor"

A.J. Foyt
6415 Toledo
Houston, TX 77008
"Auto Racer"

Jonathan Frakes
5062 Calvin Avenue
Tarzana, CA 91356
"Actor"

Peter Frampton
662 Stone Canyon
Los Angeles, CA 90077
"Singer, Guitarist"

Tony Franciosa
567 Tigertail Road
Los Angeles, CA 90049
"Actor"

Anne Francis
P.O. Box 5417
Santa Barbara, CA 93103
"Actress"

Arlene Francis
112 Central Park South
New York, NY 10019
"Actress"

Connie Francis
11 Pompton Avenue
Verona, NJ 07044
"Singer, Actress"

Dick Francis
Blewbury, Didcot
Oxfordshire 0X11 9NH
ENGLAND
"Author"

Freddie Francis
12 The Chestnuts
Jersey Road, Osterley
Middlesex ENGLAND
"TV Director"

Genie Francis
5062 Calvin Avenue
Tarzana, CA 91356
"Actress"

Rep. Barney Frank (MA)
House Rayburn Bldg. #2404
Washington, DC 20515
"Politician"

Charles Frank
9744 Wilshire Blvd. #308
Beverly Hills, CA 90212
"Actor"

Gary Frank
323 South Anita Avenue
Los Angeles, CA 90049
"Actor"

Joanna Frank
1274 Capri Drive
Pacific Palisades, CA 90272
"Actress"

Steve Franken
3604 Whitespeak Drive
Sherman Oaks, CA 91403
"Actor"

John Frankenheimer
3114 Abington Drive
Beverly Hills, CA 90210
"Director, Producer"

Frankie Goes To Hollywood
153 George Mortimer Street
London W1 ENGLAND
"Rock & Roll Group"

Aretha Franklin
P.O. Box 12137
Birmingham, MI 48012
"Singer, Songwriter"

Bonnie Franklin
15745 Royal Oak Road
Encino, CA 91436
"Actress"

Don Franklin
8749 Holloway Drive
Los Angeles, CA 90069
"Actor"

Joe Franklin
9 Broadcast Plaza
Secaucus, NJ 07094
"TV Host"

Pamela Franklin
1280 Sunset Plaza Drive
Los Angeles, CA 90069
"Actress"

Mary Frann
250 North Robertson #518
Beverly Hills, CA 90212
"Actress"

Arthur Franz
32960 Pacific Coast Hwy
Malibu, CA 90265
"Actor"

Dennis Franz
11805 Bellagio Road
Los Angeles, CA 90049
"Actor"

Dawn Franz
87 Birchgrove Road
Balmain NSW AUSTRALIA
"Swimmer"

Douglas Fraser
800 East Jefferson Street
Detroit, MI 48214
"Union Leader"

Linda Fratianne
18214 Septo Street
Northridge, CA 91324
"Skater"

Joe Frazier
2917 North Broad Street
Philadelphia, PA 19132
"Boxer Champion"

Walt Frazier
675 Flamingo Drive
Atlanta, GA 30311
"Basketball Player"

Stan Freberg
911 North Beverly Drive
Beverly Hills, CA 90210
"Actor, Director"

Peter Frechette
38 Park Place
Brooklyn, NY 11217
"Actor"

Bert Freed
418 North Bowling Green Way
Los Angeles, CA 90049
"Actor"

Kathleen Freeman
6247 Orion Avenue
Van Nuys, CA 91406
"Actress"

Mona Freeman
608 North Alpine Drive
Beverly Hills, CA 90210
"Actor"

Morgan Freeman
645 West End Avenue
New York, NY 10025
"Actor"

Orville Freeman
1800 "M" Street N.W. #300
Washington, DC 20036
"Government Official"

Phyllis Frelich
139 Spring Street
New York, NY 10012
"Actress"

Jourdan Fremin
128 1/2 North Hamilton Drive
Beverly Hills, CA 90211
"Actor"

Leigh French
1850 North Vista Avenue
Los Angeles, CA 90046
"Actor"

Fresh
306 South Salina Street #316
Syracuse, NY 13202
"Rock & Roll Group"

Matt Frewer
5007 Roma Court
Marina del Rey, CA 90292
"Actor"

Glen Frey
345 North Maple Drive #205
Beverly Hills, CA 90210
"Singer, Guitarist"

Janie Fricke
P. O. Box 680785
Santa Antonio, TX 78268
"Singer"

Brenda Fricker
68 Old Brompton Road
London SW7 3LQ ENGLAND
"Actress"

Betty Friedan
U.S.C.
Taper Hall, Room 331-M
Los Angeles, CA 90089
"Author"

William Friedkin
668 Perugia Way
Los Angeles, CA 90077
"Film Director"

Milton Friedman
Quadrangle Office
Hoover Institute
Stanford University
Palo Alto, CA 94305
"Econominist"

Sonya Friedman
208 Harriston Road
Glen Rock, NJ 07452
"TV Host"

Chuck Fries
1192 Cabrillo Drive
Beverly Hills, CA 90210
"TV Executive"

Lynette Fromme
Reformatory for Women
Alderson, WV 24910
"Prisnor"

Dominic Frontiere
3815 West Olive Avenue #202
Burbank, CA 91505
"Composer, Conductor"

Georgia Frontiere
2327 West Lincoln Avenue
Anaheim, CA 92801
"Football Team Owner"

David Frost
130 West 57th Street
New York, NY 10019
"TV Host"

Lindsay Frost
9200 Sunset Blvd. #625
Los Angeles, CA 90069
"Actress"

Rep. Martin Frost (TX)
House Rayburn Bldg. #2459
Washington, DC 20515
"Politician"

Leo Fuchs
609 North Kilkea Drive
Los Angeles, CA 90048
"Actor"

Alan Fudge
355 South Rexford Drive
Beverly Hills, CA 90212
"Actor"

J. William Fulbright
2527 Belmont Road N.W.
Washington, DC 20036
"Ex-Senator"

Robert Fulghum
219-1st Avenue North
Box 369
Seattle, WA 98109
"Author, Clergyman"

Lance Fuller
8831 Sunset Blvd. #402
Los Angeles, CA 90069
"Actor"

Penny Fuller
12428 Hesby Street
North Hollywood, CA 91607
"Actress"

Robert Fuller
1930 Century Park West #403
Los Angeles, CA 90067
"Actor"

Samuel Fuller
7628 Woodrow Wilson Drive
Los Angeles, CA 90046
"Film Writer, Producer"

Wendy Fulton
9169 Sunset Blvd.
Los Angeles, CA 90069
"Actor"

Annette Funicello
16102 Sandy Lane
Encino, CA 91316
"Actress"

Allen Funt
2359 Nichols Canyon
Los Angeles, CA 90068
"TV Host, Director"

John Furey
1000 Santa Monica Blvd. #305
Los Angeles, CA 90067
"Actor"

Betty Furness
30 Rockefeller Plaza
New York, NY 10112
"Consumer Advocate"

Stephen Furst
3900 Huntercrest Court
Moopark, CA 93021
"Actor"

George Furth
307 West 4th Street
New York NY 10014
"Actor, Writer"

Rep. Jaime Fuster (PR)
House Cannon Bldg. #427
Washington, DC 20515
"Politician"

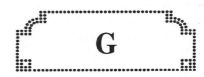

Kenny G
21940 Lamplighter Lane
Malibu, CA 90265
"Singer"

Christopher Gable
60 St. James's Street
London SW1 ENGLAND
"Actor"

Eva Gabor
100 Delfern Drive
Los Angeles, CA 90077
"Actress"

"Princess" Zsa Zsa Gabor
1001 Bel Air Road
Los Angeles, CA 90024
"Actress"

John Gabriel
100 West 57th Street #5-Q
New York, NY 10019
"Actor"

Peter Gabriel
13 Abbie Churchyard
Bath, ENGLAND
"Singer, Songwriter"

Roman Gabriel
377 Carowinds Blvd. #117
Fort Mill, SC 29715
"Football Player"

Col. Moammar Gaddafi
Bab el Aziziya
Tripoli, LIBYA
"Politician"

Max Gail
29451 Bluewater
Malibu, CA 90265
"Actor"

Boyd Gaines
2121 Avenue of the Stars #950
Los Angeles, CA 90067
"Actor"

John Kenneth Galbraith
30 Francis Avenue
Cambridge, MA 02138
"Economist"

Dr. Robert Gale
UCLA Medical Center
Dept. of Medicine, Rm. 42-121
Los Angeles, CA 90024
"Medical Doctor"

Helen Gallagher
260 West End Avenue
New York, NY 10023
"Actress"

Megan Gallagher
442 Landfair Avenue
Los Angeles, CA 90024
"Actress"

Peter Gallagher
151 El Camino Drive
Beverly Hills, CA 90212
"Actor"

Silvano Gallardo
3800 Barham Blvd. #303
Los Angeles, CA 90068
"Actress"

Rep. Elton Gallegly (CA)
House Cannon Bldg.# 107
Washington, DC 20515
"Politician"

Joe Gallison
3760 Green Vista Drive
Encino, CA 91436
"Actor"

Rep. Dean Gallo (NJ)
House Longworth Blgd. #1318
Washington, DC 20515
"Politician"

Lew Gallo
915 North Beverly Drive
Beverly Hills, CA 90210
"Director, Producer"

Don Galloway
23913 Bar Harbor Court
Valencia, CA 91355
"Actor"

James Galway
73 Baker Street
London W1M 1AH ENGLAND
"Flutist"

Rita Gam
180 West 58th Street
New York, NY 10019
"Actress"

Teresa Ganzel
9744 Wilshire Blvd. #308
Beverly Hills, CA 90212
"Actress"

Joe Garagiola
6221 East Huntress Drive
Paradise Valley, AZ 85253
"TV Host, Baseball"

Kaz Garas
31276 Bailard Road
Malibu, CA 90265
"Actor, Director"

Terri Garber
10100 Santa Monica Blvd. #700
Los Angeles, CA 90067
"Actress"

Victor Garber
888-7th Avenue #1602
New York, NY 10019
"Actor"

Andy Garcia
4519 Varna Avenue
Sherman Oaks, CA 91423
"Actor"

Vincent Gardenia
1350 Avenue of the Americas
New York, NY 10119
"Actor"

Booth Garder (WA)
Legislative Building
Olympia, WA 98504
"Governor"

Hy Gardner
5601 North Bayshore Drive
Miami, FL 33137
"TV-Radio Personality"

Randy Gardner
4640 Glencove Avenue #6
Marina Del Rey, CA 90291
"Ice Skater"

Jack Garfein
412 West 42nd Street
New York, NY 10036
"Director Producer"

Allen Garfield
9973 Durant Drive #2
Beverly Hills, CA 90212
"Actor"

Art Garfunkel
9 East 79th Street
New York, NY 10021
"Singer, Songwriter"

Beverly Garland
8014 Briar Summit Drive
Los Angeles, CA 90046
"Actress"

Sen. Jake Garn (UT)
Senate Dirksen Bldg. #505
Washington, DC 20510
"Politician"

James Garner
33 Oakmont Drive
Los Angeles, CA 90049
"Actor, Director"

Teri Garr
1462 Rising Glen
Los Angeles, CA 90069
"Actress"

Anne Garrels
c/o National Public Radio
2025 "M" Street N.W.
Washington, DC 20036
"News Correspondent"

Betty Garrett
3231 Oakdell Road
Studio City, CA 91604
"Actress"

Leif Garrett
9000 Sunset Blvd. #515
Los Angeles, CA 90069
"Actor, Singer"

Snuff Garrett
6255 Sunset Blvd. #1019
Los Angeles, CA 90028
"Talent Agent"

Zina Garrison
9417 Denbury Way
Houston, TX 77025
"Tennis Player"

Greer Garson Fogelson
2400 Republic Bank, Tower II
Dallas, TX 75201
"Actress"

Kathy Garver
170 Woodbridge Road
Hillsborough, CA 94010
"Actress"

Cyndy Garvey
3516 Malibu Country Drive
Malibu, CA 90265
"TV-Radio Personality"

Steve Garvey
228 South Anita
Los Angeles, CA 90049
"Baseball Player"

John Gray
32500 Concord Drive #221
Madison Heights, MI 48071
"Singer"

Lorraine Gary
1158 Tower Drive
Beverly Hills, CA 90210
"Actress"

Vittorio Gassman
c/o Giuseppe Prosa
Via San Dominico
2 bis Rome, ITALY
"Actor"

Mark Gastineau
1000 Fulton Avenue
Hempstead, NY 11550
"Football Player"

Daryl Gates
P.O. Box 30158
Los Angeles, CA 90030
"Police Chief"

Larry Gates
1015 Gayley Avenue
Los Angeles, CA 90024
"Actor"

Larry Gatlin
7003 Chadwick Drive #360
Brentwood, TN 37027
"Singer, Songwriter"

Dick Gautier
11156 Valley Spring Lane
North Hollywood, CA 91602
"Actor, Writer"

John Gavin
2415 Century Hill
Los Angeles, CA 90067
"Actor"

Rep. Joseph Gaydos (PA)
House Rayburn Bldg. #2186
Washington, DC 20515
"Politician"

Crystal Gayle
51 Music Square East
Nashville, TN 37203
"Singer"

Jackie Gayle
13109 Chandler Blvd.
Van Nuys, CA 91401
"Comedian"

Mitch Gaylord
100 North Woodburn Drive
Los Angeles, CA 90049
"Actor"

George Gaynes
3344 Campanil Drive
Santa Barbara, CA 93109
"Actor, Director"

Gloria Gaynor
15 Atherton Place Southall
Middlesex UB1 3QT ENGLAND
"Singer"

Mitzi Gaynor
610 North Arden Drive
Beverly Hills, CA 90210
"Actor, Dancer"

Ben Gazzara
1080 Madison Avenue
New York, NY 10028
"Actor"

Michael V. Gazzo
2047 Malcolm Avenue
Los Angeles, CA 90025
"Actor"

Tony Geary
7010 Pacific View Drive
Los Angeles, CA 90068
"Actor"

Gunther Gebel-Williams
3201 New Mexico Avenue N.W.
Washington, DC 20016
"Animal Trainer"

Nicolei Gedda
Valhavagen 128
S-11441 Stockholm, SWEDEN
"Tenor"

Jason Gedrick
9560 Wilshire Blvd. #500
Beverly Hills, CA 90212
"Actor"

Ellen Geer
21418 West Entrada Road
Topanga, CA 90290
"Actress"

David Geffen
9130 Sunset Blvd.
Los Angeles, CA 90069
"Record Executive"

J. Geils Band
8 Cadman Plaza West
Brooklyn, NY 11201
"Rock & Roll Group"

Rep. Sam Gejdenson (CT)
House Rayburn Bldg. #2416
Washington, DC 20515
"Politician"

Rep. George W. Gekas (PA)
House Longworth Bldg. #1519
Washington, DC 20515
"Politician"

Larry Gelbart
807 North Alpine Drive
Beverly Hills, CA 90210
"Writer, Producer"

Sir Bob Geldof, KBE
Davington Priory
Faversham Kent, ENGLAND
"Singer"

Daniel Gelin
92 Boulevard Murat
75015 Paris, FRANCE
"Film Director"

Uri Geller
Sonning-on-Thames
Berkshire, ENGLAND
"Psychic"

The X Generation
185 Glochester Place
London NW1 ENGLAND
"Rock & Roll Group"

Bryan Genesse
654 South Cloverdale #302
Los Angeles, CA 90036
"Actor"

Genesis
81-83 Walton Street
London SW3 ENGLAND
"Rock & Roll Group"

Peter Gennaro
115 Central Park West
New York, NY 10024
"Choreographer"

Hans-Dietrich Genscher
Auswartiges Amt.
Adenauerallee 99-103
5300 Bonn, GERMANY
"Diplomat"

Boy George(O'Dowd)
34A Green Lane
Northwood, Middlesex
ENGLAND
"Singer, Composer"

Gorgeous George
(aks George Grant)
Blessed Hope Baptist Church
York, SC 29745
"Wrestler"

Lynda Day George
10310 Riverside Drive #104
Toluca Lake, CA 91602
"Actress"

Phyllis George
Cave Hill, Box 4308
Lexington, KY 40503
"TV Personality"

Susan George
1221 North King Road #104
Los Angeles, CA 90069
"Actress"

Wally George
14155 Magnolia Blvd. #127
Sherman Oaks, CA 91423
"TV Host"

Rep. Richard Gephardt (MO)
House Longworth Bldg. #1432
Washington, DC 20515
"Politician"

Helen Gerald
969 Hilgard Avenue #408
Los Angeles, CA 90024
"Actress"

Gil Gerard
32 Hurricane Street
Marina del Rey, CA 90292
"Actor"

Richard Gere
45 East 98th Street #98
New York, NY 10003
"Actor"

Gordon Gerry
2880 Broadway
San Francisco, CA 94115
"Executive, Composer"

Jami Gertz
8899 Beverly Blvd.
Los Angeles, CA 90048
"Actress"

Vitas Gerulaitas
200 East End Avenue #15-P
New York, NY 10028
"Tennis Player"

Estelle Getty
68-85 218th Street
Bayside, NY 11364
"Actress"

Gordon Getty
2880 Broadway
San Francisco, CA 94115
"Executive, Composer"

Mrs. J. Paul Getty
1535 North Beverly Drive
Beverly Hills, CA 90210
"Philanthropist"

John Getz
P.O. Box 5617
Beverly Hills, CA 90210
"Actor"

Alice Ghostley
3800 Reklaw Drive
North Hollywood, CA 91604
"Actress"

Giancarlo Giannini
Via Mercalli 46
Rome, ITALY
"Actor"

Joey Giardello
1214 Severn Avenue
Cherry Hill, NJ 08802
"Boxer"

Barry Gibb
3088 South Mann
Las Vegas, NV 89102
"Singer"

Cynthia Gibb
151 El Camino Drive
Beverly Hills, CA 90212
"Actress"

Maurice Gibb
4744 North Bay Road
Miami Beach, FL 33140
"Singer, Songwriter"

Robin Gibb
4744 North Bay Road
Miami Beach, FL 33140
"Singer, Songwriter"

Leeza Gibbons
5555 Melrose Avenue #"L"
Los Angeles, CA 90038
"TV Host"

Rep. Sam Gibbons (FL)
House Rayburn Bldg. #2204
Washington, DC 20515
"Politician"

Georgia Gibbs
965 Fifth Avenue
New York, NY 10021
"Singer"

Marla Gibbs
2323 West M. L. King Jr Blvd.
Los Angeles, CA 90008
"Actress"

Terri Gibbs
110-30th Avenue
Nashville, TN 37203
"Singer, Songwriter"

Althea Gibson-Darbeu
275 Prospect Street #768
East Orange, NJ 07017
"Tennis Player"

Bob Gibson
215 Belleview Road
Belleview, NE 68005
"Baseball Player"

Charles Gibson
1965 Broadway #500
New York, NY 10023
"TV Host"

Debbie Gibson
P.O. Box 489
Merrick, NY 11566
"Singer"

Don Gibson
P.O. Box 50474
Nashville, TN 37205
"Singer, Songwriter"

Henry Gibson
26740 Latigo Shore Drive
Malibu, CA 90265
"Actress"

Kirk Gibson
1082 Oak Pointe Drive
Pontiac, MI 48054
"Baseball Player"

Mel Gibson
23333 Palm Canyon
Malibu, CA 90265
"Actor, Writer"

Sir John Gielgud
South Pavillion, Wotten
Underwood Aylesbury
Buckinghamshire, ENGLAND
"Actor"

Frances Gifford
940 East Colorado Blvd. #306
Pasadena, CA 91106
"Actress"

Frank Gifford
625 Madison Avenue #1200
New York, NY 10022
"Sportscaster"

Kathie Lee Gifford
625 Madison Avenue #1200
New York, NY 10022
"TV Host"

Elaine Giftos
10351 Santa Monica Blvd. #211
Los Angeles, CA 90025
"Actress"

Elsie Gilbert
1016 North Orange Grove #4
Los Angeles, CA 90046
"Actress"

Herschel Burke Gilbert
2451 Nichols Canyon
Los Angeles, CA 90046
"Composer, Conductor"

Melissa Gilbert
337 West 12th Street
New York, NY 10014
"Actress"

Sara Gilbert
16254 High Valley Drive
Encino, CA 91346
"Actress"

Nancy Giles
433 South Shirley Place #4
Beverly Hills, CA 90212
"Actress"

Johnny Gill
17539 Corinthian Drive
Encino, CA 91316
"Singer, Songwriter"

Vance Gill
1514 South Street
Nashville, TN 37212
"Singer, Songwriter"

Dizzy Gillespie
477 North Woodlands
Englewood, NJ 07632
"Trumpeter"

Anita Gillette
328 South Beverly Drive #A
Beverly Hills, CA 90212
"Actress"

Mickey Gilley
P.O. Box 1242
Pasadena, TX 77501
"Singer, Songwriter"

Terry Gilliam
The Old Hall
South Grove Highgate
London W6 ENGLAND
"Actor, Writer, Director"

Richard Gilliland
4545 Noeline Avenue
Encino, CA 91436
"Actor"

Rep. Paul E. Gillmor (OH)
House Longworth Bldg. #1203
Washington, DC 20515
"Politician"

Rep. Benjamin Gilman (NY)
House Rayburn Bldg. #2185
Washington, DC 20515
"Politician"

Frank Gilroy
6 Magnin Road
Monroe, NY 10950
"Dramatist"

Erica Gimpel
888-7th Avenue #201
New York, NY 10019
"Actress"

Jack Ging
10000 Santa Monica Blvd. #305
Los Angeles, CA 90067
"Actor"

Rep. Newt Gingrich (GA)
House Rayburn Bldg. #2438
Washington, DC 20515
"Politician"

Allen Ginsberg
P.O. Box 582
Stuyvesant Station
New York, NY 10009
"Poet"

Robert Ginty
9834 Wanda Park Drive
Beverly Hills, CA 90210
"Actor"

The Girls Next Door
P.O. Box 22765
Nashville, TN 37202
"C&W Group"

Annabeth Gish
P.O. Box 5617
Beverly Hills, CA 90210
"Actress"

Miss Lillian Gish
430 East 57th Street
New York, NY 10022
"Actress"

Carlo Giuffre
via Massimi 45
00132 Rome, ITALY
"Conductor"

Hubert Givenchy
3 Avenue George V
75008 Paris, FRANCE
"Fashion Designer"

Robin Givens
8818 Thrasher Avenue
Los Angeles, CA 90069
"Actress"

Glaser Brothers
916-19th Avenue South
Nashville, TN 37212
"Music Group"

Paul Michael Glaser
317 Georgina Avenue
Santa Monica, CA 90402
"Actor, Director"

Philip Glass
231-2nd Avnue
New York, NY 10003
"Composer"

Ron Glass
2485 Wild Oak Drive
Los Angeles, CA 90068
"Actor"

Glass Tiger
238 Davenport #126
Toronto, Ontario M5R 1J6
CANADA
"Rock & Roll Group"

Mrs. Marilyn Gleason
Invarry
Lauderhill, FL 33319
"Widower of Jackie Gleason"

Paul Gleason
1999 Avenue of the Stars #2850
Los Angeles, CA 90067
"Actor"

Sen. John Glenn (OH)
Senate Hart Bldg. #503
Washington, DC 20210
"Politician, Astronaut"

Scott Glenn
P.O. Box 1902
Santa Fe, NM 87501
"Actor"

Sharon Gless
4709 Teesdale Avenue
Studio City, CA 91604
"Actress"

Yoram Globus
640 San Vicente Blvd.
Los Angeles, CA 90048
"Producer, Executive"

Crispin Glover
1811 North Whitley #1400
Los Angeles, CA 90028
"Actor"

Danny Glover
P.O. Box 1648
San Francisco, CA 94101
"Actor"

John Glover
2517 Micheltorena Street
Los Angeles, CA 90039
"Actor"

Julian Glover
19 Ullswater Road
London SW13 ENGLAND
"Actor"

Jean-Luc Godard
15 rue du Nord
1180 Rolle
SWITZERLAND
"Film Director"

Alexander Godunov
98787 Shoreham Drive #101
Los Angeles, CA 90069
"Dancer"

Alexander Goehr
11 West Road
Cambridge, ENGLAND
"Composer"

Bob Goen
3816 Marber Avenue
Long Beach, CA 90808
"TV Performer"

Bernhard Goetz
55 West 14th Street
New York, NY 10011
"Subway Shooter"

Menachem Golan
640 San Vicente Blvd.
Los Angeles, CA 90048
"Producer, Executive"

Jack Gold
18 Avenue Road
London N6 5DW ENGLAND
"Film-TV Director"

Missy Gold
3500 West Avenue #1400
Burbank, CA 91505
"Actress"

Tracey Gold
12631 Addison Street
North Hollywood, CA 91607
"Actress"

Gary David Goldberg
P.O. Box 84168
Los Angeles, CA 90077
"Writer, Producer"

Leonard Goldberg
235 Ladera Drive
Beverly Hills, CA 90210
"TV-Film, Producer"

Whoopi Golberg
33012 Pacific Coast Highway
Malibu, CA 90265
"Actress, Comedienne"

Jeff Goldblum
8033 Sunset Blvd. #367
Los Angeles, CA 90046
"Actor"

William Lee Golden
P.O. Box 1795
Hendersonville, TN 37077
"Singer, Songwriter"

William Golding
Ebble Thatch
Bowerchalke, Wiltshire
ENGLAND
"Author"

William Goldman
50 East 77th Street #30
New York, NY 10021
"Screenwriter"

Bobby Goldsboro
P.O. Box 5250
Ocala, FL 32678
"Singer, Songwriter"

Judy Goldsmith
1111 Army-Navy Drive
Arlington, VA 22202
"Feminist"

Bob Goldthwait
3950 Fredonia Drive
Los Angeles, CA 90068
"Actor, Comedian"

Barry Goldwater
6250 Hogahn
Paradise Valley, AZ 85253
"Ex-Senator"

Sam Goldwyn, Jr.
10203 Santa Monica Blvd. #500
Los Angeles, CA 90067
"Director, Producer"

Tony Goldwyn
751 Ozone Street
Santa Monica, CA 90405
"Actor"

Arlene Golonka
1835 Pandora Avenue #3
Los Angeles, CA 90025
"Actress"

Richard Golub
42 East 64th Street
New York, NY 10021
"Lawyer"

Pedro Gonzalez-Gonzalez
4154 Charles Avenue
Culver City, CA 90203
"Wrestler"

Jane Goodall
P.O. Box 26846
Tucson, AZ 85726
"Anthropologist, Ethnologist"

Dwight Gooden
3101 East Elm Street
Tampa, FL 33610
"Baseball Player"

Grant Goodeve
21416 N.E. 68th Court
Redmond, WA 98053
"Actor"

Linda Goodfriend
5700 Etiwanda #150
Tarzana, CA 91365
"Actress"

Dody Goodman
10144 Culver Blvd. #21
Culver City, CA 90232
"Actress"

John Goodman
2412 Jupiter Drive
Los Angeles, CA 90046
"Actor"

Gail Goodrich
601-26th Street
Santa Monica, CA 90402
"Basketball Player"

Mark Goodson
375 Park Avenue
New York, NY 10022
"TV Producer"

Ron Goodwin
70 Charlotte Street
London W1 ENGLAND
"Actor"

Lecy Goranson
8457 Melrose Place #200
Los Angeles, CA 90069
"Actress"

Mikhail S. Gorbachev
4 Straya Ploschad
Moscow RUSSIA
"Former U.S.S.R. Chairman"

Barry Gordon
12725-E Ventura Blvd.
Studio City, CA 91604
"Actor"

Don Gordon
8485-E Melrose Place
Los Angeles, CA 90069
"Actor"

Gale Gordon
P.O. Box 179
Borrego Springs, CA 92004
"Actor"

Richard Gordon
1 Craven Hill
London W2 3EP ENGLAND
"Writer"

Berry Gordy
6464 Sunset Blvd.
Los Angeles, CA 90028
"Record Executive"

Sen. Albert Gore, Jr. (TN)
Senate Russell Bldg. #393
Washington, DC 20510
"Politician"

Lesley Gore
170 East 77th Street #2-A
New York, NY 10162
"Actress, Singer"

Michael Gore
310 West End Avenue #12C
New York, NY 10023
"Composer"

Tipper Gore
Rt. #2
Carthage, TN 37030
"Wife of Sen. Albert Gore, Jr."

Marius Goring
Middlecourt, The Green
Hampton Court, Surrey
ENGLAND
"Actor"

Cliff Gorman
333 West 57th Street
New York, NY 10019
"Actor"

Eydie Gorme
820 Greenway Drive
Beverly Hills, CA 90210
"Singer"

Karen Lynn Gorney
853-7th Avenue #7-C
New York, NY 10019
"Actress"

Frank Gorshin
74 South Morningside
Westport, CT 06880
"Actor, Comedian"

Sen. Slade Gorton (WA)
Senate Hart Bldg. #730
Washington, DC 20510
"Politician"

Vern Gosdin
818-18th Avenue South #300
Nashville, TN 37203
"Singer, Songwriter"

Rep. Perter Goss (FL)
House Cannon Bldg. #224
Washington, DC 20515
"Politician"

Goose Gossage
1565 Viacha Way
San Diego, CA 92124
"Baseball Player"

Louis Gossett, Jr.
P.O. Box 6187
Malibu, CA 90264
"Actor, Director"

Elliott Gould
21250 Califa #201
Woodland Hills, CA 91367
"Actor"

Harold Gould
912 El Medio
Pacific Palisades, CA 90272
"Actor"

Jason Gould
446 North Orlando Avenue
Los Angeles, CA 90048
"Financier"

Morton Gould
231 Shoreward Drive
Great Neck, NY 10201
"Composer, Conductor"

Robert Goulet
3110 Monte Rosa
Las Vegas, NV 89120
"Singer"

Curt Gowdy
9 Pierce Road
Wellesley Hills, MA 02188
"Sportscaster"

Lord Lew Grade
3 Audley Square
London W1Y 5DR ENGLAND
"Film Executive"

Randy Gradishar
5700 Logan Road
Denver, CO 80216
"Football Player"

Don Grady
4537 Simpson Avenue
North Hollywood, CA 91607
"Actor"

Steffi Graff
Luftschiffring 8
D-6835 Bruhl, GERMANY
"Tennis Player"

Ilene Graff
11455 Sunshine Terrace
Studio City, CA 91604
"Actress"

Rev. Billy Graham
1300 Harmon Place
Minneapolis, MN 55408
"Evangelist"

Sen. Bob Graham (FL)
Senate Dirksen Bldg. #241
Washington, DC 20510
"Politician"

Gerrit Graham
5601 Park Oak Place
Los Angeles, CA 90068
"Actor, Writer"

Katherine Graham
2920 "R" Street N.W.
Washington, DC 20007
"Publishing Executive"

Otto Graham
2241 Beneva Terrace
Sarasota, FL 33582
"Football Player"

Ronny Graham
8955 Beverly Blvd.
Los Angeles, CA 90048
"TV Writer"

Nancy Grahan
4910 Agnes Avenue
North Hollywood, CA 91607
"Actress"

Sen. Phil Gramm (TX)
Senate Russell Bldg. #370
Washington, DC 20510
"Politician"

Kelsey Grammer
13539 Hart
Van Nuys, CA 91405
"Actor"

Rep. Fred Grandy (IA)
House Cannon Bldg. #418
Washington, DC 20002
"Politician, Actor"

Dorothy Granger
11903 West Pico Blvd.
Los Angeles, CA 90064
"Actress"

Farley Granger
18 West 72nd Street #25D
New York, NY 10023
"Actor"

Stewart Granger
17331 Tramanto Drive #1
Pacifif Palisades, CA 90272
"Actor"

Amy Grant
P.O. Box 50701
Nashville, TN 37205
"Singer"

Mrs. Barbara Grant
9966 Beverly Grove Drive
Beverly Hills, CA 90210
"Cary Grant's Widower"

Faye Grant
322 West 20th Street
New York, NY 10011
"Actress"

Gogi Grant
10323 Alamo Avenue #202
Los Angeles, CA 90064
"Singer"

Lee Grant
21243 Ventura Blvd. #101
Woodland Hills, CA 91364
"Actress, Director"

Dr. Tony Grant
610 South Ardmore Avenue
Los Angeles, CA 90005
"Radio Personality"

Guenther Grass
Niedstrasse 13
1000 Berlin 41 GERMANY
"Author"

Karen Grassle
9744 Wilshire Blvd. #308
Beverly Hills, CA 90212
"Actress"

Rep. Charles Grassley (IA)
Senate Hart Bldg. #135
Washington, DC 20510
"Politician"

Grateful Dead
Box 1566, Main Station
Montclair, NJ 07043
"Rock & Roll Group"

Peter Graves
660 East Channel Road
Santa Monica, CA 90402
"Actor"

Teresa Graves
3437 West 78th Place
Los Angeles, CA 90043
"Actress"

Billy Gray
19612 Grandview Drive
Topanga, CA 90290
"Actor"

Colleen Gray
1432 North Kenwood Street
Burbank, CA 91505
"Actress"

Dulcie Gray
44 Brunswick Gardens
Flat #2
London W8 ENGLAND
"Actress, Author"

Erin Gray
10921 Alta View
Studio City, CA 91604
"Actress"

Linda Gray
6218 Rock Cliff Drive
Malibu, CA 90265
"Actress, Director"

Velekka Gray
9000 Sunset Blvd. #811
Los Angeles, CA 90069
"Actress"

William H. Gray III
500 East 62nd Street
New York, NY 10021
"U.N.C.F. President"

Helen Grayco
11500 San Vicente Blvd.
Los Angeles, CA 90049
"Singer"

Kathryn Grayson
2009 La Mesa Drive
Santa Monica, CA 90402
"Actress, Singer"

Adolph Green
529 West 42nd Street #7-F
New York, NY 10036
"Screen & Songwriter"

Al Green
P.O. Box 456
Memphis, TN 38053
"Singer, Clergy"

Rep. Bill Green (NY)
House Rayburn Bldg. #2301
Washington, DC 20515
"Politician"

Kerry Green
8899 Beverly Blvd.
Los Angeles, CA 90048
"Actress"

Daniel Greene
1999 Avenue of the Stars #2850
Los Angeles, CA 90067
"Actor"

Ellen Greene
151 South El Camino Drive
Beverly Hills, CA 90212
"Actress, Singer"

Graham Greene
59 Dawn Valley Drive
Toronto Ontario MYK 2J1
CANADA
"Author"

Michele Greene
2281 Holly Drive
Los Angeles, CA 90068
"Actress"

Shecky Greene
1220 Shadow Lane
Las Vegas, NV 89102
"Comedian"

Bud Greenspan
33 East 68th Street
New York, NY 10021
"Writer, Producer"

Lee Greenwood
1311 Elm Hill Pike
Nashville, TN 37214
"Singer, Songwriter"

Brodie Greer
5840 Shirley Avenue
Tarzana, CA 91356
"Actor"

Dabs Greer
284 South Madison
Pasadena, CA 91101
"Actor"

Germaine Greer
29 Frenshaw Road
London SW10 0TG ENGLAND
"Feminist Author"

(Betty) Jane Greer
966 Moraga Drive
Los Angeles, CA 90049
"Actress"

Judd Gregg (NH)
State House
Concord, NH 03301
"Governor"

Dick Gregory
P.O. Box 3266
Tower Hill Farm
Plymouth, MA 02361
"Activist, Comedian"

James Gregory
55 Cathedral Rock Drive #33
Sedona, AZ 86336
"Actor"

Paul Gregory
P.O. Box 38
Palm Springs, CA 92262
"Film Producer"

Bob Greise
3250 Mary Street
Miami, FL 33133
"Football Player"

Wayne Gretzky
14135 Beresford Drive
Beverly Hills, CA 90210
"Hockey Player"

Jennifer Grey
500 South Sepulveda Blvd. #500
Los Angeles, CA 90049
"Actress"

Joel Grey
888-7th Avenue #1800
New York, NY 10019
"Actor, Singer"

Virginia Grey
15101 Magnolia Blvd. #5
Sherman Oaks, CA 91403
"Actress"

Richard Grieco
15263 Mulholland Drive
Los Angeles, CA 90077
"Actor"

Pam Grier
6767 Hayvenhurst Drive
Van Nuys, CA 91406
"Actress"

Rosey Grier
11656 Montana #301
Los Angeles, CA 90049
"Actor, Football Player"

Archie Griffin
2389 Bookwood
Columbus, OH 43209
"Football Player"

Merv Griffin
603 North Doheny Road
Beverly Hills, CA 90210
"Singer, Producer"

Andy Griffith
10500 Camarillo
North Hollywood, CA 91602
"Actor"

Melanie Griffith
9555 Heather Road
Beverly Hills, CA 90210
"Actress"

Nanci Griffith
72-74 Brewer Street
London W1 ENGLAND
"Singer, Songwriter"

Thomas Ian Griffith
9301 Wilshire Blvd. #312
Beverly Hills, CA 90210
"Actor"

Florence Griffith-Joyner
11444 West Olympic Blvd.
10th Floor
Los Angeles, CA 90064
"Track Athlete"

Gary Grimes
10637 Burbank Blvd.
North Hollywood, CA 91601
"Actor"

Tammy Grimes
10 East 44th Street #700
New York, NY 10017
"Actress"

George Grizzard
400 East 54th Street
New York, NY 10022
"Actor"

Dick Groat
320 Beach Street
Pittsburgh, PA 15218
"Baseball Player"

Matt Groening
15205 Friends Street
Pacific Palisades, CA 90272
"Cartoonist"

Ferde Grofe, Jr.
18139 West Coastline
Malibu, CA 90265
"Writer"

Sam Groom
140 Riverside Drive #16-0
New York, NY 10024
"Actor"

Michael Gross
Paul Ehlich Strasse 6
D-6000 Frankfurt 70
GERMANY
"Swimmer"

Michael Gross
151 El Camino Drive
Beverly Hills, CA 90212
"Actor"

Sir Charles Groves
12 Camden Square
London NW1 9UY ENGLAND
"Conductor"

Lou Groza
5287 Parkway Drive
Berea, OH 44017
"Football Player"

Gary Grubbs
9744 Wilshire Blvd. #308
Beverly Hills, CA 90212
"Actor"

Christopher Guard
2 Geraldine Road
London W4 ENGLAND
"Actor"

Harry Guardino
9738 Arby Drive
Beverly Hills, CA 90210
"Actor"

Rep. Frank Guarini (NJ)
House Rayburn Bldg. #2458
Washington, DC 20515
"Politician"

Peter Guber
760 Lausanne Road
Los Angeles, CA 90077
"Film Producer"

Aldo Gucci
8 Via Condotti
00187, Rome, ITALY
"Fashion Designer"

Bob Guccione
909 Third Avenue
New York, NY 10022
"Publisher"

Christopher Guest
1242 South Camden Drive
Los Angeles, CA 90035
"Actor, Writer"

Cornelia Guest
2411 Briarcrest Road
Beverly Hills, CA 90210
"Actress"

Lance Guest
121 North San Vicente Blvd.
Beverly Hills, CA 90211
"Actor"

Ron Guirdy
109 Conway
Lafayette, LA 70507
"Baseball Player"

Ann Morgan Guilbert
1525 Amherst Avenue #304
Los Angeles, CA 90025
"Actress"

Nancy Guild
12 East 62nd Street
New York, NY 10021
"Actress"

Robert Guillaume
3853 Longridge Avenue
Sherman Oaks, CA 91423
"Actor"

Sir Alec Guiness
Kettle Brook Meadows
Petersfield, Hampshire
ENGLAND
"Actor, Director"

Cathy Guisewite
4900 Main Street
Kansas City, MO 64112
"Cartoonist"

Tito Guizar
Sierra Madre
640 Lomas Drive Chaupultepec
Mexico City 10 09999 MEXICO
"Actor, Guitarist"

Dorothy Gulliver
28792 Lajos Lane
Valley Center, CA 92082
"Actress"

Bryant Gumbel
30 Rockefeller Plaza #3B
New York, NY 10020
"Morning TV Show Host"

Greg Gumbel
347 West 57th Street
New York, NY 10019
"Sports Anchor"

Rep. Steve Gunderson (WI)
House Rayburn Bldg. #2235
Washington, DC 20515
"Politician"

Moses Gunn
395 Nut Plains Road
Guilford, CT 06430
"Actor"

Guns & Roses
1839 South Robertson Blvd. #201
Los Angeles, CA 90035
"Rock & Roll Group"

Dan Gurney
2334 South Broadway
Santa Ana, CA 92707
"Auto Racer"

HM King Carl Gustav XVI
Jungliga Slottet
11130 Stockholm SWEDEN
"Royalty"

Arlo Guthrie
The Farm
Washington, MA 01223
"Singer, Songwriter"

Steve Guttenburg
15237 Sunset Blvd. #48
Pacific Palisades, CA 90272
"Actor"

Lucy Gutteridge
109 Jermyn Street
London SW1 Y6HB ENGLAND
"Actress"

Jasmine Guy
21243 Ventura Blvd. #101
Woodland Hills, CA 91364
"Actress, Singer"

Anne Gwynne
4350 Colfax
North Hollywood, CA 91604
"Actress, Former Model"

James "Gypsy" Haake
1256 North Flores
Los Angeles, CA 90069
"Actor"

Lukas Haas
335 North Maple Drive #250
Beverly Hills, CA 90210
"Actor"

Philip Habib
1606 Courtland Road
Belmont, CA 94002
"Politician"

Shelley Hack
1208 Georgina
Santa Monica, CA 90402
"Actress, Model"

Joseph Hacker
211 South Beverly Drive #107
Beverly Hills, CA 90212
"Actor"

Buddy Hackett
800 North Whittier Drive
Beverly Hills, CA 90210
"Comedian, Actor"

Taylor Hackford
2003 La Brea Terrace
Los Angeles, CA 90046
"Actor"

Gene Hackman
8500 Wilshire Blvd. #801
Beverly Hills, CA 90211
"Actor"

Sammy Hagar
31740 Broad Beach Road
Malibu, CA 90265
"Singer"

Kevin Hagen
8350 Santa Monica Blvd. #103
Los Angeles, CA 90069
"Actor"

Uta Hagen
27 Washington Square North
New York, NY 10011
"Actress"

Merle Hager
P.O. Box 536
Palo Cedro, CA 96073
"Singer"

Dan Haggerty
11520 Decente Drive
Studio City, CA 91604
"Actor"

Larry Hagman
23730 Malibu Colony Road
Malibu, CA 90265
"Actor, Director"

Albert Hague
4346 Redwood Avenue #304A
Marina del Rey, CA 90292
"Actor, Composer"

Jessica Hahn
P.O. Box 54972
Phoenix, AZ 85078
"Radio Personality"

Charles Haid
4376 Forman Avenue
North Hollywood, CA 91602
"Actor, Producer"

Gen. Alexander Haig, Jr.
1155-15th Street NW #800
Washington, DC 20005
"Military Leader, Politician"

Arthur Hailey
P.O. Box N-7776
Lyford Cay
Nassau, BAHAMAS
"Writer"

Oliver Hailey
11747 Canton Place
Studio City, CA 91604
"Screenwriter"

Corey Haim
3960 Laurel Canyon Blvd. #384
Studio City, CA 91604
"Actor"

Connie Haines
1870 Caminito del Cielo
Glendale, CA 91208
"Singer"

Ron Hajak
17420 Ventura Blvd. #4
Encino, CA 91316
"Actor"

Khrystyne Haje
P.O. Box 8750
Universal City, CA 91608
"Actress"

H.R. Haleman
443 North McCadden Place
Los Angeles, CA 90004
"Politician"

Barbara Hale
15301 Ventura Blvd. #345
Sherman Oaks, CA 91403
"Actress"

Monte Hale
11732 Moorpark #B
Studio City, CA 91604
"Actor"

Jack Haley, Jr.
1443 Devlin Drive
Los Angeles, CA 90069
"Writer, Producer"

Jackie Earle Haley
843 North Sycamore Avenue
Los Angeles, CA 90038
"Actor"

Bill Haley's Comets
2011 Ferry Avenue #U19
Camden, NJ 08104
"Rock & Roll Group"

Anthony Michael Hall
65 Roosevelt Stream
Valley Stream, NY 11581
"Actor"

Arsenio Hall
10987 Bluffside Drive #4108
Studio City, CA 91604
"TV Host, Actor"

Daryl Hall
130 West 57th Street #2A
New York, NY 10019
"Singer"

Deidre Hall
9023 Norman Place
Los Angeles, CA 90069
"Actress"

Fawn Hall
8339 Chapel Lake Court
Annandale, VA 22003
"Secretary, Model"

Gus Hall
235 West 23rd Street
New York, NY 10011
"Politician"

Huntz Hall
12512 Chandler Blvd. #307
North Hollywood, CA 91607
"Actor"

Jerry Hall
2 Munro Terrace
London SW10 ODL ENGLAND
"Model"

Lani Hall
31930 Pacific Coast Highway
Malibu, CA 90265
"Singer, Songwriter"

Monty Hall
519 North Arden Drive
Beverly Hills, CA 90210
"TV Host"

Rep. Ralph M. Hall (TX)
House Rayburn Bldg. #2236
Washington, DC 20515
"Politician"

Tom T. Hall
P.O. Box 1246
Franklin, TN 37065
"Singer, Songwriter"

Rep. Tony P. Hall (OH)
House Rayburn Bldg. #2162
Washington, DC 20515
"Politician"

Johnny Halladay
19 rue Vignon
F-75008 Paris, FRANCE
"Singer"

Charles Hallahan
1975 West Siverlake Drive
Los Angeles, CA 90039
"Actor"

Holly Hallstrom
5750 Wilshire Blvd. #475-W
Los Angeles, CA 90036
"Model"

Brett Halsey
141 North Grand Avenue
Pasadena, CA 91103
"Actor"

Alan Hamel
10342 Mississippi Avenue
West Los Angeles, CA 90025
"TV Personality"

Veronica Hamel
2121 Avenue of the Stars #900
Los Angeles, CA 90067
"Actress"

Dorothy Hamill
2331 Century Hill
Los Angeles, CA 90067
"Ice Skater"

Mark Hamill
P.O. Box 124
Malibu, CA 90265
"Actor"

Carrie Hamilton
2114 Ridgemont
Los Angeles, CA 90046
"Carol Burnett's Daughter"

Donald Hamilton
984 Acequia Madre
P.O. Box 1045
Santa Fe, NM 87501
"Author"

George Hamilton
9141 Burton Way #3
Beverly Hills, CA 90210
"Actor"

Guy Hamilton
22 Mont Port
Puerto de Andraitx
Mallorca, SPAIN
"Film Director"

Kim Hamilton
1229 North Horn Avenue
Los Angeles, CA 90069
"Actress"

Rep. Lee Hamilton (IN)
House Rayburn Bldg. #2187
Washington, DC 20515
"Politician"

Linda Hamilton
8955 Norman Place
Washington, CA 90069
"Actress"

Scott Hamilton
1 Erieview Plaza
Cleveland, OH 44114
"Ice Skater"

Harry Hamlin
P.O. Box 25578
Los Angeles, CA 90025
"Actor"

Marvin Hamlisch
970 Park Avenue #65
New York, NY 10028
"Composer, Pianist"

M.C. Hammer
80 Swan Way #130
Oakland, CA 94621
"Rap Singer"

Rep. John Hammerschmidt (AR)
House Rayburn Bldg. #2110
Washington, DC 20515
"Politician"

Nicholas Hammond
1930 Century Park West #303
Los Angeles, CA 90067
"Actor"

Earl Hamner
11575 Amanda Drive
Studio City, CA 91604
"TV Writer, Producer"

Susan Hampshire
Billing Road
London SW10 ENGLAND
"Actress"

James Hampton
10552 Deering Avenue
Chatsworth, CA 91311
"Actor, Writer"

Lionel Hampton
20 West 64th Street #28K
New York, NY 10023
"Musician"

Maggie Han
9200 Sunset Blvd. #710
Los Angeles, CA 90069
"Actress"

Herbie Hancock
1250 North Doheny Drive
Los Angeles, CA 90069
"Pianist, Composer"

Rep. Melton Hancock (MO)
House Cannon Bldg. #318
Washington, DC 20515
"Politician"

Tom Hanks
23414 Malibu Colony Drive
Malibu, CA 90265
"Actor"

Bridget Hanley
16671 Oak View Drive
Encino, CA 91316
"Actress"

Daryl Hannah
8306 Wilshire Blvd. #535
Beverly Hills, CA 90212
"Actress"

Page Hannah
P.O. Box 5617
Beverly Hills, CA 90210
"Actress"

Rep. James Hansen (UT)
House Longworth Bldg. #2421
Washington, DC 20515
"Politician"

Sir James Hanson
180 Brompton Road
London SW3 1HF ENGLAND
"Film Director"

Otto Harbach
876 Park Avenue #7N
New York, NY 10021
"Lyricist"

Ernest Harden, Jr.
1052 Carol Drive
Los Angeles, CA 90069
"Actor"

Jerry Hardin
3033 Vista Crest Drive
Los Angeles, CA 90068
"Actor"

Melora Hardin
11726 San Vicent Blvd. #300
Los Angeles, CA 90049
"Actress"

Kadeem Hardison
324 North Brighton Street
Burbank, CA 91506
"Actor"

Billy Hardwick
1576 South White Station
Memphis, TN 38117
"Bowler"

Robert Hardy
Chatto & Linnit
Shaftesbury Avenue
London W1 ENGLAND
"Actor"

Dorian Harewood
1865 Hill Drive
Los Angeles, CA 90041
"Actress"

Billy James Hargis
Rose of Sharon Farm
Neosho, MO 64840
"Evangelist"

Mariska Hargitay
9274 Warbler Way
Los Angeles, CA 90069
"Actress"

Mickey Hargitay
1255 North Sycamore Avenue
Los Angeles, CA 90038
"Actor"

Marion Hargrove
244 Sheldon Avenue
Santa Cruz, CA 95060
"TV Writer"

Sen. Tom Harkin (IA)
Senate Hart Bldg. #531
Washington, DC 20510
"Politician"

Harlem Globetrotters
6121 Santa Monica Blvd.
Los Angeles, CA 90038
"Comedy Basketball Team"

Debbie Harmon
13243 Valley Heart
Sherman Oaks, CA 91423
"Actress"

Manny Harmon
8350 Santa Monica Blvd.
Los Angeles, CA 90069
"Conductor"

Mark Harmon
2236 Encinitas Blvd. #A
Encinitas, CA 92024
"Actor"

The Harmonica Rascals
P.O. Box 156
Roselle, NJ 07203
"Musical Group"

Magda Harout
13452 Vose Street
Van Nuys, CA 91405
"Actress"

Jessica Harper
3454 Glorietta Place
Sherman Oaks, CA 91423
"Actress"

Ron Harper
3800 Barham Blvd.
Los Angeles, CA 90068
"Actor"

Tess Harper
2271 Betty Lane
Beverly Hills, CA 90210
"Actress"

Valerie Harper
616 North Maple Drive
Beverly Hills, CA 90210
"Actress"

The Harptones
55 West 119th Street
New York, NY 10026
"Vocal Group"

Woody Harrelson
1642 Westwood Blvd. #3
Los Angeles, CA 90024
"Actor"

Pamela Harriman
3032 "N" Street N.W.
Washington, DC 20007
"Averell Harriman's Widower"

Curtis Harrington
6286 Vine Way
Los Angeles, CA 90028
"Film Director"

Pat Harrington
730 Marzella Avenue
Los Angeles, CA 90049
"Actor, Writer"

Bishop Barbara Harris
138 Tremont Street
Boston, MA 02111
"Clergy"

Rep. Claude Harris (AL)
House Longworth Bldg. #1009
Washington, DC 20515
"Politician"

Ed Harris
1427 North Poinsettia Place
Los Angeles, CA 90046
"Actor"

Emmylou Harris
P.O. Box 1384
Brentwood, TN 37027
"Singer, Songwriter"

Franco Harris
400 West North Avenue
Old Allegheny, CA 15212
"Football Player"

Mrs. Jean Harris
Bedford Hills Correctional Facility
Westchester County
Bedrod Hills, NY 10507
"Prisoner"

Jonathan Harris
16830 Marmaduke Place
Encino, CA 91316
"Actor"

Julie Harris
132 Barn Hill Road
West Chatham, MA 02669
"Actress"

Mel Harris
10390 Santa Monica Blvd. #300
Los Angeles, CA 90025
"Actress"

Neil Patrick Harris
11350 Ventura Blvd. #206
Studio City, CA 91604
"Actor"

Phil Harris
49400 JFK Trail
Palm Desert, CA 92660
"Orchestra Leader"

Richard Harris
520 Park Avenue
New York, NY 10022
"Actor"

Sam Harris
1253 South Hauser Blvd.
Los Angeles, CA 90019
"Singer"

Susan Harris
11828 La Grange #200
Los Angeles, CA 90025
"TV Producer"

George Harrison
Friar Park Road
Henley-On-Thames ENGLAND
"Singer, Songwriter"

Gregory Harrison
8327 Santa Monica Blvd.
Los Angeles, CA 90069
"Singer, Songwriter"

Jenilee Harrison
3800 Barham Blvd #303
Los Angeles, CA 90068
"Actress, Model"

Linda Harrison
211 North Main Street #A
Berlin, MD 21811
"Actress"

Noel Harrison
10100 Santa Monica Blvd #700
Los Angeles, CA 90067
"Singer, Actor"

Kathryn Harrold
151 El Camino Drive
Beverly Hills, CA 90212
"Actress"

Donald Harron
P.O. Box 4700
Vancouver BC V6B 4A3
CANADA
"TV Host"

Lisa Harrow
200 Fulham Road
London SW10 ENGLAND
"Actress"

Deborah Harry
425 West 21st Street
New York, NY 10011
"Singer"

Ray Harryhausen
2 Ilchester Place
West Kesington
London ENGLAND
"Special Effect Technician"

Corey Hart
81 Hymus Blvd.
Montreal, Que. H9R 1E2
CANADA
"Singer, Songwriter"

Mother Dolores
(Dolores Hart)
Regina Laudis Convent
Bethlehem, CT 06751
"Actress, Nun"

Dorothy Hart
222 Monterey Road #1603
Glendale, CA 91206
"Actress"

Freddie Hart
505 Canton Pass
Madison, TN 37115
"Singer"

Gary Hart
P.O. Box 185
Denver, CO 80201
"Ex-Senator"

John Hart
35109 Highway 79 #134
Warner Springs, CA 92086
"Actor"

Mary Hart
150 South El Camino Drive #303
Beverly Hills, CA 90212
"TV Host"

Huntington Hartford
600 Third Avenue
New York, NY 10016
"Financer, Art Patron"

John Hartford
P.O. Box 40989
Nashville, TN 37204
"Singer"

Mariette Hartley
10100 Santa Monica Blvd. #2460
Los Angeles, CA 90067
"Actress"

Lisa Hartman
8037 Sunset Blvd. #2641
Los Angeles, CA 90046
"Actress, Model"

Paul Harvey
1035 Park Avenue
River Forest, IL 60305
"News Analyst"

Rodney Harvey
1608 North Las Palmas
Los Angeles, CA 90028
"Actor"

Eugene Hasenfus
c/o General Delivery
Marinette, WI 54143
"Flight Master"

Peter Haskell
19924 Acre Street
Northridge, CA 91324
"Actor"

King Hassan II
Royal Palace
Rabat, MOROCCO
"Royalty"

David Hasselhoff
4310 Sutton Place
Van Nuys, CA 91403
"Actor"

Marilyn Hassett
8485 Brier Drive
Los Angeles, CA 90046
"Actress"

Signe Hasso
582 South Orange Grove Avenue
Los Angeles, CA 90036
"Actress"

Rep. Dennis Hastert (IL)
House Cannon Bldg. #515
Washington, DC 20515
"Politician"

Sen. Orrin G. Hatch (UT)
Senate Russell Bldg. #135
Washington, DC 20510
"Politician"

Richard Hatch
1604 North Courtney Avenue
Los Angeles, CA 90046
"Actor"

Rep. Charles Hatcher (GA)
House Rayburn Bldg. #2434
Washington, DC 20515
"Politician"

Teri Hatcher
P.O. Box 1101
Sunland, CA 91040
"Actress"

Bobby Hatfield
1824 Port Wheeler Drive
Newport Beach, CA 92660
"Singer"

Hurd Hatfield
Ballinterry House
Rathcormac, County Cork
IRELAND
"Actor"

Sen. Mark Hatfield (OR)
Senate Hart Bldg. #711
Washington, D.C. 20510
"Politician"

Rutger Hauer
151 El Camino Drive
Beverly Hills, CA 90212
"Actor"

Wings Hauser
9113 Sunset Blvd.
Los Angeles, CA 90069
"Actor"

Vaclav Havel
udejvickenho Rybnicku 4
CS-160 00 Prague 6
CZECHOLOVAKIA
"Politician"

Richie Havens
10 East 44th Street #700
New York, NY 10017
"Singer, Guitarist"

June Haver MacMurray
485 Halvern Drive
Los Angeles, CA 90049
"Actress"

Nigel Havers
125 Gloucester Road
London SW7 ENGLAND
"Actor"

June Havoc
405 Old Long Ridge Road
Stamford, CT 06903
"Actress"

Ethan Hawke
9830 Wilshire Blvd.
Beverly Hills, CA 90212
"Actor"

Edwin Hawkins
1971 Hoover Avenue
Oakland, CA 94602
"Gospel Singer"

Tramaine Hawkins
151 El Camino Drive
Beverly Hills, CA 90212
"Gospel Singer"

Goldie Hawn
1849 Sawtelle Blvd. #500
Los Angeles, CA 90025
"Actress"

Jill Haworth
300 East 51st Street
New York, NY 10019
"Actress"

Nigel Hawthorne
5 Stud Cottages, Burnt Farm
Crewes Hill, Enfield
Middlesex ENGLAND
"Actor"

Tom Hayden
10960 Wilshire Blvd.#908
Los Angeles, CA 90024
"Politician"

Julie Haydon
1310 Harold Ellen
El Dorado, AR 71414
"Actress, Model"

Julie Hayek
5645 Burning Tree Drive
La Canada, CA 91011
"Actress, Model"

Bill Hayes
4528 Beck Avenue
North Hollywood, CA 91602
"Actor"

Rep. Charles Hayes (IL)
House Longworth Bldg. #1131
Washington, DC 20515
"Politician"

Helen Hayes
235 North Broadway
Nyack, NY 10970
"Actress"

Isaac Hayes
1962 Spectrum Circle #700
Marietta, GA 30067
"Singer, Songwriter"

Rep. James Hayes (LA)
House Cannon Bldg. #503
Washington, DC 20515
"Politician"

Peter Lind Hayes
3538 Pueblo Way
Las Vegas, NV 89109
"Actor, Comedian"

Susan Seaforth Hayes
4528 Beck Avenue
North Hollywood, CA 91602
"Actress"

Robert Hays
9350 Wilshire Blvd. #324
Beverly Hills, CA 90212
"Actor"

Brooke Hayward
305 Madison Avenue #956
New York, NY 10165
"Author, Actress"

Jonathan Haze
3636 Woodhill Canyon
Studio City, CA 91604
"Actor"

Glenne Headley
7929 Hollywood Blvd.
Los Angeles, CA 90046
"Actress"

Mary Healy
3538 Pueblo Way
Las Vegas, NV 89109
"Actress"

John Heard
347 West 84th Street #5
New York, NY 10024
"Actor"

George Hearn
340 West 57th Street #7-C
New York, NY 10019
"Actor"

Tommy Hearns
19600 West McNichol Street
Detroit, MI 48219
"Boxer"

Patricia Hearst
110-5th Street
San Francisco, CA 94103
"Author"

Randolph A. Hearst
959-8th Avenue
New York, NY 10019
"Publishing Executive"

Mrs. Wm. Randolph Hearst
875 Comstock Avenue #168
Los Angeles, CA 90024
"Wife of William Hearst"

Heart
6300 South Center Blvd. #200
Seattle, WA 98188
"Rock & Roll Group"

Marla Heasley
8730 Sunset Blvd. #220 West
Los Angeles, CA 90069
"Actress"

Heatwave
P.O. Box U
Tarzana, CA 91356
"R&B Group"

Gina Hecht
5930 Foothill Drive
Los Angeles, CA 90068
"Actress"

Eileen Heckart
135 Comstock Hill Road
New Canaan, CT 06840
"Actress"

David (Al) Hedison
2940 Trudy Drive
Beverly Hills, CA 90210
"Actor"

Tippi Hedren
1006 Fallen Leaf Road
Arcadia, CA 91006
"Actress"

Frances Heflin
10 East 44th Street #700
New York, NY 10019
"Actress"

Sen. Howell Heflin (AL)
Senate Hart Bldg. #728
Washington, DC 20510
"Politician"

Rep. Joel Hefley (CO)
House Cannon Bldg. #222
Washington, DC 20515
"Politician"

Christie Hefner
10236 Charing Cross Road
Los Angeles, CA 90024
"Hugh Hefner's Daughter"

Hugh Hefner
10236 Charing Cross Road
Los Angeles, CA 90024
"Publishing Executive"

Rep. W.G. "Bill" Hefner (NC)
House Rayburn Bldg. #2161
Washington, DC 20515
"Politician"

Beth Heiden
3505 Blackhawk Drive
Madison, WI 53704
"Skater"

Eric Heiden
3505 Blackhawk Drive
Madison, WI 53704
"Skater"

Carol Heiss
809 Lafayette Drive
Akron, OH 44303
"Actress"

Katherine Helmond
2035 Davies Way
Los Angeles, CA 90046
"Actress, Director"

Sen. Jesse Helms (NC)
403 Everett Dirksen Bldg.
Washington, DC 20510
"Politician"

Harry Helmsley
Park Lane Hotel
36 Central Park South
New York, NY 10019
"Real Estate Executive"

Leona Helmsley
Park Lane Hotel
36 Central Park South
New York, NY 10019
"Hotel Executive"

Margaux Hemingway
9454 Wilshire Blvd., PH.
Beverly Hills, CA 90212
"Actress, Model"

Mariel Hemingway
P.O. Box 2249
Ketchum, ID 83340
"Actress"

Dwight Hemion
201 Ocean Avenue
Santa Monica, CA 90402
"TV Director, Producer"

David Hemmings
9113 Sunset Blvd.
Los Angeles, CA 90069
"Actor, Director"

Shirley Hemphill
539 Trona Avenue
West Covina, CA 91790
"Actress"

Sherman Hemsley
8033 Sunset Blvd. #193
Los Angeles, CA 90046
"Actor"

Florence Henderson
P.O. Box 11295
Marina del Rey, CA 90295
"Singer, Actor"

Rickey Henderson
10561 Englewood Drive
Oakland, CA 94621
"Baseball Player"

Skitch Henderson
Hunt Hill Farm
RFD #3 Upland Road
New Milford, CT 06776
"Composer, Conductor"

Don Henley
14100 Mulholland Drive
Beverly Hills, CA 90210
"Singer, Songwriter"

Marilu Henner
2101 Castilian
Los Angeles, CA 90068
"Actress"

Linda Kaye Henning
4231 Warner Blvd.
Burbank, CA 91505
"Actress"

Paul Henreid
18068 Bluesail Drive
Pacific Palisades, CA 90272
"Actor, Director, Producer"

Lance Henriksen
9255 Sunset Blvd. #1115
Los Angeles, CA 90069
"Actor"

Buck Henry
1649 Woods Drive
Los Angeles, CA 90069
"Writer, Producer"

Gregg Henry
121 North San Vicente Blvd.
Beverly Hills, CA 90211
"Actor"

Justin Henry
3 Clark Lane
Rye, NY 10580
"Child Actor"

Rep. Paul B. Henry (MI)
House Cannon Bldg. #215
Washington, DC 20515
"Politician"

Goldie Hawn
9526 Dalegrove Drive
Beverly Hills, CA 90210
"Actress"

Audrey Hepburn
Chalet Rico Bissenstrasse
Gstaad, SWITZERLAND
"Actress"

Katherine Hepburn
244 East 49th Street
New York, NY 10017
"Actress"

Richard Herd
4610 Wooster Avenue
Sherman Oaks, CA 91423
"Actor"

Rep. Wally Herger (CA)
House Longworth Bldg. #1108
Washington, DC 20515
"Politician"

Pee Wee Herman
12725 Ventura Blvd. #H
Studio City, CA 91604
"Actor"

Herman's Hermits
Box 81, Brighton, Oldham
Manchester OLD 5DG ENGLAND
"Rock & Roll Group"

Keith Hernandez
255 East 49th Street #28-D
New York, NY 10017
"Baseball Player"

Kimberly Herrin
P.O. Box 22402
Santa Barbara, CA 93121
"Actress, Model"

Lynn Herring
8485-E Melrose Place
Los Angeles, CA 90069
"Actress"

Bruce Hershensohn
4151 Prospect Avenue
Los Angeles, CA 90027
"Writer, Producer"

Barbara Hershey
9830 Wilshire Blvd.
Beverly Hills, CA 90212
"Actress"

Orel Hershiser
1199 Madia Street
Pasadena, CA 91103
"Baseball Player"

Rep. Dennis Hertel (MI)
House Rayburn Bldg. #2242
Washington, DC 20515
"Politician"

Irene Hervey
10741 Moorpark Street
North Hollywood, CA 91602
"Actress"

Jason Hervey
9200 Sunset Blvd. #625
Los Angeles, CA 90069
"Actor"

Pres. Chaim Herzog
The Knesset
Hakiria Jerusalem, ISRAEL
"Politician"

Werner Herzog
karl-Theodor-Street 18
D-8000 Munich 40 GERMANY
"Film Director"

Whitey Herzog
250 Stadium Plaza
St. Louis, MO 63102
"Baseball Manager"

Howard Hesseman
7146 La Presa
Los Angeles, CA 90068
"Actor, Director"

Charlton Heston
2859 Coldwater Canyon
Beverly Hills, CA 90210
"Actor, Director"

Christopher Hewett
1422 North Sweetzer
Los Angeles, CA 90069
"Actor, Director"

Don Hewitt
555 West 57th Street
New York, NY 10019
"Writer, Producer"

Martin Hewitt
8899 Beverly Blvd.
Los Angeles, CA 90048
"Actor"

Tor Heyerdahl
Hulen Meadows
Ketchum, ID 83340
"Ethnologist, Explorer"

Anne Heywood
9966 Liebe Drive
Beverly Hills, CA 90210
"Actress"

William Hickey
69 West 12th Street
New York, NY 10011
"Actor"

Gov. Walter J. Hickel (AK)
P.O. Box A
Juneau, AK 99811
"Governor"

Catherine Hickland
34-23rd Avenue
Venice, CA 90291
"Actress"

Darryl Hickman
10100 Santa Monica Blvd. #1600
Los Angeles, CA 90067
"Actor, Writer, Director"

Dwayne Hickman
812-16th Street #1
Santa Monica, CA 91403
"Actor"

Catherine Hicks
2801 North Keystone Street
Burbank, CA 91504
"Actress"

Jack Higgins
Septembertide
Mont De La Rocqque
Jersey Channel Islands
ENGLAND
"Writer"

Joel Higgins
246-16th Street
Santa Monica, CA 90402
"Actor"

Anita Hill
300 Timberdell Road
Norman, OK 73019
"Professor of Law"

Hildegarde
230 East 48th Street
New York, NY 10017
"Singer"

Arthur Hill
1515 Clubview Drive
Los Angeles, CA 90024
"Actor"

Benny Hill
2 Queens Gate #7
London SW7 ENGLAND
"Actor, Comedian"

Carla Hill
3125 Chain Bridge Road N.W.
Washington, DC 20018
"Government Official"

Dana Hill
848 Lincoln Blvd. #D
Santa Monica, CA 90403
"Actress"

George Roy Hill
75 Rockefeller Plaza #700
New York, NY 10019
"Film Writer, Director"

Sandy Hill
341-23rd Street
Santa Monica, CA 90402
"TV Reporter, Announcer"

Steven Hill
18 Jill Lane
Monsey, NY 10952
"Actor"

Terrence Hill
P.O. Box 818
Stockbridge, MA 01262
"Actor"

Sir Edmund Hillary
278A Remuera Road
Auckland SE2 NEW ZEALAND
"Mountaineer"

Arthur Hiller
1218 Benedict Canyon
Beverly Hills, CA 90210
"Film Director"

Dame Wendy Hiller
Spindles, Beaconsfield
Stratton Road
Buckinghamshire ENGLAND
"Actress"

John Hillerman
7102 La Presa Drive
Los Angeles, CA 90068
"Actor"

Barron Hilton
28775 Sea Ranch Way
Malibu, CA 90265
"Hotel Executive"

Kimberly Beck Hilton
28775 Sea Ranch Way
Malibu, CA 90265
"Actress"

John Hinkley, Jr.
St. Elizabeth's Hospital
2700 Martin Luther King Avenue
Washington, DC 20005
"Attempted to kill Ronald Reagan"

Art Hindle
3500 West Olive Avenue #1400
Burbank, CA 91505
"Actor"

Gregory Hines
377 West 11th Street, PH. 4-A
New York, NY 10014
"Actor"

Mimi Hines
1605 South 11th Street
Las Vegas, NV 89109
"Actress"

Jurgen Hingsen
Siedweg 92
D-4130 Moers-Schwafhei, GER-
MANY
"Decathlon Athlete"

Darby Hinton
1234 Bel Air Road
Los Angeles, CA 90024
"Actor"

James David Hinton
2808 Oak Point Drive
Los Angeles, CA 90068
"Actor"

Hiroshima
6404 Wilshire Blvd. #800
Los Angeles, CA 90048
"Jazz Group"

Elroy Hirsch
144 Monroe Street
Madison, WI 53711
"Actor"

Judd Hirsch
P.O. Box 25909
Los Angeles, CA 90025
"Actor"

Al Hirschfield
122 East 95th Street
New York, NY 10028
"Caricaturist"

Al Hirt
6135 Catina Street
New Orleans, LA 70114
"Trumpeter"

Alger Hiss
c/o Lawrence Buttenweiser
575 Madison Avenue
New York, NY 10022
"Lawyer"

Shere Hite
Box 5282, FDR Station
New York, NY 10022
"Feminist, Author"

Don Ho
277 Lewers
Honolulu, HI 96814
"Singer, Songwriter"

Rep. Peter Hoagland (NE)
House Longworth Bldg. #1710
Washington, DC 20515
"Politician"

Rose Hobart
23388 Mulholland Drive
Woodland Hills, CA 91364
"Actress"

Olveta Culp Hobby
4747 S.W. Freeway
Houston, TX 77002
"Publisher"

Valerie Hobson
Old Barn Cottage
Upton Gey
Hampshire RG25 2RM
ENGLAND
"Actress"

John Hockenberry
c/o National Public Radio
2025 "M" Street N.W.
Washington, DC 20036
"News Correspondent"

David Hockney
7506 Santa Monica Blvd.
Los Angeles, CA 90046
"Artist"

Rep. George Hochbrueckner (NY)
House Cannon Bldg. #124
Washington, DC 20515
"Politician"

Eddie Hodges
CPC Sand Hill Hospital
Gulfport, MS 39502
"Actor"

Joy Hodges Schiess
RFD #3, Box 254
Katonah, NY 10536
"Actress"

Dustin Hoffman
711 Fifth Avenue
New York, NY 10022
"Actor"

Susanna Hoffs
8033 Sunset Blvd. #3527
Los Angeles, CA 90046
"Singer"

Ben Hogan
2911 West Pafford
Fort Worth, TX 76110
"Golfer"

Hulk Hogan
10901 Winnetka
Chatsworth, CA 91311
"Wrestler"

Paul Hogan
1900 Avenue of the Stars #2270
Los Angeles, CA 90067
"Actor"

Robert Hogan
344 West 89th Street #1B
New York, NY 10024
"Actor"

Drake Hogestyn
9255 Sunset Blvd. #515
Los Angeles, CA 90069
"Actor"

Hal Holbrook
618 South Lucerne Blvd.
Los Angeles, CA 90005
"Actor"

Rebecca Holden
1105-16th Avenue South #C
Nashville, CA 37212
"Actress, Singer"

Jonathan Hole
5024 Balboa Blvd.
Encino, CA 91316
"Actor"

Xaviera Hollander
410 Park Avenue, 10th Floor
New York, NY 10022
"Author"

Jennifer Holliday
9000 Sunset Blvd. #1200
Los Angeles, CA 90069
"Singer, Actress"

Polly Holliday
888-7th Avenue #2500
New York, NY 10106
"Actress"

Earl Holliman
4249 Bellingham Avenue
Studio City, CA 91604
"Actor"

Sen. Ernest F. Hollings (SC)
125 Russell Senator Office Bldg.
Washington, DC 20510
"Politician"

Rep. Clyde Holloway (LA)
House Longworth Bldg. #1206
Washington, DC 20515
"Politician"

Sterling Holloway
4168 Dorsey Street
Los Angeles, CA 90011
"Actor"

Celeste Holm
88 Central Park West
New York, NY 10023
"Actress"

Ian Holm
80 Ivera Court
London W8 ENGLAND
"Actor"

Jennifer Holmes
5329 Sunnyslope
Van Nuys, CA 91401
"Actress"

Larry Holmes
413 Northhampton Street
Easton, PA 18042
"Boxer Champion"

Charlene Holt
151 El Camino Drive
Beverly Hills, CA 90212
"Actress"

Georgia Holt
12341 Hesby Street
North Hollywood, CA 91602
"Cher's Mother"

Jack Holt, Jr.
504 Temple Drive
Harrah, OK 73045
"Actor"

Jennifer Holt
Apartado Postal 170
Cuernavaca, Morelos MEXICO
"Actress"

Victoria Holt
84 Kingston House South
Ennismore Gardens
London EW7 1NG ENGLAND
"Author"

Evander Holyfield
310 Madison Avenue #804
New York, NY 10017
"Boxer Champion"

Rick Honeycutt
2237 Valle Drive
La Habra Heights, CA 90631
"Baseball Player"

Honeymoon Suite
Box 70 - Station C
Queens St. West
Toronto, Ontario
M6J 3M7 CANADA
"Rock & Roll Group"

James Hong
8235 Santa Monica Blvd. #309
Los Angeles, CA 90046
"Actor"

Dr. Hook
P.O. Box 121017
Nashville, TN 37212
"Rock & Roll Group"

Benjamin Hooks
260 Fifth Avenue
New York, NY 10027
"N.A.A.C.P. Executive"

Kevin Hooks
401 South Ardmore Street #119
Los Angeles, CA 90020
"Actor, Director"

Robert Hooks
145 North Valley Street
Burbank, CA 91505
"Actor"

Burt Hooten
3619 Grandby Court
San Antonio, TX 78217
"Baseball Player"

The Hooters
P.O. Box 205
Ardmore, PA 19003
"Rock & Roll Group"

William Hootkins
16 Berners Street
London W1 ENGLAND
"Actor"

Bob Hope
10346 Moopark
North Hollywood, CA 91602
"Actor, Comedian"

Dolores Hope
10346 Moopark
North Hollywood, CA 91602
"Mrs. Bob Hope"

Leslie Hope
151 El Camino Drive
Beverly Hills, CA 90212
"Actress"

Anthony Hopkins
7 High Park Road
Kew, Surrey TW9 3BL ENGLAND
"Actor"

Bo Hopkins
6620 Ethel Avenue
North Hollywood, CA 91606
"Actor"

Rep. Larry Hopkins (KY)
House Rayburn Bldg. #2437
Washington, DC 20515
"Politician"

Linda Hopkins
2055 North Ivar PH
Los Angeles, CA 90068
"Singer"

Telma Hopkins
9200 Sunset Blvd. #428
Los Angeles, CA 90069
"Actress, Singer"

Dennis Hopper
330 Indiana
Venice, CA 90291
"Actor, Director"

Jeffrey Hornaday
132 South Spalding Drive #101
Beverly Hills, CA 90212
"Actor"

Lena Horne
23 East 74th Street
New York, NY 10021
"Singer"

Marilyn Horne
165 West 57th Street
New York, NY 10019
"Mezzo-Soprano"

Harry Horner
728 Brooktree Road
Pacific Palisades, CA 90272
"Film Director"

Bruce Hornsby
P.O. Box 3545
Williamburg, VA 23187
"Rock & Roll Group"

David Horowitz
P.O. Box 49915
Los Angeles, CA 90049
"TV Host"

Anna Maria Horsford
P.O. Box 29765
Los Angeles, CA 90029
"Actress"

Lee Horsley
1941 Cummings Drive
Los Angeles, CA 90027
"Actor"

Rep. Frank Horton (NY)
House Rayburn Bldg. #2108
Washington, DC 20515
"Politician"

Peter Horton
222 Adelaide Drive
Santa Monica, CA 90402
"Actor"

Robert Horton
5317 Anadsol Avenue
Encino, CA 91316
"Actor"

Bob Hoskins
40 Belmont Road
Exeter, Devon, ENGLAND
"Actor"

Robert Hossein
33 rue Galilee
75116 Paris, FRANCE
"Actor"

Rep. Amo Houghton (NY)
House Longworth Bldg. #1217
Washington, DC 20515
"Politician"

James Houghton
8585 Walnut Drive
Los Angeles, CA 90046
"Actor, Writer"

Katharine Houghton
134 Steele Road
West Hartford, CT 06119
"Actress"

Jerry Houser
3236 Brenda Street
Los Angeles, CA 90068
"Actor"

Cissy Houston
2160 North Central Road
Ft. Lee, NJ 07024
"Singer"

Thelma Houston
4296 Mount Vernon
Los Angeles, CA 90008
"Singer"

Whitney Houston
2160 North Central Road
Ft. Lee, NJ 07024
"Singer"

Clint Howard
4286 Clay Bourne Avenue
Burbank, CA 91505
"Actor"

John Howard
14155 Magnolia Blvd. #303
Sherman Oaks, CA 91423
"Actor"

Ken Howard
59 East 54th Street
New York, NY 10022
"Actor"

Ron Howard
1925 Century Park East #2300
Los Angeles, CA 90067
"Actor, Director"

Susan Howard
8505 Amestoy Avenue
Northridge, CA 91325
"Actress"

Gordie Howe
32 Plank Avenue
Glastonbury, CT 06033
"Hockey Player"

Steve Howe
318 West 6th Street
Whitefish, MT 59937
"Baseball Player"

C. Thomas Howell
926 North La Jolla Avenue
Los Angeles, CA 90046
"Actor"

Anne Howells
Milestone, Broomclose
Esher, Surrey, ENGLAND
"Opera Singer"

Frankie Howerd
306-16 Euston Road
London NW 13 ENGLAND
"Comedian"

Sally Ann Howes
19 West 44th Street
New York, NY 10036
"Actress"

Beth Howland
8428-C Melrose Place
Los Angeles, CA 90069
"Actress"

Rep. Steny H. Hoyer (MD)
House Longworth Bldg. #1705
Washington, DC 20515
"Politician"

Rep. Carroll Hubbard, Jr. (KY)
House Rayburn Bldg. #2267
Washington, DC 20515
"Politician"

Hubcaps
P.O. Box 1388
Dover, DE 19003
"Rock & Roll Group"

Season Hubley
2645 Outpost Drive
Los Angeles, CA 90068
"Actress"

Cooper Huckabee
1800 East Cerrito Place #34
Los Angeles, CA 90068
"Actor"

Rep. Jerry Huckaby (LA)
House Rayburn Bldg. #2182
Washington, DC 20515
"Politician"

David Huddleston
10100 Santa Monica Blvd. #1600
Los Angeles, CA 90067
"Actor"

Hudson Brothers
10100 Santa Monica Blvd. #1600
Los Angeles, CA 90067
"Vocal Group"

Ernie Hudson
3800 Barham Blvd. #303
Los Angeles, CA 90068
"Actor"

Hues Corporation
P.O. Box 5295
Santa Monica, CA 90405
"Vocal Trio"

Brent Huff
2203 Ridgemont Drive
Los Angeles, CA 90046
"Actor"

Billy Hufsey
19134 Gayle Place
Tarzana, CA 91356
"Actor"

Daniel Hugh-Kelly
130 West 42nd Street #2400
New York, NY 10036
"Actor"

Barnard Hughes
250 West 94th Street
New York, NY 10025
"Actor"

Finola Hughes
250 West 94th Street
New York, NY 10025
"Actor"

Irene Hughes
500 North Michigan Avenue #1039
Chicago, IL 60611
"Journalist"

Kathleen Hughes
8818 Rising Glen Place
Los Angeles, CA 90069
"Actress"

Rep. William Hughes (NJ)
House Cannon Bldg. #341
Washington, DC 20515
"Politician"

Thomas Hulce
2305 Stanley Hills
Los Angeles, CA 90046
"Actor"

Bobby Hull
15-1430 Maroons Road
Winnipeg, Manitoba R3G OL5
CANADA
"Hockey Player"

Human League
P.O. Box 153
Sheffield SL 1DR ENGLAND
"Rock & Roll Group"

Rev. Rex Hubbard
2690 State Road
Cuyahoga Falls, OH 44421
"Evangelist"

Mary Margaret Humes
P.O. Box 1168-714
Studio City, CA 91604
"Actress, Model"

Englebert Humperdinck
10100 Sunset Blvd.
Los Angeles, CA 90024
"Singer"

Leann Hunley
1888 North Crescent Heights
Los Angeles, CA 90069
"Actress, Model"

Gayle Hunnicutt
174 Regents Park Road
London NW1 ENGLAND
"Actress"

Guy Hunt (AL)
Executive Department
11 South Union Street
Montgomery, AL 36130
"Governor"

Lamar Hunt
1 Arrowhead Drive
Kansas City, MO 64129
"Football Team Owner"

Linda Hunt
457 West 57th Street
New York, NY 10019
"Actress"

Marsha Hunt
400 South Drive #216
Beverly Hills, CA 90212
"Actress"

Peter Hunt
2229 Roscomare Road
Los Angeles, CA 90077
"Film Director"

Holly Hunter
9169 Sunset Blvd.
Los Angeles, CA 90069
"Actress"

Jim "Catfish" Hunter
RR #1, Box 895
Hertford, NC 27944
"Baseball Player"

Kim Hunter
42 Commerce Street
New York, NY 10014
"Actress"

Rachel Hunter
391 North Carolwood Avenue
Los Angeles, CA 90077
"Model"

Ross Hunter
370 Trousdale Place
Beverly Hills, CA 90210
"Film Producer"

Tab Hunter
P.O. Box 1048
La Tierra
Santa Fe, NM 87501
"Actor"

Isabelle Huppert
10 Avenue George V
75008 Paris, FRANCE
"Actress"

Gale Ann Hurd
270 North Canon Drive #1195
Beverly Hills, CA 90210
"Film Producer"

George Hurrell
6702 St. Clair Avenue
North Hollywood, CA 91606
"Photographer"

John Hurt
388/396 Oxford Street
London W1 ENGLAND
"Actor"

Mary Beth Hurt
1619 Broadway #900
New York, NY 90019
"Actress"

William Hurt
R.D. 1, Box 251-A
Palisades, NY 10964
"Actor"

Ferlin Husky
38 Music Square East
Nashville, CA 37203
"Singer, Songwriter"

Rick Husky
13565 Lucca Dive
Pacific Palisades, CA 90272
"Actor, Writer, Producer"

King Hussein I
P.O. Box 1055
Amman, JORDAN
"Royalty"

Saddam Hussein
Al-Sijoud Palace
Baghdad, IRAQ
"Politician"

Olivia Hussey
12097 Summit Circle
Beverly Hills, CA 90210
"Actress"

Ruth Hussey
3361 Don Pablo Drive
Carlsbad, CA 92008
"Actress"

Angelica Huston
2771 Hutton Drive
Beverly Hills, CA 90210
"Actress"

Will Hutchins
3461 Waverly Drive #108
Los Angeles, CA 90027
"Actor"

Josephine Hutchinson
360 East 55th Street
New York, NY 10022
"Actress"

Don Hutson
1265 Lombardi Avenue
Green Bay, WI 54307
"Football Player"

Rep. Earl Hutto (FL)
House Rayburn Bldg. #2435
Washington, DC 20515
"Politician"

Betty Hutton
Harrison Avenue
Newport, RI 02840
"Actress"

Danny Hutton
2437 Horseshoe Canyon Road
Los Angeles, CA 90046
"Singer, Songwriter"

Lauren Hutton
124 Waverly Place
New York, NY10011
"Actress, Model"

Laura Huxley
6233 Mulholland Drive
Los Angeles, CA 90068
"Author"

Joe Hyams
1250 South Beverly Glen #108
Los Angeles, CA 90024
"Author"

Rep. Henry J. Hyde (IL)
House Rayburn Bldg. #2262
Washington, DC 20515
"Politician"

Alex Hyde-White
8271 Melrose Avenue #110
Los Angeles, CA 90046
"Actor"

Martha Hyer Wallis
4100 West Alameda Avenue #204
Toluca Lake, CA 91505
"Actress"

Scott Hylands
10000 Santa Monica Blvd. #305
Los Angeles, CA 90067
"Actor"

Kenneth Hyman
Sherwood House
Tilehouse Lane
Denham, Bucks. ENGLAND
"Film Executive"

Phyllis Hyman
P.O. Box 50
Philadelphia, PA 19103
"Singer"

Joyce Hyser
190 North Canon Drive #201
Beverly Hills, CA 90210
"Actress"

Lee Iacocca
30 Scenic Oaks
Bloomfield Hills, MI 48304
"Automobile Executive"

Janis Ian
611 Broadway #822
New York, NY 10022
"Singer"

Carl Icahn
100 South Bedford Drive
Mt. Kisco, NY 10549
"Businessman"

Ice Cube
(Oshea Jackson)
2155 Van Wick Street
Los Angeles, CA 90047
"Rap Singer"

Ice Tea
9560 Wilshire Blvd. #500
Beverly Hills, CA 90212
"Rap Singer"

Eric Idle
c/o Roger Hancock
8 Waterloo Place
Pall Mall
London SW! ENGLAND
"Actor, Director"

Billy Idol
8209 Melrose Avenue
Los Angeles, CA 90046
"Singer, Songwriter"

Julio Iglesias
5 Indian Creek Drive
Miami, FL 33154
"Singer"

Rev. Ike
4140 Broadway
New York, NY 10004
"Evangelist"

Gary Imhoff
113 North San Vicente Blvd. #202
Beverly Hills, CA 90211
"Actor"

Marty Ingels
8322 Beverly Blvd.
Los Angeles, CA 90048
"Actor"

James Ingram
867 Muirfield Road
Los Angeles, CA 90005
"Singer"

Rep. James M. Inhofe (OK)
House Cannon Bldg. #408
Washington, DC 20515
"Politician"

The Ink Spots
1385 York Avenue #15H
New York, NY 10021
"Vocal Group"

Roy Innis
800 Riverside Drive #6E
New York, NY 10032
"Activist"

Sen. Daniel Inouye (HI)
Senate Hart Bldg. #722
Washington, DC 20510
"Politician"

Adm. Bobby Inman
9430 Research Blvd.
Austin, TX 78759
"Military Leader"

INXS
9229 Sunset Blvd. #710
Los Angeles, CA 90069
"Rock & Roll Group"

Eugene Ionesco
96 Blvd. du Montparnasse
75014 Paris, FRANCE
"Dramatist"

Rep. Andy Ireland (FL)
House Rayburn Bldg. #2466
Washington, DC 20515
"Politician"

John Ireland
P.O. Box 5211
Santa Barbara, CA 93101
"Actor"

Kathy Ireland
1900 Avenue of the Stars #739
Los Angeles, CA 90069
"Model"

The Irish Rovers
747 Cardero Street
Vancouver, B.C. V6E 2G3
CANADA
"Vocal Group"

Iron Maiden
22 Danbury Street
London N1 ENGLAND
"Rock & Roll Group"

Jeremy Irons
194 Old Brompton Street
London SW5 ENGLAND
"Actor"

Michael Ironside
10100 Santa Monica Blvd. #1600
Los Angeles, CA 90067
"Actor"

Monte Irvin
11 Douglas Court South
Homosassa, FL 32646
"Baseball Player"

Amy Irving
11693 San Vicente Blvd. #335
Los Angeles, CA 90049
"Actress"

Hale Irwin
P.O. Box 12458
Palm Beach Garden, FL 33410
"Golfer"

Peter Isaacksen
4635 Placidia Avenue
North Hollywood, CA 91602
"Actor"

Chris Isaak
9560 Wilshire Blvd. #500
Beverly Hills, CA 90212
"Singer"

Isley Brothers
446 Liberty Road
Englewood, NJ 07631
"R&B Group"

Ragib Ismail
Exhibition Stadium
Exhibition Place
Toronto Ontario N6K 3C3
CANADA
"Football Player"

Robert Ito
3918 South Sycamore
Los Angeles, CA 90008
"Actor"

Zeljko Ivanek
145 West 45th Street #1204
New York, NY 10036
"Actor"

Burl Ives
2804 Oaks Avenue
Anacortes, WA 98221
"Actor, Singer"

Jackee
8649 Metz Place
Los Angeles, CA 90069
"Actress"

Anne Jackson
90 Riverside Drive
New York, NY 10024
"Actress"

Bo Jackson
P.O. Box 2517
Auburn, AL 36831
"Baseball & Football Player"

Freddie Jackson
231 West 58th Street
New York, NY 10019
"Singer"

Glenda Jackson
51 Harvey Road
Blackheath
London SE3 ENGLAND
"Actress"

Janet Jackson
12546 The Vista
Los Angeles, CA 90049
"Singer, Songwriter"

Jermaine Jackson
4641 Hayvenhurst Avenue
Encino, CA 91316
"Singer"

Rev. Jesse Jackson
400 "T" Street N.W.
Washington, DC 20001
"Politician, Evangelist"

Jesse Jackson, Jr.
733-15th Street N.W.
Washington, DC 20005
"Son of Jesse Jackson"

Joe Jackson
6 Pembridge Road
Trinity House #200
London W11 ENGLAND
"Singer, Songwriter"

Kate Jackson
1628 Marlay Drive
Los Angeles, CA 90069
"Actress"

LaToya Jackson
301 Park Avenue #1970
New York, NY 10022
"Singer"

Marlon Jackson
4704 Balboa Blvd.
Encino, CA 91436
"Singer"

Mary Ann Jackson
1242 Alessandro Drive
Newbury Park, CA 91320
"Actress"

Maynard Jackson
68 Mitchell
Atlanta, GA 30303
"Mayor of Atlanta, GA"

Melody Jackson
6269 Selma Avenue #15
Los Angeles, CA 90028
"Actress"

Michael Jackson
Neverland Ranch
Los Olivos, CA 93441
"Singer, Songwriter"

Michael Jackson
1420 Moraga Drive
Los Angeles, CA 90049
"Talk Show Host"

Paul Jackson, Jr.
888-7th Avenue #1602
New York, NY 10019
"Actor"

Randy Jackson
4641 Hayvenhurst Drive
Encino, CA 91316
"Singer"

Rebbie Jackson
200 West 51st Street #1410
New York, NY 10019
"Singer"

Reggie Jackson
22 Yankee Hill
Oakland, CA 94616
"Baseball Player"

Sherry Jackson
4933 Encino Avenue
Encino, CA 91316
"Actress"

Stonewall Jackson
6007 Cloverland Drive
Brentwood, TN 37027
"Singer, Songwriter

Stoney Jackson
1602 North Fuller Avenue #102
Los Angeles, CA 90046
"Actor"

Tito Jackson
15255 Del Gado Drive
Sherman Oaks, CA 91403
"Singer"

Victoria Jackson
8330 Lookout Mountain
Los Angeles, CA 90046
"Actress"

Derek Jacobi
22 Chelsham Road
London SW4 ENGLAND
"Actor"

Lou Jacobi
240 Central Park South
New York, NY 10019
"Actor"

Rep. Andrew Jacobs (IN)
House Rayburn Bldg. #2313
Washington, DC 20515
"Politician"

Helen Hull Jacobs
26 Joanne Lane
Weston, CT 06883
"Tennis Player, Author"

Billy Jacoby
P.O. Box 46324
Los Angeles, CA 90046
"Actor"

Scott Jacoby
1006 North Edinburgh Avenue
Los Angeles, CA 90046
"Actor"

Richard Jaeckel
P.O. Box 1818
Santa Monica, CA 90406
"Actor"

Henry Jaffe
7920 Sunset Blvd. #18-D
Los Angeles, CA 90046
"Film Producer"

Bianca Jagger
530 Park Avenue #18-D
New York, NY 10021
"Actress, Model"

Mick Jagger
2 Munro Terrace
London SW10 0DL ENGLAND
"Singer"

John Jakes
P.O. Box 3248
Harbor Town Station
Hilton Head Island, SC 29928
"Author"

Rep. Craig James (FL)
House Longworth Bldg. #1408
Washington, DC 20515
"Politician"

Dennis James
3581 Caribeth Drive
Encino, CA 91316
"TV Personality"

Etta James
4031 Panama Court
Piedmont, CA 94611
"Singer"

John James
10000 Santa Monica Blvd. #305
Los Angeles, CA 90067
"Actor"

Rick James
8116 Mulholland Terrace
Los Angeles, CA 90046
"Singer"

Jan & Dean
6310 Rodgerton Drive
Los Angeles, CA 90068
"Vocal Duo"

Eliot Janeway
15 East 80th Street
New York, NY 10021
"Economist"

Jane's Addiction
8800 Sunset Blvd. #401
Los Angeles, CA 90069
"Rock & Roll Group"

Conrad Janis
300 North Swall Drive #251
Beverly Hills, CA 90211
"Actor"

Vic Janowitz
1966 Jervis Road
Columbus, OH 43221
"Football Player"

Don January
P.O. Box 12458
Palm Beach Garden, FL 33410
"Golfer"

Lois January
225 North Crescent Drive #103
Beverly Hills, CA 90210
"Actress"

Al Jardine
P.O. Box 36
Big Sur, CA 93920
"Singer, Musician"

Claude Jarman, Jr.
11 Dos Encinas
Orinda, CA 94563
"Actor"

Maurice Jarre
27011 Sea Vista Drive
Malibu, CA 90265
"Composer"

Al Jarreau
1621 Morrison
Encino, CA 91316
"Musician"

Tom Jarrell
641 Fifth Avenue
New York, NY 10022
"New Correspondent"

Gen.Wojciech Jaruzelski
Ministerstwo Obrony Narodowej
ul Klonowa 1
009909 Warsaw, POLAND
"Military, Politician"

Graham Jarvis
15351 Via De Las Olas
Pacific Palisades, CA 90272
"Actor"

Lucy Jarvis
171 West 57th Street
New York, NY 10019
"TV Executive, Producer"

Jason & The Scorchers
P.O. Box 120-235
Nashville, TN 37212
"Rock & Roll Group"

Harvey Jason
1280 Sunset Plaza Drive
Los Angeles, CA 90069
"Writer"

Rick Jason
132-B South Lasky Drive
Beverly Hills, CA 90212
"Actor"

Sybil Jason Drake
345 South Elm Drive #208
Beverly Hills, CA 90212
"Actress"

Terry Jastrow
13201 Old Oak Lane
Los Angeles, CA 90049
"Director, Producer"

Jay & The Americans
P.O. Box 262
Carteret, NJ 07008
"Rock & Roll Group"

Michael Jayston
60 St. James's Street
London SW1 ENGLAND
"Actor"

D.J. Jazzy Jeff &
The Fresh Prince
298 Elizabeth Street #100
New York, NY 10012
"Rap Duo"

Gloria Jean
20309 Leadwell
Canoga Park, CA 91303
"Actress"

ZiZi Jeanmaire
22 rue de la Paix
75002 Paris, FRANCE
"Actress"

Sen. Jim Jeffords (VT)
Senate Hart Bldg. #530
Washington, DC 20510
"Politician"

Anne Jeffreys
121 South Bentley Avenue
Los Angeles, CA 90049
"Actress"

Herb Jeffries
P.O. Box C
River Edge, NJ 07601
"Singer"

Lionel Jeffries
8 Harley Street
London W1 ENGLAND
"Actor, Director"

Carol Mayo Jenkins
606 North Larchmont Blvd. #309
Los Angeles, CA 90004
"Actress"

Rep. Ed Jenkins (GA)
House Rayburn Bldg. #2427
Washington, DC 20515
"Politician"

Hayes Alan Jenkins
809 Lafayette Drive
Akron, OH 44303
"Skater"

Jackie "Butch" Jenkins
Route 6, Box 541G
Fairview, NC 28730
"Actor"

Bruce Jenner
P.O. Box 655
Malibu, CA 90265
"Athlete, Actor"

Peter Jennings
47 West 66th Street
New York, NY 10023
"News Anchor"

Waylon Jennings
62 East Starrs Plain
Danbury, CT 06810
"Singer, Songwriter"

Salome Jens
9400 Readcrest Drive
Beverly Hills, CA 90210
"Actress"

Adele Jergens Langan
32108 Village 32
Camarillo, CA 93010
"Actress"

The Jets
P.O. Box 290097
Brooklyn Center
Minneapolis, MN 55429
"R&B Group"

Joan Jett
5700-39th Avenue
Hyattsville, MD 20781
"Rock & Roll Group"

Norman Jewison
23752 Malibu Road
Malibu, CA 90265
"Director, Producer"

Ann Jillian
4241 Woodcliff Road
Sherman Oaks, CA 91403
"Actress, Singer"

Joyce Jillson
64 East Concord Street
Orlando, FL 32801
"Astrologer, Columnist"

Jim & Jesse
P.O. Box 27
Gallatin, TN 37066
"C&W Group"

Marlene Jobert
8-10 Blvd. de Courcelles
75008 Paris, FRANCE
"Actress"

Billy Joel
200 West 57th Street #308
New York, NY 10019
"Singer, Songwriter"

Antonio Carlos Jobin
233 1/2 East 48th Street
New York, NY 10017
"Guitarist, Songwriter"

Steve Jobs
900 Chesapeake Drive
Redwood City, CA 94063
"Computer Executive"

Zita Johann
P.O. Box 302
West Nyack, NY 10994
"Actress"

Ingemar Johansson
c/o Sven Ekstrom
Rakegaton 9 S-41320
Goteborg SWEDEN
"Boxer"

Elton John
32 Galenda Road
London W6 0LT ENGLAND
"Singer, Songwriter"

Pope John Paul II
Palazzo Apostolico Vaticano
Vatican City, ITALY
"Pope"

Tommy John
32 Adams Street
Cresskill, NY 07626
"Baseball Player"

Johnny Hates Jazz
321 Fulham Road
London ZW10 9QL ENGLAND
"Rock & Roll Group"

Glynis Johns
3 Wilshire Blvd. #600
Los Angeles, CA 90048
"Actress"

Anne-Marie Johnson
2606 Ivan Hill Terrace
Los Angeles, CA 90024
"Actress"

Arte Johnson
2725 Bottlebrush Drive
Los Angeles, CA 90077
"Actor, Comedian"

Ben Johnson
2465 Leisure World
Mesa, AZ 85206
"Actor"

Ben Johnson
62 Blacktoft
Scarborough, Ontario M1B 2N6
CANADA
"Track Athlete"

The Brothers Johnson
9200 Sunset Blvd. #823
Los Angeles, CA 90069
"Vocal Group"

Don Johnson
9555 Heather Road
Beverly Hills, CA 90210
"Actor"

Georgann Johnson
218 North Glenroy Place
Los Angeles, CA 90049
"Actress"

Howard Johnson
141-17 11th Avenue
Whitston, NY 11357
"Singer"

Jill Johnson
43 Matheson Road
London W14 ENGLAND
"Actress"

Kevin Johnson
2910 North Central Avenue
Phoenix, AZ 85012
"Basketball Player"

Lamont Johnson
601 Paseo Miramar
Pacific Palisades, CA 90272
"Director, Producer"

Laura Johnson
1917 Weepah
Los Angeles, CA 90046
"Actress"

Mrs. Lady Bird Johnson
LBJ Ranch Stonewall
Austin, TX 78701
"Ex-First Lady"

Lucie Baines Johnson
13809 Research Blvd. #400
Austin, TX 78750
"Ex-President's Daughter"

Lynn-Holly Johnson
335 North Maple Drive #250
Beverly Hills, CA 90210
"Actress"

Earvin "Magic" Johnson
12 Beverly Park
Beverly Hills, CA 90210
"Basketball Player"

Michelle Johnson
10351 Santa Monica Blvd. #211
Los Angeles, CA 90025
"Actress"

Rep. Nancy Johnson (CT)
House Cannon Bldg. #227
Washington, DC 20515
"Politician"

Rafer Johnson
4217 Woodcliff Road
Sherman Oaks, CA 91403
"Actor"

Russell Johnson
6310 San Vicente Blvd. #407
Los Angeles, CA 90048
"Actor"

Rep. Tim Johnson (SD)
House Cannon Bldg. #428
Washington, DC 20515
"Politician"

Van Johnson
405 East 54th Street
New York, NY 10022
"Actor"

Rep. Harry A. Johnston (FL)
House Longworth Bldg. #1028
Washington, DC 20515
"Politician"

Sen. J. Bennett Johnston (LA)
Senate Hart Bldg. #136
Washington, DC 20510
"Politician"

Tom Johnston Band
P.O. Box 878
Sonoma, CA 95476
"Rock & Roll Group"

Allan Jones
10 West 66th Street
New York, NY 10023
"Actor"

Rep. Ben Jones (GA)
House Cannon Bldg. #514
Washington, DC 20515
"Politician"

Chuck Jones
P.O. Box 2319
Costa Mesa, CA 92628
"Animated Cartoon Producer"

Davey Jones
21 Elms Road
Fareham, Hants. ENGLAND
"Singer, Actor"

Dean Jones
5055 Casa Drive
Tarzana, CA 91356
"Actor"

Gemma Jones
3 Goodwins Court
London WC2 ENGLAND
"Actor"

George Jones
38 Music Square East #300
Nashville, TN 37203
"Singer, Songwriter"

The Jones Girls
P.O. Box 6010, Dept. 761
Sherman Oaks, CA 91413
"Vocal Group"

Grace Jones
166 Bank Street
New York, NY 10014
"Model, Actress"

Grandpa Jones
P.O. Box 57
Mountain View, AR 72560
"Singer, Guitarist"

Dame Gwyneth Jones
P.O Box 380
8040 Zurich, SWITZERLAND
"Soprano"

Henry Jones
12221 Tweed Lane
Los Angeles, CA 90049
"Actor"

Jack Jones
3965 Deervale
Sherman Oaks, CA 91403
"Singer, Actor"

James Earl Jones
P.O. Box 55337
Sherman Oaks, CA 91413
"Actor"

Janet Jones
14135 Beresford Drive
Beverly Hills, CA 90210
"Actress"

Jennifer Jones
P.O. Box 2248
Beverly Hills, CA 90213
"Actress"

Jesue Jones
193 Joralemon Street #300
Brooklyn, NY 11201
"Singer"

L.Q. Jones
11938 Collin Street
North Hollywood, CA 91607
"Actor, Director"

Marcia Mae Jones
4541 Hazeltine Avenue #4
Sherman Oaks, CA 91423
"Actress"

Parnelli Jones
20550 Earl Street
Torrance, CA 90503
"Auto Racer"

Quincy Jones
P.O. Box 48248
Los Angeles, CA 90048
"Composer, Producer"

Rickie Lee Jones
888-7th Avenue #1602
New York, NY 10019
"Singer, Songwriter"

Sam J. Jones
10100 Santa Monica Blvd. #1600
Los Angeles, CA 90067
"Actor"

Shirley Jones
701 North Oakhurst Drive
Beverly Hills, CA 90210
"Actress"

Terry Jones
25 Newman Street
London W1 ENGLAND
"Actor, Writer, Director"

Tom Jones
363 Copa de Oro Drive
Los Angeles, CA 90077
"Singer"

Tommy Lee Jones
P.O. Box 966
San Saba, TX 76877
"Actor"

Rep. Walter B. Jones (NC)
House Cannon Bldg. #241
Washington, DC 20515
"Politician"

Erica Jong
121 Davis Hills Road
Weston, CT 06883
"Poet, Author"

Rep. Jim Jontz (IN)
House Longworth Bldg. #1317
Washington, DC 20515
"Politician"

Barbara Jordan
L.B.J. School
University of Texas
Austin, TX 78705
"Ex-Congresswoman"

Hamilton Jordan
1100 Spring Street #450
Atlanta, GA 30344
"Former Government Offical"

James Carroll Jordan
8333 Lookout Mountain Avenue
Los Angeles, CA 90046
"Actor"

Michael Jordan
980 N. Michigan Avenue #1600
Chicago, IL 60611
"Basketball Player"

Richard Jordan
3704 Carbon Canyon
Malibu, CA 90265
"Actor"

Vernon E. Jordan, Jr.
1333 New Hampshire Avenue NW
Suite #400
Washington, DC 20036
"Politician"

Will Jordan
435 West 57th Street #10-F
New York, NY 10019
"Comedian"

William Jordan
10806 Lindbrook Avenue #4
Los Angeles, CA 90024
"Actor"

Jackie Joseph
111 North Valley
Burbank, CA 91505
"Actress, Writer"

Erland Josephson
Valhallavagen 10
11-422 Stockholm, SWEDEN
"Actor"

Louis Jourdan
1139 Maybrook
Beverly Hills, CA 90210
"Actor"

Journey
P.O. Box 404
San Francisco, CA 94101
"Rock & Roll Group"

Elaine Joyce
724 North Roxbury Drive
Beverly Hills, CA 90210
"Actress"

Odette Joueux
1 rue Seguier
75006 Paris, FRANCE
"Writer"

Jackie Joyner-Kersee
20214 Leadwell
Canoga Park, CA 91304
"Track & Field Athlete"

Wally Joyner
2186 Tudor Castle Way
Decatur, GA 30033
"Baseball Player"

Judas Priest
3 East 54th Street #1400
New York, NY 10022
"Raggae Group"

Edward Judd
25 Cottenham Park Road
Wimbledon
London SW20 ENGLAND
"Actor"

The Judds
P.O. Box 17087
Nashville, TN 37217
"Vocal Duo"

Raul Julia
200 West 54th Street #7-G
New York, NY 10019
"Actor"

Gordon Jump
1631 Hillcrest
Glendale, CA 91202
"Actor, Director"

Katy Jurado
Apartado Postal 209
Cuernavaca, Moro. MEXICO
"Actress"

Sonny Jurgensen
P.O. Box 53
Mt. Vernon, VA 22121
"Football Player"

Ish Kabibble
(a.k.a. Mervyn Bogue)
P.O. Box 536
Indio, CA 92201
"Trumpeter, Singer, Comedian"

Pauline Kael
2 Berkshire Heights Raod
Great Barrington, MA 02130
"Film Critic, Author"

Marvin Kalb
4001 Nebraska Avenue N.W
Washington, DC 20016
"Journalist"

Patricia Kalember
P.O. Box 5617
Beverly Hills, CA 90210
"Actress"

Madeline Kahn
975 Park Avenue #9A
New York, NY 10028
"Actress, Singer"

Al Kaline
945 Timberlake Drive
Bloomfield Hills, MI 48013
"Baseball Player"

Helena Kallianides
12830 Mulholland Drive
Beverly Hills, CA 90210
"Actress, Writer, Director"

Herbert Kalmbach
1056 Santiago Drive
Newport Beach, CA 92660
"Watergate Participant"

Stanley Kamel
9300 Wilshire Blvd. #410
Beverly Hills, CA 90210
"Actor"

Steve Kampmann
812 Jacon Way
Pacific Palisades, CA 90272
"Actor, Writer"

Steven Kanaly
3611 Longridge Avenue
Sherman Oaks, CA 91423
"Actor"

Sean Kanan
1999 Avenue of the Stars #2850
Los Angeles, CA 90067
"Actor, Karate Expert"

Big Daddy Kane
151 El Camino Drive
Beverly Hills, CA 90212
"Rap Singer"

Bob Kane
8455 Fountain Avenue #725
Los Angeles, CA 90069
"Cartoonist"

Carol Kane
1416 North Havenhurst #1-C
Los Angeles, CA 90046
"Actress"

Fay Kanin
653 Ocean Front
Santa Monica, CA 90402
"Screenwriter"

Garson Kanin
210 Central Park South
New York, NY 10019
"Writer, Producer"

Stan Kann
570 North Rossmore Avenue
Los Angeles, CA 90004
"Actor"

Rep. Paul Kanjorski (PA)
House Cannon Bldg. #424
Washington, DC 20515
"Politician"

Hal Kanter
15941 Woodvale Road
Encino, CA 91316
"Writer, Producer"

Gabriel Kaplan
9551 Hidden Valley Road
Beverly Hills, CA 90210
"Comedian, Actor"

Marvin Kaplan
1418 North Highland Avenue #102
Los Angeles, CA 90028
"Actor"

Rep. Marcy Kaptur (OH)
House Longworth Bldg. #1228
Washington, DC 20515
"Politician"

James Karen
4455 Los Feliz Blvd. #807
Los Angeles, CA 90027
"Actor"

Anna Karina
12 rue St. Severin
75005 Paris, FRANCE
"Actress"

John Karlen
428 East Larraine
Glendale, CA 91207
"Actor"

Bela Karolyi
17911 Grand Valley Circle
Houston, TX 77090
"Gymnastic Coach"

Alex Karras
7943 Woodrow Wilson Drive
Los Angeles, CA 90046
"Football Player, Actor"

Yousuf Karsh
18 East 62nd Street
New York, NY 10003
"Photographer"

Lawrence Kasdan
708 North Elm Drive
Beverly Hills, CA 90210
"Director, Producer"

Casey Kasem
138 North Mapleton Drive
Los Angeles, CA 90077
"Radio-TV Personality"

Jean Kasem
138 North Mapleton Drive
Los Angeles, CA 90077
"Radio-TV Personality"

Lawrence Kasha
2229 Gloaming Drive
Beverly Hills, CA 90210
"TV Writer, Producer"

Rep. John R. Kasich (OH)
House Longworth Bldg. #1133
Washington, DC 20515
"Politician"

Sen. Nancy Kassebaum (KS)
302 Russell Office Bldg.
Washington, DC 20510
"Politician"

Dr. Irene Kassorla
10231 Charing Cross Road
Los Angeles, CA 90024
"Psychologist, Author"

Sen. Bob Kasten (WI)
Senate Hart Bldg. #110
Washington, DC 20510
"Politician"

William Katt
25218 Malibu Road
Mailbu, CA 90265
"Actor"

Julie Kayner
25154 Malibu Road #2
Malibu, CA 90265
"Actress"

Dianne Kay
1559 Palisades Drive
Pacific Palisades, CA 90272
"Actress"

Monte Kay
7655 Curson Terrace
Los Angeles, CA 90046
"Talent Agent"

Caren Kaye
217-16th Street
Santa Monica, CA 90402
"Actress"

Melvina Kaye
P.O. Box 6085
Burbank, CA 90510
"Singer"

Elia Kazan
174 East 95th Street
New York, NY 10128
"Director, Producer"

Lainie Kazan
9903 Santa Monica Blvd #283
Beverly Hills, CA 90212
"Singer, Actress"

James Keach
9229 Sunset Blvd. #607
Los Angeles, CA 90069
"Actor"

Stacy Keach, Jr.
27525 Winding Way
Malibu, CA 90265
"Actor"

Jane Kean
4332 Coldwater Canyon
Studio City, CA 91604
"Actress"

Diane Keane
23 Primrose Hill
Charleston Mackrell
Nr. Someton, Summerset
ENGLAND
"Actress"

Noel P. Keane
930 Mason
Dearborn, MI 48124
"Surrogate Birth Lawyer"

Diane Keaton
2255 Verde Oak Drive
Los Angeles, CA 90068
"Actress, Director"

Michael Keaton
9830 Wilshire Blvd.
Beverly Hills, CA 90212
"Actor"

Lila Kedrova
50 Forest Manor Road #3
Willowdale Ontario M2J 1M1
CANADA
"Actress"

Don Keefer
4146 Allot Avenue
Sherman Oaks, CA 91403
"Actor"

Howard Keel
15353 Longbow Drive
Sherman Oaks, CA 91403
"Actor, Singer"

Ruby Keeler
71029 Early Time Road
Rancho Mirage, CA 92270
"Actress"

Bob Keeshan
(Capt. Kangaroo)
40 West 57th Street #1600
New York, NY 10019
"TV Host"

Garrison Keillor
300 Central Park West
New York, NY 10024
"Author, Radio Personality"

Harvey Keitel
P.O. Box 49
Palisades, NY 10964
"Actor"

Brian Keith
23449 Malibu Colony Road
Malibu, CA 90265
"Actor"

David Keith
8221 Sunset Blvd.
Los Angeles, CA 90069
"Actor"

Penelope Keith
66 Berkeley House
Hay Hill
London SW3 ENGLAND
"Actress"

Marthe Keller
5 rue St. Dominique
75007 Paris, FRANCE
"Actress"

Mary Page Keller
24789 Master Cup Way
Valencia, CA 91355
"Actress"

Sally Kellerman
7944 Woodrow Wilson Drive
Los Angeles, CA 90046
"Actress"

DeForrest Kelley
822 South Robertson Blvd. #200
Los Angeles, CA 90035
"Actor"

Kitty Kelley
3037 Dunbarton Avenue N.W.
Washington, DC 20007
"Author"

Gene Kelly
725 North Rodeo Drive
Beverly Hills, CA 90210
"Actor, Dancer"

Jack Kelly
P.O. Box 31
Huntington Beach, CA 92648
"Actor"

Jim Kelly
One Bill Drive
Orchard Park, NY 14127
"Football Player"

Paula Kelly
1801 Avenue of Stars #1250
Los Angeles, CA 90067
"Actress, Dancer"

Petra Kelly
Bundeshaus-HT 718
D-5300 Bonn
GERMANY
"Politician"

Roz Kelly
5614 Lemp Avenue
North Hollywood, CA 91601
"Actress"

Linda Kelsey
1999 Avenue of the Stars #2850
Los Angeles, CA 90067
"Actress"

Ed Kemmer
11 Riverside Drive #17PE
New York, NY 10022
"Actor"

Sec. Jack Kemp
4571-7th Street S.W.
Washington, DC 20410
"Secretary of H.U.D."

Suzy Kendall
Dentham House #4
The Mount, Hampstead
NW 3 ENGLAND
"Actress"

The Kendalls
1522 Demonbreun Street
Nashville, TN 37203
"C&W Group"

Eddie Kendricks
200 West 57th Street #907
New York, NY 10019
"Singer"

Adams Kennedy
P.O. Box 679
Kent, CT 06757
"Screenwriter"

Justice Anthony Kennedy
1-1st Street N.E.
Washington, DC 20543
"Supreme Court Justice"

Burt Kennedy
13138 Magnolia Blvd.
Sherman Oaks, CA 91423
"Film Writer, Director"

Caroline Kennedy-Schlosseberg
888 Park Avenue
New York, NY 10021
"Ex-President's Daughter"

Sen. Edward Kennedy (MA)
315 Russell Office Bldg.
Washington, DC 20510
"Politician"

Ethel Kennedy
1147 Chain Bridge Road
McLean, VA 22101
"Mrs. Robert Kennedy"

George Kennedy
10100 Santa Monica Blvd. #700
Los Angeles, CA 90067
"Actor"

Jayne Kennedy
944-17th Street #1
Santa Monica, CA 90403
"Actress, Model"

Joan Kennedy
Squaw Island
Hyannisport, MA 02647
"Ted Kennedy's Ex-Wife"

John F. Kennedy, Jr.
1041 Fifth Avenue
New York, NY 10028
"Ex-President's Son"

Rep. Joseph Kennedy II (MA)
1208 Longworth House Bldg.
Washington, DC 20510
"Politician"

Leon Isaac Kennedy
P.O. Box 361039
Los Angeles, CA 90036
"Actor, Producer"

Mimi Kennedy
10100 Santa Monica Blvd. #1600
Los Angeles, CA 90067
"Actress"

Robert F. Kennedy, Jr.
78 North Broadway
White Plains, CA 10603
"Robert Kennedy's Son"

Rose Fitzgerald Kennedy
The Compond
Hyannis, MA 02647
"Ex-President's Mother"

Ted Kennedy, Jr.
636 Chain Bridge Road
McLean, VA 22101
"Sen. Ted Kennedy's Son"

Rep. Barbara Kennelly (CT)
House Cannon Bldg. #204
Washington, DC 20515
"Politician"

Mr. Kenneth
19 East 54th Street
New York, NY 10022
"Hairstylist"

Patsy Kensit
50 Lisson S., Unit 18
London NW1 5DF ENGLAND
"Actress"

Jean Kent
22-23 Marlebone High #80
London W1 ENGLAND
"Actress"

Lord Philip Kentner
1 Mallord Street
London SW3 ENGLAND
"Musician"

Kentucky Headhunters
447 East 65th Street #3C
New York, NY 10021
"Music Group"

Shell Kepler
3123 Belden Drive
Los Angeles, CA 90068
"Actress"

Ken Kercheval
P.O. Box 1350
Los Angeles, CA 90078
"Actor"

Kirk Kerkorian
9333 Wilshire Blvd.
Beverly Hills, CA 90210
"Business Executive"

Joanna Kerns
178 North Carmelina
Los Angeles, CA 90049
"Actress"

Sandra Kerns
620 Resolano Drive
Pacific Palisades, CA 90272
"Actress"

Deborah Kerr
Los Monteras
E-29600 Marbella
Malaga, SPAIN
"Actress"

Jean Kerr
1 Beach Avenue
Larchmont, NY 10538
"Dramatist"

John Kerr
1570 Abajo Drive
Monterey Park, CA 91754
"Actor"

Linda Kerridge
9812 West Olympic Blvd.
Beverly Hills, CA 90212
"Actress, Model"

Sen. Robert Kerrey (NE)
Senate Hart Bldg. #316
Washington, DC 20510
"Politician"

Sen. John Kerry (MA)
Senate Russell Bldg. #421
Washington, DC 20510
"Politician"

Brian Kerwin
10402 1/2 Wheatland Avenue
Sunland, CA 91040
"Actor"

Hank Ketcham
P.O. Box 800
Pebble Beach, CA 93953
"Cartoonist"

Ted Key
1694 Glenhardie Road
Wayne, PA 19087
"Cartoonist"

Evelyn Keyes
999 North Doheny Drive
Los Angeles, CA 90069
"Actress"

Mark Keyloun
3500 West Olive Avenue #1400
Burbank, CA 91505
"Actor"

Persis Khambatta
113 North San Vicente Blvd. #202
Beverly Hills, CA 90211
"Actress, Model"

Chaka Khan
P.O. Box 3125
Beverly Hills, CA 90212
"Singer"

Princess Yasmin Khan
279 Central Park West
New York, NY 10024
"Royalty"

Adnan Khashoggi
P.O. Box 6
Riyadh SAUDIA-ARABIA
"Arms Dealer"

Victor Kiam
60 Main Street
Bridgeport, CT 06602
"Businessman"

Billy Kidd
P.O. Box 803291
Santa Clarita, CA 91380
"Skier"

Margot Kidder
335 North Maple Drive #250
Beverly Hills, CA 90210
"Actress"

Nicole Kidman
12725-H Ventura Blvd.
Studio City, CA 91604
"Actress"

Richard Kiel
500 Grand Avenue
South Pasadena, CA 91030
"Actor"

Kaleena Kiff
1800 North Vine Street #120
Los Angeles, CA 90028
"Actress"

Terry Kilburn
Meadowbrook Theater
Oberland University
Walton & Squirrel
Rochester, MI 48063
"Actor, Teacher"

Rep. Dale E. Kildee (MI)
House Rayburn Bldg. #2239
Washington, DC 20515
"Politician"

Richard Kiley
Ryerson Road
Warwick, NY 10990
"Actor"

Harmon Killebrew
R.R. 2, Box 626
Ontario, OR 97914
"Baseball Player"

Jean-Claude Killey
73 Val-d'Isere
FRANCE
"Skier"

Val Kilmer
P.O. Box 362
Tesuque, NM 87574
"Actress"

James L. Kilpatrick
White Walnut Hill
Woodville, VA 22749
"Columnist, Journalist"

Lincoln Kilpatrick
12834 McLennan Avenue
Granada Hills, CA 91344
"Actor"

Bruce Kimball
405 Beverly Blvd.
Brandon, FL 33511
"Swimmer"

Bruce Kimmel
12230 Otsego Street
North Hollywood, CA 91607
"Writer, Director"

Roslyn Kind
8871 Burton Way, #303
Los Angeles, CA 90048
"Actress"

Alan King
888-7th Avenue, 38th Floor
New York, NY 10106
"Comedian, Actor"

Andrea King
1225 Sunset Plaza Drive #3
Los Angeles, CA 90069
"Actress"

B.B. King
P.O. Box 4396
Las Vegas, CA 89107
"Singer, Guitarist"

Ben E. King
1301 Princeton Road
Teaneck, NJ 07666
"Singer, Songwriter"

Billie Jean King
101 West 79th Street
New York, NY 10024
"Tennis Player"

Cammie King Conlon
6000 North Highway #1
Little River, CA 95456
"Actress"

Carole King
P.O. Box 7308
Carmel, CA 93921
"Singer, Songwriter"

Coretta Scott King
234 Sunset Avenue N.W.
Atlanta, GA 30314
"Mrs. Martin Luther King, Jr."

Don King
968 Pinehurst Drive
Las Vegas, NV 89109
"Fight Promoter"

Evelyn "Champagne" King
119 West 57th Street #901
New York, NY 10019
"Singer"

Larry King
111 Massachusetts Avenue N.W.
Suite #300
Washington, DC 20001
"Radio-TV Personality"

Mabel King
7100 Teesdale Avenue
North Hollywood, CA 91605
"Actress"

Perry King
3647 Wrightwood Drive
Studio City, CA 91604
"Actor"

Regina King
3800 Barham Blvd. #303
Los Angeles, CA 90068
"Actress"

Stephen King
49 Florida Avenue
Bangor, ME 04401
"Novelist"

Tony King
9615 Brighton Way
Beverly Hills, CA 90210
"Illustrator"

Zalman King
1393 Rose Avenue
Venice, CA 90291
"Writer"

Roger Kingdom
146 South Fairmont Street #1
Pittsburg, PA 15206
"Track & Field Athlete"

Ben Kingsley
Stratford Upon Avon
New Penworth House
Warwickshire 0V3 7QX
ENGLAND
"Actor"

The Kingsmen
P.O. Box 2622
Asheville, NC 28801
"Rock & Roll Group"

The Kingston Trio
P.O. Box 34397
San Diego, CA 92103
"Vocal Trio"

Sam Kinison
32248 Pacific Coast Hwy.
Malibu, CA 90265
"Comedian, Actor"

The Kinks
29 Rushton Mews
London W11 1RB ENGLAND
"Rock & Roll Group"

Kathleen Kinmont
8551 Wonderland
Los Angeles, CA 90046
"Actress"

Leonid Kinskey
11652 Huston
North Hollywood, CA 91604
"Actor"

Klaus Kinski
9169 Sunset Blvd.
Los Angeles, CA 90069
"Actor"

Nastassja Kinski
11 West 81st Street
New York, NY 10024
"Actress, Model"

Durward Kirby
Rt. 37, Box 374
Sherman, CT 06784
"Screenwriter"

George Kirgo
178 North Carmelina
Los Angeles, CA 90049
"TV Writer"

Phyllis Kirk Bush
1225 Sunset Plaza Drive #1
Los Angeles, CA 90069
"Actress"

Tommy Kirk
833 South Beacon Avenue
Los Angeles, CA 90017
"Actor"

Clare Kirkconnell
515 South Irving Blvd.
Los Angeles, CA 90020
"Actress"

Billy Kirkland
1112 North Sherbourne Drive
Los Angeles, CA 90069
"Singer"

Gelsey Kirkland
945 Fifth Avenue
New York, NY 10021
"Dancer"

Lane Kirkland
815-16th Street N.W.
Washington, DC 20006
"Union Executive"

Sally Kirkland
1930 Ocean Avenue
Santa Monica, CA 90405
"Actress"

Jeane Kirkpatrick
6812 Granby Street
Bethesda, MD 20817
"Politician"

Dorothy Kirsten French
271 Tavistock Avenue
Los Angeles, CA 90049
"Soprano"

Terry Kiser
5750 Wilshire Blvd. #512
Los Angeles, CA 90036
"Actor, Comedian"

KISS
6363 Sunset Blvd. #417
Los Angeles, CA 90028
"Rock & Roll Group"

Dr. Henry Kissinger
435 East 52nd Street
New York, NY 10022
"Politician"

Michael Kitchen
4 Windmill Street
London W1P 1HF ENGLAND
"Actor"

Tawny Kitaen
17820 Merridy Street #16
Northridge, CA 91325
"Actress"

Eartha Kitt
1524 Labaig Avenue
Los Angeles, CA 90028
"Singer, Actress"

Franz Klammer
Mooswald 22
A-9712 Friesach, AUSTRIA
"Skier"

Rep. Gerald D. Kleczka (WI)
House Cannon Bldg. #226
Washington, DC 20515
"Politician"

Calvin Klein
55 Central Park West #19-F
New York, NY 10023
"Fashion Designer"

Werner Klemperer
44 West 62nd Street, 10th Floor.
New York, NY 10023
"Actor"

Kevin Kline
136 East 57th Street #1001
New York, NY 10022
"Actor"

Richard Kline
14322 Mulholland Drive
Los Angeles, CA 9007
"Actor"

Robert Kline
Edgehill Sleepy Hollow Road
Briarcliff Manor, NY 10510
"Comedian, Actor"

Don Klosterman
2220 Avenue of the Stars #2502
Los Angeles, CA 90067
"Football Player"

Patricia Klous
18095 Karen Drive
Encino, CA 91316
"Actress"

Jack Klugman
22548 Pacific Coast Highway #8
Malibu, CA 90265
"Actor, Writer"

Hildegard Knef
Maria-Theresia-Street
800 Munich Bogenhausen
GERMANY
"Actress, Singer"

Gladys Knight
98 Cuttermill Road
Box 82 #342-A
Great Neck, NY 11022
"Singer"

Holly Knight
1585 Stone Canyon Road
Los Angeles, CA 90077
"Singer, Songwriter"

Michael E. Knight
9301 Wilshire Blvd. #312
Beverly Hills, CA 90210
"Actor"

Shirley Knight
24 Mailmains Way
Beckenham Kent ENGLAND
"Actress"

Don Knotts
1854 South Beverly Glen #402
Los Angeles, CA 90025
"Actor"

Patric Knowles
6243 Randi Avenue
Woodland Hills, CA 91367
"Actor"

Alexander Knox
8 Harley Street
London W1N 2AB ENGLAND
"Actor"

Buddy Knox
P.O. BOX 244, Dominion City
Manitoba R0A 0H0 CANADA
"Singer, Songwriter"

Chuck Knox
11220 N.E. 53rd Street
Kirkland, WA 98033
"Football Coach"

Elyse Knox-Harmon
320 North Gunston
Los Angeles, CA 90049
"Actress"

Terence Knox
1440 South Sepulvede Blvd. #200
Los Angeles, CA 90025
"Actor"

Mayor Edward I. Koch
1290 Avenue of the Stars
30th Floor
New York, NY 10104
"Ex-Mayor"

Howard W. Koch
704 North Crescent Drive
Beverly Hills, CA 90210
"Director, Producer"

Fanny Blankers Koen
"Nachtegaal"
Strat. NO.67
Utrecht HOLLAND
"Track Athlete"

Walter Koenig
P.O. Box 4395
North Hollywood, CA 91607
"Actor, Writer"

Helmut Kohl
Marbacher Str. 11
D-6700 Ludwigshafen/Rhein
GERMANY
"Politician"

Sen. Herbert Kohl (WI)
Senate Hart Bldg. #330
Washington, DC 20510
"Politician"

Susan Kohner
710 Mark Avenue #14-E
New York, NY 10021
"Actress"

Rep. Jim Kolbe (AZ)
House Cannon Bldg. #410
Washington, DC 20515
"Politician"

Mayor Teddy Kollek
22 Jaffa Road
Jerusalem, ISRAEL
"Politician"

Rep. Joe Kolter (PA)
House Cannon Bldg. #212
Washington, DC 20515
"Politician"

James Komack
617 North Beverly Drive
Beverly Hills, CA 90210
"Actor, Writer, Director"

Dorothy Konrad
10650 Missouri Avenue #2
Los Angeles, CA 90025
"Actress"

Kool & The Gang
641 Lexington Avenue #1450
New York, NY 10022
"R & B Group""

Kool Moe Dee
151 El Camino Drive
Beverly Hills, CA 90212
"Rap Singer"

Dean R. Koontz
P.O. Box 5686
Orange, CA 92613
"Writer"

Dr. C. Everett Koop
1123 Rock Creek Road
Glandwyne, PA 19035
"Ex-Surgeon General"

Bernie Kopel
19413 Olivos
Tarzana, CA 91356
"Actor, Writer"

Karen Kopins
10989 Bluffside Drive
Studio City, CA 91604
"Actress"

Ted Koppel
1717 DeSales N.W. #300
Washington, DC 20036
"TV Host"

Olga Korbut
Youg Communist League Street
Minsk, Russia
"Gymnast"

Michael Korda
1230 Avenue of the Americas
New York, NY 10020
"Writer"

Harvey Korman
10960 Wilshire Blvd. #826
Los Angeles, CA 90024
"Actor, Director"

Lauren Koslow
2020 Avenue of the Stars #500
Los Angeles, CA 90067
"Actress"

Rep. Peter Kostmayer (PA)
House Rayburn Bldg. #2436
Washington, DC 20515
"Politician"

Yaphet Kotto
1930 Century Park West #303
Los Angeles, CA 90067
"Actor"

Martin Kove
8705 Wonderland Park
Los Angeles, CA 90046
"Actor"

Ron Kovic
507 North Lucia Avenue
Redondo Beach, CA 90277
"Author, Soldier"

Harley Jane Kozak
8730 Sunset Blvd. #480
Los Angeles, CA 90069
"Actor"

Linda Kozlowski
1900 Avenue of the Stars #2270
Los Angeles, CA 90067
"Actress"

Jeroen Krabbe
107 Van Eeghenstraat
1071 EZ Amsterdam, HOLLAND
"Actor"

Ken Kragen
240 Baroda
Los Angeles, CA 90077
"Talent Agent"

Jack Kramer
231 North Glenroy Place
Los Angeles, CA 90049
"Tennis Player"

Stanley Kramer
12386 Ridge Circle
Los Angeles, CA 90049
"Film Director"

Stephanie Kramer
8455 Beverly Blvd. #505
Los Angeles, CA 90048
"Actress, Director"

Judith Krantz
166 Groverton Place
Los Angeles, CA 90077
"Author"

Lenny Kravitz
6435 Balcom
Reseda, CA 91335
"Singer"

Paul Kreppel
14300 Killion Street
Van Nuys, CA 91401
"Actor"

Kreskin
201-A North Robertson Blvd.
Beverly Hills, CA 90211
"Psychic"

Robbie Krieger
2548 Hutton Drive
Beverly Hills, CA 90210
"Actress'

Alice Krige
9830 Wilshire Blvd.
Beverly Hills, CA 90212
"Actress'

Sylvia Kristal
8955 Norma Place
Los Angeles, CA 90069
"Actress"

Kris Kristofferson
3179 Sumack Ridge
Malibu, CA 90265
"Singer, Actor, Writer"

Joan Kroc
8939 Villa La Jolla Drive #201
La Jolla, CA 92037
"Ray Kroc's Widower"

Marty Krofft
7710 Woodrow Wilson Drive
Los Angeles, CA 90046
"Puppeteer, Producer"

Sid Krofft
7710 Woodrow Wilson Drive
Los Angeles, CA 90046
"Puppeteer, Producer"

Hardy Kruger
P.O. Box 726
Crestline, CA 92325
"Actor"

Jack Kruschen
6948 Vista del Mar
Playa del Rey, CA 90291
"Actor"

Tony Kubek
8323 North Shore Road
Menosha, WI 43952
"Sportscaster"

Stanley Kubrick
P.O. Box 123
Borehamwood, Herts.
ENGLAND
"Film Director"

Bowie Kuhn
320 North Murray Avenue
Ridgewood, NJ 07450
"Ex-Baseball Commissioner"

Mitch Kupchak
1123 Manning Avenue
Los Angeles, CA 90024
"Basketball Player"

Irv Kupcinet
5400 North St. Louis Avenue
Chicago, IL 60625
"Columnist, TV Host"

Charles Kuralt
524 West 57th Street
New York, NY 10019
"Journalist"

Akira Kurosawa
Matsubara-Cho
Setagaya-Ku
Tokyo, JAPAN
"Film Director"

Swoosie Kurtz
320 Central Park West
New York, NY 10025
"Actress"

Nancy Kwan
4154 Woodman Avenue
Sherman Oaks, CA 91403
"Actress"

Burt Kwouk
235-241 Regent Street
London W1A 2JT ENGLAND
"Actor"

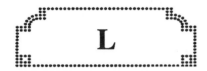

L

Patti LaBelle
1212 Grennox Road
Wynnewood, PA 19096
"Singer, Actress

Matthew Laborteaux
15301 Ventura Blvd. #345
Sherman Oaks, CA 91405
"Actor"

Patrick Laborteaux
1450 Belfast Drive
Los Angeles, CA 90069
"Actor"

Jerry Lacy
28980 Newton Canyon
Malibu, CA 90265
"Actor, Writer, Director"

Alan Ladd, Jr.
1010 North Crescent Drive
Beverly Hills, CA 90210
"Film Executive"

Cheryl Ladd
2485 Janin Way
Solvang, CA 93463
"Actress, Singer"

David Ladd
9212 Hazen Drive
Beverly Hills, CA 90210
"Actor"

Diane Ladd
8440 De Longpre Avenue #203
Los Angeles, CA 90069
"Actress"

Margaret Ladd
444-21st Street
Santa Monica, CA 90402
"Actress"

Rep. John J. LaFalce (NY)
House Rayburn Bldg. #2367
Washington, DC 20515
"Politician"

Dr. Arthur Laffer
P.O. Box 1167
Rancho Santa Fe, CA 92067
"Economist"

Perry Lafferty
335 South Bristol
Los Angeles, CA 90049
"TV Executive"

Guy LaFleur
2313 St. Catherine Street
West Montreal, PQ H3H 1N2
CANADA
"Hockey Player"

Rep. Robert Lagomarsion (CA)
House Rayburn Bldg. #2332
Washington, DC 20515
"Politician"

Christine Lahti
10 West 86th Street
New York, NY 10024
"Actress"

Francis Lai
23 rue Franklin
F-75016 Paris, FRANCE
"Composer"

Cleo Laine
101 West 79th Street
New York, NY 10024
"Singer"

Frankie Laine
352 San Gorgonia Street
San Diego, CA 92106
"Singer, Actor"

Melvin Laird
1730 Rhode Island Avenue
Washington, DC 20036
"Politician"

Ricki Lake
7419 Woodrow Wilson Drive
Los Angeles, CA 90068
"Actress"

Jack LaLanne
P.O. Box 1249
Burbank, CA 91507
"Exercise Instructor"

Donny Lalonde
33 Howard Street
Toronto, Ont. M4X 1J6
CANADA
"Boxer"

Hedy Lamarr
568 Orange Drive #47
Altamonte Springs, FL 32701
"Actress"

Lorenzo Lamas
641 South Mariposa Drive
Burbank, CA 91506
"Actor"

Gil Lamb
7755 Madrid Circle
Palm Springs, CA 92262
"Actor"

Christopher Lambert
9220 Sunset Blvd. #201
Los Angeles, CA 90069
"Actor"

Jack Lambert
222 Highland Drive
Carmel, CA 93921
"Football Player"

Jerry Lambert
P.O. Box 25371
Charlotte, NC 28212
"Singer"

L.W. Lambert
Route #1
Olin, NC 28868
"C&W Singer"

Jake Lamotta
400 East 57th Street
New York, NY 10022
"Boxer"

Dorothy Lamour
5309 Goodland Avenue
North Hollywood, CA 91607
"Actress"

Richard Lamparski
924-D Garden Street
Santa Barbara, CA 93101
"Author"

Zohra Lampert
8899 Beverly Blvd.
Los Angeles, CA 90048
"Actress"

Jim Lampley
3347 Tareco Drive
Los Angeles, CA 90068
"Sportscaster"

Mark LaMura
9301 Wilshire Blvd. #312
Beverly Hills, CA 90210
"Actor"

Burt Lancaster
P.O. Box 67-B-38
Los Angeles, CA 90067
"Actor"

Rep. H. Martin Lancaster (NC)
House Longworth Bldg. #1417
Washington, DC 20515
"Politician"

Bert Lance
409 East Line Street
Calhoun, GA 30701
"Politician"

Martin Landau
7455 Palovista Drive
Los Angeles, CA 90046
"Actor"

David L. Lander
7009 West Senalda Drive
Los Angeles, CA 90069
"Actor, Writer"

Ann Landers
435 North Michigan Avenue
Chicago, IL 60611
"Columnist"

Audrey Landers
1913 North Beverly Drive
Beverly Hills, CA 90210
"Actress, Singer"

Judy Landers
9849 Denbigh
Beverly Hills, CA 90210
"Actress, Model"

Steve Landesburg
355 North Genesee Avenue
Los Angeles, CA 90036
"Actor"

John Landis
9369 Lloydcrest Drive
Beverly Hills, CA 90210
"Film Writer, Director"

Michael Landon, Jr
1370 Kelton Avenue #303
Los Angeles, CA 90024
"Actor"

Tom Landry
P.O. Box 9108
Dallas, TX 75209
"Football Coach"

Vytatis Landsbergis
Parliment House
Vilnius, LITHUANIA
"President of Lithuania"

Valerie Landsburg
22745 Chamera Lane
Topanga, CA 90290
"Actress"

Abby Lane
444 North Faring Road
Los Angeles, CA 90077
"Actress, Singer"

Charles Lane
321 Gretna Green Way
Los Angeles, CA 90049
"Actor"

Christy Lane
1225 Apache Lane
Madison, TN 37115
"Singer"

Diane Lane
151 South El Camino Drive
Beverly Hills, CA 90212
"Actress"

Dick "Night Train" Lane
18100 Meyer
Detroit, MI 48235
"Football Player"

Mark Lane
1177 Central Avenue
Memphis, TN 38104
"Lawyer"

Priscilla Lane
R.R. 1 North Shore Drive
Derry, NH 03038
"Actress"

Eric Laneuville
8383 Wilshire Blvd. #923
Beverly Hills, CA 90211
"Actor"

June Lang-Morgan
12756 Kahlenberg Lane
North Hollywood , CA 91607
"Actress"

Katherine Kelly Lang
317 South Carmelina Avenue
Los Angeles, CA 90049
"Actress"

K.D. Lang
1616 West 3rd Avenue
Vancouver BC V6J TK2
CANADA
"Singer"

SueAnne Langdon
3800 Barham Blvd.
Los Angeles, CA 90068
"Actress"

Hope Lange
803 Bramble
Los Angeles, CA 90049
"Actress"

Jessica Lange
9830 Wilshire Blvd.
Beverly Hills, CA 90212
"Actress"

Ted Lange
19305 Redwing Street
Tarzana, CA 91355
"Actor, Writer, Director"

Frank Langella
1999 Avenue of the Stars
Suite #2850
Los Angeles, CA 90067
"Actor"

Bernhard Langer
1120 S.W. 21st Lane
Boca Raton, FL 33486
"Golfer"

Frances Langford
P.O. Box 96
Jensen Beach, FL 33457
"Singer"

Murray Langston
3701 Willowcrest Avenue
Studio City, CA 91604
"Comedian, Actor"

Lester Lanin
157 West 57th Street
New York, NY 10019
"Band Leader"

Kim Lankford
9000 Sunset Blvd. #1200
Los Angeles, CA 90069
"Actress"

Angela Lansbury
635 Bonhill Road
Los Angeles, CA 90049
"Actress"

Robert Lansing
10 East 4th Street #700
New York, NY 10017
"Actor, Director"

Sherry Lansing
1500 San Ysidro Drive
Beverly Hills, CA 90210
"Film Executive"

Rep. Tom Lantos (CA)
House Longworth Bldg. #1526
Washington, DC 20515
"Politician"

Walter Lantz
1715 Carla Ridge
Beverly Hills, CA 90210
"Cartoonist"

Georganne La Pierre
22801 Trigger
Chatsworth, CA 91311
"Actress"

Alison La Placa
555 North Bronson Avenue
Los Angeles, CA 90004
"Actress"

Laura La Plante Asher
Motion Picture Country Home
23388 Mulholland Drive
Woodland Hills, CA 91364
"Actress"

Guy LaPointe
2313 West St. Catherine Street
Montreal PQ H3H 1N2 CANADA
"Hockey Player"

John Larch
4506 Varna Avenue
Sherman Oaks, CA 91403
"Actor"

Ring Lardner, Jr.
55 Central Park West
New York, NY 10023
"Writer"

Sheila Larkin
1626 North Orange Grove
Los Angeles, CA 90046
"Actress"

Julius LaRosa
67 Sycamore Lane
Irvington, NY 10533
"Actor, Singer"

Lyndon La Rouche
2110 Center Street East
Rochester, MN 55904
"Politician, Cult Leader"

John Larroquette
P.O. Box 6303
Malibu, CA 90264
"Actor"

Don Larsen
17090 Cooper Hill Drive
Morgan Hill, CA 95037
"Baseball Player"

Darrell Larson
8380 Melrose Avenue #207
Los Angeles, CA 90069
"Actor"

Gary Larson
4900 Main Street #900
Kansas City, MO 62114
"Cartoonist"

Glen Larson
351 Delfern Drive
Los Angeles, CA 90024
"TV Writer, Producer"

Jack Larson
449 Skyway Road North
Los Angeles, CA 90049
"Actor"

Nicolette Larson
2980 Beverly Glen Circle #302
Los Angeles, CA 90077
"Singer"

Danny LaRue
57 Gr. Cumberland Place
London W1M 7LJ ENGLAND
"Actor"

Florence La Rue
4300 Louis Avenue
Encino, CA 91316
"Singer"

Lash LaRue
9145 Hinson Drive
Matthews, NC 28105
"Actor"

Tony LaRussa
338 Golden Meadow Place
Danville, CA 94526
"Baseball Manager"

Frank Lary
RR #8, Box 142
Northport, AL 35476
"Actress"

Tommy Lasorda
1473 West Maxzim Avenue
Fullerton, CA 92633
"Baseball Manager"

Louise Lasser
200 East 71st Street #20C
New York, NY 10021
"Actor, Writer"

Fred Lasswell
1111 North Westshore Blvd. #604
Tampa, FL 33607
"Cartoonist"

Louise Latham
9229 Sunset Blvd. #607
Los Angeles, CA 90069
"Actress"

Queen Latifah
151 El Camino Drive
Beverly Hills, CA 90212
"Rap Singer"

Matt Lattanzi
P.O. Box 2710
Malibu, CA 90265
"Actor"

Niki Lauda
Can Costa de Baix
Santa Eucalia IBIZA
SPAIN
"Auto Racer, Author"

Paula Kelly
767 Fifth Avenue
New York, NY 10153
"Fashion Designer"

Rep. Greg Laughlin (TX)
House Cannon Bldg. #218
Washington, DC 20515
"Politician"

Tom Laughlin
20933 Big Rock Drive
Malibu, CA 90265
"Actor, Producer"

Cyndi Lauper
853-7th Avenue #9-D
New York, NY 10019
"Singer, Songwriter"

Matthew Laurance
1951 Hillcrest Road
Los Angeles, CA 90068
"Actor"

Mitchell Laurance
2250 Malcolm Avenue
Los Angeles, CA 90064
"Actor"

Ralph Lauren
1107-5th Avenue
New York, NY 10028
"Fashion Designer"

Arthur Laurents
P.O. Box 582
Quoque, NY 11959
"Writer"

Piper Laurie
907-12th Street
Santa Monica, CA 90403
"Actress"

Ed Lauter
P.O. Box 5617
Beverly Hills, CA 90210
"Actor"

Rod Laver
P.O. Box 4798
Hilton Head, SC 29928
"Tennis Player"

Daliah Lavi
5900 S.W. 117th Street
Miami, FL 33156
"Actress, Model"

Linda Lavin
20781 Big Rock Road
Malibu, CA 90265
"Actress, Director"

John Phillip Law
1339 Miller Drive
Los Angeles, CA 90069
"Actor"

Patricia Kennedy Lawford
1 Sutton Place South
New York, NY 10021
"Widower of Peter Lawford"

Barbara Lawrence
760 Thayer Avenue
Los Angeles, CA 90024
"Actress"

Carol Lawrence
12337 Ridge Circle
Los Angeles, CA 90049
"Actress, Singer"

Linda Lawrence
4926 Commonwealth
La Canada, CA 91011
"Actress"

Marc Lawrence
14016 Bora Way
Marina del Rey, CA 90292
"Actor, Director"

Steve Lawrence
820 Greenway Drive
Beverly Hills, CA 90210
"Singer, Writer"

Vicki Lawrence-Schultz
6000 Lido Avenue
Long Beach, CA 90803
"Actress, Singer"

Hubert Laws
1078 South Ogden Drive
Los Angeles, CA 90019
"Flutist"

Richard Lawson
3728 Broadlawn Drive
Los Angeles, CA 90068
"Actor"

Paul Laxalt
412 North Divison Street
Carson City, NV 89701
"Government Official"

Irving Paul Lazar
1840 Carla Ridge Drive
Beverly Hills, CA 90210
"Talent Agent"

George Lazenby
1127-21st Street
Santa Monica, CA 90403
"Actor"

Rep. Jim Leach (IA)
House Longworth Bldg. #1514
Washington, DC 20515
"Politician"

Robin Leach
875 Third Avenue #1800
New York, NY 10022
"TV Personality"

Cloris Leachman
13127 Boca De Canon Lane
Los Angeles, CA 90049
"Actress"

Sen. Patrick J. Leahy (VT)
Senate Russell Bldg. #433
Washington, DC 20510
"Politician"

Amanda Lear
Postfach 800149
D-8000 Munich 80
GERMANY
"Singer, Actress"

Norman Lear
255 Chadbourne Avenue
Los Angeles, CA 90049
"TV Writer, Producer"

Michael Learned
145 Central Park West
New York, NY 10023
"Actress"

Brianne Leary
9229 Sunset Blvd. #607
Los Angeles, CA 90069
"Actress"

Dr. Timothy Leary
10106 Sunbrook
Beverly Hills, CA 90210
"Author, Lecturer"

Sabrina LeBeauf
133 St. Nichols Avenue
Englewood, NJ 07632
"Actress"

Simon Le Bon
25 Tewkesbury Avenue
Pinner, Middlesex, ENGLAND
"Singer"

Kelly LeBrock
P.O. Box 727
Los Olivos, CA 93441
"Actress, Model"

John Le Carre
Tregiffian, St. Buryan
Penzance, Cornwall ENGLAND
"Writer"

Francis Lederer
23134 Sherman Way
Canoga Park, CA 91307
"Actor, Director"

Led Zeppelin
57-A Gr. Titchfield Street
London W1 7FL ENGLAND
"Rock & Roll Group"

Anna Lee
1240 North Doheny Drive
Los Angeles, CA 90069
"Actress"

Brandon Lee
2005 La Brea Terrace
Los Angeles, CA 90046
"Actor, Bruce Lee's Son"

Brenda Lee
2174 Carson Street
Nashville, TN 37210
"Singer"

Christopher Lee
c/o J. Sharkey Associates
15 Golden Square
Soho, London W1R 3AG
ENGLAND
"Actor"

Dorothy Lee
434 Santa Dominga
Solana Beach, CA 92075
"Actress"

Hyapatia Lee
P.O. Box 1924
Indianapolis, IN 46206
"Actress, Model"

Johnny Lee
9225 Sunset Blvd. #411
Los Angeles, CA 90069
"Singer, Songwriter"

Michelle Lee
830 Birchwood
Los Angeles, CA 90024
"Actress, Singer"

Peggy Lee
2331 Century Hill
Los Angeles, CA 90067
"Singer, Actress"

Pinky Lee
7110 Highway #22
Commerce City, CO 80022
"Actor"

Ruta Lee
2623 Laurel Canyon Road
Los Angeles, CA 90046
"Actress"

Dr. Sammy Lee
16537 Harbour Lane
Huntington Beach, CA 92649
"Physician, Athlete"

Spike Lee
40 Acres & A Mule Film Works
124 De Kalb Avenue #2
Brooklyn, NY 11217
"Actor, Film Director"

Tommy Lee
4970 Summit View Drive
Westlake Village, CA 91362
"Drummer"

Peter Leeds
626 North Screenland Drive
Burbank, CA 91505
"Actor"

Jim Lefebvre
5999 East Van Burern
Phoenix, AZ 85008
"Actor"

Michel Legrand
Le Grand Moulin
Rovres 28 FRANCE
"Pianist, Composer"

Rep. Richard Lehman (CA)
House Longworth Bldg. #1319
Washington, DC 20515
"Politician"

Jim Lehrer
P.O. Box 2626
Washington, DC 20013
"Broadcast Journalist"

Ron Leibman
10530 Strathmore Drive
Los Angeles, CA 90024
"Actor, Writer"

Janet Leigh
1625 Summitridge Drive
Beverly Hills, CA 90210
"Actress"

Jennifer Jason Leigh
856 North Genesee Avenue
Los Angeles, CA 90046
"Actress"

Mike Leigh
8 Earlham Grove
London N22 ENGLAND
"Film Writer, Director"

Erich Leinsdorf
209 East 56th Street
New York, NY 10022
"Conductor"

David Leisure
1999 Avenue of the Stars #2850
Los Angeles, CA 90067
"Actor"

Donovan Leitch
1959 North Wilton Place
Los Angeles, CA 90068
"Actor"

Claude LeLouch
15 Avenue Foch
8e Paris, FRANCE
"Director, Producer"

Paul Le Mat
1100 North Alta Loma #805
Los Angeles, CA 90069
"Actor"

Michael Lembeck
3960 Laurel Canyon Blvd.
Studio City, CA 91604
"Actor"

Christopher Lemmon
7887 Hillside Avenue
Los Angeles, CA 90046
"Actor"

Jack Lemmon
141 South El Camino Drive #201
Beverly Hills, CA 90212
"Actor, Director"

Bob Lemon
1141 Claiborne Drive
Long Beach, CA 90807
"Baseball Manager"

Meadowlark Lemon
P.O. Box 398
Sierra Vista, AZ 85635
"Basketball Player"

Greg Lemond
1101 Wilson Blvd. #1800
Washington, DC 22209
"Bicyclist"

Mark Lenard
845 Via de la Paz #A243
Pacific Palisades, CA 90272
"Actor"

Ivan Lendl
800 North Street
Greenwich,CT 06830
"Tennis Player"

Julian Lennon
7319 Woodrow Wilson Drive
Los Angeles, CA 90046
"Singer, Composer"

Sean Lennon
1 West 72nd Street
New York, NY 10023
"Singer, Composer"

Lennon Sisters
944 Harding Avenue
Venice, CA 90291
"Vocal Group"

Annie Lennox
P.O. Box 245
London N8 9QG ENGLAND
"Singer"

Jay Leno
9000 Sunset Blvd. #400
Los Angeles, CA 90069
"TV Host, Comedian"

Rep. Norman F. Lent (NY)
House Rayburn Bldg. #2408
Washington, DC 20515
"Politician"

Kay Lenz
5930 Manola Way
Los Angeles, CA 90068
"Actress"

Rick Lenz
12955 Calvert Street
Van Nuys, CA 91401
"Actor"

Michael Leon
P.O. Box 241609
Los Angeles, CA 90024
"Actor"

Lu Leonard
12245 Chandler Blvd.
North Hollywood, CA 91607
"Actress"

Sheldon Leonard
1141 Loma Vista
Beverly Hills, CA 90210
"Actor, Director"

Sugar Ray Leonard
1505 Brady Court
Mitchellville, MD 20716
"Boxer"

Gloria LeRoy
3500 West Olive Avenue #1400
Burbank, CA 91505
"Actress"

Aleen Leslie
1700 Lexington Road
Beverly Hills, CA 90210
"Writer"

Bethel Leslie
393 West End Avenue #11C
New York, NY 10024
"Actress, Writer"

Joan Leslie Caldwell
2228 North Catilina Avenue
Los Angeles, CA 90027
"Actress"

Doris Lessing
11 Kingscroft Road #3
London NW2 3QE ENGLAND
"Author"

Ketty Lester
5931 Comey Avenue
Los Angeles, CA 90034
"Actress"

Richard Lester
River land
Petersham Surrey, ENGLAND
"Film Director, Composer"

Terry Lester
9200 Sunset Blvd. #710
Los Angeles, CA 90069
"Actor"

David Letterman
30 Rockefeller Plaza
Suite #1410-W
New York, NY 10020
"TV Host"

Shelby Leverington
11325 Morrison #211
North Hollywood, CA 91607
"Actress"

Le Vert
110-112 Lantoga Road #D
Wayne, PA 19087
"Singer, Songwriter"

Sen. Carl Levin (MI)
Senate Russell Bldg. #459
Washington, DC 20510
"Politician"

Ira Levin
40 East 49th Street
New York, NY 10017
"Author"

Rep. Sander Levin (MI)
House Cannon Bldg. #323
Washington, DC 20515
"Politician"

Rep. Mel Levine (CA)
House Rayburn Bldg. #2443
Washington, DC 20515
"Politician"

Gene Levitt
9200 Sunset Blvd., PH. 25
Los Angeles, CA 90069
"TV Writer, Director"

Al Lewis
252 Bleeker Street
New York, NY 10016
"Actor"

Carl Lewis
1801 Ocean Park Blvd. #112
Santa Monica, CA 90405
"Track & Field Athlete"

Daniel Day Lewis
65 Connaught Street
London W2 ENGLAND
"Actor"

Dawnn Lewis
9229 Sunset Blvd. #607
Los Angeles, CA 90069
"Actress"

Geoffrey Lewis
19756 Collier
Woodland Hills, CA 91364
"Actor"

Huey Lewis
P.O. Box 819
Mill Valley, CA 94942
"Singer"

Jerry Lewis
1701 Waldman Avenue
Las Vegas, NV 89102
"Comedian, Actor"

Rep. Jerry Lewis (CA)
House Rayburn Bldg. #2312
Washington, DC 20515
"Politician"

Jerry Lee Lewis
P.O. Box 3864
Memphis, TN 38173
"Singer, Composer"

Rep. John Lewis (GA)
House Rayburn Bldg. #5329
Washington, DC 20515
"Politician"

Robert Q. Lewis
2032 North Beverly Drive
Beverly Hills, CA 90210
"TV Personality"

Sagan Lewis
1416 North Hayvenhurst #1E
Los Angeles, CA 90046
"Actress"

Shari Lewis
603 North Alta Drive
Beverly Hills, CA 90210
"Ventriloquist"

Rep. Tom Lewis (FL)
House Longworth Bldg. #1216
Washington, DC 20515
"Politician"

Richard Libertini
29235 Heathercliff Road #1
Malibu, CA 90265
"Actor"

Jeremy Licht
2659 South Barrington Avenue #202
Los Angeles, CA 90064
"Actor"

G. Gordon Liddy
9113 Sunset Blvd
Los Angeles, CA 90069
"Author"

Sen. Joseph I Lieberman (CT)
Senate Hart Bldg. #502
Washington, DC 20510
"Politician"

Judith Light
3960 Laurel Canyon Blvd. #280
Studio City, CA 91604
"Actress"

Gordon Lightfoot
1365 Yonge Street #207
Toronto, Ont. M4T 2P7
CANADA
"Singer, Songwriter"

Rep. Jim Lightfoot (IA)
House Longworth Bldg. #1222
Washington, DC 20515
"Politician"

Candy Lightner
2245 Park Town Circle
Sacramento, CA 95825
"Social Activist"

Tom Ligon
227 Waverly Place
New York, NY 10014
"Actor"

Arthur L. Liman
1285 Avenue of the Americas
New York, NY 10019
"Laywer"

Rush Limbaugh
342 Madison Avenue #920
New York, NY 10173
"Radio Personality"

Ann Morrow Lindbergh
Scotts Cove
Darien, CT 06820
"Aviatrix, Author"

Eric Linden
31791-5th Avenue
South Laguna, CA 92677
"Actor"

Hal Linden
9200 Sunset Blvd., PH. #20
Los Angeles, CA 90069
"Actor, Director"

Kate Linden
9111 Wonderland
Los Angeles, CA 90046
"Actress"

Vivica Lindfors
172 East 95th Street
New York, NY 10028
"Actress"

Astrid Lindgren
Dalagatan 46
11314 Stockholm, SWEDEN
"Author"

Audra Lindley
9229 Sunset Blvd. #607
Los Angeles, CA 90069
"Actress"

George Lindsey
10000 Santa Monica Blvd.
Suite #305
Los Angeles, CA 90067
"Actor, Singer, Comedian"

Mort Lindsey
6970 Fernhill Drive
Malibu, CA 90265
"Composer, Conductor"

Pia Lindstrom
30 Rockefeller Plaza
7th Floor
New York, NY 10020
"Film Critic"

Art Linkletter
1100 Bel Air Road
Los Angeles, CA 90024
"TV Personality"

Jack Linkletter
765 Baker Street
Costa Mesa, CA 92626
"TV Personality"

Mark Linn-Baker
2700 Neilson Way #1624
Santa Monica, CA 90405
"Actor"

Teri Ann Linn
4267 Marina City Drive
Marina del Rey, CA 90292
"Actress"

Joanne Linville
3148 Fryman Road
Studio City, CA 91604
"Actress"

Larry Linville
10100 Santa Monica Blvd. #700
Los Angeles, CA 90067
"Actor"

Ray Liotta
9830 Wilshire Blvd.
Beverly Hills, CA 90212
"Actor"

Rep. William O. Lipinski (IL)
House Longworth Bldg. #1501
Washington, DC 20515
"Politician"

Peggy Lipton
15250 Ventura Blvd. #900
Sherman Oaks, CA 91403
"Actress"

Robert Lipton
9300 Wilshire Blvd. #410
Beverly Hills, CA 90212
"Actor"

Lisa Lisa
747-10th Avenue
New York, NY 10019
"R&B Group"

Virna Lisi
Via di Filomarino 4
Rome, ITALY
"Actress"

John Lithgow
1319 Warnall Avenue
Los Angeles, CA 90024
"Actor"

Cleavon Little
4374 Ventura Canyon #4
Sherman Oaks, CA 91403
"Actor"

Little River Band
87-91 Palmerstin Cres.
Albert Park
Melbourne, Vic 3206
AUSTRALIA
"Rock & Roll Group"

Rich Little
24800 Pacific Coast Highway
Malibu, CA 90265
"Actor, Comedian"

Little Richard
Hyatt Sunset Hotel
8401 Sunset Blvd.
Los Angeles, CA 90069
"Singer, Songwriter"

Tawny Little
4151 Prospect Avenue
Los Angeles, CA 90027
"TV Host"

Big Tiny Little
West 3985 Taft Drive
Spokane, WA 98208
"Singer, Songwriter"

Gene Littler
P.O. Box 1949
Rancho Santa Fe, CA 92067
"Golfer"

Barry Livingston
9255 Sunset Blvd. #603
Los Angeles, CA 90069
"Actor"

Rep. Bob Livingston (LA)
House Rayburn Bldg. #2368
Washington, DC 20515
"Politician"

Kari Lizer
8543 Walnut Drive
Los Angeles, CA 90046
"Actress"

LL Cool J
298 Elizabeth Street
New York, NY 10012
"Rap Singer"

Doug Llewelyn
9300 Wilshire Blvd. #410
Beverly Hills, CA 90212
"Actor"

Christopher Lloyd
742 North Sycamore Avenue
Los Angeles, CA 90038
"Actor"

Emily Lloyd
10100 Santa Monica Blvd. #1600
Los Angeles, CA 90067
"Actress"

Rep. Marilyn Lloyd (TN)
House Rayburn Bldg. #2266
Washington, DC 20515
"Politician"

Norman Lloyd
1813 Old Ranch Road
Los Angeles, CA 90049
"Actor, Director"

Tony Lo Bianco
365 West End Avenue #4C
New York, NY 10024
"Actor, Writer, Director"

Sondra Locke
P.O. Box 69865
Los Angeles, CA 90069
"Actress"

Brad Lockerman
10351 Santa Monica Blvd.
Suite #211
Los Angeles, CA 90025
"Actor"

Anne Lockhart
28245 Driver Avenue
Agoura Hills, CA 91301
"Actress"

June Lockhart
404 San Vicente Blvd. #208
Santa Monica, CA 90402
"Actress"

Heather Locklear
4970 Summit View Drive
Westlake Village, CA 91362
"Actress, Model"

Hank Locklin
Rt. 1, Box 123
Milton, FL 32570
"Singer, Songwriter"

Gary Lockwood
3083 1/2 Rambla Pacifica
Malibu, CA 90265
"Actor"

Julia Lockwood
112 Castlenan
London SW13 ENGLAND
"Actress"

David Lodge
8 Sydney Road
Richmond, Surrey, ENGLAND
"Actor"

Robert Logan
10637 Burbank Blvd.
North Hollywood, CA 91601
"Actor"

Robert Loggia
1718 Angelo Drive
Beverly Hills, CA 90210
"Actor, Director"

Kenny Loggins
985 Hot Springs Road
Santa Barbara, CA 93108
"Singer, Songwriter"

Gina Lollobrigida
Via Appino Antica 223
Rome, ITALY
"Actress"

Herbert Lom
147-149 Wardour Street
London W1V 3TB ENGLAND
"Actor"

Julie London
16074 Royal Oaks
Encino, CA 91436
"Actress, Singer"

John Lone
1341 Ocean Avenue #104
Santa Monica, CA 90401
"Actor"

Howie Long
26 Strawberry Lane
Rolling Hills, CA 90274
"Football Player"

Shelley Long
15237 Sunset Blvd
Pacific Palisades, CA 90272
"Actress"

Johnny Longdon
Bar JL Ranch
247 West Lemon Avenue
Arcadia, CA 91006
"Actor"

Tony Longo
24 Westwind Street
Marina del Rey, CA 90292
"Actor"

Davey Lopes
16984 Avenida de Santa Ynez
Pacific Palisades, CA 90272
"Baseball Player"

Al Lopez
3601 Beach Street
Tampa, FL 33609
"Baseball Player"

Mario Lopez
11350 Ventura Blvd. #206
Studio City, CA 91604
"Actor"

Nancy Lopez
Rt. 2, Box 380-C
Albany, GA 31707
"Golfer"

Trini Lopez
1139 Abrigo Road
Palm Springs, CA 92762
"Singer, Actress"

Stefan Lorant
215 West Mountain Road
Lenox, MA 01240
"Photojournalist, Author"

Jack Lord
4999 Kahala Avenue
Honolulu, HI 96816
"Actor"

Marjorie Lord
1110 Maytor Place
Beverly Hills, CA 90210
"Actress"

Traci Lords
3349 Cahuenga Blvd. West
Suite #2-B
Los Angeles, CA 90068
"Actress"

Sophia Loren
1151 Hidden Valley Road
Thousand Oaks, CA 91360
"Actress"

Gloria Loring
14746 Valley Vista
Sherman Oaks, CA 91403
"Singer, Actress"

Lynn Loring
506 North Camden Drive
Beverly Hills 90210
"Actress, TV Producer"

Joan Lorring
345 East 68th Street
New York, NY 10021
"Actress"

Los Lobos
P.O. 1304
Burbank, CA 91507
"Rock & Roll Group"

Sen. Trent Lott (MS)
Senate Russell Bldg. #487
Washington, DC 20510
"Politician"

Dorothy Loudon
101 Central Park West
New York, NY 10023
"Actress"

Greg Louganis
P.O. Box 4068
Malibu, CA 90265
"Diver"

Lori Loughlin
9279 Sierra Mar Drive
Los Angeles, CA 90069
"Actress"

Tina Louise
9565 Lime Orchard Road
Beverly Hills, CA 90210
"Actress"

Love & Rockets
The Lakes
Bushey, Hertsfordshire
WD2 1HS ENGLAND
"Rock & Roll Group"

Linda Lovelace Marciano
120 Enterprise
Secaucus, NJ 07094
"Actress"

Patty Loveless
P.O. Box 363
Groveport, OH 43125
"Singer"

James Lovell
5725 East River Road
Chicago, IL 60611
"Astronaut"

Loverboy
406-68 Water Street
Gastown, Vancouver B.C.
VGB 1AY CANADA
"Rock & Roll Group"

Lyle Lovett
4155 East Jewell Avenue #412
Denver, CO 80222
"Singer"

Chad Lowe
975 Hancock #126
Los Angeles, CA 90069
"Actor"

Rob Lowe
2817 Nichols Canyon
Los Angeles, CA 90046
"Actor"

Carey Lowell
8899 Beverly Blvd.
Los Angeles, CA 90048
"Model, Actress"

Rep. Bill Lowery (CA)
House Rayburn Bldg. #2433
Washington, DC 20515
"Politician"

Rep. Nita M. Lowey (NY)
House Longworth Bldg. #1313
Washington, DC 20515
"Politician"

Myrna Loy
425 East 63rd Street
New York, NY 10021
"Actress"

George Lucas
P.O. Box 2009
San Rafael, CA 94912
"Writer, Producer, Director"

Susan Lucci
16 Carteret Place
Garden City, NY 11530
"Actress"

Gloria Luchenbill
415 South Shirley Place
Beverly Hills, CA 90212
"Actress"

Laurance Lukenbill
470-K Main Street
Ridgefield, CT 06877
"Actor"

William Lucking
10100 Santa Monica Blvd. #700
Los Angeles, CA 90067
"Actor"

Sid Luckman
5303 St. Charles Road
Bellwood, IL 60104
"Football Player"

Robert Ludlum
58 West 10th Street
New York, NY 10011
"Author, Actor, Producer"

Lorna Luft
1901 Avenue of the Stars #1600
Los Angeles, CA 90067
"Actress"

Sen. Richard Lugar (IN)
306 Hart Office Bldg.
Washington, DC 20510
"Politician"

Bela Lugosi, Jr.
600 Wilshire Blvd. #1700
Los Angeles, CA 90017
"Actor"

James Luisi
14315 Riverside Drive
Sherman Oaks, CA 91423
"Actor"

Johnny Lujack
3700 Harrison Street
Davenport, IA 52806
"Football Player"

Rep. Charles Luken (OH)
House Longworth Bldg. #1632
Washington, DC 20515
"Politician"

Lulabel & Scottie
P.O. Box 171132
Nashville, TN 37217
"Vocal Group"

Carl Lumbly
9744 Wilshire Blvd. #206
Beverly Hills, CA 90212
"Actor"

Sidney Lumet
1380 Lexington Avenue
New York, NY 10028
"Film Writer, Director"

Joanna Lumley
200 Fulham Road
London SW10 ENGLAND
"Actress"

Barbara Luna
18026 Rodarte Way
Encino, CA 91316
"Actress"

Deanna Lund
1948 Benecia Avenue
Los Angeles, CA 90025
"Actress"

John Lund
2777 Coldwater Canyon
Beverly Hills, CA 90210
"Actor"

Lucille Lund Higgins
3424 Shore Heights Drive
Malibu, CA 90265
"Actress"

Joan Lunden
707 Westchester Avenue
White Plains, NY 10604
"TV Host"

Dolf Lundgren
29055 Cliffside Drive
Malibu, CA 90265
"Bodybuilder, Actor"

Steve Lundquist
3448 Southbay Drive
Jonesboro, GA 30236
"Swimmer"

Ida Lupino
11666 Wedding Street
North Hollywood, CA 91601
"Actress, Writer"

Patti LuPone
130 West 42nd Street #2400
New York, NY 10036
"Singer"

John Lupton
2528 Tilden Avenue
Los Angeles, CA 90064
"Actor"

Peter Lupus
11375 Dona Lisa Drive
Studio City, CA 91604
"Actor"

Nellie Lutcher
1524 La Baig Avenue
Los Angeles, CA 90028
"Pianist, Vocalist"

Frank Luz
606 North Larchmont Blvd. #309
Los Angeles, CA 90004
"Actor"

Greg Luzinski
320 Jackson Road
Medford, NJ 08055
"Baseball Player"

Jacki Lyden
c/o National Public Radio
2025 "M" Street NW
Washington, DC 20036
"News Correspondent"

Jimmy Lydon
1317 Los Arboles Avenue N.W.
Albuquerque, NM 87107
"Actor"

A.C. Lyles
2115 Linda Flora
Los Angeles, CA 90024
"Writer, Producer"

Dorothy Lyman
1870 North Vista Street
Los Angeles, CA 90046
"Actress"

David Lynch
P.O. Box 93624
Los Angeles, CA 90093
"TV Writer

Carol Lynley
P.O. Box 2190
Malibu, CA 90265
"Actress"

Betty Lynn
10424 Tennessee Avenue
Los Angeles, CA 90264
"Actress"

Fred Lynn
24 Haykey Way
Boston, MA 02115
"Baseball Player"

Janet Lynn
4215 Marsh Avenue
Rockford, IL 61111
"Skater"

Jeffrey Lynn
11600 Acama Street
Studio City, CA 91604
"Actor"

Loretta Lynn
1010-18th Avenue South
Nashville, TN 37212
"Singer"

Dame Vera Lynn
4 Sandhurst, Bispham
Blackpool
Lancashire FY2 OAV ENGLAND
"Singer, Actress"

Jeff Lynne
2621 Deep Canyon Drive
Beverly Hills, CA 90210
"Musician, Composer"

Lynyrd Skynyrd
3 East 54th Street #1400
New York, NY 10022
"Music Group"

M

Andrea McArdle
713 Disston Street
Philadelphia, PA 19111
"Actress"

Alex McArthur
8899 Beverly Blvd.
Los Angeles, CA 90048
"Actor"

Amanda McBroom
22903 Mariano
Woodland Hills, CA 91364
"Singer, Songwriter"

Frances Lee McCain
8075 West 3rd Street #303
Los Angeles, CA 90048
"Actress"

Sen. John McCain (AZ)
Senate Russell Bldg. #111
Washington, DC 20510
"Politician"

C.W. McCall
206 South 44th Street
Omaha, NE 68131
"Singer, Songwriter"

Mary Ann McCall
1546 North Gordon Street
Los Angeles, CA 90028
"Actor"

Mitzi McCall
3635 Wrightwood Drive
Studio City, CA 91604
"Actress"

Irish McCalla
920 Oak Terrace
Prescott, AZ 86301
"Actress"

Lon McCallister
P.O. Box 396
Little River, CA 95456
"Actor"

David McCallum
10 East 44th Street #700
New York, NY 10017
"Actor"

Napoleon McCallum
332 Center Street
El Segundo, CA 90245
"Football Player"

Mercedes McCambridge
1001 Gentry Street #8-1
La Jolla, CA 92037
"Actress"

Rep. Al McCandless (CA)
House Rayburn Bldg. #2422
Washington, DC 20515
"Politician"

Chuck McCann
2941 Briar Knoll Drive
Los Angeles, CA 90046
"Actor, Comedian"

Fred McCarren
9200 Sunset Blvd. #1210
Los Angeles, CA 90069
"Actor"

Chris McCarron
315 South Beverly Drive #216
Beverly Hills, CA 90212
"Jockey"

Andrew McCarthy
4708 Vesper Avenue
Sherman Oaks, CA 91403
"Actor"

Eugene McCarthy
P.O. Box 22
Woodville, VA 22749
"Ex-Senator"

Kevin McCarthy
1032-6th Street #3
Santa Monica, VA 90403
"Actor"

Lin McCarthy
233 North Swall Drive
Beverly Hills, CA 90210
"Actor"

Paul McCartney
Waterfall Estate
Peamarsh, St. Leonard-on-Sea
Sussex ENGLAND
"Singer, Composer"

Constance McCashin
2037 Desford Drive
Beverly Hills, CA 90210
"Actress"

Peggy McCay
8811 Wonderland Avenue
Los Angeles, CA 90046
"Actress"

Rue McClanahan
16601 Woodvale Road
Encino, CA 91436
"Actress"

Sarah McClendon
2933-28th Street N.W.
Washington, DC 20006
"News Correspondent"

Rep. Frank McCloskey (IN)
House Cannon Bldg. #127
Washington, DC 20515
"Politician"

Leigh McCloskey
6032 Philip Avenue
Malibu, CA 90265
"Actor"

Pete McCloskey
2200 Gengo Road
Palo Alto, CA 94304
"Ex-Congressman"

Doug McClure
14936 Stonesboro Place
Sherman Oaks, CA 91403
"Actor"

Jessica McClure
P.O. Box 3901
Midland, TX 79701
"Baby Trapped in Well"

Edie McClurg
9320 Wilshire Blvd. #300
Beverly Hills, CA 90212
"Actress"

Rep. Bill McCollum (FL)
House Rayburn Bldg. #2453
Washington, DC 20515
"Politician"

Judith McConnell
3300 Bennett Drive
Los Angeles, CA 90068
"Actress"

Sen. Mitch McConnell (KY)
Senate Russell Bldg. #120
Washington, DC 20510
"Politician"

Marilyn McCoo
P.O. Box 7905
Beverly Hills, CA 90212
"Singer"

John McCook
4154 Colbath Avenue
Sherman Oaks, CA 91423
"Actor, Writer, Director"

Kent McCord
1738 North Orange Grove
Los Angeles, CA 90046
"Actor"

Carolyn McCormick
15760 Ventura Blvd. #1730
Encino, CA 91436
"Actress"

Maureen McCormick
2812 North Shell Creek Place
Westlake Village, CA 91361
"Actress"

Pat McCormick
P.O. Box 250
Seal Beach, CA 90740
"Swimmer"

Pat McCormick
4303 Klump Avenue
North Hollywood, CA 91602
"Comedian"

Willie McCovey
P.O. Box 620342
Woodside, CA 94062
"Baseball Player"

Alec McCowen
3 Goodwins Court
St. Martin's Lane
London WG2 ENGLAND
"Actor"

Matt McCoy
10000 Santa Monica Blvd. #305
Los Angeles, CA 90067
"Actor"

George McCrae
495 S.E. 10th Court
Hialeah, FL 33010
"Singer, Songwriter"

Gwen McCrae
495 S.E. 10th Court
Hialeah, FL 33010
"Singer, Songwriter"

Jody McCrea
Rt#1, Box 575
Camarillo, CA 93010
"Actor"

Rep. Jim McCrery (LA)
House Cannon Bldg. #429
Washington, DC 20515
"Politician"

Julie McCullough
8306 Wilshire Blvd. #438
Beverly Hills, CA 90211
"Model"

Kimberly McCullough
9200 Sunset Blvd. #625
Los Angeles, CA 90069
"Actress"

Shanna McCullough
7920 Alabama Avenue
Canoga Park, CA 91304
"Actress"

Rep. Dave McCurdy (OK)
House Rayburn Bldg. #2344
Washington, DC 20515
"Politician"

Rep. Joseph M. McDade (PA)
House Rayburn Bldg. #2370
Washington, DC 20515
"Politician"

Mel McDaniel
191 Dickerson Bay Road
Gallatin, TN 37066
"Singer"

Rep. Jim McDermott (WA)
House Longworth Bldg. #1707
Washington, DC 20515
"Politician"

James McDivitt
P.O. Box 3105
Anaheim, CA 92803
"Astrouaut"

"Country" Joe McDonald
P.O. Box 7158
Berkeley, CA 94707
"Singer"

Grace McDonald Green
6115 Lincoln Drive
Minneapolis, MN 55436
"Singer, Dancer"

Mary McDonnell
15760 Ventura Blvd. #1730
Encino, CA 91436
"Actress"

Malcolm McDowall
388 Oxford Street
London W1 ENGLAND
"Actor"

Roddy McDowall
3110 Brookdale Road
Studio City, CA 91604
"Actor"

Ronnie McDowell
P.O. Box 53
Portland, TN 37148
"Singer"

John McEnroe
23712 Malibu Colony
Malibu, CA 90265
"Tennis Player"

Reba McEntire
511 Fairground Court
Nashville, TN 37204
"Singer"

Rep. Bob McEwen (OH)
House Rayburn Bldg. #2431
Washington, DC 20515
"Politician"

Spanky McFarland
8500 Buckner Lane
Fort Worth, TX 76180
"Actor"

Robert C. McFarlane
3414 Prospect Street N.W.
Washington, DC 20007
"Politician"

Bobby McFerrim
600 West 58th Street #9188
New York, NY 10019
"Singer"

Darren McGavin
470 Park Avenue
New York, NY 10022
"Actor"

Kirk McGee
P.O Box 626
Franklin, TN 37064
"Singer"

Vonetta McGee
9744 Wilshire Blvd. #308
Beverly Hills, CA 90212
"Actress"

Howard McGinnin
10100 Santa Monica Blvd. #1600
Los Angeles, CA 90067
"Actor, Singer"

Kelly McGillis
13428 Maxella Avenue
Marina del Rey, CA 90292
"Actress"

Ted McGinley
151 South El Camino Drive
Beverly Hills, CA 90212
"Actor"

Patrick McGoohan
16808 Bollinger Drive
Pacific Palisades, CA 90272
"Actor, Writer, Producer"

Elizabeth McGovern
17319 Magnolia Blvd.
Encino, CA 91316
"Actress"

George McGovern
P.O. Box 5591
Washington, DC 20016
"Ex-Senator"

Maureen McGovern
529 West 42nd Street #7F
New York, NY 10036
"Singer"

Rep. Raymond McGrath (NY)
House Cannon Bldg. #205
Washington, DC 20515
"Politician"

Tug McGraw
Coleshill Rose Valley Road
Media, PA 19063
"Baseball Player"

Dorothy McGuire
121 Copley Place
Beverly Hills, CA 90210
"Actress"

McGuire Sisters
5455 Wilshire Blvd. #2200
Los Angeles, CA 90036
"Vocal Group"

Stephen McHattie
9229 Sunset Blvd. #607
Los Angeles, CA 90069
"Actor"

Rep. Matthew McHugh (NY)
House Rayburn Bldg. #2335
Washington, DC 20515
"Politician"

John McIntire
1417 Samoa Way
Laguna Beach, CA 92651
"Percussionist"

Gardner McKay
445 Kawailoa Raod #10
Kailua, HI 96734
"Actor"

Jim McKay
1330 Avenue of the Americas
New York, NY 10019
"Sportscaster"

John McKay
1 Buccaneer Road
Tampa, FL 33607
"Football Coach"

Michael McKean
3570 Willowcrest Avenue
Studio City, CA 91604
"Actor"

Todd McKee
32362 Lake Pleasant Drive
Westlake Village, CA 91361
"Actor"

Danica McKellar
6212 Banner
Los Angeles, CA 90068
"Actress"

Ian McKellen
25 Earl's Terrace
London W8 ENGLAND
"Actor"

Virginia McKenna
67 Glebe Place
London SW3 5JB ENGLAND
"Actress"

Julia McKenzie
Richmond Park
Kingston Surrey, ENGLAND
"Actress"

Doug McKeon
818-6th Street #202
Santa Monica, CA 90403
"Actor"

Nancy McKeon
P.O. Box 6778
Burbank, CA 91510
"Actress"

Philip McKeon
10201 West Pico Blvd.
Building #54, Room #6
Los Angeles, CA 90035
"Actor"

Leo McKern
12 Summerhill Road
Oxford 0X2 7JY ENGLAND
"Actor"

Gov. John McKernan (ME)
Executive Department
State House Station #1
Augusta, ME 04333
"Governor"

Tamara McKinney
4935 Parkers Mill Road
Lexington, KY 40502
"Skier"

Rod McKuen
1155 Angelo Drive
Beverly Hills, CA 90210
"Singer, Poet"

Denny McLain
4933 Coventry Parkway
Ft. Wayne, IN 46804
"Baseball Player"

John McLaughlin
2918 Garfield Street N.W.
Washington, DC 20008
"News Correspondent"

Don McLean
Old Manitou Road
Garrison, NY 10524
"Singer, Songwriter"

Catherine McLeod
4146 Allott Avenue
Van Nuys, CA 91423
"Actress"

Allyn Ann McLerie
3344 Campanil Drive
Santa Barbara, CA 93109
"Actress"

Ed McMahon
12000 Crest Court
Beverly Hills, CA 90210
"TV Host"

Jim McMahon
c/o Veterans Stadium
Philadelphia, PA 19148
"Football Player"

Rep. J. Alex McMillan (NC)
House Cannon Bldg. #401
Washington, DC 20515
"Politician"

Rep. Tom McMillen (MD)
House Cannon Bldg. #420
Washington, DC 20515
"Politician"

Jim McMullen
515 Mt. Holyoke Avenue
Pacific Palisades, CA 90272
"Actor"

Stephen McNally
624 North Hillcrest Road
Beverly Hills, CA 90210
"Actor"

Terrence McNally
218 West 10th Street
New York, NY 10014
"Dramatist"

Brian McNamara
P.O. Box 5617
Beverly Hills, CA 90210
"Actor"

Julianne McNamara
3500 West Olive Avenue #1400
Burbank, CA 91505
"Actress"

Robert McNamara
2412 Tracy Place N.W.
Washington, DC 20008
"Banker, Government"

Willaim McNamara
131 South Rodeo Drive #300
Beverly Hills, CA 90212
"Actor"

Kristy McNichol
P.O. Box 5813
Sherman Oaks, CA 91413
"Actress"

Rep. Michael R. McNulty (NY)
House Cannon Bldg. #414
Washington, DC 20515
"Politician"

Butterfly McQueen
3060-A Dent Street
Augusta, GA 30906
"Actress"

Chad McQueen
8306 Wilshire Blvd. #438
Beverly Hills, CA 90211
"Actor"

Niele McQueen
2323 Bowmont Drive
Beverly Hills, CA 90210
"Actress"

Gerald McRaney
1290 Inverness
Pasadena, CA 91101
"Actor, Director"

Jim McReynolds
P.O. Box 304
Gallatin, TN 37066
"Singer, Guitarist"

Jesse McReynolds
P.O. Box 304
Gallatin, TN 37066
"Singer, Guitarist"

Ian McShane
999 North Doheny Drive
Los Angeles, CA 90069
"Actor"

Christie McVie
9477 Lloydcrest Drive
Beverly Hills, CA 90210
"Singer, Songwriter"

Gov. Ned McWherter (TN)
State Capitol
Nashville, TN 37219
"Governor"

Caroline McWilliams
2195 Mandeville Canyon
Los Angeles, CA 90049
"Actress"

Yo-Yo Ma
40 West 57th Street
New York, NY 10019
"Cellist"

Mrs. Jean MacArthur
Waldorf Towers
100 East 50th Street
New York, NY 10022
"Widower of Douglas MacArthur"

Sean MacBride
41 rue de Zurich
CH-1021 Genf
SWITZERLAND
"Diplomat"

Ralph Macchio
972 Nichols Road
Deer Park, NY 11729
"Actor"

Simon MacCorkindale
1221 North Kings Road
Los Angeles, CA 90069
"Actor"

Dr. Jeffrey MacDonald
Federal Correctional Institute
Bastrop, TX 78602
"Accused of Killing His Family"

Andie MacDowell
8899 Beverly Blvd.
Los Angeles, CA 90048
"Actress"

Ali MacGraw
1679 Alta Mura Road
Pacific Palisades, CA 90272
"Actress, Model"

Jeff MacGregor
233 South Beverly Drive #112
Beverly Hills, CA 90212
"TV Personality"

Stephen Macht
248 South Rodeo Drive
Beverly Hills, CA 90212
"Actor"

Rep. Ronald Machtley (RI)
House Cannon Bldg. #132
Washington, DC 20515
"Politician"

Sen. Connie Mack (FL)
Senate Hart Bldg. #517
Washington, DC 20510
"Politician"

Warner Mack
1136 Sunnymeade Drive
Nashville, TN 37216
"Singer, Guitarist"

Gisele MacKenzie
11014 Blix
North Hollywood, CA 91604
"Actress"

Patch MacKenzie
9744 Wilshire Blvd. #306
Beverly Hills, CA 90212
"Actress"

Bob Mackie
9314 Lloydcrest Drive
Beverly Hills, CA 90210
"Costume Designer"

Janet MacLachlan
1919 North Taft Avenue
Los Angeles, CA 90068
"Actress"

Kyle MacLachlan
760 North La Cienega Blvd.
Los Angeles, CA 90069
"Actor"

Shirley MacLaine
25200 Old Malibu Road
Malibu, CA 90265
"Actress"

Gavin MacLeod
14680 Valley Vista
Sherman Oaks, CA 91403
"Actor"

Robert Macnaughton
8899 Beverly Blvd.
Los Angeles, CA 90048
"Actor"

Patrick Macnee
P.O. Box 1685
Palm Springs, CA 92263
"Actor"

Robert Macneil
356 West 58th Street
New York, NY 10019
"News Correspondent"

Ella MacPherson
40 East 61st Street
New York, NY 10021
"Model"

Heather MacRae
4430 Hayvenhurst Avenue
Encino, CA 91436
"Actress"

Meredith MacRae
13659 Victory Blvd.
Van Nuys, CA 91401
"Actress"

Bill Macy
10130 Angelo Circle
Beverly Hills, CA 90210
"Actor"

Dave Madden
2722 Forrester
Los Angeles, CA 90064
"Actor"

John Madden
1 West 72nd Street
New York, NY 10023
"Sportscaster"

Lester Maddox
3155 Johnson Ferry Road N.E.
Marietta, GA 30062
"Former Politician"

Amy Madigan
662 North Van Ness Avenue #305
Los Angeles, CA 90004
"Actress"

Rep. Edward R. Madigan (IL)
House Rayburn Bldg. #2109
Washington, DC 20515
"Politician"

Guy Madison
35022 1/2 Avenue #H
Yucaipa, CA 92399
"Actor"

Bill Madlock
453 East Decatur Street
Decatur, IL 62521
"Baseball Player"

Madonna
8000 Beverly Blvd.
Los Angeles, CA 90048
"Singer, Actress"

Virginia Madsen
9206 Cordell Mew Drive
Los Angeles, CA 90069
"Actress"

Debra Sue Maffett
2969 Passmore Drive
Los Angeles, CA 90068
"Actress, Model"

Ann Magnuson
2865 Avenel Street
Los Angeles, CA 90039
"Proformance Artist"

Jeb Struart Magruder
720 West Monument Street
Colorado Springs, CO 80901
"Former Government Official"

John Mahaffey
3100 Richmond Avenue #500
Houston, TX 77098
"Golfer"

Taj Majal
1671 Appian Way
Santa Monica, CA 90401
"Singer, Songwriter"

George Maharis
13150 Mulholland Drive
Beverly Hills, CA 90210
"Actor"

Cardinal Roger Mahony
1531 West 9th Street
Los Angeles, CA 90012
"Clergy"

Phil Mahre
White Pass Br.
Naches, WA 98937
"Skier"

Steve Mahre
2408 North 52nd Avenue
Yakima, WA 98908
"Skier"

Norman Mailer
142 Columbia Heights
Brooklyn, NY 11201
"Author"

Beth Maitland
23555 Neargate
Santa Clarita, CA 91321
"Actress"

Lee Majors
411 Isle of Capri Drive
Ft. Lauderdale, FL 33301
"Actor"

Miriam Makebe
14011 Ventura Blvd. #2008
Sherman Oaks, CA 91423
"Singer"

Tommy Makem
2 Longmeadow Road
Dover, NH 03820
"Singer"

Chris Makepeace
15 Cleveland Street
Toronto, Ont. CANADA
"Actor"

Mako
8032 Blackburn Avenue
Los Angeles, CA 90048
"Actor"

Kristina Malandro
10647 Wilkins Avenue #307
Los Angeles, CA 90024
"Actress"

Karl Malden
1845 Mandeville Canyon
Los Angeles, CA 90049
"Actor"

John Malkovich
346 South Lucerne Blvd.
Los Angeles, CA 90020
"Actor"

Louis Malle
222 Central Park South
New York, NY 10019
"Film Director"

Carole Mallory
2300-5th Avenue
New York, NY 10037
"Model, Actress, Author"

Bruce Malmuty
9981 Robin Drive
Beverly Hills, CA 90210
"Screenwriter, Director"

Nancy Malone
11625 Sunshine Terrace
Studio City, CA 91604
"Actress, Director"

Leonard Maltin
5555 Melrose Avenue #L
Los Angeles, CA 90038
"Film Critic, Author"

The Mamas & The Papas
805-3rd Avenue #2900
New York, NY 10022
"Rock & Roll Group"

Charles T. Manatt
4814 Woodway Lane N.W.
Washington, DC 20016
"Politician"

Melissa Manchester
15822 High Knoll Road
Encino, CA 91436
"Singer, Songwriter"

William Manchester
P.O. Box 329 Wesleyan Station
Middletown, CT 06457
"Author"

Henry Mancini
9229 Sunset Blvd. #304
Los Angeles, CA 90069
"Pianist, Composer"

Ray "Boom Boom" Mancini
848-G Lincoln Blvd.
Santa Monica, CA 90404
"Boxer"

Nick Mancuso
7160 Grasswood Avenue
Malibu, CA 90265
"Actor"

Robert Mandan
10351 Santa Monica Blvd. #211
Los Angeles, CA 90025
"Actor"

Howie Mandel
208 North Canon Drive
Beverly Hills, CA 90210
"Actor, Comedian"

Loring Mandel
555 West 57th Street #1230
New York, NY 10019
"Screenwriter"

Nelson Mandela
Orlando West
Soweto, Johannesburg
SOUTH AFRICA
"Social Activist, Politician"

Winnie Mandela
Orlando West
Soweto, Johannesburg
SOUTH AFRICA
"Social Activist"

Barbara Mandrell
128 River Road
Hendersonville, TN 37075
"Singer, Singwriter"

Erline Mandrell
713 West Main Street
Hendersonville, TN 37075
"Actress, Drummer"

Louise Mandrell
Old Hickory Lake
Hendersonville, TN 37075
"Singer, Musician"

Costas Mandylor
10351 Santa Monica Blvd. #211
Los Angeles, CA 90025
"Actor"

Larry Maneti
4615 Winnetka
Woodland Hills, CA 91364
"Actor"

Manhattan Transfer
3575 Cahuenga Blvd. West #450
Los Angeles, CA 90068
"Vocal Group"

Barry Manilow
6640 Sunset Blvd. #200
Los Angeles, CA 90028
"Singer, Composer"

Joseph L. Mankiewicz
RFD #2, Box 82
Bedford, NY 10506
"Writer, Producer"

Wolf Mankowitz
Bridge House
Ahakista, County Cork
Kilcrohane 11 IRELAND
"Author, Producer, Dramatist"

Dexter Manley
P.O. Box 17247
Washington, DC 20041
"Football Player"

Elizabeth Manley
2331 Century Hill
Los Angeles, CA 90067
"Skater"

Hana Manlikova
Vymolova 8, Prague 5
150 00 CZECHOSLOVAKIA
"Tennis Player"

Abby Mann
1240 La Collina Drive
Beverly Hills, CA 90210
"Writer, Producer"

Daniel Mann
6328 Frondosa Drive
Malibu, CA 90265
"Film Director"

Delbert Mann
401 South Burnside Avenue
Suite #11D
Los Angeles, CA 90036
"Director, Producer"

Johnny Mann
20641 Celtic Street
Chatsworth, CA 91311
"Composer, Conductor"

Michael Mann
13746 Sunset Blvd.
Pacific Palisades, CA 90272
"Writer, Producer"

David Manners
3010 Foothill Road
Santa Barbara, CA 93105
"Actor"

Dorothy Manners
744 North Dohney Drive
Los Angeles, CA 90069
"Actress"

Miss Manners
1651 Harvard Street N.W.
Washington, DC 20009
"Etiquette Expert"

Irene Manning
3165 La Mesa Drive
Santa Clara, CA 94070
"Actress, Singer, Author"

Dinah Manoff
P.O. Box 5617
Beverly Hills, CA 90210
"Actress"

Charles Manson
Corcoran Prison
1002 Dairy Avenue
Corcoran, CA 93212
"Convicted Serial Killer"

Paul Mantee
8485 East Melrose Place
Los Angeles, CA 90069
"Actor"

John Mantley
4121 Longridge Avenue
Sherman Oaks, CA 91423
"Screenwriter"

Rep. Thomas J. Manton
House Cannon Bldg. #331
Washington, DC 20515
"Politician"

Randolph Mantooth
P.O. Box 280
Agoura, CA 91301
"Actor"

Martin Manulis
242 Copa de Oro Road
Los Angeles, CA 90077
"TV Producer"

Ralph Manza
550 Hygeia Avenue
Leucadia, CA 92024
"Actor"

Ray Manzarek
232 South Rodeo Drive
Beverly Hills, CA 90212
"Keyboardist"

Marla Maples
420 Madison Avenue #1400
New York, NY 10017
"Actress"

Adela Mara Huggins
1928 Mandeville Canyon
Los Angeles, CA 90049
"Dancer, Actress"

Diego Maradona
Maternidad 2
Barcelona 14 SPAIN
"Soccer Player"

Marcel Marceau
15 Ave. Montaigne
75008 Paris, FRANC
"Pantominist"

Mario Marcelino
1418 North Highland Avenue #102
Los Angeles, CA 90028
"Actress, Writer"

Muzzy Marcellino
14633 Round Valley Drive
Sherman Oaks, CA 91403
"Composer"

Guy Marchand
11 rue Eugene Labiche
75016 Paris, FRANCE
"Actor"

Nancy Marchand
250 West 89th Street
New York, NY 10024
"Actress"

Imelda Marcos
2439 Makiki Drive
Honolulu, HI 96822
"Politician"

Adrea Marcovicci
8273 West Norton Avenue
Los Angeles, CA 90046
"Actress, Singer"

Ann-Margaret Smith
2707 Benedict Canyon
Beverly Hills, CA 90210
"Actress"

HRH The Princess Margaret
Kensington Palace
London N5 ENGLAND
"Royalty"

Janet Margolin
7667 Seattle Place
Los Angeles, CA 90040
"Actress"

Stuart Margolin
9401 Wilshire Blvd. #700
Beverly Hills, CA 90212
"Actor, Director"

Stan Margulies
16965 Strawberry Drive
Encino, CA 91316
"TV Producer"

Juan Marichal
Ed. Hache 3
Piso Este, JFK Avenue
Santo Domingo
DOMINICAN REPUBLIC
"Baseball Player"

Anne Marie
120 Hickory Street
Madison, TN 37115
"Actress, Model"

Lisa Marie
3636 Freedonia Drive
Los Angeles, CA 90068
"Actress"

Teena Marie
1000 Laguna Road
Pasadena, CA 91105
"Actress"

Richard Marin
(Cheech & Chong)
32020 Pacific Coast Hwy.
Malibu, CA 90265
"Actor, Comedian"

Ed Marinaro
1466 North Doheny Drive
Los Angeles, CA 90069
"Football Player, Actor"

Dan Marino
2269 N.W. 199th Street
Miami, FL 33056
"Football Player"

Rep. Edward Markey (MA)
House Rayburn Bldg. #2133
Washington, DC 20515
"Politician"

Monte Markhan
26328 Ingleside
Malibu, CA 90265
"Actor"

Rep. Ron Marlenee (MT)
House Rayburn Bldg. #2465
Washington, DC 20515
"Politician"

Ziggy Marley
Jack's Hill
Kingston, JAMAICA
"Raggae Singer"

Scott Marlowe
132-B South Lasky Drive
Beverly Hills, CA 90212
"Actor"

Christian Marquand
45 rue de Belle Chasse
75007 Paris, FRANCE
"Actor"

Gabriel Garcia Marques
Fuego 144
Pedregal de Santa Angel
Mexico City D.F. MEXICO
"Author"

Kenneth Mars
144 South Beverly Blvd. #405
Beverly Hills, CA 90212
"Actor"

Branford Marsalis
3 Hasting Square
Cambridge, MA 02139
"Saxophonist"

Wynton Marsalis
327 East 18th Street
New York, NY 10003
"Trumpeter"

Jean Marsh
The Pheasant, Chinnor Hill
Oxfordshire OX9 4BN ENGLAND
"Actress"

Linda Marsh
4041 Alta Mesa
Studio City, CA 91604
"Actress"

Marian Marsh
P.O. Box 1, 73597 Pinyon
Palm Desert, CA 92260
"Actress"

Catherine Marshall
3003 Fernwood Drive
Boynton Beach, FL 33435
"Author"

Don Marshall
9021 Melrose Avenue #304
Los Angeles, CA 90069
"Actor"

E.G. Marshall
RFD #2, Oregon Road
Mt. Kisco, NY 10549
"Actor"

Garry Marshall
10067 Riverside Drive
Toluca Lake, CA 91602
"Writer, Producer"

James Marshall
1999 Avenue of the Stars #2850
Los Angeles, CA 90067
"Author"

Ken Marshall
9301 Wilshire Blvd. #312
Beverly Hills, CA 90210
"Actor"

Mike Marshall
4641 Fulton Avenue #105
Sherman Oaks, CA 91423
"Actor"

Penny Marshall
7150 La Presa Drive
Los Angeles, CA 90068
"Actress"

Peter Marshall
4337 Marina City Drive #247-E
Marina del Rey, CA 90291
"Actor, TV Host"

Trudy Marshall
1852 Marcheeta Place
Los Angeles, CA 90069
"Actress"

William Marshall
11351 Dronfield Avenue
Pacoima, CA 91331
"Actor"

Frank Marta
8538 Eastwood Road
Los Angeles, CA 90069
"Actor, Singer"

Martika
947 Fairway Drive
Walnut, CA 91789
"Actress"

Barney Martin
12838 Milbank Street
Studio City, CA 91604
"Actor"

Rep. David Martin (NV)
House Cannon Bldg. #442
Washington, DC 20515
"Politician"

Dean Martin
613 North Linden Drive
Beverly Hills, CA 90210
"Actor, Singer"

Dick Martin
11030 Chalon Road
Los Angeles, CA 90077
"Actor, Writer, Comedian"

Eric Martin Band
P.O. Box 5952
San Francisco, CA 94101
"Rock & Roll Band"

Helen Martin
1440 North Fairfax #109
Los Angeles, CA 90046
"Actress"

Jared Martin
15060 Ventura Blvd. #350
Sherman Oaks, CA 91403
"Actor"

Millicent Martin
P.O. Box 101
Redding, CT 06875
"Singer, Actress"

Nan Martin
33604 Pacific Coast Hwy.
Malibu, CA 90265
"Actress"

Pamela Sue Martin
P.O. Box 25578
Los Angeles, CA 90025
"Actress, Producer"

Steve Martin
P.O. Box 929
Beverly Hills, CA 90213
"Actor"

Tony Martin
10390 Wilshire Blvd. #1507
Los Angeles, CA 90024
"Actor, Singer"

Wink Martindale
1650 Veteran Avenue #104
Los Angeles, CA 90024
"Game Show Host"

A. Martinez
6835 Wild Life Road
Malibu, CA 90265
"Actor"

Rep. Matthew Martinez (CA)
House Rayburn Bldg. #2446
Washington, DC 20515
"Politician"

Al Martino
927 North Rexford Drive
Beverly Hills, CA 90210
"Singer'

Arthur Marx
1244 Bel Air Road
Los Angeles, CA 90024
"Dramatist"

Greg Marx
8322 Beverly Blvd. #202
Los Angeles, CA 90048
"Actor"

Mrs. Harpo Marx
37631 Palm View Road
Rancho Mirage, CA 92270
"Harpo Marx's Widower"

Richard Marx
15250 Ventura Blvd. #900
Sherman Oaks, CA 91403
"Conductor"

Ron Masak
5440 Shirley Avenue
Tarzana, CA 91356
"Actor"

Hugh Masekela
52 Gover Court
Paradise Road
London SW4 ENGLAND
"Trumpeter"

Giulietta Masina
141a Via Margutta 110
Rome, ITALY
"Actress"

Jackie Marsalis
30 Park Avenue
New York, NY 10016
"Comedian"

Marlyn Mason
P.O. Box 1648
Studio City, CA 91604
"Actress, Singer"

Marsha Mason
c/o Collett & Levy
10100 San Monica Blvd. #400
Los Angeles, CA 90067
"Actress"

Tom Mason
853-7th Avenue #9A
New York, NY 10019
"Actor"

Osa Massen
10501 Wilshire Blvd. #704
Los Angeles, CA 90024
"Actress"

Andrew Masset
11635 Huston
North Hollywood, CA 91607
"Actor"

Anna Massey
388-396 Oxford Street
London W1 ENGLAND
"Actress"

Daniel Massey
35 Tynehan Road
London SW11 ENGLAND
"Actor"

Masters & Johnson
3530 Camino Del Rio North
San Diego, CA 92108
"Physician & Psychologist"

Mary Stuart Masterson
40 West 57th Street
New York, NY 10067
"Actress"

Marcello Mastroianni
Av. Cav, Via Maria Adelaide 8
Rome, ITALY
"Actor"

Richard Masur
121 North San Vicente Blvd.
Beverly Hills, CA 90211
"Actor, Writer"

Jerry Mathers
23965 Via Aranda
Valencia, CA 91355
"Actor"

Don Matheson
10275 1/2 Missouri Avenue
Los Angeles, CA 90025
"Actor"

Tim Matheson
1221 Stone Canyon Road
Los Angeles, CA 90077
"Actor"

Carmen Mathews
101 Marchant Road
West Redding, CT 06896
"Actress"

Eddie Mathews
13744 Recuerdo Drive
Del Mar, CA 92014
"Baseball Player"

Bob Mathias
7469 East Pine Avenue
Fresno, CA 93727
"Athlete, Actor"

Mirielle Mathieu
122 Avenue de Wagram
75017 Paris, FRANCE
"Singer"

Johnny Mathis
3500 West Olive Avenue
Suite #750
Burbank, CA 91505
"Singer"

Samantha Mathis
1861 Midvale Avenue #2
Los Angeles, CA 90025
"Orchestra Leader"

Melissa Mathison
655 MacCulloch Drive
Los Angeles, CA 90049
"Screenwriter"

Marlee Matlin
335 North Maple Drive #270
Beverly Hills, CA 90210
"Actress"

Ollie Matson
1319 South Hudson
Los Angeles, CA 90019
"Football Player"

Rep. Robert T. Matsui (CA)
House Rayburn Bldg. #2353
Washington, DC 20515
"Politician"

Kathy Mattea
P.O. Box 158482
Nashville, TN 37215
"Singer"

Walter Matthau
278 Toyopa Drive
Pacific Palisades, CA 90272
"Actor"

Roland Matthes
Storkower Str. 118
1055 Berlin, Germany
"Swimmer"

Kerwin Matthews
67-A Buena Vista Terrace
San Francisco, CA 94117
"Actor"

Don Mattingly
RR #5, Box 74
Evansville, IN 47711
"Baseball Player"

Robin Mattson
917 Manning Avenue
Los Angeles, CA 90024
"Actress"

Victor Mature
P.O. Box 706
Rancho Santa Fe, CA 92067
"Actor"

Peter Matz
18926 Pacific Coast Highway
Malibu, CA 90265
"Composer, Conductor"

Billy Mauch
23427 Canzonet Street
Woodland Hills, CA 91364
"Actor"

Bobby Mauch
23427 Canzonet Street
Woodland Hills, CA 91364
"Actor"

Gene Mauch
46 La Ronda Drive
Rancho Mirage, CA 92270
"Baseball Player"

Bill Mauldin
401 North Wabash Avenue
Chicago, IL 60611
"Cartoonist

Brad Maule
151 South El Camino Drive
Beverly Hills, CA 90212
"Actor"

Nicole Maurey
21 Chemin Vauillons
78160 Marly-le-roi FRANCE
"Actress"

Claire Maurier
11 rue de la Montague-le-Breuil
91360 Epinay sur Orge, FRANCE
"Actress"

Max Maven
1746 North Orange Drive #1106
Los Angeles, CA 90046
"Mind Reader"

Rep. Nicholas Mavroules (MA)
House Rayburn Bldg. #2334
Washington, DC 20515
"Politician"

Peter Max
118 Riverside Drive
New York, NY 10024
"Artist, Designer"

Frank Maxwell
447 San Vicente Blvd. #301
Santa Monica, CA 90401
"Actor"

Lois Maxwell
150 Carlton Street #200
Toronto, Ontario CANADA
"Actress"

Elaine May
146 Central Park West #4E
New York, NY 10023
"Actress, Writer, Director"

Eddie Mayehoff
369 Paseo de Playa #411
Ventura, CA 93001
"Actor"

Ferdianand Mayne
100 South Doheny Drive
Los Angeles, CA 90048
"Actor"

Asa Maynor
P.O. Box 1641
Beverly Hills, CA 90213
"Actress, Producer"

Virginia Mayo
109 East Avenue De Los Arboles
Thousand Oaks, CA 91360
"Actress"

Whitman Mayo
9000 Fifth Avenue
Inglewood, CA 90305
"Actor"

Melanie Mayron
1418 North Ogen Drive
Los Angeles, CA 90046
"Actress, Writer"

Willie Mays
3333 Henry Hudson Parkway
New York, NY 10463
"Baseball Player"

Bill Mazeroski
RR 6, Box 130
Greensburg, PA 15601
"Baseball Player"

Paul Mazursky
16 East 11th Street #3A
New York, NY 10003
"Writer, Producer"

Rep. Romano L. Mazzoli (KY)
House Rayburn Bldg. #2246
Washington, DC 20515
"Politician"

Julia Meade
1010 Fifth Avenue
New York, NY 10021
"Actress"

Audrey Meadows
350 Trousdale Place
Beverly Hills, CA 90210
"Actress"

Jayne Meadows
16185 Woodvale
Encino, CA 91316
"Actress"

Kristen Meadows
15301 Ventura Blvd. #345
Sherman Oaks, CA 91403
"Actress"

Mary T. Meagher
4100 Ormond Drive
Louisville, KY 40207
"Swimmer"

Russell Means
444 Crazy Horse Drive
Porcupine, SD 57772
"Indian Leader"

Anne Meara
118 Riverside Drive #5-A
New York, NY 10024
"Actress, Comedienne"

Meatloaf
Box 68, Stockport
Cheshire SK3 0JY ENGLAND
"Singer, Composer"

Patricia Medina Cotton
1993 Mesa Drive
Palm Springs, CA 92264
"Actress"

Michael Medved
1224 Ashland Avenue
Santa Monica, CA 90405
"Writer, Film Critic"

Evan Meecham
4510 West Glendale Avenue
Glendale, AZ 85301
"Ex-Governor"

Thomas Meehan
Brook House
Obtuse Road
Newtown, CT 06470
"Screenwriter"

Edwin Meese
1075 Springhill Road
McLean, VA 22102
"Politician"

Gunter Meisner
Schildhornstrasse 74
D-1000 Berlin 41
GERMANY
"Actor"

John Cougar Mellencamp
Rt. 1, Box 361
Nashville, IN 47448
"Singer, Songwriter"

Daniel Melnick
1123 Sunset Hills Drive
Los Angeles, CA 90069
"Film Producer"

Sid Melton
5347 Cedros Avenue
Van Nuys, CA 91411
"Actor"

Allen Melvin
271 North Bowling Green Way
Los Angeles, CA 90049
"Actor"

Harold Melvin
P.O. Box 82
Great Neck, NY 11021
"Singer, Songwriter"

Men AT Work
P.O. Box 289, Abbotsford
Victoria 3067 AUSTRALIA
"Rock & Roll Group"

Gian Carlo Menotti
27 East 62nd Street
New York, NY 10021
"Composer"

Menudo
Padosa Hato Rey
157 Ponce de Leon
San Juan, PUERTO RICO
"Rock & Roll Group"

Sir Yehudi Menuhin
Buhlstr
CH-3780 Gstaad-Neuret
SWITZERLAND
"Violinist"

Heather Menzies Urich
15930 Woodvale Road
Encino, CA 91436
"Actress"

Marion Mercer
25901 Piuma
Calabasas, CA 91302
"Actress"

Melina Mercouri
Anagnostropoulon 25
Athens, GREECE
"Actress"

Freddie Mercury
5 Campden Street
London W8 ENGLAND
"Singer, Songwriter"

Burgess Meredith
25 Malibu Colony Road
Malibu, CA 90265
"Actress, Writer, Director"

Don Meredith
P.O. Box 597
Santa Fe, NM 87504
"Football Player"

Lee Ann Meriwether
P.O. Box 260402
Encino, CA 91316
"Actress"

Jan Merlin
9016 Wonderland Avenue
Los Angeles, CA 90046
"Actor, Director"

David Merrick
970 Park Avenue
New York, NY 10028
"Motion Picture Producer"

Dina Merrill
870 United Nations Plaza
New York, NY 10017
"Actress"

Robert Merrill
79 Oxford Drive
New Rochelle, NY 10801
"Baritone"

Teresa Merritt
192-06 110th Road
St. Albans, NY 11412
"Actress"

Dale Messick
64 East Concord Street
Orlando, FL 32801
"Cartoonist"

Don Messick
1360 North Ritchie Court
Chicago, IL 60610
"Actor"

Reinhold Messner
139040 Villnoss
St. Magdalena 52 ITALY
"Mountaineer, Author"

Laurie Metcalf
11845 Kling Street
North Hollywood, CA 91607
"Actress"

Burt Metcalfe
11800 Brookdale Lane
Studio City, CA 91604
"TV Writer, Producer"

Sophie Metral
20 rue Sauffrey
75017 Paris, FRANCE
"Actress"

Art Metrano
1330 North Doheny Drive
Los Angeles, CA 90069
"Actor"

Sen. Howard Metzenbaum (OH)
140 Russell Office Bldg.
Washington, DC 20515
"Politician"

Nicholas Meyer
2109 Stanley Hills Drive
Los Angeles, CA 90046
"Writer, Producer"

Russ Meyer
3121 Arrowhead Drive
Los Angeles, CA 90068
"Film Writer, Producer"

Ari Meyers
301 North Canon Drive #203
Beverly Hills, CA 90210
"Actress"

Rep. Jan Meyers (KS)
House Longworth Bldg. #1230
Washington, DC 20515
"Politician"

Rep. Kweisi Mfume (MD)
House Cannon Bldg. #217
Washington, DC 20515
"Politician"

Miami Sound Machine
8390 S.W. 4th Street
Miami, FL 33144
"Rock & Roll Group"

Rep. Bob Michael (IL)
House Rayburn Bldg. #2112
Washington, DC 20515
"Politician"

George Michael
1149 Calle Vista
Beverly Hills, CA 90210
"Singer, Composer"

Prince Michael of Kent
Kensington Palace
London N5 ENGLAND
"Royalty"

Princess Michael of Kent
Kensington Palace
London N5 ENGLAND
"Royalty"

Lorne Michaels
88 Central Park West
New York, NY 10023
"TV Writer, Producer"

Marilyn Michaels
185 West End Avenue
New York, NY 10023
"Comedienne"

Kari Michaelson
1717 North Highland Avenue #414
Los Angeles, CA 90028
"News Correspondent"

Michael Michele
424 West End Avenue #7B
New York, NY 10023
"Actress"

Keith Michell
130 West 57th Street #10-A
New York, NY 10019
"Actor"

Gov. George Mickelson (SD)
State Capitol, 2nd Floor
Pierre, SD 57501
"Governor"

Dale Midkiff
6369 La Punta Drive
Los Angeles, CA 90068
"Actor"

Bette Midler
P.O. Box 46703
Los Angeles, CA 90046
"Singer, Actress, Comedy"

Mighty Clouds of Joy
9220 Sunset Blvd. #823
Los Angeles, CA 90069
"Gospel Group"

Mike & The Mechanics
P.O. Box 107
London N65 ARU ENGLAND
"Rock & Roll Group

Sen. Barbara A. Mikulski (MD)
Senate Hart Bldg. #320
Washington, DC 20510
"Politician"

Alyssa Milano
12952 Woodbridge
Studio City, CA 91604
"Actress"

Joanna Miles
2062 North Vine Street
Los Angeles, CA 90028
"Actress"

Sarah Miles
7 Windmill Street
London W1 ENGLAND
"Actor, Singer"

Sylvia Miles
240 Central Park South
New York, NY 10019
"Actress"

Vera Miles
P.O. Box 1704
Big Bear Lake, CA 92315
"Actress"

Mike Milken
4543 Tara Drive
Encino, CA 91436
"Stock Broker"

Ann Miller
618 North Alta Drive
Beverly Hills, CA 90210
"Actress, Dancer"

Arthur Miller
Box 320 RR #1 Tophet Road
Roxbury, CT 06783
"Author, Dramatist"

Barry Miller
121 North San Vicente Blvd.
Beverly Hills, CA 90211
"Actor, Singer"

Cheryl Miller
6767 Forest Lawn Drive #115
Los Angeles, CA 90068
"Basketball Analyst"

Rep. Clarence E. Miller (OH)
House Rayburn Bldg. #2308
Washington, DC 20515
"Politician"

Denny Miller
1104 Foothill Road
Ojai, CA 93023
"Actor"

Rep. George Miller (CA)
House Rayburn Bldg. #2228
Washington, DC 20515
"Politician"

Jason Miller
10000 Santa Monica Blvd.
Suite #305
Los Angeles, CA 90067
"Actor, Writer, Director"

Rep. John Miller (WA)
House Cannon Bldg. #322
Washington, DC 20515
"Politician"

Johnny Miller
P.O. Box 2260
Napa, CA 94558
"Golfer"

Mitch Miller
345 West 58th Street
New York, NY 10019
"Musician, Composer"

Nolan Miller
816 North Whittier Drive
Beverly Hills, CA 90210
"Fashion Designer"

Patsy Ruth Miller
425 Sierra Madre North
Palm Desert, CA 92260
"Actress"

Gov. Robert J. Miller (NV)
State Capitol
Carson City, NV 89710
"Governor"

Sidney Miller
3284 Barham Blvd. #304
Los Angeles, CA 90068
"Actor, Director"

Milli Vanilli
8730 Sunset Blvd. PH.-H
Los Angeles, CA 90069
"Music Duo"

Spike Milligan
9 Orme Court
London W2 ENGLAND
"Actor, Director"

Alley Mills
15301 Ventura Blvd. #345
Sherman Oaks, CA 91403
"Actress"

Donna Mills
2660 Benedict Canyon
Beverly Hills, CA 90210
"Actress, Model"

Hayley Mills
81 High Street
Hampton, Middlesex, ENGLAND
"Actress"

Sir John Mills
Hill House
Denham Village
Buckinghamshire ENGLAND
"Actor"

Juliet Mills
4036 Foothill Road
Carpinteria, CA 93013
"Actress"

Stephanie Mills
P.O. Box K-350
Tarzana, CA 91356
"Singer"

Martin Milner
9000 Sunset Blvd. #1200
Los Angeles, CA 90069
"Actor, Radio Personality"

Ronnie Milsap
12 Music Circle South
Nashville, TN 37203
"Singer, Songwriter"

Nathan Milstein
17 Chester Square
London SW1 ENGLAND
"Violinist"

Yvette Mimieux
500 Perugia Way
Los Angeles, CA 90077
"Actress, Writer"

Jan Miner
300 East 46th Street #9-J
New York, NY 10017
"Actress"

Rep. Norman Mineta (CA)
House Rayburn Bldg. #2350
Washington, DC 20515
"Politician"

Liza Minnelli
150 East 69th Street #21-G
New York, NY 10021
"Actress, Singer"

Minnesota Fats
(aka R.W. Wanderone, Jr.)
231-6th Avenue North
Nashville, TN 37219
"Billiard Player"

Minnie Minoso
4250 Marin Drive
Chicago, IL 60613
"Baseball Player"

Miou-Miou
10 Avenue George V
75008 Paris, FRANCE
"Actress"

Walter Mirisch
647 Warner Avenue
Los Angeles, CA 90024
"Film Executive, Producer"

Helen Mirren
55 Park Lane
London W1 ENGLAND
"Actress"

Missing Persons
11935 Laurel Hills Road
Studio City, CA 91604
"Rock & Roll Group"

Mr. Mister
P.O. Box 69343
Los Angeles, CA 90069
"Rock & Roll Group"

Brian Mitchell
14980 Valley Vista
Sherman Oaks, CA 91403
"Actor"

Cameron Mitchell
9744 Wilshire Blvd. #308
Beverly Hills, CA 90212
"Actor"

Don Mitchell
1930 South Marvin
Los Angeles, CA 90016
"Actor"

Edgar Mitchell
P.O. Box 3163
Palm Beach, FL 33480
"Astronuat"

Sen. George Mitchell (ME)
Senate Russell Bldg. #176
Washington, DC 20510
"Politician"

James Mitchell
330 West 72nd Street #12C
New York, NY 10023
"Actor"

Joni Mitchell
10960 Wilshire Blvd. #938
Los Angeles, CA 90024
"Singer, Songwriter"

Kim Mitchell
41 Britain Street #305
Toronto, Ont. M5A 1R7 CANADA
"Singer, Guitarist"

Scoey Mitchell
664 West Broadway #A
Glendale, CA 91204
"Comedian"

Shirley Mitchell
133 South Oakhurst Drive
Beverly Hills, CA 90212
"Actress"

Marvin Mitchelson
1801 Century Park East #1900
Los Angeles, CA 90067
"Talent Agent"

Robert Mitchum
860 San Ysidro Road
Santa Barbara, CA 93108
"Actor"

Rosi Mittermaier
Winkelmoosalm
D-8216 Reit im Winkel
GERMANY
"Skier"

Francois Mitterrand
Palais de l'Elysee
55 et 57 rue de Faubourg
75008 Paris, FRANCE
"Politician"

Steve Mittleman
8821 Beverly Blvd.
Los Angeles, CA 90048
"Comedian"

Kim Miyori
121 North San Vicente Blvd.
Beverly Hills, CA 90211
"Actress"

Johnny Mize
P.O. Box 112
Demorest, GA 30535
"Baseball Player"

Rep. Joe Moakley (MA)
House Cannon Bldg. #221
Washington, DC 20515
"Politician"

Mary Ann Mobley
2751 Hutton Drive
Beverly Hills, CA 90210
"Actress"

Jayne Modean
10000 Santa Monica Blvd.
Suite #305
Los Angeles, CA 90025
"Actress"

Matthew Modine
1632 North Beverly Drive
Beverly Hills, CA 90210
"Actor"

Anna Moffo
380 Madison Avenue
New York, NY 10017
"Soprano"

Rep. Susan Molinari (NY)
House Cannon Bldg. #315
Washington, DC 20515
"Politician"

Richard Moll
7561 West 82nd Street
Playa del Rey, CA 90293
"Actor"

Rep. Alan Mollohan (WV)
House Cannon Bldg. #229
Washington, DC 20515
"Politician"

Paul Monash
912 Alto Cedro Drive
Beverly Hills, CA 90210
"Writer, Producer"

Walter Mondale
2200-1st Bank Place East
Minneapolis, MN 55402
"Ex-Vice President"

Eddie Money
P.O. Box 1994
San Francisco, CA 94101
"Singer"

Monkees
P.O. Box 1461
Radio City Station
New York, NY 10101
"Rock & Roll Group"

Bob Monkhouse
118 Beaufort Street
London SW3 6BU ENGLAND
"Actor, Writer"

Bill Monroe
2804 Opryland Drive
Nashville, TN 37214
"Singer, Guitarist"

Earl Monroe
113 West 88th Street
New York, NY 10025
"Basketball Player"

Renee Montagne
c/o National Public Radio
2025 "M" Street NW
Washington, DC 20036
"News Correspondent"

Ashley Montague
321 Cherry Hill Road
Princeton, NJ 08540
"Model"

Ricardo Montalban
1423 Oriole Drive
Los Angeles, CA 90069
"Actor, Director"

Joe Montana
664 Oak Park Way
Redwood City, CA 94062
"Football Player"

Monte Montana
520 Murray Canyon Drive #412
Palm Springs, CA 92262
"Actor"

Belinda Montgomery
15301 Ventura Blvd. #345
Sherman Oaks, CA 91403
"Actress"

Elizabeth Montgomery
1230 Benedict Canyon
Beverly Hills, CA 90210
"Actress"

George Montgomery
P.O. Box 69983
Los Angeles, CA 90069
"Actor"

Rep. "Sonny" Montgomery (MS)
House Rayburn Bldg. #2184
Washington, DC 20515
"Politician"

Carlotta Monti
7946 Fountain Avenue
Los Angeles, CA 90046
"Actress, Writer"

Carlos Montoya
345 West 58th Street
New York, NY 10019
"Guitarist"

Rep. Jim Moody (WI)
House Longworth Bldg. #1019
Washington, DC 20515
"Politician"

Ron Moody
Ingleside
41 The Green, Southgate
London N14 ENGLAND
"Actor"

Rev. Donn Moomaw
3124 Corda Drive
Los Angeles, CA 90049
"Clergy"

Rev. Sun Myung Moon
4 West 43rd Street
New York, NY 10010
"Cult Leader"

Warren Moon
6910 Fannin Street
Houston, TX 77030
"Football Player"

Alvy Moore
8546 Amestov Avenue
Northridge, CA 91324
"Actor"

Clayton Moore
4720 Parkolivo
Calabasas, CA 91302
"Actor"

Constance Moore
1661 Ferrari Drive
Beverly Hills, CA 90210
"Actress"

Demi Moore
1453-3rd Street #420
Santa Monica, CA 90401
"Actress"

Dickie Moore
165 West 46th Street #907
New York, NY 10036
"Actor"

Dudley Moore
73 Market Street
Venice, CA 90291
"Actor, Writer, Pianist"

Juanita Moore
3802-L Dunsford Lane
Inglewood, CA 90305
"Actress"

Mary Tyler Moore
927 Fifth Avenue
New York, NY 10021
"Actress"

Melba Moore
200 Central Park South #8R
New York, NY 10019
"Singer"

Roger Moore
Chalet Fenil
Grund bei Staad
SWITZERLAND
"Actor"

Sara Jane Moore
Fed. Ref. For Women
Alderson, WV 24910
"Prisoner"

Terry Moore
833 Ocean Avenue #104
Santa Monica, CA 90403
"Actress"

Rep. Carlos Moorhead (CA)
House Rayburn Bldg. #2346
Washington, DC 20515
"Politician"

Esai Morales
1147 South Wooster Street
Los Angeles, CA 90035
"Actor"

Erin Moran
11075 Santa Monica Blvd. #150
Los Angeles, CA 90025
"Actress"

Peggy Moran Koster
3101 Village #3
Camarillo, CA 93010
"Actress"

Rick Moranis
90 Riverside Drive #14-E
New York, NY 10024
"Actor"

Tony Mordente
4541 Comber
Encino, CA 91316
"Film Director"

Jeanne Moreau
193 rue de l'Universite
75007 Paris, FRANCE
"Actress"

Rep. Constance Morella (MD)
House Longworth Bldg. #1024
Washington, DC 20515
"Politician"

Rita Moreno
1620 Amalfi Drive
Pacific Palisades, CA 90272
"Actress"

Deddie Morgan
9000 Sunset Blvd. #1200
Los Angeles, CA 90069
"Actress"

Dennis Morgan
SKJ Ranch
Ahwahnee, CA 93601
"Actor, Singer"

Harry Morgan
13172 Boca De Canon Lane
Los Angeles, CA 90049
"Actor, Director"

Henry Morgan
350 East 84th Street
New York, NY 10028
"TV Personality"

Jane Morgan Weintraub
277740 Pacific Coast Highway
Malibu, CA 90265
"Actress"

Jaye P. Morgan
30130 Cuthbert
Malibu, CA 90265
"Actress"

Joe Morgan
5588 Fernhoff Road
Oakland, CA 94619
"Baseball Player"

Lorrie Morgan
P.O. Box 22765
Nashville, TN 37202
"Singer"

Michelle Morgan
5 rue Jacques Dulud
92200 Neuily, FRANCE
"Actress"

Robert M. Morganthau
1085 Park Avenue
New York, NY 10028
"Lawyer"

Cathy Moriarity
4139 Via Marina #901
Marina del Rey, CA 90292
"Actress"

Michael Moriarty
200 West 58th Street #3B
New York, NY 10019
"Actor"

Patricia Morison
400 South Hauser Blvd.
Los Angeles, CA 90036
"Actress, Singer"

Noriyuki "Pat" Morita
P.O. Box 491278
Los Angeles, CA 90049
"Actor, Comedian"

Louisa Moritz
120 South Reeves Drive
Beverly Hills, CA 90212
"Actress, Model"

Karen Morley Gough
4411 Matilija Avenue
Sherman Oaks, CA 91423
"Actress"

Robert Morley
Fairmans, Wargrave
Berkshire, ENGLAND
"Actor"

Giorgio Moroder
9348 Civic Center Drive #101
Beverly Hills, CA 90210
"Composer, Conductor"

David Morphet
101 Honor Oak Road
London SE23 3LB ENGLAND
"Writer, Producer"

Anita Morris
13758 Mulholland Drive
Beverly Hills, CA 90210
"Actress"

Dr. Desmond Morris
78 Danbury Road
Oxford, ENGLAND
"Zoologist, Author"

Garret Morris
3740 Barham Blvd. #E-116
Los Angeles, CA 90068
"Actor"

Gary Morris
6027 Church Drive
Sugarland, TX 77478
"Actor, Singer"

Greg Morris
3191 Bel Air Road
Las Vegas, NV 89109
"Actor"

Howard Morris
18457 Clifftop Way
Malibu, CA 90265
"Actor, Director"

Phil Morris
704 Strand
Manhattan Beach, CA 90266
"Actor"

Rep. Sid Morrison (WA)
House Longworth Bldg. #1434
Washington, DC 20515
"Politician"

Van Morrison
12304 Santa Monica Blvd. #300
Los Angeles, CA 90025
"Singer, Songwriter"
"Actor"

Karen Morrow
9400 Readcrest Drive
Beverly Hills, CA 90210
"Actress"

Rob Morrow
151 South El Camino Drive
Beverly Hills, CA 90212
"Actor"

Carleton E. Morse
Box 50 - Star Route
Redwood City, CA 94062
"Writer"

David Morse
3200 Oakshire Drive
Los Angeles, CA 90068
"Actor"

Robert Morse
13554 Valley Vista
Sherman Oaks, CA 91423
"Actor"

Gary Morton
40241 Clubview Drive
Rancho Mirage, CA 92270
"Comedian"

Howard Morton
12311 Cantura Street
Studio City, CA 91604
"Actor"

Joe Morton
606 North Larchmont Blvd.
Suite #309
Los Angeles, CA 90004
"Actor"

John Moschitta, Jr.
8033 Sunset Blvd. #41
Los Angeles, CA 90046
"Actor"

Willie Mosconi
1804 Prospect Ridge
Hidden Heights, NJ 08035
"Billard Player"

Ted Mosel
400 East 57th Street
New York, NY 10022
"Dramatist"

Mark Mosley
P.O. Box 17247
Washington, DC 20041
"Football Player"

Billy E. Moses
405 Sycamore Road
Santa Monica, CA 90402
"Actor"

Edwin Moses
20 Kimberly Circle
Dayton, OH 45408
"Track & Field Athlete"

Rick Mose
14720 Ventura Blvd. #4
Encino, CA 91316
"Actor, Singer"

Roger E. Moseley
3756 Prestwick Drive
Los Angeles, CA 90027
"Actor"

Moss Back Mule Band
306 South Saline Street #316
Syracuse, NY 13202
"Music Group"

Ronn Moss
2401 Nottingham Avenue
Los Angeles, CA 90027
"Actor"

Sterling Moss
46 Shepherd Street, Mayfair
London W1Y 8JN ENGLAND
"Actor"

Donny Most
3811 Multiview Drive
Los Angeles, CA 90068
"Actor"

Manny Mota
3920 Los Olivos Lane
La Crescenta, CA 91214
"Baseball Player"

Motley Crue
40/42 Newman Street
London W1P 3PA ENGLAND
"Rock & Roll Group"

Stewart Mott
515 Madison Avenue
New York, NY 10022
"Philanthropist"

Movita
2766 Motor Avenue
Los Angeles, CA 90064
"Actress"

Bill Moyers
524 West 57th Street
New York, NY 10019
"News Correspondent"

Sen. Daniel Moynihan (NY)
Senate Russell Bldg. #464
Washington, DC 20510
"Politician"

Rep. Robert J. Mrazek (NY)
House Cannon Bldg. #306
Washington, DC 20515
"Politician"

Pres. Hosni Mubarak
Royal Palace
Cairo, EGYPT
"President of Egypt"

Roger Mudd
7167 Old Dominion Drive
McLean, VA 22101
"News Correspondent"

Wallace Muhamred
7351 South Stony Island
Chicago, IL 60617
"Religious Leader"

Esther Muir
587-D Heritage Hills Drive
Somer, NY 10589
"Actress"

Jean Muir
University of New Mexico
Theatre Arts Department
Albuquerque, NM 87313
"Actress"

Diana Muldaur
259 Quadro Vecchio Drive
Pacific Palisades, CA 90272
"Actress"

Maria Muldaur
P.O. Box 5535
Mill Valley, CA 94942
"Singer, Songwriter"

Shirley Muldowney
16755 Parthenia Street #4
Sepulveda, CA 91343
"Actor Racer"

Kate Mulgrew
11938 Foxboro Drive
Los Angeles, CA 90049
"Actress"

Edward Mulhare
6045 Sunnyslope Avenue
Van Nuys, CA 91401
"Actor"

Martin Mull
338 Chadbourne Avenue
Los Angeles, CA 90049
"Actor, Comedian, Writer"

Greg Mullavey
4444 Hayvenhurst Avenue
Encino, CA 91436
"Actor"

Richard Mulligan
145 South Beachwood Drive
Los Angeles, CA 90004
"Actor"

Robert Mulligan
1120 Stone Canyon Road
Los Angeles, CA 90077
"Director, Producer"

Gardner Mulloy
1 Fisher Island Drive
Fisher Island, FL 33109
"Tennis Player"

Brian Mulroney
"Stornoway"
Ottawa, Ontario CANADA
"Prime Minister of Canada"

Billy Mumy
9169 Sunset Blvd.
Los Angeles, CA 90069
"Actor"

Caroline Munro
22 Grafton Street
London W1 ENGLAND
"Actress, Model"

George Murdock
5733 Sunfield Avenue
Lakewood, CA 90712
"Actor"

Rupert Murdoch
210 South Street
New York, NY 10002
"Publisher"

Sen. Frank Murkowski (AK)
Senate Hart Bldg. #709
Washington, DC 20510
"Politician"

Rep. Austin Murphy (PA)
House Rayburn Bldg. #2210
Washington, DC 20515
"Politician"

Ben Murphy
3601 Vista Pacifica #17
Malibu, CA 90265
"Actor"

Dale Murphy
3384 Townley Place
Lawrenceville, GA 30245
"Baseball Player"

Eddie Murphy
2727 Benedict Canyon Drive
Beverly Hills, CA 90210
"Actor, Comedian"

George Murphy
100 Worth Avenue #419
Palm Beach, FL 33480
"Ex-Senator"

Michael Murphy
P.O. Box FFF
Taos, NM 87571
"Actor"

Rosemary Murphy
220 East 73rd Street
New York, NY 10021
"Actress"

Anne Murray
4881 Yonge Street #412
Toronto, Ont. M4S 2B9 CANADA
"Singer"

Bill Murray
RFD 1, Box 250-A
Washington Springs Road
Palisades, NY 10964
"Actor"

Don Murray
15301 Ventura Blvd. #345
Sherman Oaks, CA 91403
"Actor, Writer, Director"

Jan Murray
1157 Calle Vista
Beverly Hills, CA 90210
"Actor, Comedian"

Katherine Murray
2877 Kalakaua Avenue
Honolulu, HI 96815
"Dance Instructor"

Kate Murtagh
15146 Moorpark Street
Sherman Oaks, CA 91403
"Actress"

Rep. John P. Murtha (PA)
House Rayburn Bldg. #2423
Washington, DC 20515
"Politician"

Tony Musante
38 Bedford Street
New York, NY 10014
"Actor, Writer"

Brent Musburger
51 West 52nd Street
New York, NY 10019
"Sportscaster"

Edmund Muskie
1101 Vermont Avenue N.W.
Washington, DC 20005
"Ex-Senator"

Marjorie Ann Mutchie
1169 Mary Circle
La Verne, CA 91750
"Actress"

Ornella Muti
376 Dalehurst Avenue
Los Angeles, CA 90024
"Actress"

Rep. John T. Myers (IN)
House Rayburn Bldg. #2372
Washington, DC 20517
"Politician"

Bess Myerson
2 East 71st Street
New York, NY 10021
"Columnist"

The Mystics
88 Anador Street
Staten Island, NY 10303
"Vocal Group"

John Naber
P.O. Box 50107
Pasadena, CA 91105
"Swimmer"

Jim Nabors
151 South El Camino Drive
Beverly Hills, CA 90212
"Actor, Singer"

George Nader
52 South Iwa Place
La Haina, CA 96761
"Actor"

Michael Nader
7565 Jalmia Way
Los Angeles, CA 90046
"Actor"

Ralph Nader
P.O. Box 19367
Washington, DC 20036
"Consumer Advocate"

Rep. David R. Nagle (IA)
House Cannon Bldg. #214
Washington, DC 20515
"Politician"

Joe Namath
300 East 51st Street #11-A
New York, NY 10022
"Football Player"

Nantucket
3924 Browning Place #200
Raleigh, NC 27609
"Rock & Roll Group"

Jack Narz
1905 Beverly Place
Beverly Hills, CA 90210
"TV Host"

Grahan Nash
584 North Lachmont Blvd.
Hollywood, CA 90004
"Singer, Songwriter"

Johnny Nash
Chalet Nival, Oberbort
CH-3780 Gstaad, SWITZERLAND
"Singer, Songwriter"

Ille Nastase
15 East 69th Street
New York, NY 100021
"Tennis Player"

Rep. William Natcher (KY)
House Rayburn Bldg. #2333
Washington, DC 20515
"Politician"

Marie-Jose Nat
10 rue Royale
75008 Paris, FRANCE
"Actress"

Mildred Natwick
1001 Park Avenue
New York, NY 10028
"Actress"

Melinda Naud
12330 Viewcrest Road
Studio City, CA 91604
"Actress"

David Naughton
15301 Ventura Blvd. #345
Sherman Oaks, CA 91403
"Actor, Singer"

James Naughton
8899 Beverly Blvd.
Los Angeles, CA 90048
"Actor"

Martina Navratilova
2665 South Bay Shore Drive #1002
Miami, FL 33133
"Tennis Player"

Patricia Neal
P.O. Box 1043
Edgartown, MA 02539
"Actress"

Rep. Richard Neal (MA)
House Cannon Bldg. #437
Washington, DC 20515
"Politcis"

Rep. Stephen Neal (NC)
House Rayburn Bldg. #2463
Washington, DC 20515
"Politician"

Christopher Neame
5 Belsize Square #2
London NW3 ENGLAND
"Actor"

Ronald Neame
2317 Kimridge Drive
Beverly Hills, CA 90210
"Film Director"

Holly Near
1514-A Electric Avenue
Venice, CA 90291
"Singer"

Lynn Neary
c/o National Public Radio
2025 "M" Street NW
Washington, DC 20036
"News Correspondent"

Connie Needham
19721 Castlebar Drive
Rowland Heights, CA 91748
"Actress"

Hal Needham
2220 Avenue of the Stars #302
Los Angeles, CA 90067
"Writer, Producer"

Liam Neeson
1999 Avenue of the Stars
Suite #2850
Los Angeles, CA 90067
"Actress"

Jean Negulesco
20508 Mandel Street
Canoga Park, CA 91306
"Director, Producer"

Noel Neill
331 Sage Lane
Santa Monica, CA 90402
"Actress"

Sam Neill
40 West 57th Street
New York, NY 10019
"Actor"

LeRoy Neiman
1 West 67th Street
New York, NY 10023
"Artist"

Stacey Nelkin
2770 Hutton Drive
Beverly Hills, CA 90210
"Actress"

Kate Nelligan
3 Goodwin's Court
London WC2 ENGLAND
"Actress"

Barry Nelson
134 West 58th Street
New York, NY 10019
"Actor"

Byron Nelson
Fairway Ranch, Rt. 2
Roanoke, TX 76262
"Golfer"

Craig T. Nelson
9350 Wilshire Blvd. #324
Beverly Hills, CA 90212
"Actor, Writer"

David Nelson
4179 Valley Meadow Road
Encino, CA 91316
"Actor, Director"

Ed Nelson
9255 Sunset Blvd. #603
Los Angeles, CA 90069
"Actor"

Frank Nelson
8906 Evanview Drive
Los Angeles, CA 90069
"Actor"

Gene Nelson
2 Stern Lane
Atherton, CA 94025
"Actor, Director"

Harriet Hilliard Nelson
4179 Valley Meadow
Encino, CA 91316
"Actress, Singer"

John Allen Nelson
9000 Sunset Blvd. #1200
Los Angeles, CA 90069
"Actor"

Judd Nelson
P.O. Box 69170
Los Angeles, CA 90069
"Actor"

Kris Nelson
209 South Carmelina Avenue
Los Angeles, CA 90049
"Actress"

Lori Nelson Mann
8831 Sunset Blvd. #402
Los Angeles, CA 90069
"Actress"

Tracy Nelson
405 Sycamore Road
Santa Monica, CA 90402
"Actress"

Willie Nelson
P.O. Box 33280
Austin, TX 78764
"Singer, Songwriter"

Corin "Corkey" Nemec
9348 Civic Center Drive #407
Beverly Hills, CA 90210
"Actor"

Franco Nero
Paolo Petri-Marina Diberty
Via Margutta la
00187 Rome, ITALY
"Actor"

Michael Nesmith
50 North La Cienga Blvd. #210
Beverly Hills, CA 90211
"Singer, Producer"

Ron Nessen
1835 "K" Street N.W. #805
Washington, DC 20006
"News Correspondent"

Benjamin Netanyahue
Hakirya Romema
Jerusalem 91950 ISRAEL
"Government Official"

Graig Nettles
13 North Lane
Del Mar, CA 92014
"Baseball Player"

Lois Nettleton
1801 Avenue of the Stars #1250
Los Angeles, CA 90067
"Actress"

Aaron Neville
P.O. Box 24752
New Orleans, LA 70184
"Singer"

Mickey Newbury
2510 Franklin Road
Nashville, TN 27204
"Singer, Songwriter"

Don Newcombe
22507 Peale Drive
Woodland Hills, CA 91364
"Baseball Player"

John Newcome
P.O. Box 469
New Braunfels, TX 78130
"Tennis Player"

New Editon
P.O. Box 77505
San Francisco, CA 94107
"R&B Group"

New Grass Revival
P.O. Box 128037
Nashville, TN 37212
"C&W Group"

Bob Newhart
420 Amapola Lane
Los Angeles, CA 90077
"Actor, Comedian"

New Kids on the Block
P.O. Box 7001
Quincy, MA 02269
"Rock & Roll Group"

John Newland
1727 Nichols Canyon
Los Angeles, CA 90046
"Actor"

Anthony Newley
9000 Sunset Blvd. #1200
Los Angeles, CA 90069
"Singer, Actor, Writer"

Barry Newman
425 North Oakhurst Drive
Beverly Hills, CA 90210
"Actor"

Laraine Newman
10480 Ashton Avenue
Los Angeles, CA 90024
"Actress"

Nanette Newman
Seven Pines, Wentworth
Surrey GU25 4QP ENGLAND
"Actress"

Paul Newman
1120-5th Avenue #1-C
New York, NY 10128
"Actor, Auto Racer"

Phyllis Newman
529 West 42nd Street #7
New York, NY 10036
"Actress"

Randy Newman
470-26th Street
Santa Monica, CA 90402
"Singer, Songwriter"

Robert Newman
151 South El Camino Drive
Beverly Hills, CA 90212
"Actor"

Julie Newmar
204 South Carmelina Avenue
Los Angeles, CA 90049
"Actress, Model"

New Order
86 Palatin Road
Dudsbury, Manchester 20
ENGLAND
"Rock & Roll Group"

New Riders of the Purple Sage
P.O. Box "O"
Minneapolis, MN 55331
"Rock & Roll Group"

Tommy Newson
19315 Wells Drive
Tarzana, CA 91356
"Conductor"

Juice Newton
P.O. Box 2156
Santa Monica, CA 90406
"Singer"

Wayne Newton
6629 South Pecos
Las Vegas, NV 89120
"Singer, Actor"

Olivia Newton-John
P.O. Box 2710
Malibu, CA 90265
"Singer, Actress"

Richard Ney
800 South San Rafael Avenue
Pasadena, CA 91105
"Actor"

Dr. Haing S. Ngor
945 North Beaudry Avenue
Los Angeles, CA 90012
"Actor"

Dustin Nguyen
9301 Wilshire Blvd. #312
Beverly Hills, CA 90210
"Actor"

Stavros Niarchos
41-43 Park Street
London W1 ENGLAND
"Shipping Executive"

Denise Nicholas
932 Longwood Avenue
Los Angeles, CA 90019
"Actress, Singer"

Fayard Nicholas
Motion Picture Home
23450 Calabasas Avenue
Woodland Hills, CA 91302
"Dancer"

Mike Nichols
211 Central Park West
New York, NY 10024
"Film Writer, Director"

Nichele Nichols
23281 Leonora Drive
Woodland Hills, CA 91367
"Actress"

Stephen Nichols
6287 View Way
Los Angeles, CA 90068
"Actor"

Jack Nicholson
15760 Ventura Blvd. #1730
Encino, CA 91436
"Actor"

Jack Nicklaus
11760 U.S. Highway 1 #6
North Palm Beach, FL 33408
"Golfer"

Sen. Don Nickles (OK)
Senate Hart Bldg. #713
Washington, DC 20510
"Politician"

Stevie Nicks
P.O. Box 6907
Alhambra, CA 91802
"Singer, Songwriter"

Julia Nickson Soul
2232 Moreno Drive
Los Angeles, CA 90039
"Actress"

Alex Nicol
1496 San Leandro Park
Santa Barbara, CA 93108
"Actor"

Joe Niekro
501 Chicago Avenue South
Minneapolis, MN 55415
"Baseball Player"

Phil Niekro
4781 Castlewood Drive
Liburn, GA 30247
"Baseball Player"

Brigitte Nielsen
12488 Wilshire Blvd. #930
Los Angeles, CA 90025
"Actress"

Toni Nieminen
c/o Finnish Olympic Committee
Radiokatu 20
00240 Helsinki, FINLAND
"Skater"

Leslie Nielsen
1622 Wilshire Blvd.
Los Angeles, CA 90069
"Actor"

Night Ranger
P.O. Box 1000
Glen Ellen, CA 95442
"Rock & Roll Group"

Wendell Niles
10357 Valley Spring Lane
North Hollywood, CA 91602
"Annoucer"

Birgit Nilsson
P.O. Box 527
Stockholm, SWEDEN
"Soprano"

Harry Nilsson
23960 Long Valley Road
Hidden Valley, CA 91302
"Singer, Songwriter"

Leonard Nimoy
801 Stone Canyon
Los Angeles, CA 90077
"Actor, Writer, Director"

Paul Nitze
3120 Woodley Road
Washington, DC 20008
"Statesman"

Mrs. Hjordis Niven
Chateau D'Oex
Vaud SWITZERLAND
"David Niven's Widower"

David Niven, Jr.
1457 Blue Jay Way
Los Angeles, CA 90069
"Son of David Niven"

Marni Nixon
9000 Sunset Blvd. #1200
Los Angeles, CA 90069
"Singer, Actress"

Norm Nixon
607 Marguerita Avenue
Santa Monica, CA 90402
"Basketball Player"

Mrs. Patricia Nixon
577 Chestnut Ridge Road
Woodcliff Lake, NJ 07675
"Ex-First Lady"

Richard Nixon
577 Chestnut Ridge Road
Woodcliff Lake, NJ 07675
"Ex-President"

Louis Nizer
40 West 57th Street
New York, NY 10019
"Actor"

Chelsea Noble
8730 Sunset Blvd. #220-W.
Los Angeles, CA 90069
"Actress"

James Noble
80 Bywater Lane
Black Rock, CT 06605
"Actor"

Dr. Thomas Noguchi
1110 Avoca Avenue
Pasadena, CA 91105
"Coroner"

Christopher Nolan
158 Vernon Avenue
Dublin, IRELAND
"Poet, Author"

Jeanette Nolan
1417 Samoa Way
Laguna Beach, CA 92651
"Actress"

Kathleen Nolan
360 East 55th Street
New York, NY 10022
"Actress"

Chuck Noll
300 Stadium Circle
Pittsburg, PA 15212
"Football Coach"

Nick Nolte
6174 Ronsall Drive
Malibu, CA 90265
"Actor"

Peter Noone
9265 Robin Lane
Los Angeles, CA 90069
"Singer"

Clayton Norcross
951 Galloway Street
Pacific Palisades, CA 90272
"Actor"

Gen. Manuel Noriega
#38699-079
Metro Correctional Center
1531 N. W. 12th Street
Miami, FL 33125
"Prisoner of War"

Greg Norman
P.O. Box 12458
Palm Beach Gardens, FL 33410
"Golfer"

Jessye Norman
c/o Shaw
1900 Broadway
New York, NY 10023
"Soprano"

Maide Norman
455 East Charleston Road #132-B
Palo Alto, CA 94306
"Actress"

Christopher Norris
9016 Wilshire Blvd. #434
Beverly Hills, CA 90211
"Actress"

Chuck Norris
P.O. Box 872
Navosota, TX 77868
"Actor"

Jay North
4101 Beck Avenue
North Hollywood, CA 91602
"Actor"

Oliver North
703 Kentland Drive
Great Falls, VA 22066
"Former Military Lt. Col."

Sheree North
27 Village Park Way
Santa Monica, CA 90405
"Actress"

Wayne Northrup
21919 West Canon Drive
Topanga, CA 90290
"Actor"

Ken Norton
16 South Peck Drive
Laguna Niguel, CA 92677
"Boxer, Actor"

Judy Norton-Taylor
6767 Forest Lawn Drive #115
Los Angeles, CA 90068
"Actress, Model"

Deborah Norville
829 Park Avenue #10-A
New York, NY 10021
"Radio-TV Host"

Michael Nouri
6036-C Hazelhurst Place
North Hollywood, CA 91607
"Actor"

William Novack
3 Ashton
Newton, MA 02149
"Author"

Kim Novak
Rt. 3, Box 524
Carmel Highland, CA 93921
"Actress"

Robert Novak
1750 Pennsylvania Avenue N.W.
Suite #1312
Washington, DC 20006
"News Journalist, Columnist"

Don Novello
P.O. Box 245
Fairfax, CA 94930
"Actor, Writer, Comedian"

Jamila Novotna
162 East 80th Street
New York, NY 10021
"Opera Singer"

Rep. Henry Nowak (NY)
House Rayburn Bldg. #2240
Washington, DC 20515
"Politician"

Eddie Nugent
419 Devonshire Street
San Antonio, TX 78209
"Actor"

Ted Nugent
P.O. Box 15108
Ann Arbor, MI 49106
"Singer, Guitarist"

Gary Numan
39/41 North Road
London N7 7DP ENGLAND
"Singer, Songwriter"

Sen. Sam Nunn (GA)
303 Dirksen Bldg.
Washington, DC 20510
"Politician"

Rudolf Nureyev
35 Dover Street
London W1 ENGLAND
"Dancer"

France Nuyen
1930 Century Park West #303
Los Angeles, CA 90067
"Actress"

Diana Nyad
151 East 86th Street
New York, NY 10028
"Swimmer"

Carrie Nye
109 East 79th Street
New York, NY 10010
"Actress"

Louis Nye
1241 Corsica Drive
Pacific Palisdaes, CA 90272
"Actor, Comedian"

Russell Nype
178 East 78th Street
New York, NY 10021
"Actor"

Sven Nyquist
4 Floragatan
Stockholm 11431 SWEDEN
"Photographer"

Laura Nyro
P.O. Box 186
Shoreham, NY 11786
"Singer, Songwriter"

Rep. Mary Rose Oakar (OH)
House Rayburn Bldg. #2231
Washington, DC 20515
"Politician"

Oak Ridge Boys
5800 East Skelly Drive, PH.
Tulsa, OK 74135
"C&W Group"

Randi Oaks
3681 Alomar Drive
Sherman Oaks, CA 91423
"Actress"

Oasis
P.O. Box 28082
Columbus, OH 43228
"Gospel Group"

John Oates
130 West 57th Street #12B
New York, NY 10019
"Singer, Songwriter"

Rep. James Oberstar (MN)
House Rayburn Bldg. #2209
Washington, DC 20515
"Politician"

Rep. David Obey (WI)
House Rayburn Bldg. #2462
Washington, DC 20515
"Politician"

Hugh O'Brian
3195 Benedict Canyon
Beverly Hills, CA 90210
"Actor"

Cubby O'Brien
11274 Dulcet Avenue
Northridge, CA 91324
"Actor"

Ken O'Brien
598 Madison Avenue
New York, NY 10022
"Football Player"

Margaret O'Brien
1250 La Peresa Drive
Thousand Oaks, CA 91362
"Actress"

Parry O'Brien
851 Euclid
Santa Monica, CA 90403
"Track Athlete"

Billy Ocean
32 Willesden Lane
London NW1 ENGLAND
"Singer"

Helen O'Connell
1260 South Beverly Glen
Los Angeles, CA 90024
"Singer"

Carroll O'Connor
30826 Broad Beach Road
Malibu, CA 90265
"Actor, Writer, Director"

Des O'Connor
235-241 Regent Street
London W1A 2JT ENGLAND
"Singer"

Donald O'Connor
P.O. Box 4524
North Hollywood, CA 91607
"Actor, Director"

Sandra Day O'Connor
1-1st Street, Northeast
Washington, DC 20543
"Supreme Court Justice"

Sinead O'Connor
41 Britain Street #200
Toronto, Ontario M5A 1R7
CANADA
"Singer"

Tim O'Connor
10000 Santa Monica Blvd. #305
Los Angeles, CA 90067
"Actor"

Anita O'Day
R.D. 1, BOX 91
Tannersville, PA 18372
"Entertainer, Singer"

Molly O'Day
P.O. Box 2123
Avila Beach, CA 93424
"Actress"

Tony O'Dell
417 Griffith Park Drive
Burbank, CA 91506
"Actor"

Martha O'Driscoll Appleton
22 Indian Creek Village
Miami Beach, FL 33154
"Actress"

Al Oerter
135 West Islip Road
West Islip, NY 11797
"Executive, Discus Thrower"

Ian Oqilvy
17 Great Cumberland Plaza
London W1A 146 ENGLAND
"Actor"

Lani O'Grady
33861 Calle Primavera
Dana Point, CA 92629
"Actress"

Soon-Teck Oh
8235 Santa Monica Blvd. #202
Los Angeles, CA 90046
"Actor"

Jenny O'Hara
8663 Wonderland Avenue
Los Angeles, CA 90046
"Actress"

Maureen O'Hara
P.O. Box 1400
Christiansted 00820
St. Croix, VIRGIN ISLANDS
"Actress"

Madelyn Murray O'Hare
2210 Handcock Drive
Austin, TX 78756
"Atheist"

Dan O'Herlihy
9113 Sunset Blvd.
Los Angeles, CA 90069
"Actor"

Carol Ohmart
P.O. Box 5435
Lahaina, HI 96761
"Actress"

Oingo Boingo
8335 Sunset Blvd. #300
Los Angeles, CA 90069
"Rock & Roll Group"

O'Jays
113 North Robertson Blvd.
Los Angeles, CA 90069
"R&B Group"

Michael O'Keeffe
P.O. Box 216
Malibu, CA 90265
"Actor"

Miles O'Keeffe
P.O. Box 69365
Los Angeles, CA 90069
"Actor"

Ken Olandt
5701 Cahill Avenue
Tarzana, CA 91356
"Actor"

Mike Oldfield
"Little Halings"
Tilehouse Lane
Denham, Bucks ENGLAND
"Musician, Composer"

Gary Oldham
235 Regent Street
London W1 ENGLAND
"Actor"

Rep. Jim Olin (VA)
House Longworth Bldg. #1410
Washington, DC 20515
"Politician"

Ken Olin
11840 Chapparal Street
Los Angeles, CA 90049
"Actor"

David Oliver
4185 Arch Drive #303
Studio City, CA 91604
"Actor"

Gordon Oliver
200 North Swall Drive #453
Beverly Hills, CA 90210
"Actor, Director"

Edward James Olmos
10000 Santa Monica Blvd. #305
Los Angeles, CA 90067
"Actor"

Gerald O'Loughlin
P.O. Box 832
Arleta, CA 91331
"Actor, Director"

Merlin Olsen
1080 Lorain Road
San Marino, CA 91108
"Sportscaster, Actor"

Nancy Olsen Livingston
945 North Alpine Drive
Beverly Hills, CA 90210
"Actress"

Susan Olsen
4506 Saugus Avenue
Sherman Oaks, CA 91403
"Actress"

James Olson
250 West 57th Street #2223
New York, NY 10019
"Actor"

Peter O'Malley
Doger Stadium
Los Angeles, CA 90012
"Baseball Executive"

Kate O'Mara
2121 Avenue Of The Stars #950
Los Angeles, CA 90067
"Actress"

Sydney Omarr
201 Ocean Avenue #1706-B
Santa Monica, CA 90402
"Astrologer, Writer"

Jacqueline Kennedy Onassis
1040 Fifth Avenue
New York, NY 10028
"Ex-First Lady, Editor"

Griffin O'Neal
21368 Pacific Coast Highway
Malibu, CA 90265
"Screenwriter"

Patrick O'Neal
8428-C Melrose Place
Los Angeles, CA 90006
"Actor, Director"

Ryan O'Neal
21368 Pacific Coast Highway
Malibu, CA 90265
"Actor"

Tatum O'Neal
23712 Malibu Colony Road
Malibu, CA 90265
"Actress"

Dick O'Neil
230 South Lasky Drive
Beverly Hills, CA 90212
"Actor"

Jennifer O'Neil
32356 Mulholland Highway
Malibu, CA 90265
"Actress, Model"

Ed O'Neill
2607 Grand Canal
Venice, CA 90291
"Actor"

Kitty O'Neill
P.O. Box 604
Medina, OH 44256
"Stuntwoman, Auto Racer"

Thomas P. "Tip" O'Neill
Cape Cod
Harwich Port, MA 02646
"Ex-House Speaker"

Yoko Ono Lennon
1 West 72nd Street
New York, NY 10023
"Singer, Songwriter"

Michael Ontkean
7120 Grasswood
Malibu, CA 90265
"Actor"

David Opatashu
4161 Dixie Canyon Avenue
Sherman Oaks, CA 91423
"Actor, Writer"

Marcel Ophuls
10 rue Ernst-Deloison
92200 Neuilly, FRANCE
"Director, Producer"

Peter Oppegard
2331 Century Hill
Los Angeles, CA 90067
"Skater"

Cyril O'Reilly
P.O. Box 5617
Beverly Hills, CA 90210
"Actor"

Tony Orlando
804 North Crescent Drive
Beverly Hills, CA 90210
"Singer"

Yuri Orlov
Cornell University
Newman Laboratory
Ithica, NJ 14853
"Scientist"

Bobby Orr
1800 West Madison Street
Chicago, IL 60612
"Hockey Player"

Brian Orser
1600 James Naismith Drive
Gloucester Ontario K1B 5N4
CANADA
"Skater"

Rep. Solomon Ortiz (TX)
House Longworth Bldg. #1524
Washington, DC 20515
"Politician"

Jeffrey Osborne
5800 Valley Oak Drive
Los Angeles, CA 90068
"Singer, Songwriter"

John Osborne
162 Wardour Street
London W1 ENGLAND
"Dramatist"

Ozzy Osbourne
Flat #2, Merchant House
184 Sutherland Avenue
London W9 ENGLAND
"Singer, Songwriter"

Milo O' Shea
The Bancroft
40 West 72nd Street #17-A
New York, NY 10023
"Actor"

K.T. Oslin
1103-16th Avenue
Nashville, TN 37212
"Singer"

Alan Osmond
754 East Osmond Lane
Provo, UT 84604
"Singer"

Cliff Osmond
630 Bienvenida
Pacific Palisades, CA 90272
"Screenwriter"

Donny Osmond
1570 Brookhollow Drive #118
Santa Ana, CA 92705
"Singer"

Jimmy Osmond
7106 South Highway Drive
Salt Lake City, UT 84121
"Singer"

Ken Osmond
9863 Wornom Avenue
Sunland, CA 91040
"Actor"

Marie Osmond
3325 North University #375
Provo, UT 84605
"Singer, Actress"

Merrill Osmond
7106 South Highland Drive
Salt Lake City, UT 84121
"Singer"

The Osmonds
1420 East 800 North
Orem, UT 84059
"Vocal Group"

Jeff Osterhage
210-D North Cordova
Burbank, CA 91505
"Actor"

Bibi Osterwald
341 Carrol Park West
Long Beach, CA 90815
"Actress"

Maureen O'Sullivan
1839 Union Street
Schnectady, NY 12309
"Actress"

Annette O'Toole
360 Morton Street
Ashland, OR 97520
"Actress"

Peter O'Toole
98 Heath Street
London NW3 ENGLAND
"Actor"

Otto of Austria
Hindenburger- Strasse 15
8134 Pocking GERMANY
"Ex-King"

Park Overall
4904 Sancola Avenue
North Hollywood, CA 91602
"Actress"

Paul Overstreet
P.O. Box 2977
Hendersonville, TN 37077
"Singer"

Michael Ovitz
457 Rockingham Avenue
Los Angeles, CA 90049
"Talent Agent"

Randy Owen
Rt. #4
Ft. Payne, AL 35967
"Guitarist, Singer"

Buck Owens
818-18th Avenue South
Nashville, CA 37203
"Singer, Songwriter"

Gary Owens
17856 Via Vallarta
Encino, CA 91316
"Radio/TV Performer"

Geoffrey Owens
19 West 44th Street #1500
New York, NY 10036
"Newspaper Editor"

Rep. Major R. Owens (NY)
House Cannon Bldg. #114
Washington, DC 20515
"Politician"

Marie Owens
2401-12th Avenue South
Nashville, TN 37204
"Singer"

Patricia Owens
410 Gretna Green Way
Los Angeles, CA 90049
"Actress"

Rep. Wayne Owens (UT)
House Longworth Bldg. #1728
Washington, DC 20515
"Politician"

Earl Owensby
P.O. Box 184
Shelby, NC 28150
"Director, Producer"

Catherine Oxenberg
P.O. Box 25909
Los Angeles, CA 90025
"Actress, Model"

Rep. Michael G. Oxley (OH)
House Longworth Bldg. #2448
Washington, DC 20515
"Politician"

Frank Oz
117 East 69th Street
New York, NY 10024
"Puppeteer"

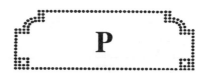

Jack Paar
9 Chateau Ridge Drive
Greenwich, CT 06830
"Ex-TV Host"

Pablo Cruise
P.O. Box 779
Mill Valley, CA 94941
"Rock & Roll Group"

Judy Pace
4139 Cloverdale
Los Angeles, CA 90008
"Actress"

Al Pacino
301 West 57th Street #16-C
New York, NY 10017
"Actor"

David Packard
1501 Page Mill Road
Palo Alto, CA 94304
"Business Executive"

Rep. Ron Packard (CA)
House Cannon Bldg. #434
Washington, DC 20515
"Politician"

Vance Packard
Mill Road
New Canaan, CT 06840
"Author"

Sen. Robert Packwood (OR)
259 Russell Bldg.
Washington, DC 20510
"Politician"

Jimmy Page
57-A Gr. Titchfield Street
London W1P 7FL ENGLAND
"Guitarist"

Patti Page
1412 San Lucas Court
Solana Beach, CA 92075
"Singer"

Janis Paige
1700 Rising Glen Road
Los Angeles, CA 90069
"Actress"

Rev. Ian Paisley
'The Parsonage'
17 Cyprus Avenue
Belfast BT5 5NT
NORTHERN IRELAND
"Clergyman"

Alan Pakula
330 West 58th Street #5-H
New York, NY 10019
"Writer, Producer"

Holly Palance
2753 Roscomare
Los Angeles, CA 90077
"Actress"

Jack Palance
Star Route 1, Box 805
Cielo Ranch
Tehachapi, CA 93561
"Actor, Director"

Ron Palillo
5750 Wilshire Blvd. #512
Los Angeles, CA 90036
"Actor"

Michael Palin
68a Delancey Street
London NW1 70W ENGLAND
"Actor, Writer"

Rep. Frank Pallone (NJ)
House Cannon Bldg. #213
Washington, DC 20515
"Politician"

Arnold Palmer
P.O. Box 52
Youngstown, PA 15696
"Golfer"

Betsy Palmer
4040 Farmdale
Studio City, CA 91604
"Actress"

Gregg Palmer
5726 Graves Avenue
Encino, CA 91316
"Actor"

Jim Palmer
P.O. Box 145
Brooklandville, MD 21022
"Baseball Player, Model"

Peter Palmer
1930 Century Park West #403
Los Angeles, CA 90067
"Actor"

Robert Palmer
2A Chelsea Manor
Blood Street
London SW3 ENGLAND
"Singer, Songwriter"

Rep. Leon. Panetta (CA)
House Cannon Bldg. #339
Washington, DC 20515
"Politician"

May Pang
1619 Third Avenue #9D
New York, NY 10128
"John Lennon's Mistress"

Stuart Pankin
15010 Ventura Blvd. #219
Sherman Oaks, CA 91403
"Actor"

Joe Pantaliano
2313-30th Street
Santa Monica, CA 90405
"Actor"

Irene Papas
Xenokratous 39
Athens-Kolanaki, GREECE
"Actress"

Ara Paraseghian
1326 East Washington Street
South Bend, IN 46601
"Football Coach"

Michael Pare
2804 Pacific Avenue
Venice, CA 90291
"Actor"

Gail Parent
2001 Mandeville Canyon
Los Angeles, CA 90024
"Screenwriter"

Johnny Paris
1764 Parkway Drive South
Maumee, OH 43537
"Rock & Roll Singer"

Cecelia Parker
5298 Teton Lane
Ventura, CA 93003
"Actress"

Dave Parker
7864 Ridge Road
Cincinnati, OH 45237
"Baseball Player"

Eleanor Parker
2195 La Paz Way
Palm Springs, CA 92262
"Actress"

Fess Parker
P.O. Box 50440
Santa Barbara, CA 93150
"Actor"

Frank Parker
4225 Huntley Avenue
Culver City, CA 90230
"Actor"

Jameson Parker
419 North Larchmont Blvd. #288
Los Angeles, CA 90004
"Actor"

Lara Parker
1441 Bonnell
Topanga, CA 90290
"Actress"

Rep. Mike Parker (MS)
House Longworth Bldg. #1504
Washington, DC 20515
"Politician"

Sarah Jessica Parker
1494 North Kings Road
Los Angeles, CA 90069
"Actress"

Suzy Parker Dillman
770 Hot Springs Road
Santa Barbara, CA 93103
"Actress"

Col. Tom Parker
P.O. Box 220
Madison, TN 37118
"Talent Agent"

Willard Parker
73311 Broadmore Drive
Thousand Oaks, CA 91362
"Actor"

Barbara Parkins
1930 Century Park West #403
Los Angeles, CA 90067
"Actress"

Dian Parkinson
4655 Natick Avenue #1
Sherman Oaks, CA 91403
"Actress, Model"

Michael Parkinson
58 Queen Anne Street
London W1M 0DX ENGLAND
"Writer"

Andrew Parks
1860 Grace Avenue
Los Angeles, CA 90028
"Actor"

Hildy Parks
225 West 44th Street
New York, NY 10036
"Producer, Writer, Actress"

Michael Parks
9000 Sunset Blvd. #1200
Los Angeles, CA 90069
"Actor"

Rosa Parks
231 West Lafayette Street
Detroit, MI 48226
"Mother of Civil Rights"

Julie Parrish
11620 Oxnard Street #H
North Hollywood, CA 91604
"Actress"

Peter Parros
7651 Camellia Avenue
North Hollywood, CA 91605
"Actor"

Alan Parsons
30 The Avenue Muswell Hill
London N10 ENGLAND
"Rock & Roll Singer"

Nancy Parsons
4220 Cahuenga Blvd. West
North Hollywood, CA 91602
"Actress"

Estelle Parsons
505 West End Avenue
New York, NY 10024
"Actress"

Dolly Parton
Rt. #1, Crockett Road
Brentwood, TN 37027
"Singer, Actress"

Randy Parton
821-19th Avenue South
Nashville, TN 37202
"Singer"

Stella Parton
P.O. Box 120295
Nashville, TN 37212
"Singer"

Francoise Pascal
89 Riverview Gardens
London SW12 ENGLAND
"Actress"

Jean-Claude Pascal
133 Bd. Exelmans
75016 Paris, FRANCE
"Actor"

Mary Ann Pascal
9744 Wilshire Blvd. #308
Beverly Hills, CA 90212
"Actress"

Adrian Pasdar
3176 Lindo Street
Los Angeles, CA 90068
"Actor"

Joseph Pasternak
9454 Wilshire Blvd. #405
Beverly Hills, CA 90212
"Producer"

Robert Pastorelli
2751 Holly Ridge Drive
Los Angeles, CA 90068
"Actor"

Michael Pate
21 Bukdarra Road
Bellevue Hill 2023
AUSTRALIA
"Actor"

Mandy Patinkin
200 West 90th Street
New York, NY 10024
"Actress"

Jason Patric
335 North Maple Drive #250
Beverly Hills, CA 90210
"Actor"

Butch Patrick
P.O. Box 587
Farmingville, NY 11738
"Child Actor"

Floyd Patterson
Springtown Road
P.O. Box 336
New Paltz, NY 12561
"Boxer"

Rep. Liz Patterson (SC)
House Longworth Bldg. #1641
Washington, DC 20515
"Politician"

Lorna Patterson
5028 Willow Crest Avenue
North Hollywood, CA 91601
"Actress"

Neva Patterson
2498 Maneville Canyon Road
Los Angeles, CA 90049
"Actress"

Sandi Patti
530 Grand Avenue
Anderson, IN 46012
"Singer"

Alexandra Paul
P.O. Box 491246
Los Angeles, CA 90049
"Actress"

Les Paul
78 Deerhaven Road
Mahwah, NJ 07430
"Guitarist"

Richard Paul
3614 Willowcrest Avenue
Studio City, CA 91604
"Actor"

Jane Pauley
271 Central Park West #10-B
New York, NY 10024
"TV Host"

Dr. Linus Pauling
Deer Flat Ranch
Big Sur, CA 93920
"Chemist"

Morgan Paull
4104 Camellia Avenue
North Hollywood, CA 91604
"Actor"

Pat Paulsen
37 Old Court House Square #312
Santa Rosa, CA 95404
"Comedian, Actor

Marisa Pavan
27 rue de Richelieu
75001 Paris, FRANCE
"Actress"

Luciano Pavarotti
150 Central Park West
New York, NY 10019
"Tenor"

Bill Paxton
7920 Sunset Blvd. #350
Los Angeles, CA 90046
"Actor"

Rep. L. William Paxton (NY)
House Longworth Bldg. #1314
Washington, DC 20515
"Politician"

Johnny Paycher
38 Music Square East #300
Nashville, TN 37203
"Singer"

Rep. Donald M. Payne (NJ)
House Cannon Bldg. #417
Washington, DC 20515
"Politician"

Freda Payne
10160 Cielo Drive
Beverly Hills, CA 90210
"Singer"

Amanda Pays
1724 Las Flores Drive
Glendale, CA 91207
"Actress, Model"

Walter Payton
1251 East Golf Road
Schaumburg, IL 60195
"Football Player"

Octavio Paz
Revista Vuelta
Leonardo de Vinci 17
Mexico 19 DF MEXICO
"Poet, Diplomat"

Vinnie Pazienda
64 Waterman Avenue
Cranston, RI 02910
"Boxer"

E. J. Peaker
4935 Densmore Avenue
Encino, CA 91436
"Actress"

Dr. Norman Vincent Peale
1025 Fifth Avenue
New York, NY 10028
"Evangelist, Author"

Minnie Pearl
874 Curtiswood Lane
Nashville, TN 37204
"Singer, Actress"

Durk Pearson
P.O. Box 1067
Hollywood, FL 33022
"Scientist, Author"

Rep. Don Pease (OH)
House Rayburn Bldg. #2410
Washington, DC 20515
"Politician"

Patsy Pease
13538 Valley Heart Drive
Sherman Oaks, CA 91403
"Actress"

Pebbles
8730 Sunset Blvd. PH-W
Los Angeles, CA 90069
"Singer"

Gregory Peck
P.O. Box 837
Beverly Hills, CA 90213
"Actor"

Nia Peebles
26012 Fiona Circle
Calabasas, CA 91302
"Actress"

I. M. Pei
600 Madison Avenue
New York, NY 10022
"Architect"

Pele
75 Rockerfeller Plaza
New York, NY 10019
"Soccer Player"

Lisa Pelikan
3708 Whitespeak Drive
Sherman Oaks, CA 91403
"Actress"

Sen. Claiborne Pell (RI)
335 Russell Bldg.
Washington, DC 20510
"Politician"

Meeno Peluce
2713 North Keystone
Burbank, CA 91504
"Actor"

Elizabeth Pena
9301 Wilshire Blvd. #312
Beverly Hills, CA 90210
"Actress"

Teddy Pendergrass
1505 Flat Rock Road
Narberth, PA 19072
"Singer, Songwriter"

Austin Pendleton
155 East 76th Street
New York, NY 10021
"Comedian"

Thao Penghlis
9320 Wilshire Blvd. #310
Beverly Hills, CA 90212
"Actor"

The Penguins
708 West 137th Street
Gardena, CA 90247
"Vocal Group"

Christopher Penn
6728 Zumirez Drive
Malibu, CA 90265
"Actor"

Leo Penn
6728 Zumirez Drive
Malibu, CA 90265
"Filmwriter, Director"

Sean Penn
P.O. Box 2630
Malibu, CA 90265
"Actor"

Janice Pennington
5750 Wilshire Blvd. #475-W
Los Angeles, CA 90036
"Model, Actress"

Joe Penny
10453 Sarah
North Hollywood, CA 91602
"Actor"

Sidney Penny
3090 Calvert Court
Camarillo, CA 93010
"Actress"

Rep. Timothy J. Penny (MN)
House Cannon Bldg. #436
Washington, DC 20515
"Politician"

Willie Pep
36 Wayland Street
Hartford, CT 06114
"Boxer"

George Peppard
P.O. Box 1643
Beverly Hills, CA 90213
"Actor, Director"

Joe Pepitone
667 East 79th Street
Brooklyn, NY 112336
"Baseball Player"

Lance Percival
18-20 York Bldg.
Adelphi
London WC2 ENGLAND
"TV Personality"

Shimon Peres
10 Hayarkon Street
Box 3263
Tel Aviv 3263 ISRAEL
"Politician"

Javier Perez de Cuellar
1 United Nations Plaza
New York, NY 10917
"United Nations Official"

Carl Perkins
459 Country Club Lane
Jackson, TN 38301
"Singer, Songwriter"

Rep. Carl C. Perkins (KY)
House Longworth Bldg. #1004
Washington, DC 20515
"Politician"

Elizabeth Perkins
930 Wilshire Blvd.
Beverly Hills, CA 90212
"Actress"

Millie Perkins
4311 Alcove Avenue #9
Studio City, CA 91604
"Actress"

Tony Perkins
2840 Seattle Drive
Los Angeles, CA 90046
"Actor"

Rhea Perlman
31020 Broad Beach Road
Malibu, CA 90265
"Actress"

Ron Perlman
345 North Maple Drive #183
Beverly Hills, CA 90210
"Actress"

Ytzhak Perlman
173 Riverside Drive #3-C
New York, NY 10024
"Violinist"

Mme. Isabel Peron
Moreto 3
Los Jeronimos
Madrid SPAIN
"Politician"

H. Ross Perot
7171 Forest Lane
Dallas, TX 75320
"Data Executive"

Gigi Perreau
268 North Bowling Green Way
Los Angeles, CA 90049
"Actress"

Valerie Perrine
8271 Melrose Avenue
Los Angeles, CA 90046
"Actress, Model"

Felton Perry
540 South St. Andrews Place
Suite #5
Los Angeles, CA 90020
"Actor"

Frank Perry
655 Park Avenue
New York, NY 10021
"Director, Producer"

Gaylord Perry
515 Oakwood Avenue
Raleigh, NC 27604
"Baseball Player"

John Bennett Perry
10100 Santa Monica Blvd. #1600
Los Angeles, CA 90067
"Actor"

Roger Perry
3800 Barham Blvd. #303
Los Angeles, CA 90068
"Actor"

Steve Perry
P.O. Box 97
Larkspur, CA 94939
"Singer, Composer"

William "Refrigerator" Perry
250 North Washington Road
Lake Forest, IL 60045
"Football Player"

Nehemia Persoff
5847 Tampa Avenue
Tarzana, CA 91356
"Actor"

Joe Pesci
9830 Wilshire Blvd. #1825
Beverly Hills, CA 90212
"Actor"

Donna Pescow
P.O. Box 93575
Los Angeles, CA 90093
"Actress"

Pet Shop Boys
101-109 Ladbroke Grove
London W11 ENGLAND
"Rock & Roll Group"

Peter, Paul & Mary
853-7th Avenue
New York, NY 10019
"Vocal Trio"

Bernadette Peters
277 West End Avenue
New York, NY 10023
"Actress"

Brock Peters
1420 Rising Glen Road
Los Angeles, CA 90069
"Actor, Writer, Director"

Jean Peters
507 North Palm Drive
Beverly Hills, CA 90210
"Actress"

Jon Peters
9 Beverly Park
Beverly Hills, CA 90210
"Motion Picture Producer"

Roberta Peters
64 Garden Road
Scarsdale, NY 10583
"Singer"

Pat Petersen
1634 Ventura Avenue
Los Angeles, CA 90025
"Actor"

Paul Petersen
145 South Fax Avenue
Los Angeles, CA 90036
"Actor"

William L. Petersen
8899 Beverly Blvd.
Los Angeles, CA 90048
"Actor"

Roland Petit
Auguste-Carli
13001 Marseilles
FRANCE
"Dancer, Choreographer"

Rep. Thomas E. Petri (WI)
House Rayburn Bldg. #2445
Washington, DC 20515
"Politician"

Dan Petry
1808 Carlen Drive
Placentia, CA 92670
"Baseball Player"

Bob Pettit
1837 Longwood Drive
Baton Rouge, LA 70808
"Basketball Player"

Joanna Pettit
10100 Santa Monica Blvd. #700
Los Angeles, CA 90067
"Actress"

Richard Petty
Rt. #3, Box 631
Randleman, NC 27317
"Auto Racer"

Tom Petty
500 South Sepulvede Blvd.#500
Los Angeles, CA 90049
"Rock & Roll Singer"

Penny Peyser
22039 Alizondo Drive
Woodland Hills, CA 91367
"Actress"

Michelle Pfeiffer
3930 Legion Lane
Los Angeles, CA 90039
"Actress"

Mary Philbin
8788 Coral Spring Court
Huntington Beach, CA 92646
"Actress"

Regis Philbin
955 Park Avenue
New York, NY 10028
"TV Host"

HRH Prince Philip
Duke of Edinburgh
Buckingham Palace
London SW1 ENGLAND
"Royalty"

Chynna Phillips
938-2nd Street #302
Santa Monica, CA 90403
"Actress"

Dial "Bum" Phillips
c/o Oak Tree Ranch
Rosharon, TX 77583
"Football Coach"

Julianne Phillips
10390 Santa Monica Blvd.
Suite #300
Los Angeles, CA 90025
"Actress, Model"

Lou Diamond Phillips
1999 Avenue of the Stars #2850
Los Angeles, CA 90067
"Actor"

Mackenzie Phillips
13743 Victory Blvd.
Van Nuys, CA 91401
"Actress, Singer"

Michelle Phillips
10557 Troon Avenue
Los Angeles, CA 90064
"Actress, Singer"

River Phoenix
P.O. Box 521
Royal Palm Beach, FL 33411
"Actor"

Robert Picardo
4926 Commonwealth Avenue
La Canada, CA 91011
"Actor"

Paloma Picasso
1021 Park Avenue
New York, NY 10021
"Designer"

Michel Piccoli
11 rue de Lions St. Paul
4e Paris, FRANCE
"Actor"

Paul Picerni
19119 Wells Drive
Tarzana, CA 91356
"Actor"

Cindy Pickett
2423 Green Valley Road
Los Angeles, CA 90046
"Actress"

Rep. Owen B. Pickett (VA)
House Longworth Bldg. #1204
Washington, DC 20515
"Politician"

Wilson Pickett
200 West 57th Street #907
New York, NY 10019
"Singer"

Rep. J.J. Pickle (TX)
House Cannon Bldg. #242
Washington, DC 20515
"Politician"

Christina Pickles
137 South Westgate Avenue
Los Angeles, CA 90049
"Actress"

Vivian Pickles
91 Regent Street
London W1R 8RU ENGLAND
"Actress"

Molly Picon
One Lincoln Plaza #35-E
New York, NY 10023
"Actress"

Charles Pierce
4445 Cartwright Avenue #309
North Hollywood, CA 91602
"Impersonator"

Webb Pierce
1521 Clayton Avenue
Nashville, TN 37212
"Singer"

Eric Pierpoint
10929 Morrison Street #14
North Hollywood, CA 91601
"Actor"

Jimmy Piersall
1105 Oakview Drive
Wheaton, IL 60187
"Baseball Player"

Tim Pigott-Smith
11726 San Vicente Blvd. #300
Los Angeles, CA 90049
"Actor"

Bronson Pinchot
9200 Sunset Blvd. #428
Los Angeles, CA 90069
"Actor"

Robert Pine
3975 Van Noord Avenue
Studio City, CA 91604
"Actor, Director"

Pink Floyd
43 Portland Road
London W11 ENGLAND
"Rock & Roll Group"

Gordon Pinsent
180 Bloor Street West
Toronto, Ontario M5S 2V6
CANADA
"Actor, Writer"

Sir Harold Pinter
16 Cadogan Lane
London SW1 ENGLAND
"Screenwriter"

Marie-France Pisier
19 rue Servandoni
75006 Paris, FRANCE
"Actress"

Dean Pitchford
1701 Queens Road
Los Angeles, CA 90069
"Lyricist, Producer"

Gene Pitney
8901 6 Mile Road
Caledonia, WI 53108
"Singer"

Mary Kay Place
2739 Motor Avenue
Los Angeles, CA 90064
"Actress, Writer"

Platinum Blonde
P.O. Box 1223, Station F.
Toronto, Ontario M4Y 2T8
CANADA
"Rock & Roll Group"

Marc Platt
1915 Maravilla #10
Ft. Myers, FL 33901
"Dancer, Actor"

The Platters
P.O. Box 39
Las Vegas, NV 89101
"Vocal Group"

Gary Player
270 Cypress Point Road
Palm Beach Gardens, FL 33418
"Golfer"

Donald Pleasance
7 West Eton Place Mews
London W1 ENGLAND
"Actor"

John Pleshette
2643 Creston Drive
Los Angeles, CA 90068
"Actor, Writer"

Suzanne Pleshette
P.O. Box 1492
Beverly Hills, CA 90213
"Actress"

George Plimpton
541 East 72nd Street
New York, NY 10021
"Author"

Martha Plimpton
502 Park Avenue #15-G
New York, NY 10022
"Model, Actress"

Joan Plowright
4388-396 Oxford Street
London W1 ENGLAND
"Actress"

Eve Plumb
145 South Fairfax Avenue #310
Los Angeles, CA 90036
"Actress"

Amanda Plummer
49 Wampum Hill Road
Weston, CT 06883
"Actress"

Christopher Plummer
49 Wampum Hill Road
Weston, CT 06883
"Actor"

Jim Plunkett
51 Kilroy Way
Atherton, CA 94025
"Football Player"

Rosanna Podesta
Via Bartolemeo Ammanatti 8
00187 Rome, ITALY
"Actress"

Sylvia Poggioli
c/o National Public Radio
2025 "M" Street NW
Washington, DC 20036
"News Correspondent"

Buster Poindexter
200 West 58th Street
New York, NY 10019
"Singer"

Adm. John Poindexter
1322 Merry Ridge Road
McLean, VA 22101
"Former Government Official"

Anita Pointer
12060 Crest Court
Beverly Hills, CA 90210
"Singer"

Priscilla Pointer
2051 North Vine Street
Los Angeles, CA 90068
"Actress"

Pointer Sisters
10100 Santa Monica Blvd.#1600
Los Angeles, CA 90067
"Vocal Trio"

Sydney Poitier
1007 Cove Way
Beverly Hills, CA 90210
"Actor, Writer, Producer"

Roman Polanski
43 Avenue Montaigne
75008 Paris, FRANCE
"Actor, Writer, Director"

The Police
194 Kensington Park Road
London W11 2ES ENGLAND
"Rock & Roll Group"

Sydney Pollack
13525 Lucca Drive
Pacific Palisades, CA 90272
"Writer, Producer"

Cherl Pollak
P.O. Box 5617
Beverly Hills, CA 90210
"Model"

Tracy Pollan
3960 Laurel Canyon Blvd. #281
Studio City, CA 91604
"Actress"

Jonathan Pollard
Federal Reformatory
Marion, IL 62959
"Israeli Spy, Traitor"

Michael J. Pollard
520 S. Burnside Avenue #12-A
Los Angeles, CA 90036
"Actor"

Jeff Pomerantz
5930 Franklin Avenue
Los Angeles, CA 90028
"Actor"

Danny Ponce
14539 Peton Drive
Hacienda Heights, CA 91745
"Actor"

LuAnne Ponce
14539 Peton Drive
Hacienda Heights, CA 91745
"Actress"

Carlo Ponti
rue Charles Bonnet 6
Geneve, SWITZERLAND
"Motion Picture Producer"

Iggy Pop
449 South Beverly Drive #102
Beverly Hills, CA 90212
"Singer"

Paulina Porizkova
111 East 22nd Street #200
New York, NY 10010
"Model"

Darrell Porter
P.O. Box 1111
Arlington, TX 76010
"Baseball Player"

Don Porter
1900 Avenue of the Stars #2270
Los Angeles, CA 90067
"Actor, Director"

Rep. John Edward Porter (IL)
House Longworth Bldg. #1026
Washington, DC 20515
"Politician"

Marina Oswald Porter
Rt. #1, Rockwell County
Heath, TX 75087
"Widower of Lee Harvey Oswald"

Nyree Dawn Porter
28 Berkeley Square
London W1X 6HD ENGLAND
"Actress"

Rep. Glenn Poshard (IL)
House Cannon Bldg. #314
Washington, DC 20515
"Politician"

Vladimir Posner
1125-16th Street N.W.
Washington, DC 20036
"Russian Spokesman"

Markie Post
4425 Talofa
Toluca Lake, CA 91602
"Actress"

Tom Poston
2830 Deep Canyon Drive
Beverly Hills, CA 90210
"Actor"

Annie Potts
1601 North Campbell
Glendale, CA 91207
"Actress"

Cliff Potts
21423 Highvalle Terrace
Topanga, CA 90290
"Actor"

Paula Poundstone
1027 Chelsea Avenue
Santa Monica, CA 90403
"Comedienne"

Maury Povich
250 West 57th Street #26-W
New York, NY 10019
"Newscaster"

Gen Colin L. Powell
The Pentagon - Rm. 2E872
Washington, DC 20301
"Chairman, Joint Chiefs"

Jane Powell
230 West 55th Street #14-B
New York, NY 10019
"Actress"

Jody Powell
1901 "I" Street N.W.
Washington, DC 20036
"News Correspondent"

Randolph Powell
2644 Highland Avenue
London W1 ENGLAND
"Actor"

Robert Powell
10 Pond Place
London SW3 ENGLAND
"Actor"

Mrs. William Powell
c/o Diane Lewis
383 Verde Norte
Palm Springs, CA 92262
"Wife of William Powell"

Tyrone Power, Jr.
823 North Gardner Street
Los Angeles, CA 90046
"Son of Tyrone Power"

Mala Powers
10543 Valley Spring Lane
North Hollywood, CA 91602
"Actress"

Stefanie Powers
2661 Hutton Drive
Beverly Hills, CA 90210
"Actress"

Michael Praed
235 Regent Street
London W1A 2JT ENGLAND
"Actor"

Laurie Prange
1519 Sargent Place
Los Angeles, CA 90026
"Actress"

Joan Prather
31647 Sea Level Drive
Malibu, CA 90265
"Actress"

Judson Pratt
8745 Oak Park Avenue
Northridge, CA 91325
"Actor"

Josephine Premice
755 West End Avenue
New York, NY 10023
"Actress, Singer, Dancer"

Ed Prentiss
267 Toyopa Drive
Pacific Palisades, CA 90272
"Actor"

Paula Prentiss
719 North Foothill Road
Beverly Hills, CA 90120
"Actress"

Micheline Presle
6 rue Antoine Dubois
F 75006 Paris, FRANCE
"Actress"

Lisa-Marie Presley
12614 Promontory Road
Los Angeles, CA 90049
"Actress"

Priscilla Presley
1167 Summit Drive
Beverly Hills, CA 90210
"Actress, Model"

Vester Presley
3764 Elvis Presley Blvd.
Memphis, TN 38116
"Elvis's Dad"

Sen. Larry Pressler (SD)
133 Senate Hart Bldg.
Washington, DC 20510
"Politician"

Laurence Pressman
15033 Encanto Drive
Sherman Oaks, CA 91403
"Actor"

Kelly Preston
615 San Lorenzo Street
Santa Monica, CA 90402
"Actress"

The Pretenders
3 East 54th Street #1400
New York, NY 10022
"Vocal Group"

Andre Previn
8 Sherwood Lane
Bedford Hills, NY 10507
"Composer, Conductor"

Francoise Previne
5 rue Brenzin
75015 Paris, FRANCE
"Actor"

Hermann Prey
Fichtenstr. 14
8033 Krailling/Obb.
GERMANY
"Baritone"

Rep. David E. Price (NC)
House Longworth Bldg. #1406
Washington, DC 20515
"Politician"

Leontyne Price
9 Van Dam Street
New York, NY 10003
"Soprano"

Ray Price
P.O. Box 1986
Mt. Pleasant, TX 75230
"Singer"

Vincent Price
9255 Swallow Drive
Los Angeles, CA 90069
"Actor"

Nancy Priddy
8723 Lookout Mountain
Los Angeles, CA 90046
"Actress"

Charlie Pride
3198 Royal Lane #204
Dallas, TX 75229
"Singer"

Jason Priestley
8961 Sunset Blvd. #2-A
Los Angeles, CA 90069
"Actor"

Barry Primus
2735 Creston Drive
Los Angeles, CA 90068
"Actor, Director"

Prince
9401 Kiowa Trail
Chanhassen, MN 55317
"Singer, Songwriter, Actor"

Clayton Prince
877 Red Barn Lane
Huntingdon Valley, PA 19006
"Actor"

Jonathan Prince
10340 Calvin Avenue
Los Angeles, CA 90025
"Actor"

William Prince
750 North Kings Road
Los Angeles, CA 90069
"Actor"

Victoria Principal
9220 Sunset Blvd. #302
Los Angeles, CA 90069
"Actress"

Andrew Prine
3364 Longridge Avenue
Sherman Oaks, CA 91403
"Actor"

Robert Prosky
8899 Beverly Blvd.
Los Angeles, CA 90069
"Actress"

Sir Victor S. Pritchett
12 Regent's Park Terrace
London NW1 ENGLAND
"Author"

Dorothy Provine Day
8832 Ferncliff N.E.
Bainbridge Island, WA 98110
"Actress"

Paul Prudhomme
P.O. Box 770034
New Orleans, LA 70177
"Chef"

Dave Prowse
7 Carlyle Road
Croydon CRO 7HN ENGLAND
"Actor"

Juliet Prowse
343 South Beverly Glen
Los Angeles, LA 90024
"Actress, Dancer"

Jonathan Pryce
233 Park Avenue South
10th Floor
New York, NY 10003
"Actor"

Sen. David Pryor (AR)
Senate Russell Bldg. #267
Washington, DC 20510
"Politician"

Nicholas Pryor
8787 Shoreham Drive #302
Los Angeles, CA 90069
"Actor"

Rain Pryor
730 Clybourn Avenue
Burbank, CA 91505
"Actress, Musician"

Richard Pryor
1115 Moraga Drive
Los Angeles, CA 90049
"Actor, Comedian"

Public Enemy
298 Elisabeth Street
New York, NY 10012
"Rap Group"

Wolfgang Puck
805 North Sierra Drive
Beverly Hills, CA 91765
"Chef, Restaurateu"

Roxanne Pulitzer
Chesterfield Hotel
363 Cocoanut Row
Palm Beach, FL 33480
"Ex-Wife of Peter Pulitzer"

Keshia Knight Pulliam
P.O. Box 866
Teaneck, NJ 07666
"Actress"

Rep. Carl Pursell (MI)
House Longworth Bldg. #1414
Washington, DC 20515
"Politician"

Lee Purcell
3800 Barham Blvd. #303
Los Angeles, CA 90068
"Actress"

Sarah Purcell
460 Lincoln Blvd.
Santa Monica, CA 90402
"Actress"

Edmund Purdom
via G. Carducchi 10
I-00187 Rome ITALY
"Actor"

Linda Purl
P.O. Box 5617
Beverly Hills, CA 90210
"Actress"

John Putch
8271 Melrose Avenue #110
Los Angeles, CA 90046
"Actor"

Mario Puzo
866 Manor Lane
Bay Shore, NY 11706
"Author, Screenwriter"

Denver Pyle
10614 Whipple Street
North Hollywood, CA 91602
"Actor, Writer, Director"

Monty Python
68a Delancy Street
London NW1 70W ENGLAND
"Comedy Group"

Dennis Quaid
9830 Wilshire Blvd.
Beverly Hills, CA 90212
"Actor"

Randy Quaid
15760 Ventura Blvd. #1730
Encino, CA 91436
"Actor"

Quarterflash
P.O. Box 8231
Portland, OR 97207
"Rock & Roll Group"

Suzi Quatro
3 Grosvenor Gardens
London SW1 ENGLAND
"Singer"

Dan Quayle
Admiral House
34th & Massachusetts
Washington, DC 20005
"Vice President U.S.A."

Marilyn Quayle
Admiral House
34th & Massachusetts
Washington, DC 20005
"Wife of Dan Quayle"

Queen
46 Pemberidge Road
London W11 3HN ENGLAND
"Rock & Roll Group"

Mae Questel
27 East 65th Street
New York, NY 10021
"Actress"

Diana Quick
162 Wardour Street
London W1V 3AT ENGLAND
"Actress"

Quiet Riot
3208 Cahuenga Blvd. West #107
Los Angeles, CA 90068
"Rock & Roll GrouP"

Joan Quigley
1055 California Street #14
San Francisco, CA 94108
"Astrologer"

Linnea Quigley
12710 Blythe Street
North Hollywood, CA 91605
"Actress, Model"

Rep. James H. Quillen (TN)
House Cannon Bldg. #102
Washington, DC 20515
"Politician"

Kathleen Quinlan
P.O. Box 2465
Malibu, CA 90265
"Actress"

Adrian Quinn
9830 Wilshire Blvd.
Beverly Hills, CA 90212
"Actor"

Anthony Quinn
60 East End Avenue
New York, NY 10028
"Actor, Director"

Bill Quinn
16302 Village #16
Camarillo, CA 93010
"Actor"

Martha Quinn
3562 Laurelvale Drive
Studio City, CA 91604
"TV Personality"

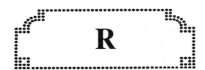

R

Eddie Rabbitt
4808 La Villa Marina #F
Marina del Rey, CA 90291
"Singer"

Alan Rachins
9348 Civic Center Drive #407
Beverly Hills, CA 90210
"Actor, Writer, Director"

Lee Radziwell
9255 Sunset Blvd. #901
Los Angeles, CA 90069
"Society Leader"

Charlotte Rae
9200 Sunset Blvd. #625
Los Angeles, CA 90069
"Actress"

Frances Rafferty Baker
221411 Burbank Blvd. #4
Woodland Hills, CA 91367
"Actress"

Gerry Rafferty
51 Paddington Street
London W1 ENGLAND
"Singer, Songwriter"

Kaye Lani Rae Rafko
4932 Frary Lane
Monroe, MI 48161
"Former Miss America"

Deborah Raffin
2630 Eden Place
Beverly Hills, CA 90210
"Actress"

Hashemi Rafsanjani
The Majlis
Tehran, IRAN
"President of Iran"

Gerald Rafshoon
3028 "Q" Street N.W.
Washington, DC 20006
"Former Presidential Aide"

Lisa Raggio
12456 Ventura Blvd. #1
Studio City, CA 91604
"Actress"

John S. Ragin
5706 Briarcliff Road
Los Angeles, CA 90068
"Actor"

Rep. Nick J. Rahall II (WV)
House Rayburn Bldg. #2104
Washington, DC 20515
"Politician"

Steve Railsback
P.O. Box 1308
Los Angeles, CA 90078
"Actor"

Luise Rainer Knittel
Vocp Morcote
6911 SWITZERLAND
"Actress"

Cristina Raines Crowe
12700 Ventura Blvd. #350
Studio City, CA 91604
"Actress"

Ford Rainey
3821 Carbon Canyon
Malibu, CA 90265
"Actor"

Bonnie Raitt
P.O. Box 626
Los Angeles, CA 90078
"Singer"

John Raitt
1164 Napoli Drive
Pacific Palisades, CA 90272
"Actor"

Sheryl Lee Ralph
938 South Longwood
Los Angeles, CA 90019
"Actress"

Esther Ralston
35 Heather Way
Ventura, CA 93003
"Actress"

Vera Hruba Ralston
4121 Crecienta Drive
Santa Barbara, CA 93110
"Actress"

Dack Rambo
Rambo Horse Farm
Earlimart, CA 93219
"Actor"

Raul Ramirez
Avenida Ruiz
65 Sur Ensenda
Baja California, MEXICO
"Tennis Player"

Harold Ramis
14198 Alisal Lane
Santa Monica, CA 90402
"Actor, Writer, Director"

Charlotte Rampling
1 Ave. Emile Augier
F-78290 Croissy-Sur Seine
FRANCE
"Actress"

Logan Ramsey
12932 Killion Street
Van Nuys, CA 91401
"Actor"

Tony Randall
1 West 81st Street #6-D
New York,NY 10024
"Actor, Director"

Teddy Randazzo
5254 Oak Island Road
Orlando, FL 32809
"Singer"

Boots Randolph
209 Printers Alley
Nashville, TN 37201
"Saxophonist"

John Randolph
1850 North Whitley Place
Los Angeles, CA 90028
"Actor"

Joyce Randolph
295 Central Park West
New York, NY 10024
"Actress"

Rep. Charles B. Rengel (NY)
House Rayburn Bldg. #2252
Washington, DC 20515
"Politician"

The Rangers
821-19th Avenue South
Nashville, TN 37203
"C&W Group"

Crown Price Ranier III
Grimaldi Palace
Monte Carlo, MONACO
"Royaly"

Kenny Rankin
8033 Sunset Blvd. #1037
Los Angeles, CA 90046
"Singer, Songwriter"

Prunella Ransome
59 Frith Street
London W1 ENGLAND
"Actress"

Sally Jessy Raphael
510 West 57th Street #200
New York, NY 10019
"TV Show Host"

David Rache
P.O. Box 5617
Beverly Hills, CA 90210
"Actor"

Ahmad Rashad
30 Rockefeller Plaza #1411
New York, NY 10020
"Football Player, Sportcaster"

Phylicia Rashad
10000 Santa Monica Blvd. #305
Los Angeles, CA 90067
"Actress"

Dan Rather
51 West 52nd Street
New York, NY 10019
"Newcaster"

RATT
1818 Illion Street
San Diego, CA 92110
Rock & Roll Group"

John Ratzerberger
1999 Avenue of the Stars #2850
Los Angeles, CA 90067
"Actor"

Eddy Raven
P.O. Box 1402
Hendersonville, TN 37075
"Singer, Songwriter"

Rep. Authur Ravenel, Jr. (SC)
House Cannon Bldg. #508
Washington, DC 20515
"Politician"

Lou Rawls
109 Fremont Place
Los Angeles, CA 90005
"Singer"

Gene Anthony Ray
10351 Santa Monica Blvd. #211
Los Angeles, CA 90025
"Actor"

James Earl Ray
Station A West
Tennessee State Prison
Nashville, TN 37203
"Martin Luthur King, Jr.'s Killer"

Rep. Richard Ray (GA)
House Cannon Bldg. #225
Washington, DC 20515
"Politician"

Marguerite Raye
1329 North Vista #106
Los Angeles, CA 90046
"Actress"

Martha Raye
1153 Roscomare Road
Los Angeles, CA 90024
"Actress, Singer"

Gene Raymond
250 Trino Way
Pacific Palisades, CA 90272
"Actor"

Guy Raymond
550 Erskine Drive
Pacific Palisades, CA 90272
"Actor"

Paula Raymond
P.O. Box 86
Beverly Hills, CA 90213
"Actress"

Peggy Rea
432 South Curson Avenue #2-K
Los Angeles, CA 90036
"Actress"

James Read
8899 Beverly Blvd.
Los Angeles, CA 90048
"Actor"

Maureen Reagan
10317 Dunleer
Los Angeles, CA 90064
"Ex-President Daughter"

Michael Reagan
4740 Allott Avenue
Sherman Oaks, CA 91403
"Ex-President's Son"

Nancy Reagan
668 St. Cloud Road
Los Angeles, CA 90077
"Ex-First Lady, Actress"

Ronald Reagan
668 St. Cloud Road
Los Angeles, CA 90077
"Actor, Ex-President"

Ron Reagan, Jr.
1283 Devon Avenue
Los Angeles, CA 90024
"TV Host, Dancer"

Rex Reason
20105 Rhapsody Road
Walnut, CA 91789
"Actor"

Rhodes Reason
409 Winchester Avenue
Glendale, CA 914201
"Actor"

Charles "Bebe" Rebozo
490 Bay Lane
Key Biscayne, FL 33149
"Business Executive"

Peter Reckell
8033 Sunset Blvd. #4016
Los Angeles, CA 90046
"Actor"

Helen Reddy
2645 Outpost Road
Los Angeles, CA 90068
"Singer"

Quinn Redeker
17931 Welby Way
Reseda, CA 91335
"Actor, Writer"

Orville Redenbacher
1780 Avendia del Mundo #704
Coronado, CA 92118
"Pop Corn Executive"

Robert Redford
P.O. Box 837
3 Provo Canyon Road
Provo, UT 84601
"Actor, Director"

Lynn Redgrave
21342 Colina Drive
Topanga, CA 90290
"Actress"

Vanessa Redgrave
31/32 Soho Square
London W1 ENGLAND
"Actress"

Marge Redmond
101 Central Park West
New York, NY 10023
"Actress"

Alaina Reed-Hall
10636 Rathburn
Northridge, CA 91326
"Actress"

Jerry Reed
45 Music Square West
Nashville, TN 37203
"Singer, Actor"

Lou Reed
38 East 68th Street
New York, NY 10021
"Singer, Songwriter"

Oliver Reed
Pinehurst Farm
Oakwood Hills
Dorking, Surrey ENGLAND
"Actor"

Pamela Reed
2450 El Contento Drive
Los Angeles, CA 90068
"Actress"

Philip Reed
969 Bel Air Road
Los Angeles, CA 90077
"Actor"

Rex Reed
1 West 72nd Street #86
New York, NY 10023
"Film Critic"

Robert Reed
980 Stoneridge Drive
Pasadena, CA 91105
"Actor"

Shanna Reed
1649 South Sterns Drive
Los Angeles, CA 90035
"Actress"

Harry Reems
2372 Geronimo Court
Park City, UT 84060
"Actor"

Della Reese
1910 Bel Air Road
Los Angeles, CA 90024
"Singer, Actress"

Christopher Reeve
100 West 78th Street #5-A
New York, NY 10024
"Actor"

Dan Reeves
5700 Lincoln Way
Denver, CO 80216
"Football Coach"

Del Reeves
991 Highway #100
Centerville, TN 37033
"Singer"

Keanu Reeves
7920 Sunset Blvd. #350
Los Angeles, CA 90046
"Actor"

Martha Reeves
168 Orchid Drive
Pearl River, NY 10965
"Singer"

Steve Reeves
P.O. Box 807
Valley Center, CA 92082
"Actor, Bodybuilder"

Joe Regalbuto
724-24th Street
Santa Monica, CA 90402
"Actor"

Donald T. Regan
11 Canal Center Plaza #301
Alexandria, VA 22314
"Former Secretary of Treasury"

Phil Regan
1123 South Orange Grove Blvd.
Pasadena, CA 91105
"Singer"

Duncan Regehr
5319 Wilkinson Avenue
North Hollywood, CA 91607
"Actor"

Sen. Harry Reid (NV)
Senate Hart Bldg. #324
Washington, DC 20510
"Politician"

Paul Regina
9200 Sunset Blvd. #710
Los Angeles, CA 90069
"Actor"

Regine
502 Park Avenue
New York, NY 10022
"Singer"

Rep. Ralph Regula (OH)
House Rayburn Bldg. #2207
Washington, DC 20515
"Politician"

William Rehnquist
1-1st Street N.E.
Washington, DC 20543
"Supreme Court Chief Justice"

Beryl Reid
Honeypot Cottage
Wraysbury, Nr. Staines
Middlesex, ENGLAND
"Actor, Comedian"

Daphne Maxwell Reid
16540 Adlon Road
Encino, CA 91436
"Actress"

Frances Reid
9165 Sunset Blvd. #202
Los Angeles, CA 90069
"Actress"

Tim Reid
16540 Aldon Road
Encino, CA 91436
"Actor"

Charles Nelson Reilly
2341 Gloaming Way
Beverly Hills, CA 90210
"Actor"

John Reilly
335 North Maole Drive #360
Beverly Hills, CA 90210
"Actor"

Tom Reilly
8033 Sunset Blvd. #3333
Lso Angeles, CA 90046
"Actor"

Carl Reiner
714 North Rodeo Drive
Beverly Hills, CA 90210
"Actor, Director"

Rob Reiner
255 Chadbourne Avenue
Los Angeles, CA 90049
"Actor, Director"

Judge Reinhold
1341 Ocean Avenue #113
Santa Monica, CA 90401
"Actor"

Paul Reiser
1134 Alta Loma Road #303
Los Angeles, CA 90069
"Actor"

R.E.M.
P.O. Box 8032
Athens, CA 30603
"Rock & Roll Group"

Bert Remsen
5722 Mammoth Avenue
Van Nuys, CA 91401
"Actor"

Line Renaud
1417 North Spaulding Avenue
Los Angeles, CA 90046
"Actress"

Liz Renay
3708 San Angelo Avenue
Las Vegas, NV 89102
"Burlesque"

Jack Reno
P.O. Box 901
Cincinnati, OH 45201
"Singer"

Alain Resnis
70 rue des Plantes
75014 Paris, FRANCE
"Film Director"

James Reston
1804 Kallorama Square N.W.
Washington, DC 20008
"Columnist"

Tommy Rettig
13802 N.W. Passage #302
Marina del Rey, CA 90291
"Actor"

Mary Lou Retton
R.R. 9, Box 493
Fairmont, WV 26554
"Gymnast, Actress"

Clive Revill
15029 Encanto Drive
Sherman Oaks, CA 91403
"Actor"

Fernando Rey
Orense 62
Madrid 20 SPAIN
"Actor"

Ernie Reyes, Jr.
1800 North Vine Street
Los Angeles, CA 90028
"Actor"

Allie Reynolds
2709 Cashion Place
Oklahoma City, OK 73112
"Baseball Player"

Burt Reynolds
1001 Indiantown Road
Jupiter, FL 33458
"Actor, Director"

Debbie Reynolds
11595 La Madia
North Hollywood, CA 91602
"Actress"

Gene Reynolds
2034 Castillian Drive
Los Angeles, CA 90068
"Actor, Director"

James Reynolds
1925 Hamscom Drive
South Pasadena, CA 91109
"Actor"

Marjorie Reynolds Haffen
3 Catalina Court
Manhattan Beach, CA 90266
"Actress"

Patrick Reynolds
260 South Rodeo Drive
Beverly Hills, CA 90212
"Actor, Anti-Smoking Advocate"

Alicia Rhett
50 Tradd Street
Charleston, SC 29401
"Actress"

Barbara Rhoades
12366 Ridge Circle
Los Angeles, CA 90049
"Actress"

Betty (Jane) Rhodes
10693 Chalon Road
Los Angeles, CA 90024
"Actress"

Cynthia Rhodes
7471 Woodrow Wilson Drive
Los Angeles, CA 90046
"Actress, Dancer"

Donnelly Rhodes
9744 Wilshire Blvd. #308
Beverly Hills, CA 90212
"Actor"

Hari Rhodes
7826 Topanga Canyon #317
Canoga Park, CA 91309
"Actor"

Rep. John J. Rhodes III (AZ)
House Cannon Bldg. #326
Washington, DC 20515
"Politician"

Madlyn Rhue
148 South Maple Drive, Apt. #D
Beverly Hills, CA 90212
"Actress"

Alfonso Ribeiro
19122 Halsted Street
Northridge, CA 91324
"Actor"

Abraham Ribicoff
425 Park Avenue
New York, NY 10022
"Ex-Governor"

Donna Rice
1204 Ina Lane
McLean, VA 22102
"Actress, Model"

Jerry Rice
4949 Centennial Blvd.
Santa Clara, CA 95054
"Football Player"

Jim Rice
135 Woden Way
Winter Haven, FL 33880
"Baseball Player"

Tim Rice
118 Wardour Street
nr. Chichester, Sussex, ENGLAND
"Lyricist"

Adam Rich
21848 Vantage
Chatsworth, CA 91311
"Actor"

Christopher Rich
15760 Ventura Blvd. #1730
Encino, CA 91436
"Actor"

Elaine Rich
9300 Hazen Drive
Beverly Hills, CA 90210
"TV Personality"

Cliff Richard
St. George Hill
Weybridge, ENGLAND
"Singer, Actor"

Maurice Richard
10950 Peloquin
Montreal PQ H2C 2KB CANADA
"Hockey Player"

Gov. Ann Richard (TX)
P.O. Box 12428
Austin, TX 78711
"Governor"

Beah Richards
1308 South New Hampshire
Los Angeles, CA 90019
"Actress"

Evan Richards
10351 Santa Monica Blvd. #211
Los Angeles, CA 90025
"Actor"

Kieth Richards
"Redlands" West Whittering
Near Chicester Sussex
ENGLAND
"Actor"

Rep. Bill Richardson (NM)
House Cannon Bldg. #332
Washington, DC 20515
"Politician"

Elliot Richardson
1100 Crest Lane
McLean, VA 22101
"Diplomat"

Ian Richardson
131 Lavender Sweep
London SW11 ENGLAND
"Actor"

Miranda Richardson
195 Devonshire Road
Forest Hill
London SE 23 ENGLAND
"Actress"

Natasha Richardson
180 West 59th Street
New York, NY 10019
"Actress, V. Redgrave's Daughter"

Lionel Richie
5750 Wilshire Blvd. #590
Los Angeles, CA 90036
"Singer, Songwriter"

Peter Mark Richman
5114 Del Moreno Drive
Woodland Hills, CA 91364
"Actor"

Debi Richter
11726 San Vicente Blvd. #300
Los Angeles, CA 90049
"Actress"

Don Rickles
925 North Alpine Drive
Beverly Hills, CA 90210
"Comeidan, Actor"

Dr. Sally Ride
9500 Gillman Drive
MS 0221
La Jolla, CA 92093
"Astronaut"

Rep. Tom Ridge (PA)
House Longworth Bldg. #1714
Washington, DC 20515
"Politician"

Andrew Ridgeley
8800 Sunset Blvd. #401
Los Angeles, CA 90069
"Singer, Composer"

Gen. Matthew Ridgeway
918 Waldheim Road
Pittsburgh, PA 15215
"Military Leader"

Leni Riefenstahl
Tengstrasse 20
8000 Munich 40
GERMANY
"Film Director"

Sen. Donald Riegle, Jr. (MI)
Senate Dirksen Bldg. #105
Washington, DC 20510
"Politician"

Victor Riesel
30 East 42nd Street
New York, NY 10017
"Columinist"

Joshua Rifkind
6216 Orange Street
Los Angeles, CA 90048
"Conductor"

Ron Rifkin
5604 Holly Oak
Los Angeles, CA 90068
"Actor"

Cathy Rigby McCoy
110 East Wilshire #200
Fullerton, CA 92632
"Gymnast"

Diana Rigg
235 Regent Street
London W7 ENGLAND
"Actress"

Bobby Riggs
508 East Avenue
Coronado, CA 92118
"Tennis Player"

Righteous Brothers
9841 Hot Springs Drive
Huntington Beach, CA 92646
"Vocal Group"

Meshulam Riklis
23720 Malibu Colony Road
Malibu, CA 90265
"Producer"

Jeaniie C. Riley
P.O. Box 454
Brentwood, TN 37027
"Singer"

Pat Riley
285 Homewood Road
Los Angeles, CA 90049
"Basketball Coach"

Rep. Matthew Rinaldo (NJ)
House Rayburn Bldg. #2469
Washington, DC 20515
"Politician"

Molly Ringwald
7680 Mulholland Drive
Los Angeles, CA 90046
"Actress"

Rodney Allen Rippey
9420 Topanga Canyon Blvd.
Chatsworth, CA 91311
"Actor"

Robby Rist
P.O. Box 867
Woodland Hills, CA 91365
"Actor"

The Ritchie Family
4100 West Flagler #B-2
Miami, FL 33134
"Vocal Group"

Lee Ritenour
P.O. Box 6774
Malibu, CA 90265
"Guitarist"

Rep. Don Ritter (PA)
House Rayburn Bldg. #2202
Washington, DC 20515
"Politician"

John Ritter
236 Tigertail Road
Los Angeles, CA 90049
"Actor"

Mrs. Tex Ritter
14151 Valley Vista
Sherman Oaks, CA 91423
"Tex Ritter's Widower"

Chita Rivera
19 West 44th Street #1500
New York, NY 10017
"Actress, Singer, Dancer"

Geraldo Rivera
311 West 43rd Street
New York, NY 10036
"TV Host, Author"

Jorge Rivero
Salvador Novo 71
Cuyoacan 21 D.F. MEXICO
"Actor"

Joan Rivers
1 East 62nd Street
New York, NY 10021
"Comedienne, TV Host"

Mickey Rivers
350 N.W. 48th Street
Miami, FL 33127
"Baseball Player"

Jacques Rivette
20 Blvd. de la Bastille
75012 Paris, FRANCE
"Director"

Phil Rizzuto
912 Westminister Avenue
Hillside, NJ 07205
"Baseball Player"

Hal Roach, Sr.
1183 Stradella Road
Los Angeles, CA 90077
"Film Producer"

Adam Roarkd
4520 Aida Place
Woodland Hills, CA 91364
"Actor"

Jason Robards
40 West 57th Street
New York, NY 10019
"Actor"

Sam Robards
2530 Riverbend Drive
Crested Butte, CO 81224
"Actor"

Sen. Charles Robb (VA)
Senate Dirksen Bldg. #493
Washington, DC 20510
"Politician"

Lynda Bird Johnson-Robb
3050 Chain Bridge Raod
Mc Lean, VA 22101
"Ex-President's Daughter"

Seymour Robbie
9980 Liebe Drive
Beverly Hills, CA 90210
"TV Director"

Brian Robbins
7743 Woodrow Wilson Blvd.
Los Angeles, CA 90046
"Actor"

Harold Robbins
990 North Patencio
Palm Springs, CA 92262
"Novelist"

Jerome Robbins
117 East 81st Street
New York, NY 10028
"Choreographer"

Mrs. Marty Robbins
713-18th Avenue South
Nashville, TN 37203
"Marty Robbins's Widower"

Tim Robbins
25 East 9th Street
New York, NY 10003
"Actor"

Cokie Roberts
c/o National Public Radio
2025 "M" Street NW
Washington, DC 20036
"News Correspondent"

Doris Roberts
6225 Quebec Drive
Los Angeles, CA 90068
"Actress, Director"

Eric Roberts
853-7th Avenue #1606
New York, NY 10019
"Actor"

Jake "The Snake" Roberts
P.O. Box 3859
Stamford, CT 06905
"Wrestler"

Julia Roberts
2410 Astral Drive
Los Angeles, CA 90046
"Actress"

Louie Roberts
2401-12th Avenue South
Nashville, TN 37203
"Singer, Guitarist"

Oral Roberts
7777 Lewis Street
Tulsa, OK 74130
"Evangelist"

Rep. Pat Roberts (KS)
House Longworth Bldg. #110
Washington, DC 20515
"Politician"

Pernell Roberts
1999 North Sycamore
Los Angeles, CA 90028
"Actor"

Robin Roberts
403 Terrace Hill Road
Temple Terrace, FL 33617
"Baseball Player"

Tanya Roberts
10090 Cielo Drive
Beverly Hills, CA 90210
"Actress"

Tony Roberts
970 Park Avenue #8-N
New York, NY 10028
"Actor"

Beverly Robertson
30912 Ariana Lane
Laguna Niguel, CA 92677
"Actress"

Cliff Robertson
325 Dunmere Drive
La Jolla , CA 92037
"Actor, Writer, Director"

Dale Robertson
P.O. Box 850707
Yukon, OK 73085
"Actor"

Oscar Robertson
P.O. Box 179
Springfield, MA 01101
"Basketball Player"

Rev. Pat Robertson
CBN Centre
Virginia Beach, VA 23463
"Evangelist"

Robbie Robertson
109 South Sycamore Avenue
Los Angeles, CA 90036
"Guitarist, Singer"

Brooks Robinson
1506 Sherbrook Road
Lutherville, MD 21093
"Baseball Player"

Charles Knox Robinson
330 North Screenland Drive #116
Burbank, CA 91505
"Actor"

Chris Robinson
843 North Sycamore Avenue
Los Angeles, CA 90038
"Actor, Director"

Frank Robinson
15557 Aqua Verde Drive
Los Angeles, CA 90024
"Baseball Player & Manager"

Holly Robinson
7743 Woodrow Wilson Drive
Los Angeles, CA 90046
"Actress"

Jay Robinson
14755 Ventura Blvd. #1-497
Sherman Oaks, CA 91403
"Actor"

Smokey Robinson
17085 Rancho Street
Encino, CA 91316
"Singer, Songwriter"

Andy Robustelli
74 Wedgemere Road
Stamford, CT 06901
"Football Player"

Alex Rocco
1755 Ocean Oaks Road
Carpinteria, CA 93013
"Actor"

Eugene Roche
451 1/2 Kelton Avenue
Los Angeles, CA 90024
"Actor"

David Rockefeller
30 Rockefeller Plaza #5600
New York, NY 10112
"Businessman"

Sen. John D. Rockefeller (WV)
Senate Hart Bldg. #109
Washington, DC 20510
"Politician"

Mrs. Nelson Rockefeller
812 Fifth Avenue
New York, NY 10024
"Wife of Nelson Rockefeller"

Sharon Rochefeller
2121 Park Road N.W.
Washington, DC 20010
"Wife of John D. Rockefeller"

Robert Rockwell
650 Toyopa Drive
Pacific Palisades, CA 90272
"Actor"

Marcia Rodd
11738 Moorpark Street #C
Studio City, CA 91604
"Actress"

Jimmie Rodgers
1961 Falcon Court
Thousand Oaks, CA 91362
"Singer, Songwriter"

Judy Rodman
7 Music Square North
Nashville, TN 37203
"Singer"

Johnny Rodriguez
P.O. Box 2671
Nashville, TN 37219
"Singer, Songwriter"

Paul Rodriguez
2036 Hanscom Drive
South Pasadena, CA 91030
"Comedian"

Rep. Robert A. Roe (NJ)
House Rayburn Bldg. #2243
Washington, DC 20515
"Politician"

Tommy Roe
P.O. Box 26037
Minneapolis, MN 55426
"Singer, Songwriter"

Gov. Roy Romer (CO)
136 State Capitol Bldg.
Denver, CO 80203
"Governor"

Bill Rogers
372 Chestnut Hills Avenue
Boston, MA 02146
"Runner"

Charles "Buddy" Rogers
1147 Pickfair Way
Beverly Hills, CA 90210
"Actor"

Mr. Rogers (Fred)
4802-5th Avenue
Pittsburgh, PA 15213
"TV Host"

Ginger Rogers
18745 Crater Lake Hwy. 62
Eagle Point, OR 97524
"Actress, Dancer"

Rep. Harold Rogers (KY)
House Cannon Bldg. #343
Washington, DC 20515
"Politician"

Joy Rogers
12016 Moorpark Street
Studio City, CA 91604
"Actress"

Kenny Rogers
P.O. Box 100
Colbert, GA 30628
"Singer, Songwriter"

Melody Rogers
2051 Nicols Canyon
Los Angeles, CA 90046
"Actress, TV Host"

Mimi Rogers
12324-24th Helena Drive
Los Angeles, CA 90049
"Actress"

Roy Rogers
15650 Seneca Road
Victorville, CA 92392
"Actor, Singer, Guitarist"

Suzanne Rogers
11266 Canton Drive
Studio City, CA 91604
"Actress"

Tristan Rogers
2121 Avenue of the Stars #950
Los Angeles, CA 90067
"Actor"

Wayne Rogers
11828 La Grange Avenue
Los Angeles, CA 90025
"Actor, Writer, Director"

Will Rogers, Jr.
P.O. Box 1206
Tubac, AZ 85646
"Actor"

Fred Roggin
3000 West Alameda Avenue
Burbank, CA 91523
"TV Host"

Eric Rohmer
26 Ave. Pierre-Ler-De-Serbie
75116 Paris, FRANCE
"Film Director"

Clayton Rohner
P.O. Box 5617
Beverly Hills, CA 90210
"Actor"

Rep. Dana Rohrabacher (CA)
House Longworth Bldg. #1039
Washington, DC 20515
"Politician"

Roxie Roker
4061 Cloverdale Avenue
Los Angeles, CA 90008
"Actress"

Gilbert Roland
518 North Roxbury Drive
Beverly Hills, CA 90210
"Actor"

Ether Rolle
P.O. Box 8986
Los Angeles, CA 90008
"Actress"

Rolling Stones
1776 Broadway #507
New York, NY 10019
"Rock & Roll Group"

Howard E. Rollins, Jr.
123 West 85th Street #4-F
New York, NY 10024
"Actor"

Sonny Rollins
Rt. 9-G
Germantown, NY 12526
"Saxophonist"

Freddie Roman
c/o Jones
101 West 57th Street
New York, NY 10019
"Comedian"

Roman Holiday
P.O. Box 475
London W1 ENGLAND
"Rock & Roll Group"

Lulu Roman
P.O. Box 140400
Nashville, TN 37214
"Actress"

Ruth Roman
1220 Cliff Drive
Laguna Beach, CA 92651
"Actress"

The Romantics
P.O. Box 133-LV
Lathrop Village, MI 48076
"Rock & Roll Group"

Richard Romanus
1850 Camino Palmero
Los Angeles, CA 90046
"Actor"

Lina Romay
1303 Lyndon Street #6
South Pasedena, CA 91030
"Actress"

Sydne Rome
Via di Porta Piniciana 14
I-00100 Rome, ITALY
"Actress"

Cesar Romero
12115 San Vicente Blvd.#302
Los Angeles, CA 90049
"Actor"

George Romero
3364 Lake Road North
Sanibel, FL 33957
"Filmmaker, Screenwriter"

George Romney
1840 East Valley Road
Bloomfield Hills, MI 48013
"Ex-Governor"

The Ronettes
5218 Almont Street
Los Angeles, CA 90032
"Vocal Group"

Linda Ronstadt
5750 Wilshire Blvd. #590
Los Angeles, CA 90036
"Singer"

Andy Rooney
254 Rowayton Avenue
Rowayton, CT 06853
"Writer, Actor, Director"

Mickey Rooney
4165 Thousand Oaks Blvd. #300
Westlake Village, CA 91362
"Actor"

Axl Rose
2738 Hollyridge
Los Angeles, CA 90068
"Singer"

Rep. Charlie Rose (NC)
House Rayburn Bldg. #2230
Washington, DC 20515
"Politician"

Jamie Rose
335 North Maple Drive #250
Beverly Hills, CA 90210
"Actress"

Murray Rose
3305 Carse Drive
Los Angeles, CA 90028
"Swimmer"

Pete Rose
10415 Stonebridge Blvd.
Boca Raton, FL 33498
"Baseball Player"

Rose Marie
6916 Chisholm Avenue
Van Nuys, CA 91406
"Singer"

Barney Rosenzweig
308 North Sycamore #502
Los Angeles, CA 90036
"TV Writer, Producer"

Ken Rosewall
111 Pentacost Avenue
Turramurra NSW 2074
AUSTRALIA
"Tennis Player"

Francesco Rosi
Via Gregoriana 36
I-00187 Rome, ITALY
"Film Director"

Diana Ross
22028 West Pacific Coast
Malibu, CA 90265
"Singer, Actress"

Herbert Ross
9255 Sunset Blvd. #901
Los Angeles, CA 90069
"Director, Producer"

Katherine Ross
33050 Pacific Caost Hwy.
Malibu, CA 90265
"Actress"

Marion Ross
14159 Riverside Drive #101
Sherman Oaks, CA 91423
"Actress"

Stan Ross
1410 North Gardner
Los Angeles, CA 90046
"Actor"

Isabella Rossellini
260 West Broadway #5-B
New York, NY 10013
"Actress"

Carol Rossen
1119-23rd Street #8
Santa Monica, CA 90403
"Actress"

Rep. Dan Rostenkowski (IL)
House Rayburn Bldg. #2111
Washington, DC 20515
"Politician"

Walt Rostow
1 Wildwind Point
Austin, TX 78746
"Economist"

Miklos Rosza
2936 Montcalm Drive
Los Angeles, CA 90046
"Composer"

Kyle Rote
1175 York Avenue
New York, NY 10021
"Football Player"

David Lee Roth
3960 Laurel Canyon #430
Studio City, CA 91604
"Singer, Songwriter"

Rep. Toby Roth (WI)
House Rayburn Bldg. #2352
Washington, DC 20515
"Politician"

Sen. William Roth, Jr. (DE)
Senate Hart Bldg. #104
Washington, DC 20510
"Politician"

Rep. Marge Roukema (NJ)
House Rayburn Bldg. #2244
Washington, DC 20515
"Politician"

Richard Roundtree
8383 Wilshire Blvd. #1018
Beverly Hills, CA 90212
"Actor"

Mickey Rourke
1020 Benedict Canyon Drive
Beverly Hills, CA 90210
"Actor"

Edd Roush
122 Main Street
Oakland City, IN 47560
"Baseball Player"

The Roustabouts
P.O. Box 25371
Charlotte, NC 28212
"Bluegrass Group"

Misty Rowe
880 Greenleaf Canyon
Topanga, CA 90290
"Actress"

Nicholas Rowe
200 Fulham Road
London SW 10 ENGLAND
"Poet, Dramatist"

Betty Rowland
217 Broadway
Santa Monica, CA 90405
"Burlesque"

Dave Rowland
8 Cadman Plaza West
Brooklyn, NY 11201
"Singer"

Rep. J. Roy Rowland (GA)
House Cannon Bldg. #423
Washington, DC 20515
"Politician"

Gena Rowlands
7917 Woodrow Wilson Drive
Los Angeles, CA 90046
"Actress"

Billy Joe Royal
819-18th Street South
Nashville, TN 37203
"Singer, Songwriter"

Darrell Royal
10507 La Costa Drive
Austin, TX 78747
"Football Coach"

Rep. Edward R. Roybal (CA)
House Rayburn Bldg. #2211
Washington, DC 20515
"Politician"

Mike Royko
435 North Michigan Avenue
Chicago, IL 60611
"Columnist"

Pete Rozelle
410 Park Avenue
New York, NY 10022
"Former Football Commissioner"

Jerry Rubin
24001 Highway 140
Eagle Point, OR 97524
"Former Political Activist"

John Rubinstein
10420 Scenario Lane
Los Angeles, CA 90077
"Actor"

Zelda Rubinstein
8730 Sunset Blvd. #22-W
Los Angeles, CA 90069
"Actress"

Paul Rudd
222 North Canon Drive #201
Beverly Hills, CA 90210
"Actor"

Al Ruddy
1601 Clearview Drive
Beverly Hills, CA 90210
"Film Writer, Producer"

Sen. Warren B. Rudman (NH)
Senate Hart Bldg. #530
Washington, DC 20510
"Politician"

Rita Rudner
2447 Benedict Canyon
Beverly Hills, CA 90210
"Comedienne"

Wilma Rudolph
3500 Centennial Blvd.
Nashville, TN 37203
"Track Athlete"

Mercedes Ruehl
306 West 100th Street
New York, NY 10025
"Actress"

Rufus
7250 Beverly Blvd #200
Los Angeles, CA 90036
"R&B Group"

Heinz Rhumann
D-8137 Berg 3
Starnberger Sea
GERMANY
"Actor"

Tracy Ruiz-Conforto
14314-174th Avenue N.E.
Redmond, WA 98052
"Swimmer"

Janice Rule
3681 Empire Drive
Los Angeles, CA 90034
"Actress"

Donald Rumsfeld
135 South La Salle Street #3910
Chicago, IL 60603
"Government Official"

Dr. Robert Runcie
Archbishop of Canterbury
Lambeth Palace
London SW1 7JU ENGLAND
"Archbishop"

Run D.M.C.
296 Elizabeth Street
New York, NY 10012
"Rap Group"

Barbara Rush
1709 Tropical Avenue
Beverly Hills, CA 90120
"Actress"

Deborah Rush
10100 Santa Monica Blvd.
Suite #1600
Los Angeles, CA 90067
"Actress"

Salman Rushdie
49 Belenheim Crescent
London W11 ENGLAND
"Author"

Patrice Rushen
1090 South La Brea Avenue
Los Angeles, CA 90010
"Singer"

Jared Rushton
12801 Owen Street
Garden Grove, CA 92645
"Actor"

Dean Rusk
1 Lafayette Square
620 Hill Street
Athens, GA 30601
"Former Secretary of State"

Bill Russell
P.O. Box 58
Mercer Island, WA 98040
"Basketball Player"

Brenda Russell
9000 Sunset Blvd. #1200
Los Angeles, CA 90069
"Singer"

Harold Russell
34 Old Town Road
Hyannis, MA 02601
"Government Official"

Jane Russell
2934 Lorito Road
Santa Barbara, CA 93108
"Actress"

Johnny Russell
P.O. Box Drawer 37
Hendersonville, TN 37075
"Singer, Songwriter"

Ken Russell
7 Bellmount Wood Land
Watford, Hert. ENGLAND
"Film Director"

Kimberly Russell
10231 Riverside Drive #205
Toluca Lake, CA 91602
"Actress"

Kurt Russell
229 East Gainsborough Road
Thousand Oaks, CA 91360
"Actor"

Mark Russell
2800 Wisconsin Avenue #810
Washington, DC 20007
"Satirist, Comedian"

Nipsey Russell
353 West 57th Street
New York, NY 10019
"Comedian, Writer, Director"

Theresa Russell
2 East Oxford & Cambridge
Old Maybone Road
London NW1 ENGLAND
"Actress"

Rep. Marty Russo (IL)
House Rayburn Bldg. #2233
Washington, DC 20515
"Politician"

Dick Rutan
614 Sandydale Road
Nipomo, CA 93444
"Aviator"

Ann Rutherford
826 Greenway Drive
Beverly Hills, CA 90210
"Actress"

Johnny Rutherford
4919 Black Oak Lane
Fort Worth, TX 76114
"Auto Racer"

Susan Ruttan
2677 La Cuesta Drive
Los Angeles, CA 90046
"Actress"

Fran Ryan
4204 Woodland
Burbank, CA 91505
"Actress"

Meg Ryan
8033 Sunset Blvd. #4048
Los Angeles, CA 90046
"Actress"

Mitchell Ryan
30355 Mulholland Drive
Cornell, CA 91301
"Actor"

Nolan Ryan
P.O. Box 670
Alvin, TX 77512
"Baseball Player"

Peggy Ryan
1821 East Oakley Blvd.
Las Vegas, NV 89104
"Actress"

Bobby Rydell
917 Bryn Mawr Avenue
Narberth, PA 19072
"Singer"

Mark Rydell
1 Topsail
Marina del Rey, CA 90292
"Actor, Director"

Winona Ryder
1636 North Beverly Drive
Beverly Hills, CA 90210
"Actress"

Jim Ryun
Rt. 3, Box 62-B
Lawrence, KS 66044
"Track Athlete"

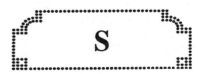

Gabriela Sabatini
2665 South Bayshore Drive
Miami, FL 31333
"Tennis Player"

Michael Sabatino
9720 Regent Street #8
Los Angeles, CA 90034
"Actor"

Brett Saberhagen
19229 Arminta Street
Reseda, CA 91335
"Baseball Player"

Rep. Martin Olay Sabo (MN)
House Rayburn Bldg. #2201
Washington, DC 20515
"Politician"

Robert Sacchi
232 South Windsor Blvd.
Los Angeles, CA 90004
"Actor"

Andrew Sachs
18/20 York Bldg. Adelphi
London WC2 ENGLAND
"Actor"

Madame Jehan El-Sadat
2310 Decatur Place N.W.
Washington, DC 20008
"Widower of Anwar"

Sade
237 Madison Avenue
New York, NY 10016
"Singer, Songwriter"

William Sadler
1114 Grant Avenue
Venice, CA 90291
"Actor"

Morley Safer
555 West 57th Street
New York, NY 10019
"News Journalist"

William Safire
6200 Elmwood Road
Chevy Chase, MD 20815
"Columnist"

Katey Sagal
3498 Troy Drive
Los Angeles, CA 90068
"Actress"

Liz Sagal
10351 Santa Monica Blvd. #211
Los Angeles, CA 90025
"Actress"

Dr. Carl E. Sagan
Cornell University
Space-Science Bldg.
Ithaca, NY 14853
"Astronomer, Writer"

Francoise Sagan
Ramsay 9, rue du Cherche-Midi
75006 Paris, FRANCE
"Author"

Jeff Sagansky
145 Ocean Avenue
Santa Monica, CA 90402
"TV Executive"

Carole Bayer Sager
658 Nimes Road
Los Angeles, CA 90077
"Singer, Songwriter"

Bob Saget
9200 Sunset Blvd. #428
Los Angeles, CA 90069
"Comedian"

Mort Sahl
2325 San Ysidro Drive
Beverly Hills, CA 90210
"Comedian, Writer"

Eva Marie Saint
8271 Melrose Avenue #110
Los Angeles, CA 90046
"Actress"

Lili St. Cyr
624 North Plymouth Blvd. #7
Los Angeles, CA 90004
"Entertainer"

Susan Saint James
P.O. Box 1252
Litchfield, CT 06759
"Actress"

Jill St. John
8271 Melrose Avenue #110
Los Angeles, CA 90046
"Actress"

Yves St. Laurent
15 Columbus Circle
New York, NY 10023
"Fashion Designer"

Buffy Sainte-Marie
RR #1, Box 368
Kapaa, Kauai, HI 96746
"Singer, Songwriter"

Pat Sajak
3400 Riverside Drive
Burbank, CA 91505
"TV Host"

Teresa Saldana
10637 Burbank Blvd.
North Hollywood, CA 91601
"Actress"

Virginia Sale
Motion Picture Country Home
23450 Calabasas Road
Woodland Hills, CA 91364
"Actress"

Meredith Salenger
10100 Santa Monica Blvd. #1600
Los Angeles, CA 90067
"Actress"

Soupy Sales
34-12 36th Street #1-123
Astoria, NY 11106
"Actor, Comedian"

Carlos Salinas de Gortari
Palacio Nacional
Mexico City 06220 MEXICO
"President of Mexico"

J. D. Salinger
RR #3, Box 176
Cornish Flat, NH 03746
"Author"

Matt Salinger
15760 Ventura Blvd. #1730
Encino, CA 91436
"Actor"

Pierre Salinger
7 Carburton Street
London W1P 7DT ENGLAND
"News Correspondent"

Dr. Jonas Salk
2444 Ellentown Road
La Jolla, CA 92037
"Scientist"

Jennifer Salt
137 1/2 South Rexford Drive
Beverly Hills, CA 90212
"Actress"

Hans J. Salter
3658 Woodhill Canyon Place
Studio City, CA 91604
"Composer, Conductor"

Juan Antonio Samaranch
Chateau de Viey
CH-1007 Lausanne
SWITZERLAND
"Sports Executive"

Emma Samms
335 North Maple Drive #360
Beverly Hills, CA 90210
"Actress"

Pete Sampras
6816 Verde Ridge Road
Rancho Palos Verdes, CA 90274
"Tennis Player"

Ron Samuels
3114 Abington Drive
Beverly Hills, CA 90210
"Talent Agent"

Paul Sand
9301 Wilshire Blvd. #312
Beverly Hills, CA 90210
"Actor"

Dominique Sanda
3 quai Malaquais
75006 Paris, FRANCE
"Actress"

Barry Sanders
1200 Featherstone Road
Pontiac, MI 48057
"Football Player"

Doug Sanders
8828 Sandringham
Houston, TX 77024
"Golfer"

Jay O. Sanders
1999 Avenue of the Stars #285
Los Angeles, CA 90067
"Actor"

Richard Sanders
2245 Maurice Avenue
La Crescenta, CA 91214
"Actor, Writer"

Willaim Sanderson
469 North Croft
Los Angeles, CA 90069
"Actor"

Jay Sandrich
1 North Star #205
Marina del Rey, CA 90291
"Actor, Director"

Johnny Sands
2333 Kapiolani Blvd.
Honolulu, HI 96814
"Actor"

Julian Sands
1287 Ozeta Terrace
Los Angeles, CA 90069
"Actor"

Tommy Sands
511 Hahaione Place
Honolulu, HI 96825
"Actor, Singer"

Baby Sandy
(Sandra Lee Henville Magee)
6846 Haywood
Tujunga, CA 91042
"Actress"

Gary Sandy
12810 Waddell Street
North Hollywood, CA 91607
"Actor"

Isabel Sanford
151 North San Vicente Blvd. #208
Beverly Hills, CA 90211
"Actress"

Sen. Terry Sanford (NC)
Senate Hart Bldg. #716
Washington, DC 20510
"Politician"

Rep. George Sangmeister (IL)
House Longworth Bldg. #1032
Washington, DC 20515
"Politician"

Olga San Juan
4845 Willowcrest Avenue
Studio City, CA 91604
"Dancer, Comedienne"

Santana
201-11th Street
San Francisco, CA 94103
"Rock & Roll Group"

Penny Santon
1918 North Edgemont Street
Los Angeles, CA 90027
"Actress"

Reni Santoni
247 South Beverly Drive #102
Beverly Hills, CA 90212
"Actor"

Mia Sara
P.O. Box 5617
Beverly Hills, CA 90210
"Actress"

HRH Sarah, Dutchess of York
Sunninghill Park
Windsor, ENGLAND
"Royalty"

Chris Sarandon
121 North San Vicente Blvd.
Beverly Hills, CA 90211
"Actor"

Susan Sarandon
25 East 9th Street
New York, NY 10019
"Actress"

Gene Sarazen
Emerald Beach
P.O. Box 677
Marco, FL 33937
"Golfer"

Sen. Paul Sarbanes (MD)
Senate Hart Bldg. #309
Washington, DC 20510
"Politician"

Vincent Sardi, Jr.
234 West 44th Street
New York, NY 10036
"Restaurateur"

Dick Sargent
7422 Palo Vista Drive
Los Angeles, CA 90046
"Actor"

Rep. Bill Sarpalius (TX)
House Cannon Bldg. #126
Washington, DC 20515
"Politician"

Michael Sarrazin
9920 Beverly Grove
Beverly Hills, CA 90210
"Actor"

Sen. Jim Sasser (TN)
Senate Russell Bldg. #363
Washington, DC 20515
"Politician"

Beverly Sassoon
738 North Holmby Avenue
Los Angeles, CA 90024
"Actress, Model"

Vidal Sassoon
2132 Century Park Lane #108
Los Angeles, CA 90067
"Hair Stylist"

Van Gordon Sauter
51 West 52nd Street
New York, NY 10019
"TV Executive"

Claude Sautet
14 Ave. des Gobelins
75013 Paris, FRANCE
"Director, Author"

Ann Savage-D'Armand
8218-B DeLongpre Avenue
Los Angeles, CA 90069
"Actress"

Fred Savage
P.O. Box 893
Tarzana, CA 91356
"Actor"

Rep. Gus Savage (IL)
House Rayburn Bldg. #2419
Washington, DC 20515
"Politician"

John Savage
8899 Beverly Blvd.
Los Angeles, CA 90048
"Actor"

Randy Savage
P.O. Box 3859
Stamford, CT 06905
"Wrestler"

Tracie Savage
6212 Banner Avenue
Los Angeles, CA 90038
"Actress"

Telly Savalas
160 Central Park South
New York, NY 10023
"Actor"

Doug Savant
460 East Santa Anita #110
Burbank, CA 91501
"Actor"

Jennifer Savidge
2705 Glendower Avenue
Los Angeles, CA 90027
"Actress"

Sawyer Brown
128 Volunteer Drive
Hendersonville, TN 37075
"Rock & Roll Group"

Diane Sawyer
211 Central Park West
New York, NY 10024
"Broadcast Journalist"

Rep. Thomas C. Sawyer (OH)
House Longworth Bldg. #1518
Washington, DC 20515
"Politician"

John Saxon
2432 Banyan Drive
Los Angeles, CA 90049
"Actor, Writer"

Peggy Say
438 Lake Shore Drive
Cadiz, KY 42211
"Sister Of American Hostage"

Rep. H. James Saxton (NJ)
House Cannon Bldg. #324
Washington, DC 20515
"Politician"

Gale Sayers
624 Buch Road
Northbrook, IL 60062
"Football Player"

Greta Scacchi
121 North San Vicente Blvd.
Beverly Hills, CA 90211
"Actress"

Boz Scaggs
345 North Maple Drive #235
Beverly Hills, CA 90210
"Singer, Songwriter"

Antonin Scalia
1-1st Street N.E.
Washington, DC 20543
"Supreme Court Justice"

Jack Scalia
2150 Cold Canyon
Calabasas, CA 91302
"Actor"

Susan Scannell
247 South Beverly Drive #102
Beverly Hills, CA 90212
"Actress"

Michele Scarabelli
4720 Vineland Avenue #216
North Hollywood, CA 91602
"Actress"

Glenn Scarpelli
3480 Barham Blvd. #320
Los Angeles, CA 90068
"Actor"

Diana Scarwid
P.O. Box 3614
Savannah, GA 31404
"Actress"

Francesco Scavullo
216 East 63rd Street
New York, NY 10021
"Photographer"

Wendy Schaal
3701 Longview Valley Road
Sherman Oaks, CA 91403
"Actress"

Gov. Wiliam Schacfer (ME)
State House
Annapolis, MD 21401
"Governor"

Rep. Dan L. Schaefer (CO)
House Longworth Bldg. #1007
Washington, DC 20515
"Politician"

George Schaeffer
1040 Woodland Drive
Beverly Hills, CA 90210
"TV Producer, Director"

Paul Schafer
24 West 60th Street
35th Floor
New York, NY 10023
"Keyboardist"

William Schallert
14920 Ramos Place
Pacific Palisades, CA 90272
"Actor"

Phyllis Schafly
68 Fairmont
Alton, IL 62002
"Author, Politician"

Anne Schedeen
11227 Hortense Street
North Hollywood, CA 91602
"Actress"

Roy Scheider
120 East 56th Street #8-N
New York, NY 10022
"Actor"

Maria Schell
D-8094 Heberthal
Bei Wasserburg/Inn
GERMANY
"Actress"

Maximilian Schell
2 Kepler Strasse
Munich 27 GERMANY
"Actor"

Ronnie Schell
4024 Sapphire Drive
Encino, CA 91316
"Comedian, Actor"

Bo Schembechler
870 Arlington Blvd.
Ann Arbor, MI 48106
"Football Coach, Baseball"

Rep. James Scheuer (NY)
House Rayburn Bldg. #2221
Washington, DC 20515
"Politician"

Bob Schieffer
524 West 57th Street
New York, NY 10019
"Broadcast Journalist"

Rep. Steven H. Schiff (NM)
House Longworth Bldg. #1427
Washington, DC 20515
"Politician"

Claudia Schiffer
5 Union Square West #500
New York, NY 10003
"Model"

Lalo Schifrin
710 North Hillcrest Road
Beverly Hills, CA 90210
"Composer, Conductor"

William Schilling
626 North Valley Street
Burbank, CA 91505
"Actor"

G. David Schine
626 South Hudson
Los Angeles, CA 90005
"Businessman"

Walter M. Schirra, Jr.
16834 Via de Santa Fe
Rancho Santa Fe, CA 92067
"Astronaut"

Charlie Schatter
9830 Wilshire Blvd.
Beverly Hills, CA 90212
"Actor"

George Schlatter
8320 Beverly Blvd.
Beverly Hills, CA 90048
"Writer, Producer"

Arthur Schlesinger, Jr.
33 West 42nd Street
New York, NY 10036
"Historian, Author"

James R. Schelsinger
1800 "K" Street N.W. #520
Washington, DC 20006
"Government Official"

John Schelssinger
1896 Rising Glen
Los Angeles, CA 90069
"Film Director"

Rep. Steve Schiff (NM)
House Longworth Bldg. #1427
Washington, DC 20515
"Politician"

Edwin Schlossberg
20 West 20th Street
New York, NY 10011
"Artist"

Max Schmeling
2115 Hallenstedt
Hamburg GERMANY
"Boxer"

Harrison Schmidt
Rt. 8, Box 226
Silver City, NM 88061
"Former Senator"

Helmut Schmidt
SPD-Parteivorstand
5300 Bonn 1 GERMANY
"Chancellor"

Mike Schmidt
P.O. Box 32
Rydal, PA 19046
"Baseball Player"

John Schneider
P.O. Box 741
Pacific Palisades, CA 90272
"Actor, Writer, Singer"

Stephen Schnetzer
448 West 44th Street
New York, NY 10036
"Actor"

Gina Schock
P.O. Box 4398
North Hollywood, CA 91617
"Drummer, Singer"

Carolyn Hunt Schoellkopf
100 Crescent #1700
Dallas, TX 75201
"Businesswoman"

Daniel Schorr
3113 Woodley Road
Washington, DC 20008
"Broadcast Journalist"

Tex Schramm
9355 Sunnybrook
Dallas, TX 75220
"Football Team Executive"

Avery Schreiber
6612 Ranchito
Van Nuys, CA 91405
"Actor, Comedian"

Barbet Schroeder
9830 Wilshire Blvd.
Beverly Hills, CA 90212
"Film Director"

Jay Schroeder
322 Center Street
El Segundo, CA 90245
"Football Player"

Rep. Fatricia Schroeder (CO)
House Rayburn Bldg. #2208
Washington, DC 20515
"Politician"

Ricky Schroeder
921 North Roxbury Drive
Beverly Hills, CA 90212
"Actor"

Mark Schubb
9744 Wilshire Blvd. #308
Beverly Hills, CA 90212
"Actor"

John Schuck
3543 Woodcliff Road
Sherman Oaks, CA 91403
"Actor"

Budd Schulberg
P.O. Box 707, Brookside
Westhampton Beach, NY 11978
"TV Writer"

Dr. Robert Schuller
464 South Esplanade
Orange, CA 92669
"Evangelist"

Dwight Schultz
2824 Nichols Canyon
Los Angeles, CA 90046
"Actor"

George Schultz
2201 "C" Street N.W.
Washington, DC 20005
"Educator"

Charles Schulz
1 Snoopy Place
Santa Rosa, CA 95401
"Cartoonist

Rep. Richard Schulze (PA)
House Rayburn Bldg. #2369
Washington, DC 20515
"Politician"

Rep. Charles Schumer (NY)
House Rayburn Bldg. #2412
Washington, DC 20515
"Politician"

Diane Schuur
9000 Sunset Blvd. #1200
Los Angeles, CA 90069
"Singer"

Neil Schwartz
23427 Schoolcraft Avenue
Canoga Park, CA 91304
"Actor"

Arnold Schwarzenegger
321 Hampton Drive #203
Venice, CA 90291
"Actor"

Elisabeth Schwarzkopf
Rebhusstr. 29
8126 Zunnikon
Zurich, SWITZERLAND
"Opera Singer"

Gen. Norman Schwarzkopf
401 Staff Loop
Tampa, FL 33621
"Military Leader"

Hanna Schygulla
4 rue de Ponthieu
F-75008 Paris, FRANCE
"Actress"

Patti Scialfa
11 Gimbel Place
Ocean, NJ 07712
"Singer"

Leonard Sciascia
Viale Scaduto 10/B
I-00144 Palermo, ITALY
"Author"

Mike Scioscia
810 Manchester Court
Claremont, CA 91711
"Baseball Player"

Paul Scofield
The Gables
Balcombe, Sussex ENGLAND
"Actor"

Tracy Scoggins
P.O. Box 2262
Malibu, CA 90265
"Actress, Model"

Peter Scolari
930 Hilgard Avenue
Los Angeles, CA 90024
"Actor"

The Scooters
15190 Encanto Drive
Sherman Oaks, CA 91403
"Rock & Roll Group"

Scorpions
P.O. Box 5220
3000 Hanover, GERMANY
"Rock & Roll Group"

Martine Scorsese
146 West 57th Street #75-B
New York, NY 10019
"Film Writer, Producer"

Byron Scott
31815 Camino Capistrano #C
San Juan Capistrano, CA 92675
"Basketball Player"

Campbell Scott
3211 Retreat Court
Malibu, CA 90265
"Actor"

Debralee Scott
19 West 44th Street #1500
New York, NY 10017
"Actress"

Fred Scott
1716 East Ramon Road #42
Palm Springs, CA 92264
"Actor"

Dr. Gene Scott
1615 Glendale Avenue
Glendale, CA 91205
"TV Host, Teacher"

Geoffrey Scott
3464 Primera Avenue
Los Angeles, CA 90068
"Actor"

George C. Scott
3211 Retreat Court
Malibu, CA 90265
"Actor, Director"

Jacqueline Scott
12456 Ventura Blvd. #1
Studio City, CA 91604
"Actress"

Jean Bruce Scott
144 South Beverly Drive #405
Beverly Hills, CA 90212
"Actress"

Judson Scott
10000 Santa Monica Blvd. #305
Los Angeles, CA 90067
"Actor"

Kathryn Leigh Scott
12161 Valleyheart Drive
Studio City, CA 91604
"Actress"

Lizabeth Scott
P.O. Box 5555
Beverly Hills, CA 90213
"Actress"

Martha Scott
10000 Santa Monica Blvd. #305
Los Angeles, CA 90067
"Actress"

Pippa Scott
10 Ocean Park Blvd.
Santa Monica, CA 90405
"Actress"

Raymond Scott
14549 Valeria Street
Van Nuys, CA 91405
"Songwriter, Band Leader"

Ridley Scott
8439 Sunset Blvd. #103
Los Angeles, CA 90069
"Film Director"

Ronnie Scott
47 Frith Street
London W1V 5TE ENGLAND
"Saxophonist"

Williard Scott
30 Rockerfeller Plaza #304
New York, NY 10012
"TV Weatherman"

Vito Scotti
20121 Ventura Blvd.
Woodland Hills, CA 91367
"Actor"

Renato Scotto
61 West 62nd Street #6F
New York, NY 10023
"Soprano"

Gen. Brent Scowcroft
The White House
1600 Pennsylvania Avenue
Washington, DC 20500
"Ex-Military, Politician"

Earl Scruggs
P.O. Box 66
Madison, TN 37115
"Banjoist, Songwriter"

John Sculley
20525 Mariani Avenue
Cupertino, CA 95014
"Computer Executive"

Vin Scully
1555 Capri Drive
Pacific Palisades, CA 90272
"Sportscaster"

Glenn T. Seaborg
1 Cyclotron Road
Berkeley, CA 94720
"Chemist"

The Seachers
1650 Broadway #611
New York, NY 10019
"Vocal Group"

Steven Seagal
P.O. Box 727
Los Olivas, CA 93441
"Actor"

Bob Seagren
120 South Thurston
Los Angeles, CA 90049
"Actor"

Jenny Seagrove
Garden Flat
10A Highbury New Park
London N5 2DB ENGLAND
"Actress"

Dan Seals
P.O. Box 1770
Hendersonville, TN 37077
"Singer, Songwriter"

Jackie Searl
7218 Chetwood Drive
Tujunga, CA 91042
"Actor"

Tom Seaver
Larkspur Lane
Greenwich, CT 06830
"Baseball Player"

John Sebastian
12744 Weddington
North Hollywood, CA 91607
"Singer, Songwriter"

Sir Harry Secombe
46 St. James's Place
London SW1 ENGLAND
"Actor, Singer"

Gen. Richard Secord
1 Pennsylvania Plaza #2400
New York, NY 10119
"Miltary Leader"

Neil Sedaka
8787 Shoreham Drive
Los Angeles, CA 90069
"Singer, Songwriter"

Frank Sedgman
28 Bolton Avenue
Hampton, Victoria 3188
AUSTRALIA
"Tennis Player"

Kyra Sedgwick
800 West End Avenue #7-A
New York, NY 10025
"Actress"

Pete Seeger
P.O. Box 431
Duchess Junction
Beacon, NY 12508
"Singer, Songwriter"

Erich Segal
53 The Pryors
East Heath Road
London NW3 1BP ENGLAND
"Author"

George Segal
8899 Beverly Blvd.
Los Angeles, CA 90211
"Actor"

Jonathan Segal
600 Radcliffe Avenue
Pacific Palisades, CA 90272
"Actor"

Vivienne Segal
152 North LaDoux Road
Beverly Hills, CA 90211
"Singer, Songwriter"

Pancho Segura
La Costa Hotel & Spas
Carlsbad, CA 92008
"Tennis Player"

Jerry Seinfeld
1222 North Kings Road #9
Los Angeles, CA 90069
"Comedian"

David Selby
15152 Encanto Drive
Sherman Oaks, CA 91403
"Actor"

Monica Seles
Balzakova 26
YU-21000 Novi Sad
YUGOSLAVIA
"Tennis Player"

Connie Selleca
14755 Ventura Blvd. #I-916
Sherman Oaks, CA 96815
"Actress"

Tom Selleck
4095 Black Point Road
Honolulu, HI 96815
"Actor"

Milton Selzer
575 San Juan Street
Santa Paul, CA 93060
"Actor"

**Rep. F. James Sensenbrenner
(WI)**
House Rayburn Bldg. #2444
Washington, DC 20515
"Politician"

Serendipity Singers
P.O. Box 399
Lisle, IL 60532
"Vocal Group"

Yahoo Serious
12/33 East Crescent Street
McMahons Point NSW 2060
AUSTRLIA
"Actor, Director"

Pepe Serna
2321 Hill Drive
Los Angeles, CA 90041
"Actor"

Brian Setzer
4161 Fulton Avenue
Sherman Oaks, CA 91423
"Musician"

Eric Sevareid
2020 "M" Street N.W.
Washington, DC 20036
"News Journalist"

Johnny Seven
11213 McLennan Avenue
Granada Hills, CA 91344
"Actor, Director"

Joan Severance
P.O. Box 67492
Los Angeles, CA 90067
"Actress, Model"

Doc Severinsen
2807 Nichols Canyon
Los Angeles, CA 90046
"Trumpeter"

Jane Seymour
930 Lilac Street
Montecito, CA 93108
"Actress, Model"

Ted Shackelford
12305 Valleyheart Drive
Studio City, CA 91604
"Actor"

Peter Shaffer
200 Fulham Road
London SW10 ENGLAND
"Screenwriter"

Sam The Sham
3667 Tetwiler Avenue
Memphis, TN 38122
"Vocal Group"

Steve Shagan
10390 Wilshire Blvd. #605
Los Angeles, CA 90024
"Writer, Producer"

Shalamar
200 West 51st Street #1410
New York, NY 10019
"R&B Group"

Gene Shalit
225 East 79th Street
New York, NY 10021
"Film Critic"

Yitzhak Shamir
Kiriyat Ben Gurian
Jerusalem 91919 ISRAEL
"Politician"

Garry Shandling
9200 Sunset Blvd. #428
Los Angeles, CA 90099
"Comedian, Actor, Director"

Ravi Shankar
17 Warden Court
Gowalia Tank Road
Bombay 36 INDIA
"Satarist"

Esther Shapiro
617 North Alta Drive
Beverly Hills, CA 90210
"TV Writer, Producer"

Richard Shapiro
617 North Alta Drive
Beverly Hills, CA 90210
"TV Writer, Producer"

Irene Sharaff
116 East 66th Street
New York, NY 10021
"Costume Designer"

Omar Sharif
31/32 Soho Square
London W1 ENGLAND
"Actor"

Jack Sharkey
P.O. Box 242, Pleasant Street
Epping, NH 03042
"Boxer"

Ray Sharkey
12424 Wilshire Blvd. #840
Los Angeles, CA 90025
"Actor"

Barbara Sharma
9000 Sunset Blvd. #801
Los Angeles, CA 90069
"Actress"

Rep. Philip R. Sharp (IN)
House Rayburn Bldg. #2217
Washington, DC 20515
"Politician"

William Shatner
3674 Berry Avenue
Studio City, CA 91604
"Actor"

Charles Shaughnessy
1817 Ashland Avenue
Santa Monica, CA 90405
"Actor"

Mel Shavelson
11947 Sunshine Terrace
North Hollywood, CA 91604
"Writer, Producer"

Helen Shaver
10390 Santa Monica Blvd. #300
Los Angeles, CA 90067
"Actress"

Artie Shaw
2127 West Palos Court
Newbury Park, CA 91320
"Orchestra Leader"

Bernard Shaw
111 Massachusetts N.W.
Washington, DC 20001
"News Correspondent"

Rep. E. Clay Shaw, Jr. (FL)
House Rayburn Bldg. #2338
Washington, DC 20515
"Politician"

Martin Shaw
204 Belswins Lane
Hemel, Hempstead
Hertfordshire, ENGLAND
"Actor"

Stan Shaw
1999 Avenue of the Stars #2850
Los Angeles, CA 90067
"Actor"

Tommy Shaw
1790 Broadway, PH
New York, NY 10019
"Singer, Songwriter"

Robert Shayne
555 Laurie Lane #J-7
Thousand Oaks, CA 91360
"Actor"

George Beverly Shea
1300 Harmon Place
Minneapolis, MN 55403
"Singer"

John Shea
955 South Carrillo Drive #300
Los Angeles, CA 90048
"Actor"

Harry Shearer
9000 Sunset Blvd. #1200
Los Angeles, CA 90069
"TV Writer, Director"

Ally Sheedy
P.O. Box 6327
Malibu, CA 90264
"Actress"

Doug Sheehan
4019-137 Goldfinch Street
San Diego, CA 92103
"Actor"

Gail Sheehy
105 Maidson Avenue
New York, NY 10016
"Author, Journalist"

Charlie Sheen
335 North Maple Drive #360
Beverly Hills, CA 90210
"Actor"

Martin Sheen
335 North Maple Drive #360
Beverly Hills, CA 90212
"Actor, TV Director"

Johnny Sheffield
834 First Avenue
Chula Vista, CA 92011
"Actor"

Sheila E.
11355 West Olympic Blvd. #555
Los Angeles, CA 90064
"Singer, Percussionist"

David Sheiner
351 South Avenue #12-F
Los Angeles, CA 90036
"Actor"

Sen. Richard C. Shelby (AL)
Senate Hart Bldg. #313
Washington, DC 20515
"Politician"

Deborah Sheldon
1690 Coldwater Canyon
Beverly Hills, CA 90210
"Actress"

Reid Sheldon
1524 Labaig Avenue
Los Angeles, CA 90028
"Actor"

Sidney Sheldon
10250 Sunset Blvd.
Los Angeles, CA 90077
"Writer"

Art Shell
30816 rue de la Pierre
Rancho Palos Verdes, CA 90274
"Football Player & Coach"

Adm. Alan B. Shepard, Jr.
3435 Westheimer Road #1005
Houston, TX 77027
"Astronaut"

Cybill Shepherd
16037 Royal Road
Encino, CA 91436
"Actress, Model"

Sam Shepherd
240 West 44th Street
New York, NY 10036
"Actor, Director"

T.G. Sheppard
P.O. Box 40484
Nashville, TN 37204
"Singer"

Mark Shera
9229 Sunset Blvd. #607
Los Angeles, CA 90069
"Actor"

Nicollette Sheridan
P.O. Box 25578
Los Angeles, CA 90025
"Actress"

Bobby Sherman
1870 Sunset Plaza Drive
Los Angeles, CA 90069
"Singer, Actor"

Jenny Sherman
P.O. Box 73
Los Angeles, CA 90078
"Actress, Model"

Richard Sherman
808 North Crescent Drive
Beverly Hills, CA 90210
"Composer, Lyricist"

Robert Sherman
808 North Crescent Drive
Beverly Hills, CA 90210
"Composer, Lyricist"

Madeline Sherwood
32 Leroy Street
New York, NY 10014
"Actress"

Roberta Sherwood
14155 Magnolia Blvd. #126
Sherman Oaks, CA 91423
"Singer, Actress"

Edward Shevardnadze
32-34 Smolenskaya
Sennaya Polschachad
Moscow, Russia
"Politician"

Brooke Shields
165 East 62nd Street
New York, NY 10021
"Actress, Model"

Robert Shields
7615 West Norton Avenue #1
Los Angeles, CA 90046
"Mime, Writer"

James Shigeta
8917 Cynthia #1
Los Angeles, CA 90069
"Actor"

Yoko Shimada
7245 Hillside Avenue #415
Los Angeles, CA 90046
"Actress"

Joanna Shimkus
1007 Cove Way
Beverly Hills, CA 90210
"Actress"

John Wesley Shipp
9200 Sunset Blvd. #710
Los Angeles, CA 90069
"Actor"

Talia Shire
16633 Ventura Blvd
Encino, CA 91436
"Actress"

William L. Shirer
P.O. Box 487
Lenox, MA 01240
"Author, Journalist"

Anne Shirley Lederer
7416 Rosewood Avenue
Los Angeles, CA 90036
"Actress"

Catherine Shirriff
12920 Dickens Street
North Hollywood, CA 91604
"Actress"

Bill Shoemaker
2545 Fairfield Place
San Marino, CA 91108
"Horse Racer"

Dinah Shore
916 Oxford Way
Beverly Hills, CA 90210
"Singer, TV Host"

Lonnie Shorr
141 South El Camino Drive #205
Beverly Hills, CA 90212
"Comedian"

Bobby Short
444 East 57th Street
New York, NY 10022
"Actor, Singer"

Martin Short
15907 Alcima Avenue
Pacific Palisades, CA 90272
"Actor"

Frank Shorter
787 Lincoln Place
Boulder, CO 80302
"Track Athlete"

Grant Show
9830 Wilshire Blvd.
Beverly Hills, CA 90212
"Actor"

Max Showalter
5 Gilbert Hill Road
Chester, CT 06412
"Actor"

Jean Shrimpton Cox
Abbey Hotel
Penzance, Cornwall
ENGLAND
"Actress"

Kin Shriner
8721 Sunset Blvd. #202
Los Angeles, CA 90069
"Actor"

Wil Shriner
5313 Quakertown Avenue
Woodland Hills, CA 91364
"Actor, Writer, Comedian"

Eunice Kennedy Shriver
1701 "K" Street, N.W.
Washington, DC 20006
"Ex-President's Sister"

Maria Shriver
321 Hampton Drive #203
Venice, CA 90291
"Newscaster"

Pam Shriever
2665 South Bay Shore #1002
Miami, FL 33133
"Tennis Player"

R. Sargent Shriver
1350 New York Avenue N.W.
Washington, DC 20005
"Politician"

Sonny Shroyer
8322 Beverly Blvd. #202
Los Angeles, CA 90048
"Actor"

Elizabeth Shue
217 Turell Avenue South
Orange, NJ 07079
"Actress"

Don Shula
16220 West Prestwick Place
Miami Lakes, FL 33014
"Football Coach"

Richard B. Shull
16 Gramercy Park
New York, NY 10003
"Actor"

Rep. Bud Shuster (PA)
House Rayburn Bldg. #2268
Washington, DC 20515
"Politician"

Michael Shuster
c/o National Public Radio
2025 "M" Street NW
Washington, DC 20036
"New Correspondent"

Jane Sibbett
570 North Rossmore Ave. #303
Los Angeles, CA 90004
"Actress"

Hugh Sidey
888-16th Street N.W.
Washington, DC 20006
"Columnist"

George Sidney
910 North Rexford Drive
Beverly Hills, CA 90210
"Director, Producer"

Sylvia Sidney
9744 Wilshire Blvd. #308
Beverly Hills, CA 90212
"Actress"

Charles Sieberg
227 Toyopa Drive
Pacific Palisades, CA 90272
"Actor, Director"

Robert Siegel
c/o National Public Radio
2025 "M" Street NW
Washington, DC 20036
"News Correspondent"

Siegfried & Roy
1639 North Valley Drive
Las Vegas, NV 89109
"Circus Act"

Casey Siemaszko
9830 Wilshire Blvd.
Beverly Hills, CA 90212
"Actor"

Sanford Sigoloff
320 Cliffwood Avenue
Los Angeles, CA 90049
"Business Executive"

Cynthia Sikes
250 Delfern Drive
Los Angeles, CA 90077
"Actress"

James B. Sikking
258 South Carmelina Avenue
Los Angeles, CA 90049
"Actor"

Rep. Gerry Sikorski (MN)
House Cannon Bldg. #403
Washington, DC 20515
"Politician"

Stirling Silliphant
P.O. Box 351119
Los Angeles, CA 90035
"Film Writer, Producer"

Beverly Sills
211 Central Park West
New York, NY 10024
"Soprano"

Henry Silva
8747 Clifton Way #305
Beverly Hills, CA 90210
"Actor"

Ron Silver
6116 Tyndall Avenue
Riverside, NY 10471
"Actor"

Fred Silverman
12400 Wilshire Blvd. #920
Los Angeles, CA 90025
TV Executive, Producer"

Jonathan Silverman
854 Birchwood Drive
Los Angeles, CA 90024
"Actor"

Gene Simmons
6363 Sunset Blvd. #417
Los Angeles, CA 90028
"Singer, Actor, Composer"

Jean Simmons
636 Adelaide Way
Santa Monica, CA 90402
"Actress"

Richard Simmons
1350 Belfast
Los Angeles, CA 90069
"Exercise Instructor"

Ginny Simms
1578 Murray Canyon Drive
Palm Springs, CA 92262
"Actress"

Larry Simms
P.O. Box 85
Gray River, WA 98621
"Actor"

Carly Simon
135 Central Park West
New York, NY 10023
"Singer, Songwriter"

Neil Simon
10100 Santa Monica Blvd. #400
Los Angeles, CA 90067
"Dramatist"

Norton Simon
411 West Colorado Blvd.
Pasadena, CA 91105
"Industrialist, Art Collector"

Sen. Paul Simon (IL)
462 Dirksen Bldg.
Washington, DC 2051
"Politician"

Paul Simon
1619 Broadway #500
New York, NY 10019
"Singer, Songwriter

Scott Simon
c/o National Public Radio
2025 "M" Street NW
Washington, DC 20036
"News Correspondent"

Simone Simon
5 rue de Tilsitt
75008 Paris, FRANCE
"Actress"

William Simon
330 South Street
Morristown, NJ 07960
"Former Secretary of Treasury"

Nina Simone
1995 Broadway #501
New York, NY 10023
"Singer, Pianist"

Simple Minds
63 Frederic Street
Edinburgh EH2 1LH SCOTLAND
"Rock & Roll Group"

Simply Red
36 Atwood Road
Didsbury, Manchester 20
ENGLAND
"Rock & Roll Group"

Sen. Alan K. Simpon (WY)
Senate Dirksen Bldg. #261
Washington, DC 20510
"Politician"

O.J. Simpson
360 Rockingham Avenue
Los Angeles, CA 90049
"Football Player"

Joan Sims
17 Esmonds Court
Thackery Street
London W8 ENGLAND
"Actress"

Sylvia Sims
135 East 63rd Street
New York, NY 10021
"Actress"

Frank Sinatra
70-558 Frank Sinatra Drive
Rancho Mirage, CA 92270
"Singer, Actor"

Frank Sinatra, Jr.
2211 Florian Place
Beverly Hills, CA 90210
"Singer"

Mrs. Nancy Sinatra
1121 North Beverly Drive
Beverly Hills, CA 90210
Ex-Mrs. Frank Sinatra"

Nancy Sinatra, Jr.
P.O. Box 69453
Los Angeles, CA 90069
"Singer, Actress"

Tina Sinatra
9461 Lloydcrest Drive
Beverly Hills, CA 90210
"Singer"

SinBad
20061 Merridy Street
Chatsworth, CA 91311
"Comedian, Actor"

Sinceros
25 Buliver Street
Shephards Bush
London W12 ENGLAND
"Rock & Roll Group"

Madge Sinclair
22976 Avenue San Luis
Woodland Hills, CA 91364
"Actress"

Donald Sinden
60 Temple Fortune Lane
London NW11 ENGLAND
"Actor"

Lori Singer
11218 Canton Drive
Studio City, CA 91604
"Actress"

Marc Singer
11218 Canton Drive
Studio City, CA 91604
"Actor"

Penny Singleton
13419 Riverside Drive #C
Sherman Oaks, CA 91423
"Actress"

Gov. George A. Sinner (ND)
1st Floor, State Capitol
Bismarck, ND 58505
"Governor"

Curt Siomak
Old Southfork Ranch
43422 South Fork Drive
Three Rivers, CA 93271
"Writer, Producer"

Sirhan Sirhan
California Men's Colony
San Luis Obispo, CA 93401
"Robert Kennedy's Killer"

John Sirica
5069 Overlook Road N.W.
Washington, DC 20016
"Judge"

Marina Sirtis
2436 Creston Way
Los Angeles, CA 90068
"Actress"

Rep. Norman Sisisky (VA)
House Cannon Bldg. #426
Washington, DC 20515
"Politician"

Gene Siskel
1301 North Astor
Chicago, IL 60610
"Film Critic"

Sister Sledge
10100 Santa Monica Blvd. #1600
Los Angeles, CA 90067
"Vocal Group"

Rep. David E. Skaggs (CO)
House Longworth Bldg. #1507
Washington, DC 20515
"Politician"

Ricky Skaggs
P.O. Box 15781
Nashville, TN 37215
"Singer, Guitarist"

Lilia Skala
42-02 Layton Street
Elmhurst, NY 11373
"Actress"

Rep. Joe Skeen (NM)
House Rayburn Bldg. #2447
Washington, DC 20515
"Politician"

Rep. Ike Skelton (MO)
House Rayburn Bldg. #2134
Washington, DC 20515
"Politician"

Red Skelton
37-801 Thompson Road
Rancho Mirage, CA 92270
"Comedian, Actor"

Tom Skerritt
1654 Shenandoah Drive East
Seattle, WA 98112
"Actor"

Skid Row
240 Central Park South #2-C
New York, NY 10019
"Rock & Roll Group"

Moose Skowron
1118 Beachcomber Drive
Schaumburg, IL 60193
"Baseball Player"

Ione Skye
3120 Hollyridge Drive
Los Angeles, CA 90068
"Actress"

Henry Slate
6310 San Vicent Blvd. #407
Los Angeles, CA 90048
"Actor"

Mark Slate
2247 Linda Flora Drive
Los Angeles, CA 90077
"Actor"

Christian Slater
5871 Allott
Van Nuys, CA 91401
"Actor"

Helen Slater
151 South Camino Drive
Beverly Hills, CA 90212
"Actress"

Rep. Jim Slattery (KS)
House Longworth Bldg. #1512
Washington, DC 20515
"Politician"

Richard X. Slattery
P.O. Box 2410
Avalon, CA 90704
"Actor"

Robert F. Slatzer
3033 Hollycrest Drive #2
Los Angeles, CA 90068
"Writer, Producer"

Enos Slaughter
Rt. #2, Box 159
Roxboro, NC 27573
"Baseball Player"

Dr. Frank Slaughter
P.O. Box 14, Ortega Station
Jacksonville, FL 32210
"Author, Surgeon"

Rep. French Slaughter (VA)
House Longworth Bldg. #1404
Washington, DC 20515
"Politician"

Rep. Louise Slaughter (NY)
House Longworth Bldg. #1424
Washington, DC 20515
"Politician"

Donald "Deke" Slayton
7015 Gulf Freeway #140
Houston, TX 77087
"Astronaut"

Percy Sledge
9850 Sandalfoot Blvd. #458
Boca Raton, FL 33438
"Singer"

Grace Slick
18 Escalon Drive
Mill Valley, CA 94941
"Singer, Songwriter"

Curtis Sliwa
982 East 89th Street
Brooklyn, NY 11236
"Guardian Angles Founder"

James Sloyan
4442 Vista del Monte #1
Sherman Oaks, CA 914903
"Actor"

Jean Smart
4545 Nocline Avenue
Encino, CA 91316
"Actress"

Eleanor Smeal
3324 Lakeside View Drive
Falls Church, VA 22041
"Feminist Leader"

Yakov Smirnoff
1123 Napoli
Pacific Palisades, CA 90272
"Comedian, Actor"

Alexis Smith
25 Central Park West
New York, NY 10023
"Actress"

Allison Smith
8899 Beverly Blvd.
Los Angeles, CA 90048
"Actress"

Bruce Smith
4385 Twilight Lane
Hamburg, NY 14075
"Football Player"

Bubba Smith
5178 Sunlight Place
Los Angeles, CA 90016
"Actor, Football Player"

Buffalo Bob Smith
Big Lake
Princeton, ME 04619
"Actor"

Charlie Martin Smith
4328 Chaumont Road
Woodland Hills, CA 91364
"Actor"

Rep. Christopher Smith (NJ)
House Rayburn Bldg. #2440
Washington, DC 20515
"Politician"

Connie Smith
P.O. Box 335
Nashville, TN 37027
"Singer"

Cotter Smith
14755 Ventura Blvd. #I-904
Sherman Oaks, CA 91403
"Actor"

Ilan Smith
104-60 Queens Blvd. #10-C
Fox Hills, NY 11375
"Actor"

Jaclyn Smith
733 Stradella Road
Los Angeles, CA 90024
"Actress, Model"

Kathy Smith
117 South Laxton Drive
Los Angeles, CA 90049
"Actress"

Rep. Lamar Smith (TX)
House Cannon Bldg. #422
Washington, DC 20515
"Politician"

Lane Smith
9320 Wilshire Blvd. #300
Beverly Hills, CA 90212
"Actor"

Rep. Lawrence J. Smith (FL)
House Cannon Bldg. #113
Washington, DC 20515
"Politician"

Lewis Smith
250 North Robertson Blvd. #518
Beverly Hills, CA 90211
"Actor"

Liz Smith
160 East 38th Street
New York, NY 10016
"Film Critic, Columnist"

Madolyn Smith
6131 1/2 Glen Oak
Los Angeles, CA 90069
"Actress"

Maggie Smith
388-396 Street
London W1 ENGLAND
"Actress"

Margaret Chase Smith
Norridgewock Avenue
Skowhegan, ME 04976
"Former Senator"

Martha Smith
9690 Heather Road
Beverly Hills, CA 90210
"Actress, Model"

Rep. Neal Smith (IA)
House Rayburn Bldg. 2373
Washington, DC 20515
"Politician"

O.C. Smith
14621 Leadwell Street
Van Nuys, CA 91405
"Singer"

Rex Smith
16986 Encino Hills Drive
Encino, CA 91436
"Actor, Singer"

Rep. Robert F. Smith (OR)
House Cannon Bldg. #118
Washington, DC 20515
"Politician"

Roger Smith
2707 Benedict Canyon
Beverly Hills, CA 90210
"Actor, Writer"

Shawnee Smith
5200 Lankershim Blvd. #260
North Hollywood, CA 91601
"Actress"

Shelley Smith
9145 Sunset Blvd. #228
Los Angeles, CA 90069
"Actress"

Stan Smith
888-17th Street N.W. #1200
Washington, DC 20006
"Tennis Player"

Toukie Smith
1608 North Las Palmas Avenue
Los Angeles, CA 90028
"Model, Actress"

Wendy Smith
2925 Tuna Canyon Road
Topanga, CA 90290
"Actress"

William Smith
2552 Laurel Canyon
Los Angeles, CA 90046
"Actor"

William Kennedy Smith
1095 North Ocean Blvd.
Palm Beach, FL 33480
"Sen. Ted Kennedy's Nephew"

Jan Smithers
2401 Colorado Avenue #160
Santa Monica, CA 90404
"Actress"

Bill Smitrovich
5052 Rubio Avenue
Encino, CA 91436
"Actor"

Jimmy Smits
110 South Westgate Avenue
Los Angeles, CA 90049
"Actor"

Dick Smothers
8489 West Third Street
Los Angeles, CA 90048
"Comedian, Actor"

Tom Smothers
1976 Warm Springs Road
Kenwood, CA 95452
"Comedian, Actor"

Reggie Smythe
Whiteglass Caladonian Road
Hartlepool Cleveland, ENGLAND
"Cartoonist"

J.C. Snead
P.O. Box 1152
Ponte Verde Beach, FL 32082
"Golfer"

Sam Snead
P.O. Box 777
Hot Springs, VA 24445
"Golfer"

Mike Snider
P.O. Box 140710
Nashville, TN 37214
"Bluegrass"

Wesley Snipes
5335 North Maple Drive #250
Beverly Hills, CA 90210
"Actor"

Carrie Snodgress
3025 Surry Street
Los Angeles, CA 90027
"Actress"

Hank Snow
P.O. Box 1084
Nashville, TN 37202
"Singer, Songwriter"

Phoebe Snow
550 Park Avenue
New York, NY 10022
"Singer"

Rep. Olympia Snowe (ME)
House Rayburn Bldg. #2464
Washington, DC 20515
"Politician"

Jimmy "The Greek" Snyder
870-7th Avenue #2049
New York, NY 10019
"Odds Maker"

Tom Snyder
2801 Hutton Drive
Beverly Hills, CA 90210
"TV Host

Barry Sobel
9000 Sunset Blvd. #1200
Los Angeles, CA 90069
"Comedian"

Steve Sohmer
2625 Larmar Road
Los Angeles, CA 90068
"TV Director"

P.J. Soles
P.O. Box 2351
Carefree, AZ 85377
"Actress"

Rep. Stephen Solarz (NY)
House Longworth Bldg. #1536
Washington, DC 20515
"Politician"

Rep. Gerald Solomon (NY)
House Rayburn Bldg. #2265
Washington, DC 20515
"Politician"

Harold Solomon
1500 South Ocean Blvd.
Pompano Beach, FL 33062
"Tennis Player"

Sir George Solti
Chalet Haut Pre
1884 Villars-sur-Ollon
SWITZERLAND
"Conductor"

Suzanne Somers
190 North Canon Drive #201
Beverly Hills, CA 90210
"Actress, Singer"

Julie Sommars
7272 Outpost Cove Drive
Los Angeles, CA 90068
"Actress"

Elke Sommer
540 North Beverly Glen
Los Angeles, CA 90024
"Actress"

Stephen Sondheim
246 East 49th Street
New York, NY 10017
"Composer, Lyricist"

Louise Sorel
10808 Lindbrook Drive
Los Angeles, CA 90024
"Actress"

Ted Sorenson
1285 Avenue of the Americas
New York, NY 10019
"Former Government Official"

Arleen Sorkin
100 South Doheny Drive #605
Los Angeles, CA 90048
"Writer, Producer"

Paul Sorvino
84 Prospect Terrace
Tenafly, NJ 07670
"Actor"

Ann Sothern
P.O. Box 2285
Ketchum, ID 83340
"Actress"

Talisa Soto
1608 North Las Palmas
Los Angeles, CA 90028
"Actress, Model"

David Soul
2232 Moreno Drive
Los Angeles, CA 90039
"Actor, Singer, Director"

Olan Soule
4010 Calle Sonora Oeste
Laguna Hills, CA 92653
"Actor"

Soul II Soul
162 Camden High Street
London ENGLAND
"R&B Group"

David Souter
1-1st Street N.E.
Washington, DC 20543
"Supreme Court Justice"

J.D. Souther
8263 Hollywood Blvd
Los Angeles, CA 90069
"Singer, Songwriter"

Southern Belles
11150 West Olympic Blvd.
Suite #1100
Los Angeles, CA 90064
"Wrestling Tag Team"

Terry Southern
RFD
East Canaan, CT 06020
"TV Writer"

Catherine Spaak
Viale Parioli 59
00197 Rome, ITALY
"Actress"

Sissy Spacek
9830 Wilshire Blvd.
Beverly Hills, CA 90212
"Actress"

James Spader
8899 Beverly Blvd.
Los Angeles, CA 90048
"Actor"

Warren Spahn
RD #2
Hartshorne, OK 74547
"Baseball Player"

Laurette Spang
4154 Colbath Avenue
Sherman Oaks, CA 91413
"Actress"

Joe Spano
9056 Santo Monica Blvd. #307
Los Angeles, CA 90069
"Actor"

Vincent Spano
8899 Beverly Blvd. #601
Los Angeles, CA 90048
"Actor"

Camilla Spary
1520 Circle Drive
Santa Marino, CA 91108
"Actress"

Billy Joe Spears
P.O. Box 23470
Nashville, TN 37202
"Singer"

Sen. Arlen Specter (PA)
Senate Hart Bldg. #303
Washington, DC 20510
"Politician"

Phil Spector
1210 South Arroyo Blvd.
Pasadena, CA 91101
"Record Producer"

Ronnie Spector
7 Maplecrest Drive
Danbury, CT 06810
"Singer"

Aaron Spelling
594 North Mapleton Drive
Los Angeles, CA 90077
"TV Producer"

Rep. Floyd Spence (SC)
House Rayburn Bldg. #2405
Washington, DC 20515
"Politician"

Bud Spencer
Via Cortina d'Ampezzo 156
00191 Rome, ITALY
"Actor"

Victor Spencer-Churchill
6 Cumberland Mansions
George Street
London W1 ENGLAND
"Viscount"

Wendy Jo Sperber
4110 Witzel Drive
Sherman Oaks, CA 91423
"Actress"

Penelope Spheeris
8301 Kirkwood Drive
Los Angeles, CA 90068
"Director, Producer"

David Spielberg
3531 Bentley Avenue
Los Angeles, CA 90034
"Actor"

Steven Spielberg
P.O. Box 6190
Malibu, CA 90264
"Director, Producer"

Mickey Spillane
c/o General Delivery
Marrells Inlet, SC 22117
"Writer"

Sandy Spillman
1353 Alvarado Terrace
Los Angeles, CA 90017
"Actor"

Klinton Spilsbury
329 North Wetherly Drive #205
Beverly Hills, CA 90211
"Actor"

Leon Spinks
223 West Ontario
Chicago, IL 60610
"Boxer"

Michael Spinks
20284 Archdale
Detroit, MI 48235
"Boxer"

Spinners
65 West 55th Street #6C
New York, NY 10019
"Vocal Group"

Mark Spitz
383 Dalenhurst
Los Angeles, CA 90024
"Swimmer"

Split Ends
136 New Kings Road
London SW6 ENGLAND
"Rock & Roll Group"

Dr. Benjamin Spock
P.O. Box 1890
St. Thomas 00803 V.I.
"Physician"

Michael Spound
4303 Farmdale Avenue
Studio City, CA 91604
"Actor"

J.D. Spradlin
P.O. Box 5617
Beverly Hills, CA 90210
"Actor, Director"

Rep. John Spratt, Jr. (SC)
House Longworth Bldg. #1533
Washington, DC 20515
"Politician"

Dusty Springfield
130 West 57th Street #8-B
New York, NY 10019
"Singer"

Rick Springfield
9200 Sunset Blvd. PH.-15
Los Angeles, CA 90069
"Singer, Guitarist"

Bruce Springsteen
9922 Tower Lane
Beverly Hills, CA 90210
"Singer, Guitarist"

Spyro Gyro
P.O. Box 7308
Carmel, CA 93921
"Jazz Group"

Billy Squier
145 Central Park West
New York, NY 10023
"Singer, Guitarist"

Robert Stack
321 St. Pierre Road
Los Angeles, CA 90077
"Actor"

James Stacy
478 Severn Avenue
Tampa, FL 33606
"Actor"

Jim Stafford
P.O. Box 6366
Branson, MO 65616
"Singer"

Jo Stafford Weston
2339 Century Hill
Los Angeles, CA 90067
"Singer"

Nancy Stafford
13080 Mindanao Way #69
Marina del Rey, CA 90292
"Actress"

Thomas Strafford
P.O. Box 75410
Oklahoma City, OK 73147
"Astronaut, Businessman"

Rep. Harley Staggers (WV)
House Longworth Bldg. #1323
Washington, DC 20515
"Politician"

Lesley Stahl
51 West 52nd Street
New York, NY 10019
"Journalist"

Joan Staley
24516-B Windsor Drive
Valencia, CA 91355
"Actress"

Lynn Stallmaster
9911 West Pico Blvd. #1580
Los Angeles, CA 90035
"Casting Director"

Frank Stallone
10668 Eastborne #206
Los Angeles, CA 90025
"Actor"

Sasha Stallone
9 Bevery Park
Beverly Hills, CA 90210
"Wife of Sylvester Stallone"

Sylvester Stallone
9750 Wanda Park Drive
Beverly Hills, CA 90210
"Actor"

Susan Stamberg
c/o National Public Radio
2025 "M" Street NW
Washington, DC 20036
"News Correspondent"

John Stamos
22139 Mulholland Drive
Woodland Hills, CA 91364
"Actor"

Terrence Stamp
The Albany, Piccadilly
London W1 ENGLAND
"Actor"

Joe Stampley
2137 Zercher Road
San Antonio, TX 78209
"Singer"

Lionel Stander
13176 Boca De Canon Lane
Los Angeles, CA 90049
"Actor"

John Standing
28 Broomhouse Road
London SW6 ENGLAND
"Actor"

Dennis Stanfill
908 Oak Grove Avenue
San Marino, CA 91108
"Businessman"

Arnold Stang
P.O. Box 786
New Canaan, CT 06840
"Actor"

Eddie Stanky
2100 Spring Hill Road
Mobile, AL 36607
"Baseball Manager"

Kim Stanley
1914 Hillcrest Road
Los Angeles, CA 90068
"Actress"

Maurice Stans
211 South Orange Grove
Pasadena, CA 91105
"Government Official"

Lisa Stansfield
43 Hillcrest Road
Rockdale ENGLAND
"Singer"

Harry Dean Stanton
14527 Mulholland Drive
Los Angeles, CA 90077
"Actor"

Jean Stapleton
635 Perugia Way
Los Angeles, CA 90024
"Actress"

Maureen Stapleton
1 Bolton Drive
Lenox, MA 01240
"Actress"

Willie Stargell
113 Ashley Place
Stone Montain, GA 30083
"Baseball Player"

Rep. Fortney Stark (CA)
House Cannon Bldg. #239
Washington, DC 20515
"Politician"

Koo Stark
52 Shaftesbury Avenue
London W1 ENGLAND
"Actress"

Ray Stark
232 South Mapleton Drive
Los Angeles, CA 90077
"TV Producer"

Bart Starr
5250 East Onyn
Paradise Valley, AZ 85253
"Football Player"

Kay Starr
223 Ashdale Avenue
Los Angeles, CA 90024
"Singer"

Ringo Starr
"Rocca Bella"
24 Avenue Princess Grace
Monte Carlo, MONACO
"Drummer, Actor"

Starship (Jefferson Airplane)
2400 Fulton Street
San Francisco, CA 94118
"Rock & Roll Group"

Harold E. Stassen
431 East Haskell
West St. Paul, MN 55118
Ex-Governor"

Arianna Stassinopoulos
2806 "Q" Street
Washington, DC 20007
"Author"

Statler Brothers
P.O. Box 2703
Staunton, VA 24401
"Vocal Group"

Roger Staubach
6750 LBJ Freeway
Dallas, TX 75109
"Football Player"

Rep. Cliff Stearns (FL)
House Longworth Bldg. #1123
Washington, DC 20515
"Politician"

Eleanor Steber
P.O. Box 342
Port Jefferson, NY 11777
"Soprano"

Amy Steel
2431 North Gower
Los Angeles, CA 90068
"Actress"

Barbara Steele
442 South Bedford Drive
Beverly Hills, CA 90212
"Actress"

Danielle Steele
P.O. Box 1637
Murray Hill Station
New York, NY 10156
"Novelist"

Tommy Steele
37 Hill Street
London W1X 8JY ENGLAND
"Actor, Singer"

Rod Steiger
6324 Zumirez Drive
Malibu, CA 90265
"Actor"

Ben Stein
7251 Pacific View Drive
Los Angeles, CA 90068
"Writer"

David Steinberg
16121 High Valley Place
Encino, CA 91436
"Comedian, Actor, Writer"

George Steinbrenner
River Avenue & East 16th Street
New York, NY 100451
"Baseball Executive"

Gloria Steinem
118 East 73rd Street
New York, NY 10021
"Author, Feminist"

Jake Steinfeld
2112 Roscomare Road
Los Angeles, CA 90077
"Actor, Bodybuilder"

Rep. Charles Stenholm (TX)
House Longworth Bldg. #1226
Washington, DC 20515
"Politician"

Ingemar Stenmark
Tarnaby, SWEDEN
"Skier"

Princess Stephanie
4725 Forman Avenue
North Hollywood, CA 91602
"Royalty"

James Stephens
822 South Robertson Blvd. #200
Los Angeles, CA 90035
"Actor, Director"

Laraine Stephens
1900 Avenue of the Stars
Suite #2270
Los Angeles, CA 90067
"Actress"

Gov. Stan Stephens (MT)
State Capitol
Helena, MT 59620
"Governor"

Jan Stephenson
6300 Ridglea #1118
Ft. Worth, TX 76116
"Golfer"

Jan Sterling
3206 Raintree Circle #206
Culver City, CA 90230
"Actress"

Philip Sterling
4114 Benedict Canyon
Sherman Oaks, CA 91423
"Actor"

Robert Sterling
121 South Bentley Avenue
Los Angeles, CA 90049
"Actor"

Tisha Sterling
P.O. Box 903
Topanga, CA 90290
"Actress"

Isaac Stern
211 Central Park West
New York, NY 10024
"Violinist"

Frances Sternahgen
152 Sutton Manor Road
New Rochelle, NY 10805
"Actress"

Andrew Stevens
9612 Arby Drive
Beverly Hills, CA 90210
"Actor"

April Stevens
19530 Superior Street
Northridge, CA 91324
"Singer"

Cat Stevens
(aka Yusef Islam)
Ariola, Steinhauser Str. 3
8000 Munich 80 GERMANY
"Singer, Songwriter"

Connie Stevens
9551 Cherokee Lane
Beverly Hills, CA 90210
"Actress, Singer"

Craig Stevens
25 Central Park West
New York, NY 10023
"Actor"

K.T. Stevens
7080 Hollywood Blvd. #201
Los Angeles, CA 90028
"Actress"

Morgan Stevens
14348 Roblar Place
Sherman Oaks, CA 91423
"Actor"

Ray Stevens
1708 Grand Avenue
Nashville, TN 37212
"Singer, Songwriter"

Rise Stevens
930 Fifth Avenue
New York, NY 10021
"Mezzo-Soprano"

Shadow Stevens
10430 Wilshire Blvd. #2006
Los Angeles, CA 90024
"Radio-TV personality"

Stella Stevens
2180 Coldwater Canyon
Beverly Hills, CA 90210
"Actress"

Sen. Ted Stevens (AK)
Senate Hart Bldg. #522
Washington, DC 20510
"Politician"

Warren Stevens
14155 Magnolia Blvd. #44
Sherman Oaks, CA 91403
"Actor"

Adlai Stevenson III
231 South La Salle Street
Chicago, IL 60604
"Ex-Governor"

McLean Stevenson
P.O. Box 1668
Studio City, CA 91604
"Actor, Writer"

Parker Stevenson
4875 Louise Avenue
Encino, CA 91316
"Actor"

Teofilo Stevenson
Comite Olimppico
Hotel Havana
Havana CUBA
"Boxer"

Alana Stewart
6384 Rodgerton Drive
Los Angeles, CA 90068
"Actress"

Catherine Mary Stewart
500 Beloit Avenue
Los Angeles, CA 90049
"Actress"

Dave Stewart
Oakland-Alameda Coliseum
Oakland, CA 94621
"Baseball Player"

Jackie Stewart
24 Rte. de Divonne
1260 Nyon, SWITZERLAND
"Auto Racer"

James Stewart
P.O. Box 90
Beverly Hills, CA 90213
"Actor, Director"

Jermaine Stewart
4A Lauceston Place
Kensington
London W8 5RL ENGLAND
"Singer"

John Stewart
7247 Birdview Avenue
Malibu, CA 90265
"Singer, Songwriter"

Patrick Stewart
8899 Beverly Blvd.
Los Angeles, CA 90048
"Actor"

Peggy Stewart
11139 Hortense Street
North Hollywood, CA 91602
"Actress"

Rod Stewart
3 East 54th Street
New York, NY 10022
"Singer, Songwriter"

Dorothy Stickney
13 East 94th Street
New York, NY 10023
"Actress"

David Ogden Stiers
121 North Vicente Blvd.
Beverly Hills, CA 90211
"Actor, Director"

Robert Stigwood
1775 Broadway
New York, NY 10023
"Film Producer"

Stephen Stills
12077 Wilshire Blvd.
Los Angeles, CA 90025
"Singer, Songwriter"

Sting
2 The Grove
Highgate Village
London N16 ENGLAND
"Singer, Actor, Composer"

Linda Stirling
4717 Laura Canyon Blvd. #206
North Hollywood, CA 91607
"Actress"

Barbara Stock
13421 Cheltenham Drive
Sherman Oaks, CA 91423
"Actress"

Karl-Heinz Stockhausen
Stockhausen-Verlag
5067 Kuerten, GERMANY
"Composer"

Dick Stockton
715 Stadium
San Antonio, TX 78212
"Tennis Player"

Dean Stockwell
P.O. Box 6248
Malibu, CA 90264
"Actor"

Guy Stockwell
4924 Cahuenga Blvd.
North Hollywood, CA 91601
"Actor"

Brandon Stoddard
240 North Glenroy Avenue
Los Angeles, CA 90049
"Film-TV Executive

Rep. Louis Stokes (OH)
House Rayburn Bldg. #2365
Washington, DC 20515
"Politician"

Eric Stoltz
2320 Vista Madera
Santa Barbara, CA 93103
"Actor"

Christopher Stone
23035 Cumorah Crest Drive
Woodland Hills, CA 91364
"Actor, Writer"

Ezra Stone
Stone Meadows Farn
P.O. Box D
Newtown, PA 18940
"Actor"

Oliver Stone
321 Hampton Drive #105
Venice, CA 90291
"Film Writer, Director"

Rob Stone
3725 Laurel Canyon Blvd.
Studio City, CA 91604
"Actor"

Sharon Stone
7809 Torreyson Drive
Los Angeles, CA 90046
"Actress, Model"

Sly Stone
6255 Sunset Blvd. #200
Los Angeles, CA 90028
"Singer, Songwriter"

Tom Stoppard
Iver Grove, Iver
Bucks. ENGLAND
"Dramatist"

Larry Storch
336 West End Avenue #17-F
New York, NY 10023
"Actor"

Gale Storm
308 North Sycamore Avenue #104
Los Angeles, CA 90036
"Actress, Singer"

John Stossel
211 Central Park West #15K
New York, NY 10024
"Broadcast Journalist"

Beatrice Straight
30 Norford Road
Soughfield, MA 01259
"Actress"

George Strait
1000-18th Avenue South
Nashville, TN 37212
"Singer, Songwriter"

Hank Stram
194 Belle Terre Blvd.
Covington, LA 70483
"Football Coach"

Robin Strand
4118 Elmer
North Hollywood, CA 91607
"Actor"

Susan Strasberg
135 Central Park West
New York, NY 10023
"Actress"

Robin Strasser
9301 Wilshire Blvd. #312
Beverly Hills, CA 90210
"Actress"

Marcia Strassman
8756 Holloway Drive
Los Angeles, CA 90069
"Actress"

Gil Stratton
4227-B Colfax Avenue #D
Studio City, CA 91604
"Sportscaster"

Peter Straub
P.O. Box 395
Greens Farms, CT 06436
"Novelist"

Peter Strauss
1900 Avenue of the Stars #1425
Los Angeles, CA 90067
"Actor"

Robert Strauss
1333 New Hampshire Ave. NW
Washington, DC 20005
"Politician"

Darryl Strawberry
4740 Zelzah Avenue
Encino, CA 91316
"Baseball Player"

Stray Cats
113 Wardour Street
London W1 ENGLAND
"Rock & Roll Group"

Meryl Streep
9830 Wilshire Blvd.
Beverly Hills, CA 90212
"Actress"

Rebecca Street
291 Amalfi Drive
Santa Monica, CA 90402
"Actress"

Barbara Streisand
301 North Carolwood
Los Angeles, CA 90077
"Singer, Actress, Director"

Amzie Strickland
1329 North Ogden Drive
Los Angeles, CA 90046
"Actress"

Gail Strickland
7280 Caverna Drive
Los Angeles, CA 90068
"Actress"

Ray Stricklyn
852 North Genesee Avenue
Los Angeles, CA 90046
"Actor"

Elaine Stritch
888-7th Avenue #1800
New York, NY 10019
"Actress"

Woody Strode
P.O. Box 501
Glendora, CA 91740
"Actor"

Don Stroud
11342 Dona Lisa
Studio City, CA 91604
"Actor"

Sally Struthers
9229 Sunset Blvd. #520
Los Angeles, CA 90059
"Actress"

Gloria Stuart Sheekman
884 South Bundy Drive
Los Angeles, CA 90049
"Actress"

Marty Stuart
38 Music Square East #218
Nashville, TN 37203
"Singer, Songwriter"

Maxine Stuart
9744 Wilshire Blvd. #308
Beverly Hills, CA 90212
"Actress"

Roy Stuart
4948 Radford Avenue
North Hollywood, CA 91602
"Actor"

Big John Studd
P.O. Box 3859
Stamford, CT 06905
"Wrestler, Actor"

Rep. Garry Studds (MA)
House Cannon Bldg. #237
Washington, DC 20515
"Politician"

Rep. Bob Stump (AZ)
House Cannon Bldg. #211
Washington, DC 20515
"Politician"

Jule Styne
237 West 51st Street
New York, NY 10019
"Songwriter"

William Styron
RFD
Roxbury, CT 06783
"Author"

Allan Sues
1492-2nd Avenue
New York, NY 10021
"Actor"

Rep. Don Sundquist (TN)
House Cannon Bldg. #230
Washington, DC 20515
"Politician"

Burt Sugarman
150 South El Camino Drive #303
Beverly Hills, CA 90212
"Rock & Roll Producer"

Barry Sullivan
14687 Round Valley Drive
Sherman Oaks, CA 91403
"Actor"

Danny Sullivan
201 South Rockingham Avenue
Los Angeles, CA 90049
"Auto Racer"

Dr Louis Sullivan
200 Independence AvenueS.W.
Washington, DC 20201
"Health & Human Services"

Gov. Mike Sullivan (WY)
State Capitol
Cheyenne, WY 82002
"Governor"

Susan Sullivan
8642 Allenwood Road
Los Angeles, CA 90046
"Actress"

Tom Sullivan
1504 Viacastilla
Palos Verdes, CA 90274
"Singer, Songwriter"

Sultan of Brunei
Hassanal Bolkiah Nuda
Bandar Seri Begawan
BRUNEI
"Royalty"

Arthur Ochs Sulzberber
229 West 43rd Street
New York, NY 10036
"Newspaper Publisher"

Yma Sumac
1524 La Baig Avenue
Los Angeles, CA 90028
"Singer"

Cree Summer
131 South Orange Drive
Los Angeles, CA 90036
"Actress"

Donna Summer
714 West Potrero Road
Thousand Oaks, CA 91361
"Singer"

Pat Summerall
12536 Marshcreed Drive
Ponte Vedra, FL 32082
"Sportscaster"

Andy Summers
Bugle House
21A Noel Street
London W1V 3PD ENGLAND
"Singer, Songwriter"

Rosalyn Sumners
9912-225th Place S.W.
Edmonds, WA 98020
"Skater"

John Sununu
24 Samoset Drive
Salem, NH 03079
"Former Governor"

Al B Sure
636 Warren Street
Brooklyn, NY 11217
"Singer"

Survivor
2114 West Pico Blvd.
Santa Monica, CA 90405
"Rock & Roll Group"

Todd Susman
10340 Keokuk
Chatsworth, CA 91311
"Actor"

Rick Sutcliff
313 N.W. North Shore Drive
Parkville, MO 64151
"Baseball Player"

Donald Sutherland
760 North La Cienega Blvd. #300
Los Angeles, CA 90069
"Actor"

Joan Sutherland
111 West 57th Street
New York, NY 10019
"Soprano"

Kiefer Sutherland
1033 Gayley Avenue #208
Los Angeles, CA 90024
"Actor"

James Sutorius
121 North San Vicente Blvd.
Beverly Hills, CA 90210
"Actor"

Don Sutton
23506 Long Meadow
Mission Viejo, CA 92692
"Baseball Player"

Grady Sutton
1207 North Orange Drive
Los Angeles, CA 90038
"Actor"

Janet Suzman
11 Keats Grove
Faircroft, Hampsted
London NW3 ENGLAND
"Actress"

Bo Svenson
801 Greentree Road
Pacific Palisades, CA 90272
"Actor"

Jimmy Swaggart
P.O. Box 2550
Baton Rouge, LA 70821
"Evangelist"

Caskey Swaim
1605 North Cahuenga Blvd. #202
Los Angeles, CA 90028
"Actor"

Lynn Swann
5750 Wilshire Blvd. #475
Los Angeles, CA 90036
"Football Player"

John Cameron Swayze
491 Riversville Road
Greenwich, CT 06830
"News Commentator"

Patrick Swayze
10100 Santa Monica Blvd. #1600
Los Angeles, CA 90067
"Actor"

Inga Swenson
3475 Cabrillo
Los Angeles, CA 90066
"Actress"

Jo Swerling, Jr.
25745 Vista Verde Drive
Calabasas, CA 91302
"Writer, Producer"

Rep. Al Swift (WA)
House Longworth Bldg. #1502
Washington, DC 20515
"Politician"

Nora Swinburne
52 Crammer Court
Whitehead's Grove
London SW3 3HW ENGLAND
"Actress"

Loretta Swit
24216 Malibu Road
Malibu, CA 90265
"Actress"

Ken Swofford
20230 Wells Drive
Woodland Hills, CA 91364
"Actor"

Tom Sykes
P.O. Box 29543
Atlanta, GA 30359
"Singer"

The Sylvers
1900 Avenue of the Stars #1600
Los Angeles, CA 90067
"Vocal Group"

Rep. Mike Synar (OK)
House Rayburn Bldg. #2441
Washington, DC 20515
"Politician"

Jeannot Szwarz
2964 Okean Place
Los Angeles, CA 90046
"Film Director"

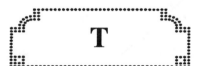

Mr. T
395 Green Bay Road
Lake Forest, IL 60045
"Actor"

Kristoffer Tabori
172 East 95th Street
New York, NY 10028
"Actor"

Taco
8124 West 3rd Street #204
Los Angeles, CA 90048
"Singer, Songwriter"

Robert A. Taft, Jr.
4300 Drake Road
Cincinnati, OH 45246
"Former Senator"

Miiko Taka
14560 Round Valley Drive
Sherman Oaks, CA 91403
"Actress"

Take Six
4404 Sumatra Drive
Nashville, TN 37218
"Vocal Group"

George Takei
3800 Barham Blvd. #303
Los Angeles, CA 90068
"Actor"

Lyle Talbot
149 Fairmount Street
San Franciso, CA 94131
"Actor"

Nita Talbot
3420 Merrimac Road
Los Angeles, CA 90049
"Actress"

Gay Talese
154 East Atlantic Blvd.
Ocean City, NJ 08226
"Writer"

Talking Heads
1775 Broadway #700
New York, NY 10019
"Rock & Roll Group"

Maria Tallchief
2739 Elston Avenue
Chicago, IL 60747
"Ballerina"

Rep. Robin Tallon (SC)
House Cannon Bldg. #432
Washington, DC 20515
"Politician"

Russ Tamblyn
2310-6th Street #2
Santa Monica, CA 90405
"Actor"

Jeffrey Tambor
5526 Calhoun Avenue
Van Nuys, CA 91401
"Actor"

Jessica Tandy
63-23 Carlton Street
Rego Park, NY 11374
"Actress"

Tangerine Dream
Box 303340
1000 Berlin 30 GERMANY
"Rock & Roll Group"

Yoko Tani
29 rue des Vignes
75018 Paris, FRANCE
"Actress"

Alain Tanner
Chemin Pt. du-jour 12
1202 Geneva, SWITZERLAND
"Film Director"

Rep. John Tanner (TN)
House Longworth Bldg. #1232
Washington, DC 20515
"Politician"

Roscoe Tanner
1109 Gnome Trail
Lookout Mountain, TN 37350
"Tennis Player"

Gordie Tapp
2401-12th Avenue South
Nashville, TN 37204
"Singer & Songwriter"

Fran Tarkington
3345 Peachtree Road N.E.
Atlanta, GA 30326
"Football Player"

Brandon Tartikoff
1479 Lindacrest Drive
Beverly Hills, CA 90210
"TV Executive"

Bernie Taupin
1422 Devlin
Los Angeles, CA 90069
"Lyricist"

Rep. W.J. "Billy" Tauzin (LA)
House Rayburn Bldg. #2342
Washington, DC 20515
"Politician"

Buck Taylor
Rt. 2, Box 150
Ennis, MT 59729
"Actor"

Clarice Taylor
35 Hamilton Terrace
New York, NY 10031
"Actress"

Delores Taylor
20933 Big Rock Drive
Malibu, CA 90265
"Actress"

Don Taylor
1111 San Vicente Blvd.
Santa Monica, CA 90402
"Film Director"

Dub Taylor
21417 Gaona Street
Woodland Hills, CA 91364
"Actor"

Elizabeth Taylor
700 Nimes Road
Los Angeles, CA 90077
"Actress"

James Taylor
644 North Doheny Drive
Los Angeles, CA 90069
"Singer"

Josh Taylor
422 South California
Burbank, CA 91505
"Actor"

Judd Taylor
1438 Rising Glen Road
Los Angeles, CA 90069
"Film Director"

Leigh Taylor-Young
1279 Beverly Estate Drive
Beverly Hills, CA 90210
"Actress"

Meldrick Taylor
2917 North 4th Street
Philadelphia, PA 19132
"Boxer"

Meshach Taylor
969 Mt. Curve Avenue
Altadena, CA 91001
"Actor"

Renee Taylor
613 North Arden Drive
Beverly Hills, CA 90210
"Actress, Writer"

Rip Taylor
1950 Sawtelle Blvd. #90025
Los Angeles, CA 90025
"Actor"

Rod Taylor
2375 Bowmont Drive
Beverly Hills, CA 90210
"Actor"

Roger Taylor
Salterwwell Farm
Moreton-In -The-Marsh
Gloucestershire ENGLAND
"Drummer"

Ludmilla Tcherina
42 cours Albert ler
75008 Paris, FRANCE
"Ballerina"

Tears For Fears
50 New Bond Street
London 1W ENGLAND
"Rock & Roll Group"

Renata Tebaldi
1 Piazza Guastalla
20100 Milan 1 ITALY
"Opera Singer"

Irene Tedrow
5763 Corteen Place
North Hollywood, CA 91602
"Actress"

Dr. Edward U. Teller
Radiation Laboratory
P.O. Box 80
Livermore, CA 94550
"Physicist, Author"

Shirley Temple-Black
115 Lakeview Drive
Woodside, CA 94062
"Actress, Ex-Ambassador"

Christopher Templeton
5309 Lemp Avenue
North Hollywood, CA 91601
"Actress"

Victoria Tennant
P.O. Box 929
Beverly Hills, CA 90213
"Actress"

Toni Tennille
P.O. Box 262
Glenbroook, NV 89143
"Singer"

Judy Tenuta
1790 Broadway #1201
New York, NY 10019
"Comedienne"

Mother Teresa
Mission of Charity
54a Lower Circular Road
7000016 Calcutta INDIA
"Missionary"

Studs Terkel
850 West Castlewood
Chicago, IL 60640
"Novelist"

Denney Terrio
1541 North Vine Street
Los Angeles, CA 90028
"Dance, TV Host"

Bill Terry
P.O. Box 2177
Jacksonville, FL 32203
"Baseball Player"

Phillip Terry
2075 Birnham Wood Drive
Santa Barbara, CA 93108
"Actor"

John Tesh
2400 Broadway #100
Santa Monica, CA 90404
"TV Host"

Vinny Testaverde
One Buccaneer Place
Tampa, FL 33607
"Football Player"

Lauren Tewes
341 North Beachwood Drive
Los Angeles, CA 90004
"Actress"

Margaret Thatcher
11 Dulwich Gate, Dulwich
London SE21 ENGLAND
"Former Prime Minister"

Phyllis Thaxer
716 Riomar Drive
Vero Beach, FL 32960
"Actress"

Brynn Thayer
9301 Wilshire Blvd. #312
Beverly Hills, CA 90210
"Actress"

Joe Theismann
150 Branch Road, S.E.
Vienna, VA 22180
"Football Player"

Brooke Theiss
11350 Ventura Blvd. #206
Studio City, CA 91604
"Actress"

Alan Thicke
10505 Sarah
Toluca Lake, CA 91602
"Actor, TV Host, Singer"

Ursula Thiess
1940 Bel Air Road
Los Angeles, CA 90024
"Actress"

Roy Thinnes
8016 Willow Glen Road
Los Angeles, CA 90046
"Actor"

Third World
10100 Santa Monica Blvd.
Suite #1600
Los Angeles, CA 90067
"Raggae Band"

Betty Thomas
3585 Woodhill Canyon
Studio City, CA 91604
"Actress"

B.J. Thomas
P.O. Box 120003
Arlington, TX 76012
"Singer, Songwriter"

Clarence Thomas
1-1st Street N.E.
Washington, DC 20543
"Supreme Court Justice"

Damien Thomas
31 Kings Road
London SW3 ENGLAND
"Actor"

Debi Thomas
22 East 71st Street
New York, NY 10021
"Ice Skater"

Heather Thomas
1433 San Vicente Blvd.
Santa Monica, CA 90402
"Actress, Model"

Helen Thomas
2501 Calvert Street N.W.
Washington, DC 20008
"News Correspondent"

Henry Thomas
9200 Sunset Blvd. #710
Los Angeles, CA 90069
"Actor"

Isaiah Thomas
c/o The Palace
Auburn Hills, MI 48057
"Basketball Player"

Jay Thomas
10351 Santa Monica Blvd. #211
Los Angeles, CA 90025
"Singer, Songwriter"

Kurt Thomas
8431 North 75th Street
Scottsdale, AZ 85258
"Actor, Athlete"

Lowell Thomas, Jr.
7022 Tanaina Drive
Anchorage, AK 99502
"Author, Lecturer"

Marlo Thomas
420 East 54th Street #22-F
New York, NY 10022
"Actress, Writer"

Melody Thomas-Scott
20620 Kingsboro Way
Woodland Hills, CA 91364
"Actress"

Michael Tilson Thomas
24 West 57th Street
New York, NY 10019
"Conductor"

Philip Michael Thomas
2501 West Burbank Blvd. #304
Burbank, CA 91505
"Actor"

Richard Thomas
4834 Bonvue
Los Angeles, CA 90027
"Actor, Director"

Rep. Robert Thomas (GA)
House Cannon Bldg. #240
Washington, DC 20515
"Politician"

Rep. William Thomas (CA)
House Rayburn Bldg. #2402
Washington, DC 20515
"Politician"

Tim Thomerson
2440 Long Jack Road
Encinitas, CA 92024
"Actor, Comedian"

Tony Thomopoulos
1280 Stone Canyon
Los Angeles, CA 90077
"Film Executive"

Daley Thompson
1 Church Row
Wandsworth Plain
London SW18 ENGLAND
"Track Athlete"

Hank Thompson
5 Rushing Creek Court
Roanoke, TX 76262
"Singer, Songwriter"

Jack Thompson
#1 Ridge Street, Unit 6
North Sydney NSW 2060
AUSTRALIA
"Actor"

John Thompson
Georgetown University Basketball
Washington, DC 20057
"Basketball Coach"

Kay Thompson
300 East 57th Street
New York, NY 10022
"Actress"

Lea Thompson
7966 Woodrow Wilson Drive
Los Angeles, CA 90046
"Actress"

Linda Thompson-Jenner
1930 Century Park West #403
Los Angeles, CA 90067
"Actress"

Sada Thompson
P.O. Box 490
Southbury, CT 06488
"Actress"

The Thompson Twins
9 Eccleston Street
London SW1 ENGLAND
"Rock & Roll Trio"

Gov. Tommy Thompson (WI)
115 East State Capitol
P.O. Box 7863
Madison, WI 53707
"Governor"

Gordon Thomson
2515 Astral Drive
Los Angeles, CA 90046
"Actor"

Malachi Thorne
13067 Greenleaf Street
Studio City, CA 91604
"Actor"

Jeremy Thorpe
2 Orme Square Bayswater
London W2 ENGLAND
"Political Leader"

Linda Thorson
308 Regent Street
London W1 ENGLAND
"Actress"

Three Degrees
19 The Willows
Maidenhead Road
Winsor, Berk. ENGLAND
"Rock & Roll Group"

Three Dog Night
151 El Camino Drive
Beverly Hills, CA 90212
"Rock & Roll Group"

Ingrid Thulin
Kevingerstrand 7b
Danderyd, SWEDEN
"Actress"

Sen. Strom Thurmond (SC)
House Russell Bldg. #217
Washington, DC 20510
"Politician"

Greta Thyssen
444 East 82nd Street
New York, NY 10228
"Actress"

Paul W. Tibbets
5574 Knollwood Drive
Columbus, OH 43227
"Former Air Force Officer"

Rachel Ticotin
14231 Margate Street
Van Nuys, CA 91404
"Actress"

Cheryl Tiegs
9219 Flicker Way
Los Angeles, CA 90069
"Model"

Lawrence Tierney
840 North Larrabee
Los Angeles, CA 90069
"Actor"

Tiffany
113378 Burbank Blvd.
North Hollywood, CA 91601
"Singer"

Pamela Tiffin
15 West 67th Street
New York, NY 10023
"Actress, Model"

Kevin Tighe
2218 East Orange Drive
Pasadena, CA 91104
"Actor"

Nadja Tiller
Via Tamporiva 26
CH6976 Castagnola
SWITZERLAND
"Actress"

Mel Tillis
46 Music Square East
Nashville, TN 37203
"Singer"

Floyd Tillman
4 Music Square East
Nashville, TN 37203
"Singer"

Jennifer Tilly
8380 Melrose Avenue #310
Los Angeles, CA 90069
"Actress"

Meg Tilly
321 South Beverly Drive #M
Beverly Hills, CA 90212
"Actress"

Charlene Tilton
4634 Azalia
Tarzana, CA 91356
"Actress"

Martha Tilton
2257 Mandeville Canyon Road
Los Angeles, CA 90049
"Singer, Actress"

Grant Tinker
531 Barnaby Road
Los Angeles, CA 90077
"TV Executive"

Tiny Tim
Hotel Olcott
27 West 72nd Street
New York, NY 10023
"Singer, Songwriter"

Sir Michael Tippett
48 Great Marlborough Street
London W1V 2BN ENGLAND
"Composer, Conductor"

Y.A. Tittle
310 South Lafayette Street
Marshall, TX 75670
"Football Player"

Kenneth Tobey
14155 Magnolia Blvd.
Sherman Oaks, CA 91403
"Actor"

Oliver Tobias
Geranienstrasse 3
8022 Grunwald
GERMANY
"Actor"

Beverly Todd
4888 Valley Ridge
Los Angeles, CA 90043
"Actress"

Hallie Todd
10100 Santa Monica Blvd.
Suite #700
Los Angeles, CA 90067
"Actress"

Richard Todd
Chinham Farm
Faringdon, Oxfordshire
ENGLAND
"Actor"

Richard Todd
598 Madison Avenue
New York, NY 10022
"Hockey Player"

Alvin Toffel
2323 Bowmont Drive
Beverly Hills, CA 90210
"Author"

215

Tokyo Rose (Iva Toguri)
851 West Belmont Avenue
Chicago, IL 60611
"Traitor"

John Toland
1 Long Ridge Road
Danbury, CT 06810
"Author"

Susan Tolsky
10815 Acama Street
North Hollywood, CA 91602
"Actress"

David Toma
P.O. Box 854
Clark, NJ 07066
"Writer"

Alberto Tomba
Rete di San Giorgio di Piano
Bologna-San Lazzaro di Savena
ITALY
"Skier"

Concetia Tomei
9200 Sunset Blvd. #710
Los Angeles, CA 90069
"Actress"

Lily Tomlin
P.O. Box 27700
Los Angeles, CA 90027
"Comedian, Actress, Writer"

David Tomlinson
Brook Cottage
Mursley, Bucks. ENGLAND
"Actor"

Angel Tompkins
1930 Century Park West #303
Los Angeles, CA 90067
"Actress"

Bruce Toms
9200 Sunset Blvd. #710
Los Angeles, CA 90069
"Actor"

Bill Toomey
1730 East Boulder Street
Colorado Springs, CO 80909
"Track Athlete"

Chaim Topol
22 Vale Court, Maidville
London W9 ENGLAND
"Actor, Director"

Mel Torme
1734 Coldwater Canyon
Beverly Hills, CA 90210
"Singer, Actor, Writer"

Rip Torn
130 West 42nd Street #2400
New York, NY 10036
"Actor, Director"

Rep. Esteban Edward Torres (CA)
House Longworth Bldg. #1740
Washington, DC 20515
"Politician"

Liz Torres
1711 North Avenue #53
Los Angeles, CA 90042
"Singer, Actress"

Rep. Robert Torricelli (NJ)
House Cannon Bldg. #317
Washington, DC 20515
"Politician"

Nina Totenberg
c/o National Public Radio
2025 "M" Street NW
Washington, DC 20036
"News Correspondent"

Toto
P.O. Box 7308
Carmel, CA 93921
"Rock & Roll Group"

Audrey Totter
1945 Glendon Avenue #301
Los Angeles, CA 90025
"Actress"

Tamara Toumanova
305 North Elm Drive
Beverly Hills, CA 90210
"Dancer, Actress"

Constance Towers
2415 Century Hill
Los Angeles, CA 90067
"Actress"

Robert Towne
1417 San Remo Drive
Pacific Palisades, CA 90272
"Film Writer, Director"

Harry Townes
100 Tempo Circle Highway
Harvest, AL 35719
"Actor"

Rep. Edolphus Towns (NY)
House Longworth Bldg. #1726
Washington, DC 20515
"Politician"

Barbara Townsend
1930 Century Park West #303
Los Angeles, CA 90067
"Actress"

Claire Townsend
2424 Laurel Pass
Los Angeles, CA 90046
"Actress"

Colleen Townsend-Evans
508 Seward Square S.E.
Washington, DC 20003
"Actress"

Robert Townsend
3000 Durand Drive
Los Angeles, CA 90068
"Director, Actor, Comedian"

Peter Townshend
The Boathouse
Ranelagh Drive
Twickensham TW1 1QT
ENGLAND
"Singer, Composer"

Arthur Tracy
350 West 57th Street
New York, NY 10019
"Actor"

Rep. James Traficant (OH)
House Cannon Bldg. #312
Washington, DC 20515
"Politician"

Jean-Claude Tramont
938 Bel Air Road
Los Angeles, CA 90077
"Writer, Director"

The Tramps
P.O. Box 82
Great Neck, NY 10021
"R&B Group"

Fred Travalana
4515 White Oak Place
Encino, CA 91316
"Comedian, Actor, Writer"

Daniel J. Travanti
14205 Sunset Blvd.
Pacific Palisades, CA 90272
"Actor"

Bill Travis
67 Glebe Place
London SW3 5JB ENGLAND
"Actor, Writer, Director"

Merle Travis
Route 1, Box 128
Park Hill, OK 74451
"Singer, Guitarist"

Nancy Travis
9200 Sunset Blvd., PH 25
Los Angeles, CA 90069
"Actress"

Randy Travis
P.O. Box 12712
Nashville, TN 37212
"Singer, Songwriter"

Ellen Travolta
5832 Nagle Avenue
Van Nuys, CA 91401
"Actress"

Joey Travolta
4975 Chimineas Avenue
Tarzana, CA 91356
"Actor"

John Travolta
1504 Live Oak Lane
Santa Barbara, CA 93105
"Actor, Singer"

Rep. Bob Traxler (MI)
House Rayburn Bldg. #2366
Washington, DC 20515
"Politician"

Alex Trebek
7966 Mulholland Drive
Los Angeles, CA 90046
"Game Show Host"

Les Tremayne
901 South Barrington Avenue
Los Angeles, CA 90049
"Actor"

Charles Trenet
2 rue Anatole FRANCE
F-11100 Narbonne, FRANCE
"Singer, Songwriter"

Lee Trevino
14901 Quorum Drive #170
Dallas, TX 75240
"Golfer"

Claire Trevor
Hotel Pierre
2 East 61st Street
New York, NY 10022
"Actress"

Travis Tritt
1112 North Sherbourne Drive
Los Angeles, CA 90069
"Singer"

Bobby Troup
16074 Royal Oaks
Encino, CA 91436
"Actor, Comedian, Singer"

Tom Troup
8829 Ashcroft Avenue
Los Angeles, CA 90048
"Actor"

Garry Trudeau
4900 Main Street
Kansas City, MO 64112
"Cartoonist"

Pierre Elliot Trudeau
10 Pine Street
Montreal, CANADA
"Former Prime Minsiter"

Mrs. Ernest Truex
3263 Via Altamura
Fallbrook, CA 92028
"Wife of Ernest Truex"

Douglas Trumbull
13335 Maxella
Venice, CA 90291
"Writer, Producer"

Donald Trump
721 Fifth Avenue
New York, NY 10022
"Real Estate Executive"

Ivana Trump
Mira Lago
1100 Palm Beach Blvd.
Palm Beach, FL 33480
"Ex-Wife of Donald Trump"

Natalie Trundy
6140 Lindenhurst Avenue
Los Angeles, CA 90048
"Actress"

Paul Tsongas
1 Post Office Square
Boston, MA 02109
"Former Senator"

Irene Tsu
2760 Hutton Drive
Beverly Hills, CA 90210
"Actress"

Barry Tubb
121 North San Vicente Blvd.
Beverly Hills, CA 90211
"Actor"

Marshall Tucker Band
300 East Henry Street
Spartanburg, SC 69302
"Rock & Roll Group"

Michael Tucker
2183 Mandeville Canyon
Los Angeles, CA 90049
"Actor"

Tanya Tucker
2325 Crestmoor Drive
P.O. Box 15245
Nashville, TN 37215
"Singer"

Jethro Tull
12 Stratford Place
London W1N 9AF ENGLAND
"Rock & Roll Goup"

Tommy Tune
50 East 89th Street
New York, NY 10128
"Dancer, Director"

HRM King Tupou IV
Palace Officiale
Nuku'alofa TONGA
"Royalty"

Ann Turkel
9877 Beverly Grove
Beverly Hills, CA 90210
"Actress"

Studs Turkel
850 West Castewood Terrace
Chicago, IL 60640
"Novelist"

Glynn Turman
9000 Sunset Blvd. #1200
Los Angeles, CA 90069
"Actor"

Debbye Turner
1325 Boardwalk
Atlantic City, NJ 08401
"Beauty Contest Winner"

Dame Eva Turner
26 Palace Court
London W2 ENGLAND
"Opera Singer"

Grant Turner
P.O. Box 414
Brentwood, TN 37027
"Singer"

Kathleen Turner
130 West 42nd Street
New York, NY 10036
"Actress"

Lana Turner
10100 Santa Monica Blvd. #700
Los Angeles, CA 90067
"Actress"

Ted Turner
1050 Techwood Drive
Atlanta, GA 30318
"Broadcast Executive"

Tina Turner
Maarweg 149
D-(W) 5000 Cologne 41
GERMANY
"Singer"

John Turturro
P.O. Box 5617
Beverly Hills, CA 90210
"Actress"

Rita Tushingham
235 Regent Street
London W1 ENGLAND
"Actress"

Dorothy Tutin Browne
13 St. Martins Road
London SW9 ENGLAND
"Actress"

Desmond Tutu
P.O. Box 31190, Braamfontein
Johannesburg, SOUTH AFRICA
"Arch-Bishop"

Shannon Tweed
9300 Wilshire Blvd. #410
Beverly Hills, CA 90212
"Actress, Model"

Conway Twitty
#1 Music Village Blvd.
Hendersonville, TN 37075
"Singer, Songwriter"

2 Live Crew
8400 N.E. 2nd Avenue
Miami, FL 33138
"Rap Group"

Beverly Tyler
14585 Geronimo Trail
Reno, NV 89551
"Actress"

Bonnie Tyler
17-19 Soho Square
London W1 ENGLAND
"Singer, Songwriter"

Susan Tyrell
826 Amoroso Place
Venice, CA 90291
"Actress"

Cicely Tyson
315 West 70th Street
New York, NY 10023
"Actress"

Mike Tyson
968 Pinehurst Drive
Las Vegas, NV 89109
"Boxer"

Richard Tyson
11500 West Olympic Drive #400
Los Angeles, CA 90064
"Actor"

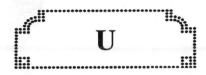

U2
Windmill Lane
Dublin 2 IRELAND
"Rock & Roll Group"

Stewart Udall
1900 "M" Street N.W.
Washington, DC 20036
"Government Official"

Peter Ueberroth
184 Emerald Bay
Laguna Beach, CA 92651
"Former Baseball Executive"

Bob Uecker
17734 Hawthorne Drive
Menomonee Falls, WI 53051
"Actor, Baseball Player"

UFO
10 Sutherland
London W9 24Q ENGLAND
"Rock & Roll Group"

Leslie Uggams
9255 Sunset Blvd. #404
Los Angeles, CA 90069
"Singer, Actress"

Dr. Art Ulene
10810 Via Verona
Los Angeles, CA 90024
"TV Doctor"

Liv Ullman
15 West 81st Street
New York, NY 10024
"Actress"

Tracey Ullman
13555 D'Este Drive
Pacific Palisades, CA 90272
"Actress, Singer"

Blair Underwood
7148 Woodrow Wilson Drive
Los Angeles, CA 90046
"Actor"

Johnny Unitas
603 West Timonium Road
Lutherville, MD 21093
"Football Player"

Al Unser
7625 Central N.W.
Albuquerque, NM 87105
"Auto Racer"

Al Unser, Jr.
73243 Calle de Deborah N.W.
Albuquerque, NM 87104
"Auto Racer"

Bobby Unser
7700 Central S.W.
Albuquerque, NM 87105
"Auto Racer"

Rep. Jolene Unsoeld (WA)
House Rayburn Bldg. #1508
Washington, DC 20515
"Politician"

John Updike
c/o General Delivery
Beverly Farm, MA 01915
"Author"

Rep. Fred Upton (MI)
House Longworth Bldg. #1713
Washington, DC 20515
"Politician"

Uriah Heep
150 Southampton Row
London WC1 ENGLAND
"Rock & Roll Group"

Robert Urich
15930 Woodvale Road
Encino, CA 91436
"Actor, Writer"

Loen Uris
P.O. Box 1559
Aspen, CO 81611
"Author"

Peter Ustinov
11 rue de Silly
92100 Boulogne, FRANCE
"Actor, Writer, Director"

Garrick Utely
12 Hanover Terrace
London NW1 ENGLAND
"News Correspondent"

Utopia
132 Nassau Street
New York, NY 10038
"Rock & Roll Group"

Brenda Vaccaro
14423 Dickens #3
Sherman Oaks, CA 91403
"Actress"

Roger Vadim
2429 Beverly Avenue
Santa Monica, CA 90406
"Film Director"

Vanessa Vadim
316 Alta Avenue
Santa Monica, CA 90402
"Daughter of Jane Fonda"

Jerry Vale
621 North Palm Drive
Beverly Hills, CA 90210
"Singer"

Nancy Valen
10000 Santa Monica Blvd.
Suite #305
Los Angeles, CA 90067
"Actress"

Jack Valenti
1600 Eye Street N.W.
Washington, D C 20006
"Director"

Karen Valentine
145 West 67th Street #42-H
New York, NY 10023
"Actress"

Scott Valentine
433 North Bowling Green Way
Los Angeles, CA 90049
"Actor"

Rep. Tim Valentine (NC)
House Longworth Bldg. #1510
Washington, DC 20515
"Politician"

Tasia Valenza
156-5th Street #1111
New York, NY 10010
"Actress"

Fernando Valenzuela
3004 North Beachwod Drive
Los Angeles, CA 90027
"Baseball Player"

Donna Valery
19 West 44th Street#1500
New York, NY 10017
"Actress"

Tannis Vallely
142 South Clark Drive #103
Los Angeles, CA 90048
"Actress"

Alida Valli
Viale Liegi 42
00100 Rome, ITALY
"Actress"

June Valli
1158 Briar Way
Fort Lee, NJ 07024
"Singer"

Raf Vallone
Viale R. Bacone
Rome, Italy
"Actor"

Richard Van Allen
18 Octavia Street
London SW11 3DN ENGLAND
"Singer"

Joan Van Ark
10950 Alta View Drive
Studio City, CA 91604
"Actress"

Abigail Van Buren
9200 Sunset Blvd. #1003
Los Angeles, CA 90069
"Columnist"

Cyrus Vance
1 Battery Park Plaza
New York, NY 10004
"Politician"

Jean-Claude Van Damme
P.O. Box 4149
Chatsworth, CA 91313
"Actor"

Gloria Vanderbilt
10 Gracie Square PH
New York, NY 10018
"Fasion Designer"

Rep. Guy Vander Jagt (MI)
House Rayburn Bldg. #2409
Washington, DC 20515
"Politician"

Trish Van Devere
3211 Retreat Court
Malibu, CA 90265
"Actress"

Titos Vandis
1930 Century Park East #303
Los Angeles, CA 90067
"Actor"

Mamie Van Doren
428-31st Street
Newport Beach, CA 92663
"Actress, Singer"

John Van Dreelen
9169 Sunset Blvd
Los Angeles, CA 90069
"Actor"

Luther Vandross
1414 Seabright Drive
Beverly Hills, CA 90210
"Singer"

Barry Van Dyke
27800 Blythdale Road
Agoura, CA 91301
"Actor"

Dick Van Dyke
23215 Mariposa De Oro
Malibu, CA 90265
"Actor"

Jerry Van Dyke
1717 North Highland Avenue #414
Los Angeles, CA 90028
"Actor"

Jo Van Fleet
54 Riverside Drive
New York, NY 10024
"Actress"

Vangelis
195 Queens Gate
London W1 ENGLAND
"Composer"

Van Halen
10100 Santa Monica Blvd.
Suite #2460
Los Angeles, CA 90067
"Rock & Roll Group"

Alex Van Halen
12024 Summit Circle
Beverly Hills, CA 90210
"Musician"

Eddie Van Halen
31736 Broad Beach Road
Malibu, CA 90265
"Guitarist, Songwriter"

Vanilla Ice
8730 Sunset Blvd. #500
Los Angeles, CA 90069
"Rap Singer"

Vanity (Denise Matthews)
151 South El Camino Drive
Beverly Hills, CA 90212
"Singer, Actress"

Nina Van Pallandt
845 East 6th Street
Los Angeles, CA 90021
"Actress"

Dick Van Patten
13920 Magnolia Blvd.
Sherman Oaks, CA 91423
"Actor"

James Van Patten
14411 Riverside Drive #15
Sherman Oaks, CA 91423
"Actor"

Joyce Van Patten
1321 North Hayworth #C
Los Angeles, CA 90046
"Actress"

Nels Van Patten
14411 Riverside Drive #18
Sherman Oaks, CA 91423
"Actor"

Tim Van Patten
400 South Beverly Drive #216
Beverly Hills, CA 90212
"Actor"

Vincent Van Patten
13926 Magnolia Blvd.
Sherman Oaks, CA 91423
"Actor"

Mario Van Peebles
40 West 57th Street
New York, NY 10019
"Actor, Writer, Director"

Melvin Van Peebles
353 West 56th Street #10-F
New York, NY 10019
"Actor, Writer, Director"

Ricky Van Sheldon
Rt. 12, Box 95
Lebanon, TN 37087
"Singer"

General Mguyen Van Thieu
Coombe Park, White House
Kingston on Thames
Surrey ENGLAND
"Military Leader"

Deborah Van Valkenburgh
2025 Stanley Hills Drive
Los Angeles, CA 90046
"Actress"

Monique Van Vooren
165 East 66th Street
New York, NY 10021
"Actress, Singer"

Randy Vanwarmer
65 Music Square West
Nashville, TN 37203
"Singer, Songwriter"

Johnny Van Zant
P.O. Box 4804
Macon, GA 31201
"Rock & Roll Singer"

Steve Van Zandt
322 West 57th Street
New York, NY 10019
"Singer, Guitarist"

The Vapors
44 Balmoral Drive
Woking, Surrey, ENGLAND
"Rock & Roll Group"

Jim Varney
12 McGovock Street
Nashville, TN 37203
"Actor"

Victor Vasarely
83 re aux Reliaues
Annet-sur-Marne, FRANCE
"Artist"

Robert Vaughn
162 Old West Mountain Road
Ridgefield, CT 06877
"Actor, Director"

Bobby Vee (Velline)
P.O. Box 41
Saulk Rapids, MN 56379
"Singer, Songwriter"

Suzanne Vega
Grand Central Station
Box 4221
New York, NY 10163
"Folk Singer"

Jorge Velasquez
770 Allerton Avenue
Bronx, NY 10467
"Jockey"

Eddie Velez
10661 Whipple
North Hollywood, CA 91602
"Actor"

Reginald Vel Johnson
9229 Sunset Blvd. #607
Los Angeles, CA 90069
"Actor"

Yolanda Veloz
19413 Olivos Drive
Tarzana, CA 91356
"Real Estate Executive"

Evelyn Venable
141 Gretna Green Way
Los Angeles, CA 90049
"Actress"

Rep. Bruce F. Vento (MN)
House Rayburn Bldg. #2304
Washington, DC 20515
"Politician"

The Ventures
P.O. Box 1646
Burbank, CA 91507
"Rock & Roll Group"

Ken Venturi
P.O. Box 12458
Palm Beach Gardens, FL 33410
"Golf Instructor"

Benay Venuta
50 East 79th Street
New York, NY 10021
"Actress"

Gwen Verdon
91 Central Park West
New York, NY 10023
"Actress, Dancer"

Elena Verdugo
P.O. Box 2048
Chula Vista, CA 92012
"Actress"

Ben Vereen
190 East Saddle River Road
Saddle River, NJ 07458
"Dancer, Actor"

Dick Vermeil
51 West 52nd Street
New York, NY 10019
"Sportcaster"

Henri Verneuil
21 rue du Bois-de-Boulogne
92200 Neuilly-sur-Seine
FRANCE
"Film Director"

John Vernon
15125 Mulholland Drive
Los Angeles, CA 90077
"Actor"

Kate Vernon
901 Bringham Avenue
Los Angeles, CA 90049
"Actress"

Yvette Vickers
P.O. Box 664
Pinon Hills, CA 92372
"Actress"

Gore Vidal
2562 Outpost Drive
Los Angeles, CA 90068
"Writer"

Peter Vidmar
14 Carnelian
Irvine, CA 92714
"Gymnast"

Meredith Viera
524 West 57th Street
New York, NY 10019
"News Correspondent"

Abe Vigoda
1215 Beverly View Drive
Beverly Hills, CA 90210
"Actor"

Richard Viguerie
7777 Leesburg Pike
Falls Church, VA 22043
"Professional Fund Raiser"

Bruce Vilanch
8730 Sunset Blvd. #600
Los Angeles, CA 90069
"Writer"

Guillermo Vilas
Avenue Foch 86
Paris, FRANCE
"Tennis Player"

Tom Villard
1999 Avenue of the Stars #2850
Los Angeles, CA 90067
"Actor"

Herve Villechaize
P.O. Box 1305
Burbank, CA 91507
"Actor"

Jan-Michael Vincent
P.O. Box 7000-690
Redondo Beach, CA 90277
"Actor"

Romo Vincent
1125 North Sherbourne Drive #A20
Los Angeles, CA 90006
"Actor"

Virginia Vincent
1001 Hammond Street
Los Angeles, CA 90069
"Actress"

Ellsworth Vines
P.O. Box 821
La Quinta, CA 92253
"Tennis & Golf Player"

Helen Vinson Haddenbrook
2213 Carol Woods
Chapel Hill, NC 27514
"Actress"

Jesse Vint
5003 Tyrone Avenue #1
Sherman Oaks, CA 91423
"Actor"

Bobby Vinton
1905 Cold Canyon Road
Calabasas, CA 91302
"Singer"

Lasse Viren
Plltihuset
Helsingfors (Helsinki)
FINLAND
"Track Athlete"

Rep. Peter Visclosky (IN)
House Cannon Bldg. #330
Washington, DC 20515
"Politician"

Sal Visculo
6491 Ivarene Avenue
Los Angeles, CA 90068
"Actor"

Nana Visitor
10390 Santa Monica Blvd.
Suite #300
Los Angeles, CA 90025
"Actress"

Monica Vitti
Via Vicenzo Tiberio 18
Rome, ITALY
"Actress"

Marina Vlady
10 Avenue de Marivauz
78800 Mission Lafitte
FRANCE
"Actress"

Karl Micheal Vogler
Auweg 60, Seehof
8110 Seehausen/ Staffelsee
GERMANY
"Actor"

Jon Voight
13340 Galewood Drive
Sherman Oaks, CA 91423
"Actor"

Paul Volcker
153 East 79th Street
New York, NY 10021
"Former Monetary Treasurer"

Rep. Harold L. Volkmer (MO)
House Rayburn Bldg. #2411
Washington, DC 20515
"Politician"

Nedra Volz
615 Tulare Way
Upland, CA 91786
"Actress"

Alexander von Auersperg
Clarendon Court
Watch Hill Station
Westerly, RI 02891
"Stepson of Claus Bulow"

Helene von Damm-Gurtler
Hotel Sacher bei der Oper
1010 Vienna, AUSTRIA
"Diplomat"

Erich Von Daniken
Baselstrasse 1
4532 Feldbrunen, SWITZERLAND
"Author"

Betsy Von Fursterberg
114 East 28th Street #203
New York, NY 10016
"Actress"

Diane von Furstenberg
745 Fifth Avenue
New York, NY 10151
"Fashion Designer"

Kurt Vonnegut, Jr.
228 East 48th Street
New York, NY 10017
"Writer"

Max Von Sydow
P.O. Box 27126
10252 Stockholm
SWEDEN
"Actor"

Richard von Weizsacker
Villa Hammerschmidt
5300 Bonn
GERMANY
"President of Germany"

Rep. Barbara Vucanovich (NV)
House Cannon Bldg. #206
Washington, DC 20515
"Politician"

Henry-Louis Vuitton
30 rue la Bletie
8th Arr. Paris, FRANCE
"Designer"

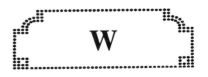

Russell Wade
Eldorado Country Club
47-287 West Eldorado Drive
Indian Wells, CA 92260
"Actor"

Virginia Wade
Sharstead Court
Sittingbourne
Kent, ENGLAND
"Tennis Player"

Lyle Waggoner
4450 Balboa Avenue
Encino, CA 91316
"Actor"

Jack Wagner
1750 North Beverly Drive
Beverly Hills, CA 90210
"Actor, Singer"

Jane Wagner
P.O. Box 27700
Los Angeles, CA 90027
"Writer, Producer"

Lindsay Wagner
P.O. Box 188
Pacific Palisades, CA 90212
"Actress"

Robert Wagner
1500 Old Oak Road
Los Angeles, CA 90049
"Actor"

Porter Wagoner
1830 Airlane Drive
Nashville, TN 37210
"Singer, Songwriter"

Ken Wahl
6622 Portshead Drive
Malibu, CA 90265
"Actor"

Gov. John Waihee III (HI)
State Capitol
Honolulu, HI 96813
"Governor"

Kurt Waldheim
Hofburg, Bullhausplatz
1010 Vienna, AUSTRIA
"President of Austria"

Marcy Walker
4403 Clybourn
North Hollywood, CA 91602
"Actress"

Bea Wain
9955 Durant Drive
Beverly Hills, CA 90212
"Singer"

Janet Waldo
15725 Royal Oak Road
Encino, CA 91316
"Actress"

Mort Walker
61 Studio Court
Stamford, CT 06903
"Cartoonist"

James Wainwright
1354 Los Robles Drive
Palm Springs, CA 92262
"Rock & Roll Group"

Lech Walesa
Ul. Pilotow 17/D3
Gdansk - Zaspa POLAND
"Politician"

Nancy Walker
3702 Eureka
North Hollywood, CA 91602
"Actress, Director"

Ralph Waite
23 Duke Drive
Rancho Mirage, CA 92270
"Actor, Director"

Christopher Walken
142 Cedar Road
Wilton, CT 06897
"Actor"

Nicholas Walker
6925 Tuna Canyon Road
Topanga, CA 90290
"Actor"

Tom Waits
P.O. Box 498
Valley Ford, CA 94972
"Singer, Songwriter"

Bree Walker
3347 Tareco Drive
Los Angeles, CA 90068
"Newscaster"

Rep. Robert S. Walker (PA)
House Rayburn Bldg. #2445
Washington, DC 20515
"Politician"

Greta Waitz
Rovnkollbakken 79
Oslo 9 NORWAY
"Track Athlete"

Clint Walker
10113 Joerschke Drive #202
Grass Valley, CA 95945
"Actor"

Robert Walker, Jr.
20828 Pacific Coast Hwy.
Malibu, CA 90265
"Actor"

Gregory Walcott
22246 Saticoy Street
Canoga Park, CA 91306
"Actor"

Doak Walker
P.O. Box TT
Steamboat Springs, CO 80477
"Football Player"

Chris Wallace
1717 DeSales Street
Washington, DC 20036
"Broadcast Journalist"

Jersey Joe Walcott
1500 Baird Avenue
Camden, NJ 08103
"Boxer"

Hershell Walker
9520 Viking Drive
Eden Prairie, MN 55344
"Football Player"

Dee-Wallace Stone
12700 Ventura Blvd. #350
Studio City, CA 91604
"Actress"

Jeff Wald
2276 Century Hill
Los Angeles, CA 90067
"Talent Agent

Jimmy Walker
220 Central Park South
New York, NY 10019
"Actor, Comedian"

George Wallace
P.O. Box 17222
Montgomery, AL 36104
"Former Governor"

Robert Walden
1450 Arroyo View Drive
Pasadena, CA 91103
"Actor"

Junior Walker
141 Dunbar Avenue
Fords, NJ 08863
"Saxophonist"

Marcia Wallace
1312 South Genesee Avenue
Los Angeles, CA 90019
"Actress"

Marjorie Wallace
901 Bundy Drive
Los Angeles, CA 90049
"Journalist"

Mike Wallace
555 West 57th Street
New York, NY 10019
"Broadcast Journalist"

Eli Wallach
90 Riverside Drive
New York, NY 10024
"Actor"

The Great Wallendas
138 Frog Hollow Road
Churchville, PA 18966
"High Wire Act"

Deborah Walley
31 1/2 -24th Avenue
Venice, CA 90291
"Actress"

Shani Wallis
303 South Crecent Height Blvd.
Los Angeles, CA 90048
"Singer"

Sen. Malcolm Wallop (WY)
Senate Russell Bldg. #237
Washington, DC 20510
"Politician"

Jon Walmsley
13810 Magnolia Blvd.
Sherman Oaks, CA 91403
"Actor"

Martin Walser
Zum Hecht 36
7700 Uberlingen, GERMANY
"Author, Dramatist"

Rep. James T. Walsh (NY)
House Longworth Bldg. #1238
Washington, DC 20515
"Politician"

John Walsh
3111 South Dixie Hwy. #244
West Palm Beach, FL 33405
"Actor"

M. Emmet Walsh
4173 Motor Avenue
Culver City, CA 90232
"Actor"

Ray Walston
423 South Rexford Drive #205
Beverly Hills, CA 90212
"Actor"

Jessica Walter
10530 Strathmore Drive
Los Angeles, CA 90024
"Actress"

Tracey Walter
257 North Rexford Drive
Beverly Hills, CA 90210
"Actor"

Barbara Walters
33 West 60th Street
New York, NY 10021
"News Journalist"

Julie Walters
153 Petherton Road
London N5 ENGLAND
"Actress"

Laurie Walters
4450 Kensington Road #5
Los Angeles, CA 9006
"Actress"

Susan Walters
10100 Santa Monica Blvd. #1600
Los Angeles, CA 90067
"Actress"

Gladys Walton
225 Main Street
Morro Bay, CA 93442
"Actress"

Jess Walton
9000 Sunset Blvd. #801
Los Angeles, CA 90069
"Actress"

Joseph Wambaugh
30 Linda Isle
Newport Beach, CA 92660
"Novelist"

Sam Wanamaker
354 North Croft Avenue
Los Angeles, CA 90048
"Actor, Director"

Joseph A. Wapner
16616 Park Lane Place
Los Angeles, CA 90049
"TV Judge"

Burt Ward
1559 Pacific Coast Hwy. #815
Hermosa Beach, CA 90049
"Actor"

Fred Ward
9301 Wilshire Blvd. #312
Beverly Hills, CA 90210
"Actor"

Jacky Ward
821-19th Avenue South
Nashville, TN 37203
"Singer"

Kelly Ward
400 South Beverly Drive #216
Beverly Hills, CA 90212
"Actor"

Rachel Ward
10100 Santa Monica Blvd. #1600
Los Angeles, CA 90067
"Actress"

Sela Ward
2102 Century Park Lane #202
Los Angeles, CA 90067
"Actress"

Skip Ward
P.O. Box 755
Beverly Hills, CA 90213
"Actor"

Jack Warden
23604 Malibu Colony Drive
Malibu, CA 90265
"Actor"

Andre Ware
1200 Featherstone Road
Pontiac, MI 48057
"Football Player"

Clyde Ware
1252 North Laurel Avenue
Los Angeles, CA 90046
"Writer, Producer"

Marsha Warfield
P.O. Box 691713
Los Angeles, CA 90069
"Actress, Comedienne"

Dr. William Warfield
706 Phoenix Drive
Champaign, IL 61820
"Actor, Singer"

Steve Wariner
1514 South Street
Nashville, TN 37212
"Actor"

Billy Warlock
9200 Sunset Blvd. #625
Los Angeles, CA 90069
"Actor"

Cornelius Warmerdam
3976 North 1st Street
Fresno, CA 93726
"Track Athlete"

Sen. John Warner (VA)
Senate Russell Bldg. #225
Washington, DC 20510
"Politician"

Malcolm-Jamal Warner
1301 The Colony
Hartsdale, NY 10530
"Actor"

Charles Marquis Warren
3250 Cornell Road
Agoura Hills, CA 91301
"Writer, Producer, Director"

Fran Warren Steinman
340 West 57th Street
New York, NY 10019
"Actress, Singer"

Jennifer Warren
1675 Old Oak Road
Los Angeles, CA 90049
"Actress"

Lesley Ann Warren
3619 Meadville
Sherman Oaks, CA 91403
"Actress"

Michael Warren
189 Greenfield
Los Angeles, CA 90049
"Actor"

Ruth Warrick
903 Park Avenue
New York, NY 10021
"Actress"

Dionne Warwick
806 North Elm Drive
Beverly Hills, CA 90210
"Singer"

Denzel Washington
4701 Sancola
Toluca Lake, CA 91602
"Actor"

Ted Wass
7667 Seattle Place
Los Angeles, CA 90046
"Actor"

Dale Wasserman
1690 Valecroft Avenue
Westlake Village, CA 91361
"Dramatist"

Lew Wasserman
911 North Foothill Road
Beverly Hills, CA 90210
"Film Executive"

Craig Wasson
1999 Avenue of the Start #2850
Los Angeles, CA 90067
"Actor"

Gedde Watanabe
3855 Lankershim Blvd.
Studio City, CA 91604
"Actor"

Waterboys
3 Monmouth Road
London W2 ENGLAND
"Rock & Roll Group"

John Waters
575-8th Avenue #1600
New York, NY 10018
"Director, Writer"

Sam Waterson
9000 Sunset Blvd #1200
Los Angeles, CA 90069
"Actor"

Carlene Watkins
15760 Ventura Blvd. #1730
Encino, CA 91436
"Actress"

Jill Watson
2331 Century Hill
Los Angeles, CA 90067
"Skater"

Mills Watson
1930 Century Park West
Los Angeles, CA 90007
"Actor"

Tom Watson
911 Main Street
1313 Commerce Towers
Kansas City, MO 64105
"Golfer"

James G. Watt
1800 North Spirit Dance Road
Jackson Hole, WY 83001
"Former Secretary of Interior"

Al Waxman
9200 Sunset Blvd. #428
Los Angeles, CA 90069
"Actor"

Rep. Henry A. Waxman (CA)
House Rayburn Bldg. #2418
Washington, DC 20515
"Politician"

Keenan Ivory Wayans
451 North Orange Drive
Los Angeles, CA 90036
"Actor"

Kristina Wayborn
9300 Wilshire Blvd. #410
Beverly Hills, CA 90212
"Actress, Model"

David Wayne
868 Napoli Drive
Pacific Palisades, CA 90272
"Actor"

Fredd Wayne
117 Strand Street
Santa Monica, CA 90405
"Actor, Writer"

Michael Wayne
10425 Kling Street
North Hollywood, CA 91602
"Film Executive"

Patrick Wayne
10502 Whipple Street
North Hollywood, CA 91602
"Actor"

Pilar Wayne
930 Mariners Drive
Newport Beach, CA 92660
"Wife of John Wayne"

Shawn Weatherly
P.O. Box 5617
Beverly Hills, CA 90210
"Actress, Model"

Carl Weathers
10000 Santa Monica Blvd. #400
Los Angeles, CA 90067
"Actor"

Bob Weatherwax
16133 Soledad Canyon Road
Canyon Country, CA 91351
"Animal Trainer"

Dennis Weaver
P.O. Box 983
Malibu, CA 90265
"Actor"

Fritz Weaver
161 West 75th Street
New York, NY 10023
"Actor"

Marjorie Weaver
13038 San Vicente Blvd.
Los Angeles, CA 90049
"Actress"

Patty Weaver
5009 Hayvenhurst Drive
Encino, CA 91316
"Actress, Singer"

Sigourney Weaver
12 West 72nd Street
New York, NY 10023
"Actress"

Jimmy Webb
1560 North Laurel Avenue #109
Los Angeles, CA 90046
"Singer, Composer"

Lucy Webb
1360 North Crescent Heights #3-B
Los Angeles, CA 90046
"Actress, Comedienne"

Richard Webb
13330 Chandler Blvd.
Van Nuys, CA 91401
"Actor"

Andrew Lloyd Webber
Trump Tower
725 Fifth Avenue
New York, NY 10022
"Composer"

Rep. Vin Weber (MN)
House Cannon Bldg. #106
Washington, DC 20515
"Politician"

William Webster
9409 Brooke Drive
Bethesda, MD 20817
"F.B.I. Director"

Ann Wedgeworth
822 South Robertson Blvd. #200
Los Angeles, CA 90035
"Actress"

Gene Weed
10405 Oklahoma Avenue
Chatsworth, CA 91311
"Writer, Producer"

Caspar Weinberger
60 Fifth Avenue
New York, NY 10011
"Former Government Official"

Carl Weintraub
151 North San Vicente Blvd.
Suite #208
Beverly Hills, CA 90211
"Actor"

Jerry Weintraub
27740 Pacific Coast Highway
Malibu, CA 90265
"Motion Picture Producer"

Rev. Benjamin Weir
Presbyterian Church of USA
Office of General Assembly
475 Riverside Drive #1201
New York, NY 10115
Ex-Hostage, Evangelist"

Tom Weiskepf
5412 East Morrison Lane
Paradise Valley, AZ 85253
"Golfer"

Michael T. Weiss
151 South El Camino Drive
Beverly Hills, CA 90212
"Actor"

Rep. Ted Weiss (NY)
House Rayburn Bldg #2467
Washington, DC 20515
"Politician"

Bruce Weitz
3061 Lake Hollywood Drive
Los Angeles, CA 90068
"Actor"

Ezer Weizman
26 Hagiffen Street
Ramat, Haseram, ISRAEL
"Politician"

Bob Welch
4150 Delphi Circle
Huntington Beach, CA 92649
"Baseball Player"

Elizabeth Welch
4a Carpenter's Close
London SW1 ENGLAND
"Actress, Singer"

Raquel Welch
200 Central Park South
New York, NY 10019
"Actress, Singer, Writer"

Tahnee Welch
200 Central Park South
New York, NY 10019
"Actress"

Tuesday Weld
300 Central Park West #14-E
New York, NY 10024
"Actress"

Ann Weldon
11555 Dona Teresa Drive
Studio City, CA 91604
"Actress"

Rep. Curt Weldon (PA)
House Cannon Bldg. #316
Washington, DC 20515
"Politician"

Lawrence Welk
1221 Ocean Avenue #602
Santa Monica, CA 90401
"Musician"

Mary Louise Weller
1416 North Havenhurst Drive #11
Los Angeles, CA 90046
"Actress"

Peter Weller
853-7th Avenue #9-A
New York, NY 10019
"Actor"

Robb Weller
4249 Beck Avenue
Studio City, CA 91604
"TV Host"

William Wellman, Jr.
410 North Barrington Avenue
Los Angeles, CA 90049
"Actor"

Dawn Wells
11684 Ventura Blvd. #364
Studio City, CA 91604
"Actress"

Kitty Wells
240 Old Hickory Blvd.
Madison, TN 35115
"Singer"

Mary Wells
9200 Sunset Blvd. #1220
Los Angeles, CA 90069
"Singer"

Eudora Welty
1119 Pinehurst Street
Jackson, MS 39202
"Author"

Señor Wences
204 West 55th Street #701A
New York, NY 10019
"Ventriliquist"

Rudolph Wendelin
4516-7th Avenue North
Arlington, VA 22203
"Illustrator"

George Wendt
3856 Vantage Avenue
Studio City, CA 91604
"Actor"

Lina Wertmuller
via Principessa Clotilde 5
00196 Rome, ITALY
"Film Director"

Linda Wertheimer
c/o National Public Radio
2025 "M" Street NW
Washington, DC 20036
"News Correspondent"

Paula Wessely
Himmelstrasse 24
1190 Vienna, AUSTRIA
"Actress"

Celeste Wesson
c/o National Public Radio
2025 "M" Street NW
Washington, DC 20036
"News Correspondent"

Adam West
P.O. Box 3446
Ketchum, ID 83340
"Actor"

Red West
10637 Burbank Blvd.
Hollywood, CA 91601
"Actor, Author"

Shelly West
P.O. Box 2977
Hendersonville, CA 37077
"Singer"

Timothy West
46 North Side
Wandsworth Common
London SW18 ENGLAND
"Actor"

Dr. Ruth Westheimer
900 West 190th Street
New York, NY 10040
"Sex Theapist"

James Westmoreland
8019 1/2 West Norton Avenue
Los Angeles, CA 90046
"Actor"

Gen. William Westmoreland
107 1/2 Tradd Street
P.O. Box 1059
Charleston, SC 29401
"Military Leader"

Jack Weston
101 Central Park West
New York, NY 10023
"Actor"

Paul Weston
2339 Century Hill
Los Angeles, CA 90067
"Musician, Composer"

Patricia Wetting
11840 Chaparal Street
Los Angeles, CA 90049
"Actress"

Rep. Alan Wheat (MO)
House Longworth Bldg. #1210
Washington, DC 20515
"Politician"

Wil Wheaton
P.O. Box 12567
La Crescenta, CA 91214
"Actor"

Arlene Whelan Cagney
P.O. Box 766
Dana Point, CA 92629
"Actress"

Jill Whelan
11628 Montana Avenue #210
Los Angeles, CA 90025
"Actress"

Lisa Whelchel
11906 Shoshone Avenue
Granada Hills, CA 91344
"Actress"

Ian Whitcomb
P.O. Box 451
Altadena, CA 91001
"Singer, Actor, Producer"

Barry White
10502 Whipple
North Hollywood, CA 91604
"Singer, Songwriter"

Betty White
P.O. Box 3713
Granada Hills, CA 91344
"Actress"

Byron White
1 First Street N.E.
Washington, D.C. 20543
"Supreme Court Justice"

Danny White
c/o General Delivery
Wylie, TX 75098
"Football Player"

Jaleel White
1450 Belfast Drive
Los Angeles, CA 90069
"Actor"

Jesse White
1944 Glendon Avenue #304
Los Angeles, CA 90025
"Actor"

Slappy White
1055 Flamingo Road #819
Las Vegas, NV 89109
"Comedian"

Vanna White
3400 Riverside Drive
Burbank, CA 91505
"TV Personality, Model"

Geoffrey Whitehead
81 Shaftesbury Avenue
London W1 ENGLAND
"Actor"

Billie Whitelaw
7 West Eaton Place Mews
London SW1X 8LY ENGLAND
"Actress"

The White's
P.O. Box 2158
Hendersonville, TN 37075
"C&W Group"

White Snake
15 Poulton Raod
Wallasey, Cheshire
ENGLAND
"Rock & Roll Group"

Barbara Whiting Smith
1085 Waddington Street
Birmingham, MI 48009
"Actress"

Leonard Whiting
91 Regent Street
London W1 ENGLAND
"Actor"

Margaret Whiting
41 West 58th Street #5A
New York, NY 10019
"Singer"

Slim Whitman
1300 Divison Street #103
Nashville, TN 37203
"Singer"

Stuart Whitman
749 San Ysidro Road
Santa Barbara, CA 93108
"Actor"

James Whitmore
88-7th Avenue #1800
New York, NY 10019
"Actor"

James Whitmore, Jr.
1284 La Brea Drive
Thousand Oaks, CA 91362
"Actor"

Grace Whitney Lee
2611 Silverside Road
Wilmington, DE 19810
"Actress"

Phyllis Whitney
310 Madison Avenue #607
New York, NY 10017
"Actress"

Roger Whittaker
2932 Hwy. A1A South #C
Augustine, FL 32084
"Singer, Songwriter"

Rep. Jamie L. Whitten (MS)
House Rayburn Bldg. #2314
Washington, DC 20515
"Politician"

Dick Whittinghill
11310 Valley Spring Lane
Toluca Lake, CA 91602
"Radio Personality"

Margaret Whitton
10100 Santa Monica Blvd.
Suite #1600
Los Angeles, CA 90067
"Actress"

The Who
48 Harley House
London NW1 ENGLAND
"Rock & Roll Group"

Mary Wickes
2160 Century Park East #503
Los Angeles, CA 90067
"Actress"

Kathleen Widdoes
888-7th Avenue #1800
New York, NY 10019
"Actress"

Richard Widmark
999 West Potrero Road
Thousand Oaks, CA 91360
"Actor"

Elie Wiesel
40 Boston University
745 Common Wealth Avenue
Boston, MA 02115
"Author, Journalist"

Bernard Wiesen
Weissger Berstrasse 2
Munich 23 GERMANY
"TV Director, Producer"

Simon Wiesenthal
Salvtorgasse 6
1010 Vienna 1 AUSTRIA
"Jewish Leader"

Mats Wilander
Vickersvagen 2
Vaxjo, SWEDEN
"Tennis Player"

The Wilburn Brothers
P.O. Box 50
Goodlettsville, TN 37072
"C&W Group"

Larry Wilcox
13 Appaloosa Lane
Bell Canyon
Canoga Park, CA 91304
"Actor, Director"

Shannon Wilcox
121 North San Vicente Blvd.
Beverly Hills, CA 90211
"Actress"

Wild Cherry
28001 Chagrin Blvd. #205
Cleveland, OH 44122
"Rock & Roll Group"

Jack Wild
47 The Grove, Ilsworth
Middlesex, ENGLAND
"Actor"

Kim Wilde
1 Stevenage Road
Newworth, Herts. ENGLAND
"Singer, Songwriter"

Billy Wilder
10375 Wilshire Blvd.
Los Angeles, CA 90024
"Writer, Producer"

Gene Wilder
9350 Wilshire Blvd. #400
Beverly Hills, CA 90210
"Actor, Writer, Director"

James Wilder
8899 Beverly Blvd.
Los Angeles, CA 90048
"Actor"

Gov. L. Douglas Wilder (VA)
State House
Richmond, VA 33219
"Governor"

Yvonne Wilder
5450 Topeka Drive
Tarzana, CA 91356
"Actress"

Michael Wilding, Jr.
8428-C Melrose Place
Los Angeles, CA 90069
"Actor"

Hoyt Wilhelm
3102 North Himes Avenue
Tampa, FL 33607
"Baseball Player"

Donna Wilkes
3802 North Earl Avenue
Rosemead, CA 91770
"Actress"

Jamaal Wilkes
7846 West 81st Street
Playa del Rey, CA 90291
"Basketball Player"

June Wilkinson
53653 Fairesta Street
La Crescenta, CA 91214
"Actress"

Gov. Wallace Wilkinson (KY)
State Capitol, Room 102
Frankford, KY 40601
"Governor"

George Will
1150-15th Street N.W.
Washington, DC 20071
"Columnist, Writer"

Fred Willard
5056 Woodley Avenue
Encino, CA 91436
"Actor"

Williams & Ree
P.O. Box 163
Hendersonville, TN 37077
"Vocal Duo"

Andy Williams
816 North La Cienega Blvd.
Los Angeles, CA 90069
"Singer, Actor"

Barry Williams
22653 Pacific Coast Hwy. #218
Malibu, CA 90265
"Actor"

Bill Williams
15301 Ventura Blvd. #345
Sherman Oaks, CA 91403
"Actor"

Billy Dee Williams
1240 Loma Vista Drive
Beverly Hills, CA 90210
"Actor"

Cara Willaims Dann
146 South Peck Drive
Beverly Hills, CA 90212
"Actress"

Cindy Williams
709-19th Street
Santa Monica, CA 90402
"Actress"

Deniece Williams
1414 Seabright
Beverly Hills, CA 90210
"Singer"

Don Williams
1103-16th Avenue South
Nashville, CA 37203
"Singer, Songwriter"

Edy Williams
1638 Blue Jay Way
Los Angeles, CA 90069
"Actress, Model"

Esther Williams
9377 Readcrest Drive
Beverly Hills, CA 90210
"Actress"

Hal Williams
6736 Laurel Canyon Blvd. #331
North Hollywood, CA 91606
"Actor"

Hank Williams, Jr.
P.O. Box 850
Paris, TN 38242
"Singer, Guitarist"

Jobeth Williams
3529 Beverly Glen Blvd.
Sherman Oaks, CA 91423
"Actress"

Joe Williams
3337 Knollwood Court
Las Vegas, NV 89121
"Singer"

John Williams
301 Massachusetts Avenue
Boston, MA 02115
"Composer, Conductor"

Mary Alice Williams
30 Rockefeller Plaza #508
New York, NY 10020
"Broadcast Journalist"

Mason Williams
P.O. Box 25
Oakbridge, OR 97463
"Singer, Songwriter"

Montel William
151 South El Camino Drive
Beverly Hills, CA 90212
"TV Host"

Rep. Pat Williams (MT)
House Rayburn Bldg. #2457
Washington, DC 20515
"Politician"

Paul Williams
645 Sand Point Road
Carpinteria, CA 93013
"Singer, Songwriter"

Robin Williams
1100 Wall Road
Napa, CA 94558
"Actor, Comedian, Writer"

Roger Williams
5710 Wallis Lane
Woodland Hills, CA 91364
"Pianist"

Stephanie Williams
1124 South Sycamore Avenue
Los Angeles, CA 90019
"Actress"

Ted Williams
P.O. Box 5127
Clearwater, FL 34618
"Baseball Player"

Treat Williams
215 West 78th Street #10-A
New York, NY 10024
"Actor"

Van Williams
1630 Ocean Park Blvd.
Santa Monica, CA 90405
"Actor"

Vanessa Williams
Rt. #100
Milwood, NY 10546
"Singer, Actress"

Wayne Williams
Classification & Diagnostic Center
Jackson, GA 30233
"Child Killer"

Wendy O. Williams
P.O. Box 837
New York, NY 10013
"Singer, Actress"

Fred Williamson
113 North San Vicente Blvd.
Suite #202
Beverly Hills, CA 90211
"Actor, Director"

Nicol Williamson
388 Oxford Street
London W1 ENGLAND
"Actor"

Bruce Willis
1453 Third Street #420
Santa Monica, CA 90401
"Actor, Singer"

Angus Wilson
Bradford Street
St. George-St. Edmunds
Suffolk, ENGLAND
"Author"

Ann Wilson
219-1st Avenue North #333
Seattle, WA 98109
"Singer, Musician"

Brian Wilson
22070 Pacific Coast Highway
Malibu, CA 90265
"Singer, Songwriter"

Carl Wilson
8860 Evan View Drive
Los Angeles, CA 90069
"Singer, Songwriter"

Rep. Charles Wilson (TX)
House Rayburn Bldg. #2265
Washington, DC 20515
"Politician"

Demond Wilson
Church of God in Christ
Ft. Washington, MD 20022
"Actor, Evangelist"

Flip Wilson
21970 Pacific Coast Highway
Malibu, CA 90265
"Comedian, Actor, Writer"

Mary Wilson
5406 Red Oak Drive
Los Angeles, CA 90068
"Singer"

Melanie Wilson
P.O. Box 93344
Los Angeles, CA 90093
"Actress"

Nancy Wilson
5455 Wilshire Blvd. #1606
Los Angeles, CA 90036
"Singer, Actress"

Nancy Wilson
202 San Vicente Blvd. #4
Santa Monica, CA 90402
"Heart Lead Singer"

Gov. Pete Wilson (CA)
State Capitol
Sacramento, CA 95814
"Governor"

Wilson Phillips
8730 Sunset Blvd. #500
Los Angeles, CA 90069
"Rock & Roll Group"

Sheree J. Wilson
22 1/2 Northstar
Marina del Rey, CA 90292
"Actress"

Tom Wilson
12120 Elmwood Avenue
Cleveland, OH 44111
"Cartoonist"

Paul Winchell
32262 Oakshore Drive
Westlake Village, CA 91361
"Actor"

William Windom
6535 Langden
Van Nuys, CA 91406
"Actor"

Marie Windsor
9501 Cherokee Lane
Beverly Hills, CA 90210
"Actress"

Dave Winfield
367 West Forest
Teaneck, NJ 07666
"Baseball Player"

Paul Winfield
5693 Holly Oak Drive
Los Angeles, CA 90068
"Actor"

Oprah Winfrey
P.O. Box 909715
Chicago, IL 60690
"TV Host, Actress"

Debra Winger
P.O. Box 1368
Pacific Palisades, CA 90272
"Actress"

Jason Wingreen
4224 Teesdale Avenue
North Hollywood, CA 91604
"Actor"

Henry Winkler
4323 Forman Avenue
Toluca Lake, CA 91604
"Actor, Producer"

Michael Winner
6/8 Sackville Street
London W1X 1DD ENGLAND
"Writer, Producer"

Mare Winningham
12256 La Maida Street
North Hollywood, CA 91607
"Actress"

Michael Winslow
19321 Palomar Place
Tarzana, CA 91356
"Actor, Comedian"

Kathleen Winsor
1271 Avenue of the Americas
New York, NY 10020
"Author"

Alex Winter
238-6th Avenue
Venice, CA 90291
"Actor"

Edward Winter
4359 Havenhurst Avenue
Encino, CA 91436
"Actor"

Judy Winter
Lamonstrasse 9
8000 Munich 80
GERMANY
"Singer"

Jonathan Winters
4310 Arcola Avenue
Toluca Lake, CA 91602
"Comedian, Actor"

Shelley Winters
457 North Oakhurst Drive
Beverly Hills, CA 90210
"Actress"

Steve Winwood
888-7th Avenue #1602
New York, NY 10106
"Singer, Songwriter"

Sen. Timothy Wirth (CO)
Senate Russell Bldg. #380
Washington, DC 20510
"Politician"

Norman Wisdom
28 Berkley Square
London 6HD ENGLAND
"Actor"

Rep. Bob Wise (WV)
House Longworth Bldg. #1421
Washington, DC 20515
"Politician"

Ernie Wise
306-16 Euston Road
London NW13 ENGLAND
"Comedian"

Robert Wise
2222 Avenue of the Stars #2303
Los Angeles, CA 90067
Director, Producer"

Bill Withers
2600 Benedict Canyon
Beverly Hills, CA 90210
Singer, Songwriter"

Googie Withers
306-316 Euston Road
London NW1 3BB ENGLAND
"Actress"

Jane Withers
1801 North Curson Avenue
Los Angeles, CA 90046
"Actress"

Jimmy Witherspoon
223 1/2 East 48th Street
New York, NY 10017
"Singer, Musician"

Katarina Witt
Reichenheiner Street
D-(0)9023
Chemnitz, GERMANY
"Ice Skater"

Paul Junger Witt
1438 North Gower Street
Los Angeles, CA 90028
"TV Producer"

Mr. Wizard (Don Herbert)
P.O. Box 83
Canoga Park, CA 91305
"TV Personality"

Charles Wolcott
P.O. Box 155
Haifa, ISRAEL
"Composer

Rep. Frank R. Wolf (VA)
House Cannon Bldg. #104
Washington, DC 20515
"Politician"

Jeanne Wolf
1375 North Wetherly Drive
Los Angeles, CA 90069
"TV Reporter"

Ian Wolfe
4652 Noble Avenue
Sherman Oaks, CA 91403
"Actor"

Michael Wolfe
41 Landowne Road
London W11 26Q ENGLAND
"Actor"

Tom Wolfe
19 Union Square West
New York, NY 10003
"Writer"

Wolfman Jack
Route 1, Box 56
Belvidere, NC 27919
"Radio Disc Jockey"

Rep. Howard Wolpe (MI)
House Rayburn Bldg. #1535
Washington, DC 20515
"Politician"

David L. Wolper
10847 Ballagio Road
Los Angeles, CA 90077
"Film Director"

Bobby Womack
10847 Bellagio Road
Los Angeles, CA 90077
"Singer"

Stevie Wonder
2270 Astral Place
Los Angeles, CA 90068
"Singer, Songwriter"

Judith Wood
1300 1/2 N. Sycamore Avenue
Los Angeles, CA 90028
"Actress"

Lane Wood
12124 Goshen Avenue #104
Los Angeles, CA 90049
"Actress"

Alfre Woodard
602 Bay Street
Santa Monica, CA 90405
"Writer"

John Wooden
17711 Margate Street #102
Encino, CA 91316
"Basketball Coach"

Cynthia Woodhead
P.O. Box 1193
Riverside, CA 92501
"Swimmer"

Barbara Woodhouse
Campions, Croxley Green
Rickmansworth, Herts
ENGLAND
"Dog Trainer, Author"

Frank Woodruff
170 North Crescent Drive
Beverly Hills, CA 90210
"Director, Producer"

Donald Woods
479 Tahquitz-McCallum
Palm Springs, CA 92262
"Actor"

James Woods
1612 Gilcrest Drive
Beverly Hills, CA 90210
"Actor, Director"

Michael Woods
9100 Sunset Blvd. #300
Los Angeles, CA 90069
"Actor"

Robert S. Woods
227 Central Park West #5-A
New York, NY 10024
"Actor"

Rosemary Woods
2500 Virginia Avenue N.W.
Washington, DC 20037
"Secretary to President Nixon"

Frank Woodruff
170 North Crescent Drive
Beverly Hills, CA 90210
"Director, Producer "

Bob Woodward
1150-15th Street N.W.
Washington, DC 20005
"News Correspondent"

Edward Woodward
10 East 40th Street #2700
New York, NY 10016
"Actor"

Joanne Woodward
1120 Fifth Avenue #1-C
New York, NY 10022
"Actress, Director"

Marjorie Woodworth
807 North La Brea Avenue
Inglewood, CA 90301
"Actress"

Chuck Woolery
1138 Coldwater Canyon
Beverly Hills, CA 90210
"TV Host"

Sheb Wooley
Route 3, Box 231
Sunset Island Trail
Gallatin, TN 37066
"Singer"

Tom Wopat
12245 Morrison Street
North Hollywood, CA 91607
"Actor, Director"

Joanne Worley
4714 Arcola
Toluca Lake, CA 91602
"Actress"

Todd Worrell
306 Harvard Drive
Arcadia, CA 91006
"Astronaut"

Irene Worty
333 West 56th Street
New York, NY 10018
"Actress"

Celebrity Directory   4th Edition

James Worthy
P.O. Box 10
Inglewood, CA 90306
"Basketball Player"

Herman Wouk
3255 "N" Street N.W.
Washington, DC 20007
"Aurhor"

Steve Wozniak
475 Alberto Way
Los Gatos, CA 95030
"Computer Builder"

Fay Wray Rothenberg
2160 Century Park East #1901
Los Angeles, CA 90067
"Actress"

Cobina Wright, Jr.
1326 Dove Meadow Road
Solvang, CA 93463
"Actress"

Jenny Wright
245 West 104th Street
New York, NY 10025
"Actress"

Jim Wright
9A10 Lanham Federal Bldg.
819 Taylor Street
Fort Worth, TX 76102
"Former House Speaker"

Max Wright
15760 Ventura Blvd. #1730
Encino, CA 91436
"Actor"

Robin Wright
P.O. Box 2630
Malibu, CA 90265
"Actress"

Steven Wright
9000 Sunset Blvd. #1200
Los Angeles, CA 90069
"Comedian"

Teresa Wright
19 West 44th Street #1500
New York, NY 10036
"Actress"

William Wrigley
410 North Michigan Avenue
Chicago, IL 60611
"Baseball Executive"

Robert Wuhl
10590 Holman Avenue
Los Angeles, CA 90024
"Comedian, Actor, Writer"

Jane Wyatt Ward
651 Siena Way
Los Angeles, CA 90024
"Actress"

Sharon Wyatt
24549 Park Grande
Calabasas, CA 91302
"Actress"

Rep. Ron Wyden (OR)
House Longworth Bldg. #2452
Washington, DC 20515
"Politician"

Andrew Wyeth
c/o General Delivery
Chadds Ford, PA 19317
"Artist"

Gretchen Wyler
15215 Weddington Street
Van Nuys, CA 91411
"Actress"

Rep. Chalmers P. Wylie (OH)
House Rayburn Bldg. #2310
Washington, DC 20515
"Politician"

Jane Wyman
P.O. Box 540148
Orlando, FL 32854
"Actress"

Patrice Wymore
Port Antonio
Jamaica BWI
"Actress"

H.M. Wynant
1021 North Beverly Glen
Los Angeles, CA 90077
"Actor"

George Wyner
3450 Laurie Place
Studio City, CA 91604
"Actor"

Tammy Wynette
P.O. Box 7532
Richboro, PA 18059
"Singer, Actress"

Early Wynn
525 Bayview Parkway
Nakomis, FL 33551
"Baseball"

Dana Wynter
9206 Monte Mar Drive
Los Angeles, CA 90035
"Actress"

Chairman Deng Xiaoping
Office of the Chairman
Beijing (Peking)
PEOPLES REPUBLIC OF CHINA
"Politician"

Andrea Yaeger
10695 Bardes Court
Largo, FL 33543
"Tennis Player"

Jeff Yagher
10000 Santa Monica Blvd.
Suite #305
Los Angeles, CA 90067
"Actor"

Kristi Yamaguchi
c/o U.S. Olympic Committee
1750 East Boulder
Colorado Spring, CA 80909
"Skater"

Sheik Ahmed Yamani
Chermignon nr
Crans Montana, FRANCE
"Former O.P.E.C. Official"

Emily Yancey
247 South Beverly Drive #102
Beverly Hills, CA 90212
"Actress"

Wierd Al Yankovic
8842 Hollywood Blvd.
Los Angeles, CA 90069
"Singer, Songwriter"

Cale Yarborough
724 Scott Drive
Fredricksburg, VA 22405
"Auto Racer"

Mollie Yard
1000-16th Street N.W.
Washington, DC 20036
"Feminist Leader"

Claire Yarlett
9300 Wilshire Blvd. #410
Beverly Hills, CA 990212
"Actress"

Amy Yasbeck
2170 Century Park East
Los Angeles, CA 90067
"Actress"

Carl Yastrzemski
4621 South Ocean Blvd.
Highland Beach, FL 33431
"Baseball Player"

Cassie Yates
627 North Rossmore Avenue #312
Los Angeles, CA 90004
"Actress"

Peter Yates
334 Caroline Avenue
Culver City, CA 90230
"Film Director"

Rep. Sidney R. Yates (IL)
House Rayburn Bldg. #2234
Washington, DC 20515
"Politician"

Rep. Gus Yatron (PA)
House Rayburn Bldg. #2205
Washington, DC 20515
"Politician"

General Chuck Yeager
P.O. Box 128
Cedar Ridge, CA 95924
"Military Test Pilot, Actor"

Jeana Yeager
614 Shadydale Road
Nipomo, CA 93444
"Avaitrix"

Steve Yeager
11550 Sumac Lane
Camarillo, CA 93010
"Baseball Player"

Yellowjackets
9220 Sunset Blvd. #320
Los Angeles, CA 90069
"Jazz Group"

Boris Yeltsin
Uliza Twerskaya
Jamskaya 2
Moscow, Russia
"President of Russia"

Dwight Yoakum
15840 Ventura Blvd #465
Encino, CA 91436
"Singer, Guitarist"

Philip Yordan
4894 Mt. Elbrus Drive
San Diego, CA 92117
"Screenwriter"

Francine York
14333 Addison Street #315
Sherman Oaks, CA 91423
"Actress"

Michael York
9100 Cordell Drive
Los Angeles, CA 90069
"Actor"

Susannah York
59 Knightsbridge
London SW1 ENGLAND
"Actress"

Bud Yorkin
124 Delfern Drive
Los Angeles, CA 90024
"Writer, Producer"

Tina Yothers
9000 Sunset Blvd. #1200
Los Angeles, CA 90069
"Actress"

Mayor Sam Yorty
12979 Blairwood Drivce
Studio City, CA 91604
"Ex-Mayor"

Alan Young
33872 Barcellona Place
Dana Point, CA 92629
"Actor"

Andrew Young
1088 Veltrie Circle S.W.
Atlanta, GA 30311
"Ex-Mayor"

Burt Young
5820 Wilshire Blvd. #503
Beverly Hills, CA 90211
"Actor, Screenwriter""

Chris Young
1722 North Orchid Avenue #9
Los Angeles, CA 90028
"Actor"

Coleman Young
2 Woodward Avenue
Detroit, MI 49226
"Mayor of Detroit"

Rep. C.W. Bill Young (FL)
House Rayburn Bldg. #2407
Washington, DC 20515
"Politician"

Dean Young
235 East 45th Street
New York, NY 10017
"Cartoonist"

Rep. Don Young (AK)
House Rayburn Bldg. #2331
Washington, DC 20515
"Politician"

Faron Young
1300 Division Street #102
Nashville, TN 37203
"Singer, Songwriter"

Freddie Young
3 Roehampton Close
London SW15 ENGLAND
"Cinematographer"

Loretta Young
1705 Ambassador
Beverly Hills, CA 90210
"Actress"

Michael Young
4570 Encino Avenue
Encino, CA 91316
"Actor"

Young M.C.
9229 Sunset Blvd. #319
Los Angeles, CA 90069
"Rap Singer"

Neil Young
3025 Surry Street
Los Angeles, CA 90027
"Singer, Songwriter"

Otis Young
6716 Zumirez Drive
Malibu, CA 90265
"Actor"

Robert Young
31589 Saddletree Drive
Westlake Village, CA 91261
"Actor"

Sean Young
300 Mercer Street #7-E
New York, NY 10003
"Actress"

William Allen Young
10000 Santa Monica Blvd. #305
Los Angeles, CA 90067
"Actor"

Barrie Youngfellow
10927 Missouri Avenue
Los Angeles, CA 90025
"Actress"

Henny Youngman
77 West 55th Street
New York, NY 10019
"Comedian"

Harris Yulin
1630 Crescent Place
Venice, CA 90291
"Actor"

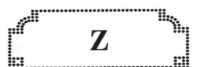

William Zabka
345 North Maple Drive #183
Beverly Hills, CA 90210
"Actor, Singer"

Grace Zabriskie
1536 Murray Drive
Los Angeles, CA 90026
"Actress"

John Zaccaro
22 Deepdene Road
Forest Hills, NY 11375
"Businessman"

Pia Zadora
8 Beverly Park
Beverly Hills, CA 90120
"Actress, Singer"

Paula Zahn
524 West 57th Street
New York, NY 10019
"TV Host"

Roxanne Zal
1450 Belfast Drive
Los Angeles, CA 90069
"Actress"

Tony Zale
3001 South King Drive #809
Chicago, IL 60616
"Boxer"

Richard Zanuck
605 North Canon Drive
Beverly Hills, CA 90210
"Motion Picture Producer"

Carmen Zapata
6107 Ethel Avenue
Van Nuys, CA 91405
"Actress"

Dweezil Zappa
7885 Woodrow Wilson Drive
Los Angeles, CA 90046
"Singer"

Frank Zappa
7885 Woodrow Wilson Drive
Los Angeles, CA 90046
"Singer, Musician"

Moon Unit Zappa
10377 Oletha Lane
Los Angeles, CA 90077
"Singer"

Emil Zatopek
Narodni Trida 33
112 93 Prague 1
CZECHOSLOVAKIA
"Track Athlete"

Franco Zefferelli
9247 Swallow Drive
Los Angeles, CA 90069
"Film Director"

Jacklyn Zeman
12186 Laurel Terrace
Studio City, CA 91604
"Actress"

Bob Zemeckis
9125 Alto Cedro Drive
Beverly Hills, CA 90210
"Film Director"

Sonja Ziemann
Via del Alp Dorf
7500 St. Moritz, SWITZERLAND
"Actress"

Efrem Zimbalist, Jr.
4750 Encino Avenue
Encino, CA 91316
"Actor"

Stephanie Zimbalist
10100 Santa Monica Blvd. #1600
Los Angeles, CA 90067
"Actress"

Don Zimmer
10124 Yacht Club Drive
St. Petersburg, FL 33706
"Baseball Manager"

Kim Zimmer
9200 Sunset Blvd #710
Los Angeles, CA 90069
"Actress"

Fred Zinneman
37 Blomfield Road
London W9 ENGLAND
"Film Director"

Adrian Zmed
23500 Daisy Trail
Calabasas, CA 91302
"Actor"

"Fuzzy" Zoeller
12 Bellewood Court
New Albany, IN 47150
"Golfer"

Vera Zorina
10 Gracie Square
New York, NY 10028
"Actress"

Adm Elmo R. Zumwalt
1500 Wilson Blvd.
Arlington, VA 22209
"Military Leader"

Daphne Zuniga
P.O. Box 1249
White River Junction, VT 05001
"Actress"

Daniel Zwerdling
c/o National Public Radio
2025 "M" Street NW
Washington, DC 20036
"News Correspondent"

ZZ Top
P.O. Box 19744
Houston, TX 77024
"Rock & Roll Group"

Other Places to write Celebrities: Movie Studios, TV Networks and Record Companies

Major Movie Studios:

Columbia Pictures
(Sony Pictures Entertainment, Inc.)
10202 West Washington Blvd.
Culver City, CA 90232

Fox, Inc.
10201 West Pico Blvd.
Los Angeles, CA 90035

Home Box Office, Inc.
2049 Century Park East, Suite 4100
Los Angeles, CA 90067

MGM-Pathe Communications Co.
10000 West Washington Blvd.
Culver City, CA 90232

Orion Pictures Corporation
1888 Century Park East
Los Angeles, CA 90067

Paramount Communication, Inc.
New York (Home Office)
15 Columbus Circle
New York, NY 10023

Paramount Communication, Inc.
West Coast Office:
5555 Melrose Avenue
Los Angeles, CA 90038

Touchstone Pictures
500 South Buena Vista Street
Burbank, CA 91521

Twentieth Century Fox
P.O. Box 900
Beverly Hills, CA 90213

Universal Pictures
100 Universal City Plaza
Universal City, CA 91608

Warner Bros., Inc.
4000 Warner Blvd.
Burbank, CA 91522

Major Television Network:

ABC
77 West 66th Street
New York, NY 10023

ABC
West Coast Studio:
2040 Avenue of the Stars
Century City, CA 90067

CBS
51 West 52nd Street
New York, NY 10019

CNN
One CNN Center
P.O. Box 105366
Atlanta, GA 30348

Fox Broadcasting Company
10201 West Pico Blvd.
Los Angeles, CA 90035

NBC
New York (Home Office)
30 Rockefeller Plaza
New York, NY 10112

NBC
West Coast Studio:
3000 Alameda Avenue
Burbank, CA 91523

Major Record Companies:

CBS Records, Inc.
51 West 52nd Street
New York, NY 10019

Capitol-EMI Music, Inc.
1750 North Vine Street
Hollywood, CA 90028

EMI
810 Seventh Avenue
8th Floor
New York, NY 10019

Elektra Entertainment
75 Rockefeller Plaza
New York, NY 10019

Emeral Records
830 Glastonbury Road
Suite 614
Nashville, TN 37217

Erika Records, Inc.
9827 Oak Street
Bellflower, CA 90706

MCA Records
70 Universal City Plaza
Universal City, CA 91608

Motown Record Company
6255 Sunset Blvd.
17th Floor
Los Angeles, CA 90028

PolyGram Records, Inc.
825 Eighth Avenue
New York, NY 10019

PolyGram Records: Nashville
901 - 18th Avenue South
Nashville, TN 37212

RCA Records, Inc.
P.O. Box 126
405 Tarrytown Road
Suite 335
Elmsford, NY 10523

SBK Records
1290 Avenue of the Americas
New York, NY 10104

Warner Music International
75 Rockefeller Plaza
New York, NY 10019

Other Places to Write Sports Celebrities: Baseball, Basketball and Football Teams

Major League Baseball
350 Park Avenue
New York, NY 10022
Commissioner:
Fay Vincent

American League Teams:

Baltimore Orioles
Memorial Stadium
Baltimore, MD 21218

Boston Red Sox
Fenway Park
Boston, MA 02215

California Angeles
P.O. Box 2000
Anaheim, CA 92803

Chicago White Sox
324 West 35th Street
Chicago, IL 60016

Cleveland Indians
Cleveland Stadium
Cleveland, OH 44114

Detroit Tigers
2121 Trumbull Avenue
Detroit, MI 48216

Kansas City Royals
P.O. Box 419969
Kansas City, MO 64141

Milwaukee Brewers
Milwaukee County Stadium
Milwaukee, WI 53214

Minnesota Twins
501 Chicago Avenue South
Minneapolis, MN 55415

New York Yankees
Yankee Stadium
Bronx, NY 10451

Oakland Athletics
Oakland Alameda County Stadium
Oakland, CA 94621

Seattle Mariners
P.O. Box 4100
Seattle, WA 98104

Texas Rangers
P.O. Box 1111
Arlington, TX 76010

Toronto Blue Jays
P.O. Box 7777, Adelaide Street
Toronto, Ont. MSC 2K7 CANADA

National League Teams:

Atlanta Braves
P.O. Box 4064
Atlanta, GA 30302

Chicago Cubs
1060 West Addison
Chicago, IL 60613

Cincinnati Reds
100 Riverfront Stadium
Cinncinnati, OH 45202

Houston Astros
P.O. Box 288
Houston, TX 77001

Los Angeles Dodgers
1000 Elysian Park Avenue
Los Angeles, CA 90012

Montreal Expos
P.O. Box 500, Station M
Montreal, Que. H1V 3P2 CANADA

New York Mets
Shea Stadium
Flushing, NY 11368

Philadelphia Phillies
P.O. Box 7575
Philadelphia, PA 19101

Pittsburgh Pirates
Three Rivers Stadium
Pittsburg, PA 15212

St. Louis Cardinals
250 Stadium Plaza
St. Louis, MO 63102

San Diego Padres
P.O. Box 2000
San Diego, CA 92120

San Francisco Giants
Candlestick Park
San Francisco, CA 94124

National Basketball Association:

Olympic Tower
645 Fifth Avenue
New York, NY 10022
Commissioner:
David Stern

Atlanta Hawks
One CNN Center
South Tower, Suite 405
Atlanta, GA 30303

Boston Celtics
151 Merrimac Street , 15th Floor
Boston, MA 02114

Charlotte Hornets
Two First Union Plaza, Suite 2600
Charlotte, NC 28282

Chicago Bulls
One Maginificent Mile
980 North Michigan Avenue
Suite 1600
Chicago, IL 60611

Cleveland Cavaliers
P.O. Box 5000
Richfield, OH 44286

Dallas Mavericks
Reunion Arena
777 Sports Street
Dallas, TX 75207

Denver Nuggets
P.O. Box 4658
Denver, CO 80204

Detroit Pistons
The Palace
3777 Lapeer Road
Auburn Hills, MI 48057

Golden State Warriors
Oakland Coliseum Arena
Oakland, CA 94621

Houston Rockets
P.O. Box 272349
Houston, TX 77277

Indiana Pacers
300 East Market Street
Indianapolis, IN 46204

Los Angeles Clippers
3939 South Figueroa
Los Angeles, CA 90037

Los Angeles Lakers
P.O. Box 10
Inglewood, CA 90306

Miami Heat
Miami Arena
Miami, FL 33136

Milwaukee Bucks
901 North Fourth Street
Milwaukee, WI 53203

Minnesota Timberwolves
730 Hennepin Avenue, Suite 500
Minneapolis, MN 55403

New Jersey Nets
Brendan Byrne Arena
East Rutherford, NJ 07073

New York Knickerbockers
Four Pennsylvania Plaza
New York, NY 10001

Orlando Magic
One Dupont Center
390 North Orange Avenue
Suite 275
Orlando, FL 32801

Philadelphia 76ers
P.O. Box 25040
Philadelphia, PA 19147

Phoenix Suns
P.O. Box 1369
Phoenix, AZ 85001

Portland Trail Blazers
700 N.E. Multnomah Street
Suite 950
Portland, OR 97232

Sacramento Kings
One Sports Parkway
Sacramento, CA 95834

San Antonio Spurs
600 East Market
Suite 102
San Antonio, TX 78205

Seattle Supersonics
P.O. Box C-900911
Seattle, WA 98109

Utah Jazz
5 Traid Center, 5th Floor
Salt Lake City, UT 84180

Washington Bullets
Capital Centre
One Harry S. Truman Drive
Landover, MD 20785

National Football League:
410 Park Avenue
New York, NY 10022
Commissioner:
Paul Tagliabue

American Football Conference:

Buffalo Bills
One Bill Drive
Orchard Park, NY 14127

Cincinnati Bengals
200 Riverfront Stadium
Cinncinnati, OH 45202

Cleveland Browns
Cleveland Stadium
Cleveland, OH 44114

Denver Broncos
5700 Logan Street
Denver, CO 80216

Houston Oilers
6910 Fannin Street
Houston, TX 77030

Indianapolis Colts
P.O. Box 24100
Indianapolis, IN 46224

Kansas City Chiefs
One Arrowhead Drive
Kansas City, MO 64129

Los Angeles Raiders
332 Center Street
El Segundo, CA 90245

Miami Dolphins
Joe Robbie Stadium
2269 N.W. 199th Street
Miami, FL 33056

New England Patriots
Sullivan Stadium-Route 1
Foxboro, MA 02035

New York Jets
598 Madison Avenue
New York, NY 10022

Pittsburgh Steelers
Three Rivers Stadium
300 Stadium Circle
Pittsburgh, PA 15212

San Diego Chargers
9449 Friars Road
San Diego, CA 92120

Seattle Seahawks
11220 N.E. 53rd Street
Kirkland, WA 98033

National Football Conference:

Atlanta Falcons
Suwanee Road at I-85
Suwanee, GA 30174

Chicago Bears
Halas Hall
250 North Washington Road
Lake Forest, IL 60045

Dallas Cowboys
1 Cowboys Parkway
Irving, TX 75063

Detroit Lions
1200 Featherstone Road
Pontiac, MI 48057

Green Bay Packers
1265 Lombardi Avenue
Green Bay, WI 54303

Los Angeles Rams
2327 West Lincoln Avenue
Anaheim, CA 92801

Minnesota Vikings
9520 Viking Drive
Eden Parairie, MN 55344

New Orleans Saints
6928 Saints Avenue
Metairie, LA 70003

New York Giants
Giants Stadium
East Rutherford, NJ 07073

Philadelphia Eagles
Veterans Stadium
Broad Street & Pattison Avenue
Philadelphia, PA 19148

Phoenix Cardinals
P.O. Box 888
Phoenix, AZ 85001

San Francisco 49ers
4949 Centennial Blvd.
Santa Clara, CA 95054

Tampa Bay Buccaneers
One Buccaneer Place
Tampa, FL 33607

Washington Redskins
P.O. Box 17247
Dulles International Airport
Washington, DC 20041

(See other side of this page for other books used to write celebrities.)